To Tip

Best wishes !

Leon Whiley Thompson

ROUGH JUSTICE

Across the yard, Whitey saw LeRoy Jackson talking to the yard officer. Whitey sauntered along to the bleachers, his eye on LeRoy. When he got within twenty feet of Jackson and the guard, Whitey stopped and began to roll a cigarette, all the while keeping his prey under surveillance. Just as he was lighting up, the guard started toward the dominoes tables, leaving LeRoy alone on the step.

"Snitching someone off, LeRoy?"

Whitey's voice startled him. "What you want, man? Why you sneak up on me?"

"That's the only way to get near a rat—sneak up on 'em."

"What you want, anyway? You stay away, you hear?"

"What do I want, LeRoy? I want to know how tall you are, and how much you weigh."

"What for you ask that?"

"I need your measurements," Whitey replied coldly.

"Why, for you need my measurements?"

"To send to the carpender shop, fool.. They need to know the size for your pine box."

LAST TRAIN TO ALCATRAZ

THE AUTOBIOGRAPHY OF A
FORMER ALCATRAZ CONVICT

LEON "WHITEY"
THOMPSON

LEON W. THOMPSON
P.O. BOX 219
FIDDLETOWN, CA 95629

DEDICATION

This book is dedicated to my wife Helen, for without her help and support it would never have been written. To the memory of Johnny House. Also to the memory of my beloved Wolf Dogs, Winter, Caribou, and Terwin; they have left a void in my heart. This book is also dedicated to my family of animals, Timber Cougar Wolf, Amorak, Bradshaw, Jude, Ebony, and Wally Bird. And to all wild animals, especially the Wolf, and may they all run free.

AUTHOR'S NOTE

LAST TRAIN TO ALCATRAZ was first published in 1988 by Leon W. Thompson. Seventy-six thousand copies were sold, and received a high review from Publishers Weekly. It attracted the attention of Pocket Books, a division of Simon & Schuster. A contract was signed, and the book was published under the name of ROCK HARD. I received many letters requesting the book in hardcover. So with permission from Simon & Schuster, I have re-published my book in hardcover under the original title of **LAST TRAIN TO ALCATRAZ.**

The writing of this book has been one of the biggest challenges of my life, for I never went past the sixth grade in school, and I received no formal education while in prison.

LAST TRAIN TO ALCATRAZ was the idea of my wife Helen Thompson, and it was she who encouraged me to write the book. Together, in 1980 we started this long project, and getting it down on paper proved to be a pains-taking chore. Each day we would put in ten to sixteen hours, and the work was tedious and tiresome. We finally completed **LAST TRAIN TO ALCATRAZ** in 1987. The book was a great success, and we received thousands of letter from all over the world wanting to know what happened to Whitey Thompson after Alcatraz. I was pressured into writing my sequel to **LAST TRAIN TO ALCATRAZ** titled **ALCATRAZ MERRY-GO-ROUND**, which is my continued autobiography.

ALCATRAZ MERRY-GO-ROUND can be purchased from the Alcatraz Bookstore, or by writing directly to me:

Leon Whitey Thompson
P.O. Box 219
Fiddletown, CA 95629, U.S.A.

The writing of both books was done without a ghost writer or professional help. It is the true story of my life, every incident actually occurred, and all the characters are real although some of the names have been changed.

Leon (Whitey) Thompson

ACKNOWLEDGEMENTS

* * *

I want to thank the following people for their help and encouragement.
First, Ron and Ellen Strope, and all their critters. Dr. William Foote who believed in me from the beginning. A thank you to Perky, Jeff and Carol Perkins, Hank and Euona Rathjen, and Terry Tyler, and Linda Nielsen. A special thanks to Steve Carney for his friendship and wisdom.

Thank you to Donna Middlemist, John Cantwell, Benny Baton, Raquel Lopez, Phil Butler, John Martini, and Naomi L.Torres, Supervisary Park Ranger of Alcatraz, and the rest of the National Park Service for their help and cooperation.

A thank you to Nicki Phelps, Stan "The man" Zbikowski, and to the staff of the Golden Gate National Park Association.

And to the Red and White Fleet, a special thank you to Al Zurawski, President, Terry Koenig, Marketing Manager, Frank Heaney, Public Relations. Carolyn Horgan, and Shannon Powell, two sweethearts who have been so kind to me, and to Paul Ruggeiro, and all the Captains, and Seamen of the Ferry Boats, and the rest of the staff of the Red and White Fleet. A thank you to Deckhand Willie D. Ramsey for his friendship and support these past few years.

To Kevin Kenny, Manager of Cell Block 41 Gift Shop, Pier 41, many thanks for your help and support.

I would like to acknowledge all my friends, but space does not permit. Last, but certainly not least, I want to thank the Man above. He never gave up on me, He has been with me all my life, and He is within my heart today.

FORWORD
****

JOHN MARTINI, Park Historian
Golden Gate National Recreation Area

Most history books are written from a distance—the distance of years that allows the "historian" to put people and events into a wider scope of reference. For four years Whitey Thompson's scope of reference was a twelve acre rock in the middle of San Francisco Bay, and the stories he tells in this book are related from a distance I can never truly appreciate—the inside of the joint.

Whitey spent his four years on Alcatraz in the same anonymity as most of the hundreds of other convicts who lived on the Rock. He was neither a "public enemy" in the Hollywood sense nor a punk kid new to prison life. He had spent time in other institutions and was well versed in the ways of prison life by the time he had arrived on Alcatraz. He knew who to trust, who to watch out for, and how and when to keep his mouth shut. In the language of the penitentiary, Whitey was a "solid con." Perhaps his main claim to fame is that he was among the handful of men ever released directly from Alcatraz to the streets of San Francisco.

This book is Whitey's highly personal history of his early life and his years on Alcatraz. Historians, with the exalted perspective of thirty years hindsight, may be able to dissect other books about the Rock, questioning dates or exact sequences of events, but no one can question Whitey's feelings, opinions and memories. They are his alone, and come from that very, very close perspective few of the rest of us can ever understand.

Whitey today comes back to Alcatraz, now part of the Golden Gate National Recreation Area, to meet with visitors and autograph copies of his book. I've seen him lecture to school groups and church tours on what life was like on the inside of the prison, answering over and over the visitors' most popular question—"What was your crime?" What few people realize is that this is the one question a man in prison never asks another convict. Whitey always answers politely, though.

"I'm a retired bank robber, ma'am." And a solid con.

PART 1.

McNEIL ISLAND AND THE

BEGINNING

CHAPTER 1.

Alcatraz Island, Federal Penitentiary, the United States most feared prison closed its doors on March 21, 1963. by order of the Attorney General Robert F. Kennedy. In 1973 the Island was turned over to the U.S. National Park Service, and became a part of Golden Gate National Recreation Area. The historic Island was reopened as a National Park to the public for daily tours. Transportation provided by the Red and White Fleet.

In September 1976 Leon Whitey Thompson made his first returned to Alcatraz. He was accompanied by his wife Helen, and stepdaughter, Dawn Hyatt.

For Whitey, his return to Alcatraz was a memorable trip. He looked across the Bay, and enjoyed the picturesque beauty of the Golden Gate Bridge, the skyline of San Francisco, and even Alcatraz Island was like a sculpture of beauty. This memorable trip to the Rock was nothing like the ill-fated day, of July 19, 1958. On this day, wearing 16 lbs. of shackles and irons, Whitey Thompson, a Federal prisoner, had been transferred from McNeil Island, Washington to Alcatraz, commonly known as "The Rock."

As he stepped off the tourist boat, many of the old feelings returned to him. As he started the trek up the tortuous hill, the cellhouse looming on the crest caught his attention. His mind was crystal clear, and it seemed like only yesterday instead of fourteen years ago, when he left this old prison. Inside the cellhouse he stood in front of his cell B-204. This had been his home for four years. As he stood there the faces of a few old friends like a roll-call flashed in front of him. Lou Peters, Johnny House, Big Longo, Mondoza, to name a few.

Trying to keep a low profile, and not disturb the Park Ranger who was giving the tour, Whitey spoke softly to his wife and stepdaughter as he told them some fascinating stories of his life on the Rock. A few tourists overheard him speaking, and before he realized it, he drew the attention of the people away from the ranger.

They crowded around Whitey as if he was a rock star, many questions were asked, "What was your crime? Did you kill anyone? Did you know Al Capone, Machine-Gun Kelly, the Birdman of

3

Alcatraz? Were you in another prison before you came to Alcatraz? And if so, which one?"

As Whitey began to speak to his new audience about his crimes, his childhood, his days on McNeil Island Federal Penitentiary and the Rock, he knew he was not proud of what he had done, but for the first time he knew too that he was not ashamed. This is his story.

It had been a long morning, and while repairing shoes his legs were tiring from standing on the concrete floor. Whitey was hard at work repairing shoes for approximately fifteen hundred men when he heard the guard shout, "Get ready for chow call."

He ceased work, and hurried out of the shop as Mr. Beard, the guard, locked the wire gate behind him.

Whitey sat on a bench next to a locked door that led upstairs to Three and Four Cell Blocks. Other prisoners who worked in the B.C.R. (basement Clothing Room) were gathered around the doorway.

McNeil Island was the oldest Federal Penitentiary in the United States located just off the coast of the state of Washington, out in Puget Sound. The prison was built in the 1880s in a rambling fashion, with buildings being added as needed. It consisted of four cell blocks, each block five tiers high. An honor dormitory was located a short distance away from the main part of the prison, but still inside the double fence and the guard towers. The hospital was at the eastern end of the prison attached to Number One Cell Block. At the south end of Four Block was the entrance to the Hole. Located here were the disciplinary cells isolated from the rest of the prison. There were many parts of the Penitentiary Whitey never saw. He was placed on close custody, and was not allowed out of the main Cell Block area.

Mr. Beard unlocked the door and swung it wide open and shouted.

"Chow—chow down."

There was a stampede as the men charged to the top of the stairs where they made a left turn out of the building into a very wide hallway. Fifty feet down the hallway, a right turn was made through an entrance into a large Dining Hall. The dining area consisted of three aisles, one on either side, and one in the middle. Whitey picked up his utensils, then turned to the steam line where food was slapped onto his tray by inmates. With loaded tray, he turned to look for a place to sit. Inmates were allowed to sit wherever they chose. Each table sat four men. He found one unoccupied, and quickly sat down and began to eat.

Throughout the Dining Room there were eight guards stationed in various places. While high up on the cat-walk, patrolled four more guards with armed rifles.

4

An inmate coffee pourer walked up to Whitey, "Coffee?" he asked. "Yeah," Whitey replied, and set his cup near the edge of the table. The coffee pourer filled the cup from a huge five-gallon container. Whitey continued eating without a word of thanks. After finishing his lunch, he sat there deep in thought, shutting out the sounds of the Dining Room. He had drifted back to his childhood days.

Marge, his older sister was calling him, "Whitey, Whitey Thompson, you come into the house right now."

Whitey was sitting alongside the tracks of the New York, New Haven, and Hartford Railroad. He often sat there to watch the railroad men switch boxcars in the train yard.

"What am I doing wrong?" he asked himself, "why does she want me?"

It was fun sitting out there. He loved watching the big freight and passenger trains as they rumbled passed.

Whitey's home was on Lyon Street right at the end of the block next to the train tracks in the city of New Haven, Connecticut. On January 23, 1923, he was given birth in this house. He never knew his mother, or whatever happened to her.

He was a lonely boy, and at the age of four he would sit by the tracks, hoping to receive attention. You could find him there most every day. The workmen would wave to him as they went about their job switching boxcars from one track to another. You could be sure he was always out there during the noon hour, because the workmen would sit under the shade of a massive oak tree, and share their lunch with him. He was a starving little boy, and from these rugged railroad men he would receive love, food, and attention, which was something he seldom received at home.

One day Whitey was playing with a jackknife. The engineer asked who had given it to him. Whitey told him he had found it.

"Would you like a brand new penny for it?" the engineer asked.

Whitey was thrilled at the thought of having a penny, and his eyes opened wide. A penny was a great deal of money for a boy who never had any, but he felt the knife was worth more than one cent.

"I'll tell you what I'll do," the engineer said as he smiled down at the small blond-headed boy. "Every day that I see you, I'll give you a penny. How does that sound to you?"

Whitey jumped up and down with joy and cried, "You bet, sure, you bet!"

He handed the engineer the knife, and every day at lunch time he was out there to receive his penny.

It was noontime, and Whitey was waiting for the engineer when his sister called again.

"Leon W. Thompson, get into the house this minute."

"But I can't," Whitey cried, "I want to wait for my penny."

"You get your ass in here right now, or I'll drag you in."

Holding back the tears, Whitey started toward the house, "I just wanted my penny," he said to himself, "and see my friends. Why does she want me now?"

"Hey Thompson—Thompson let's go."

The sharp angry voice of a guard snapped Whitey back to reality.

"Come on goddamn it," commanded the enraged guard, "get out of here before they lock the Dining Room door, do your sleeping in your cell."

Deliberately, at a snail's pace he left the Dining Room and walked toward Three Block where he lived in cell No. 3-A-5. A guard at the end of the tier pulled a long iron handle that opened the doors. Quickly Whitey jumped into his cell to avoid being pinned by the heavy steel door. It slid shut with a bang that echoed throughout the Cell House, a bell sounded.

"Count—count time," a guard shouted. "Stand up to the bars and be counted."

Whitey stood up to the cell bars just as a guard hurried by counting as he passed.

Ten minutes later there was the sound of another bell.

"Count's clear—count's clear! Work call, everybody out for work," the guards shouted.

Whitey's cell door opened, and he hurried back to his job assignment. The B.C.R. Guard was waiting to check each man off the roster as they returned to work. Then he unlocked the door to the Shoe Shop, and after Whitey entered, he re-locked it behind them.

"Won't this day ever end?" he asked himself. He started to work on another shoe when he heard a voice. "Hey Whitey—Whitey."

Whitey looked toward the speaker. Standing just outside the screen was a tall skinny redheaded inmate called Red, who worked in the B.C.R. He was a known snitch, and disliked by all convicts. He had never done anything personally to Whitey, but because of his reputation Whitey wanted nothing to do with him.

"What the hell do you want Red?"

"How about putting some crepe soles on my shoes? I'll give you five packs."

If a man had a foot problem, and approved by a doctor, he was allowed to have crepe soles put on his shoes. However every now and then Whitey would take a chance and put crepes on for people he thought were okay. For this he charged five packs of cigarettes.

Whitey received no pay for his work, and had no money in his prison account to buy commissary. Cigarettes were also used as

6

money, and could buy almost anything within the prison walls. Whitey earned his smokes by putting crepes on illegally. If he had been caught, he would go straight to Segregation, (known as the Hole).

"Get lost Red," Whitey hissed. "I don't do anything for a snitch, get the fuck out of here."

At that moment Officer Beard walked up.

"What's going on Thompson?"

Whitey snapped, "Nothing's going on, right Red?"

Looking at Whitey, Red said to the guard, "There's nothing going on," and walked away.

Whitey soon forgot the incident. That evening on his way to chow, Red dropped a kite (a note) into the Suggestion Box outside the Dining Room. This box was like a U.S. mailbox, once a note was dropped into it, it could not be retrieved. Late in the evening an officer unloaded the box, and the contents were delivered straight to the Associate Warden's office.

The next day, while at work, Whitey was interrupted by the B.C.R. Guard as he unlocked the Shoe Shop door. In walked two huge members of the Goon Squad, the name "Goon" was given them by the inmates. They were specially trained guards similar to the SWAT Teams of today's police forces. They were trained for prison riots and troublemakers, etc.

As the Goons walked into the Shoe Shop, Whitey's first thought was that they were going to search for contraband. They did this periodically without notice. He was surprised when they walked straight up to him.

"Are you Leon Thompson 27607?" one of them asked in a harsh voice.

Jokingly Whitey replied, "Who wants to know? Ya got a warrant?"

They didn't answer, both of them made a grab for Whitey, and he was pulled bodily out of the Shop.

"Hey what the hell's going on? Get your fucking hands off me, are ya crazy?"

They did not reply, but roughly manhandled him all the way back to his cell. Once there, he was told to get all his property together. He was then taken over to Number One Building where Cell Block One was located. There he was placed in a single cell.

After the door closed behind him he started to pace back and forth, and while doing so he tried to figure out just what was happening. Why did they lock him up? He had done nothing wrong that he could think of.

Whitey was a muscular man of medium height, with light blond hair and rugged good looks. He was a quiet man when left alone, but had a hair-trigger temper, and was extremely dangerous when

7

aroused.

He was angry, and the madder he got, the faster he paced the floor, until the sound of a door being slid open brought him up short. Then he heard a loud slam as the door was closed. They had put someone in the cell next to him.

Whitey stood quietly as he listened to the sound of the guard leaving the Block. After a moment or two, he heard movement in the next cell.

In a soft voice he whispered, "Hey is anyone next door?"

"Yeah, who wants to know?" came a hushed reply.

Whitey recognized the voice, "Hey is that you Lou?"

"Yes it's me, what the hell are you doing in here?"

"How the fuck do I know? They just rounded me up and here I am. How come they picked you up?"

"Hell I don't know Whitey, I'm just here."

Both men moved to the front of their cells. Their heads were only a foot apart but they couldn't see each other.

Lou was a large man standing six foot two, and weighed 195 lbs. He was good-looking with pleasant brown eyes that could turn cold as death when angered. He was not the type of person you would want to cross, but he was a loyal friend to Whitey,

"Keep ya voice down Lou, we don't know who's celling around us."

"Who gives a fuck who's celling around us? I just wished I knew why I'm here in the hole. What the hell did you do Whitey?"

"What'd ya mean what did I do? I didn't do a goddamn thing."

"Ah, bullshit, you're always doing something wrong, just because I'm your cell partner they scoop me up too."

"Ah fuck you Lou, you're full of shit."

"Full of shit am I? You're nothing but trouble Whitey, the first time I laid eyes on you, you were beating up on some dude. Hell when you first came to McNeil you weren't here a hot minute and you were in a fight with Blackie and Shorty."

"What the fuck is wrong with you Lou? You know why I got into it that day," Whitey shouted, "I won't let no bastard not even Blackie or Shorty rip me off."

"But that was ten years ago Whitey, and ever since you, Blackie and Shorty teamed up together you have been knocking in heads ever since."

"What the hell are you talking about? I haven't been in a jam for the past two years, and you damn well know it."

"Then what the hell are we doing in the hole?" Lou shouted.

In an angry voice Whitey replied, "Keep your fucking voice down fool, how the fuck do I know what we're doing in here, but believe me, when I find out, someone is gonna get hurt, you can count on it."

8

From experience Lou knew of Whitey's violent temper, and figured it best to calm him down before he did something foolish.

"Let's not get excited Whitey until we know what the score is, let's just play it cool for now."

The two men talked quietly to each other until 4:30 P.M. when dinner was brought in to them. After the meal they talked a while longer, and then tried to settle down for the night.

Whitey began to toss and turn as he lay on the hard steel bunk; sleep would not come as he pondered over the past years.

CHAPTER 2.

In June 1948 Leon W. Thompson was sentenced to fifteen years for numerous bank robberies, and various other crimes. He was sent to the Federal Penitentiary at McNeil Island, Washington.

His first thirty days of incarceration were spent in orientation, popularly known as the Fish Tank. He had just been released into the main population, and this was his first experience in the canteen line. Each prisoner was allowed to spend ten dollars a month. Whiteys had just made his purchase of cigarettes, ice cream, candy and toilet items. After placing the articles in a bag, he started to shoulder his way through the crowd, when a heavyset Mexican, and a short white man blocked his path. He knew they wanted his commissary, and were about to rip him off; this happened frequently in prison. Whitey didn't say a word, he set the paper bag on the concrete floor giving the impression he was going to show them the contents. As he rose from the bending position, he swung his left fist hitting the Mexican hard in the mouth. In the same sweeping motion he hit the other man a tremendous blow to the side of the head knocking both men backwards. The element of surprise had caught the assailants off guard. They stood for a moment shaking their heads, getting their thoughts together. Whitey made a grab for the bag, and in his haste he tore it open spilling the contents on the floor. As Whitey bent over to retrieve his articles, the two men started to move in on him just as someone yelled, "Watch out man a screw's coming."

A guard made his way through the crowd that had gathered around Whitey and his assailants. In a commanding voice the officer barked, "What the hell is going on here?"

Whitey was picking up his articles as he looked up at the guard, and in a soft voice he replied, "Nothing's going on, I dropped my bag of commissary." Then indicating the two adversaries he continued, "And these two gents were helping me pick it up. What's wrong with that?"

The guard glanced at the two men, then looking back at Whitey

10

he snapped, "Okay then pick it up, and move on out of here—NOW."

After gathering up his articles, Whitey returned to his Cell Block. He stood waiting for a guard to unlock his cell door. While he stood there the two assailants came walking along the Flats. He carefully set the bag down, and leaned it against the wall, and was prepared for another fight.

"Come on you bastards," he growled, "you want my goodies, come and get 'em."

Holding both hands up in the air in a peace sign, the Mexican smiled at Whitey, "Hey man we're not after your commissary anymore, you're an okay dude and we want to be friends."

In a skeptical voice Whitey said, "After all this bullshit now you want to be friends, why the sudden change?"

Smiling the Mexican replied, "You're people man, ya know, real people, and you don't back down, I like that. You're okay." Introducing himself, he took a step forward and held out his hand. "My name is Blackie, and this is my pal Shorty. What's your handle?"

Ignoring the handshake, Whitey replied, "The name's Whitey, Whitey Thompson."

A few weeks after this incident Whitey, Blackie, Shorty, and Whitey's new cell partner Lou Peters, formed what were to be known as the "Collectors." These men would band together and collect debts turned over to them by other inmates. If a man had someone owing him a debt he could not collect, to save face he would turn it over to Whitey and his gang, the Collectors. Once it was turned over to the Collectors the debt would be paid to them, no matter the cost. Even if it meant caving a man's head in, or tossing him off the tier, the debt would be paid. They would achieve their goal by force if necessary, and keep whatever they collected for their services.

One day, while out in the yard, Whitey sat down beside an inmate who was watching a convict baseball game.

"You're name Cann?" Whitey asked.

"Yeah that's my name, what about it?"

In a quiet whisper Whitey replied, "You owe a pal of mine one box (referring to one carton of cigarettes)."

"Yeah I owe Mitch a box, what's it to you?"

Whitey's voice turned cold as he answered, "Just this—from now on you owe the smokes to me, but instead of one box you owe me two—understand? And it's payable a week from today."

"Fuck you I don't owe you nothing, and I won't pay you nothing."

"You'll pay you son of a bitch," Whitey hissed as he moved in closer pointing his finger in anger. "Dummy up you fucker and listen carefully, a week from today you're gonna cough up two boxes, if you

11

don't I won't be responsible for what happens to you."

Not waiting for a reply, Whitey walked off.

One week later while Blackie and Shorty were playing horseshoes, Cann was sitting on a nearby bench watching the game.

Whitey walked up to Cann and stood directly in front of him.

"Get out of my way I can't see the game," Cann shouted at Whitey.

"Don't shout at me fucker I'll tear your head off. Never mind the game," Whitey hissed. "This is the payoff day. Ya got my two boxes?"

Looking up at Whitey and in a snarling voice Cann replied, "I'm not paying you anything, get lost."

Whitey turned his head toward the game in progress and nodded as a signal to the players who were keeping an eye on him.

Suddenly Blackie let a horseshoe go flying toward Whitey and Cann.

"Look out, look out," he yelled.

Whitey stepped aside just as the shoe landed in front of him.

"Hey watch out where you're throwing them shoes," Cann shouted at Blackie.

Casually Whitey bent down to pick up the horseshoe as his unsuspecting victim sat on the bench. In a swift upward motion he caught Cann alongside the head with the shoe. The sound of the impact was sickening as it tore into his skull. The force of the blow hurled him over backwards dropping him between the benches where he lay unconscious.

As if nothing happened at all, Whitey, Blackie and Shorty, nonchalantly sauntered away.

A few minutes later with most of his right ear torn off the unconscious man was discovered by a guard, and was rushed off to the hospital. He had lost much blood, suffered a concussion, but the injuries were not fatal.

Three days later, with his head bandaged, Cann, was sitting up in a hospital bed watching a prison worker sweeping the floor. The worker made his way beside his bed. "I have a message for you," he whispered quietly.

Cann did not know the man, and his eyes opened wide as he listened.

"You have a choice Cann—pay up or be covered up. Next time you're a dead man if you don't pay. So what's it gonna be?"

Terrified, Cann could hardly speak, "I'll-p-pay man, next time I draw (buy) canteen."

No one would inform on this organization for fear of their lives. For eight years the Collectors worked at their scam until 1956. The pressure was becoming too much so Whitey and his friends decided to disband the Collectors. Whitey accepted a job in the Shoe Shop on vocational training, and after a few months he became proficient at his work. Lou Peters went to work in the Furniture Factory. Blackie and Shorty were assigned to the Culinary, and during meal times they would try to slip a steak or some choice food to Whitey and Lou.

The rattle of keys interrupted Whitey's thoughts. It was the wee hours of morning and he had not slept at all. The sound of keys became louder as the guard approached the tier and pulled the bar opening the doors of Whitey and Lou's cell.

"Okay, Thompson, Peters, move out of them cells. Let's go follow me," he ordered.

They were taken directly to the Segregation Hole, and ordered to strip. They removed their clothes, were given a pair of coveralls to put on, and then individually led to the double door dark cells.

As the doors closed behind Whitey he could feel the dampness, and a shiver went up his spine. He reached out in the darkness fumbling for the wall; not finding it, he took a few steps forward until his fingers made contact. Leaning his back to the extremely cold wall, and using the wall as a brace, he slowly slid down to a sitting position on the damp floor. The five by ten foot cells was completely bare with only a hole in the concrete floor that served as a toilet. The water was controlled by a guard who pushed a button outside the cell when needed. To make life more unpleasant for the prisoner sometimes the guard would go several days before pressing the flush-button. The unfortunate prisoner was forced to breathe and smell his own human waste.

Each morning Whitey received two pieces of toilet paper for his needs. He spent most of each day trying to keep warm by doing pushups or jumping up and down until he was exhausted, then collapsed to the floor. He would lie there unmoving until his body chilled, and then repeat the same procedure. Each evening at 10:00 P.M. sharp a threadbare blanket was thrown into his cell, and taken away promptly at 5:00 A.M.. At 6:00 A.M. the outer cell door was opened and a guard slid a paper plate of food through the slot of the inner door. Immediately the guard would depart, closing and locking the outer door, leaving Whitey to fumble with his food in total darkness. Ten minutes later the outer door would slide open and the guard would retrieve the paper plate and plastic spoon. No lunch was served in Segregation, and the next time the cell door opened was at 4:30 P.M. for dinner. Time slowly passed, and Whitey knew the day had ended by the blanket he received at 10:00 P.M.. These activities were the only way he could keep track of time. If a prisoner was in

13

the dark cell long enough, he would lose all concept of time and the days stood still.

On the morning of the fourth day in Segregation Whitey's cell door opened, and the guard ordered him out. He was eager to obey; it felt good to get out of the cold and the darkness of the cell. But he was not ready for the reaction he received the moment he stepped into the light. A sharp pain shot through his head, it was like a bolt of lightning, and for a second or two he was totally blinded. He immediately covered his eyes with both hands to try to ward off the rays of light. His head began spinning and he felt dizzy, and was about to fall when the strong hands of the guard grabbed him. In almost the same instant Whitey knocked his hands away.

"Keep your grubby hands off me you filthy bastard, I don't need your fuckin' help!"

"All right," the guard replied, "I hope you fall on your face!"

The pain was severe, but Whitey's vision was slowly returning as he followed the guard into a small anteroom where he was given clean prison blues.

Lou Peters was already there getting dressed. Whitey started to say something to him, but the guard told him to shut up.

"Fuck you, make me shut up!"

"One more word and I will," the guard was getting angry now.

After both were dressed, the guard put a restraining belt around each of their waists, and their hands were cuffed to their belts. They were led out of Segregation, and after traveling through a number of locked gates, they were escorted to the Associated Warden's Conference Room. While Lou sat outside to wait his turn, a guard opened the door to admit Whitey. He entered the room, and sitting behind a long table were three men dressed in civilian clothes. The Associate Warden was seated at one end, and without a second glance Whitey knew who the other two men were. They were FBI Agents.

The guard ordered Whitey to be seated, and just before he obeyed the command he looked at the two agents, and held his nose as if there was a bad smell in the room. The Associate Warden, who had been leafing through a folder, looked up just as Whitey made the gesture. He was a large middle-aged man, with a receding hairline, and he looked at Whitey with a plastic face, and cold gray eyes. When he spoke, his resonant voice echoed throughout the room.

"Well Thompson, you just can't seem to stay out of trouble can you?" he asked.

Whitey did not reply; instead he sat staring at the man with contempt in his eyes.

14

"I have to admit, I've had no trouble out of you for the past two years, but that doesn't change the fact that I have always suspected you of being a Collector."

One of the agents asked the Associate Warden, "What is a Collector?"

"They are inmates who have formed a small clique known as the Collectors. No one knows for sure who they are. If an inmate has a gambling debt and refuses to pay, the person he owes it to turns the debt over to the Collectors, and they collect by force."

"How can they force a person to pay?" the agent asked, "won't they inform on him?"

"They're afraid to. Usually the Collectors throw a blanket over the culprit and beat him half to death. When he recovers, he receives word to pay up or the next time he won't be so lucky, and he's afraid to talk. It is difficult to catch these inmates in the act, and no one will inform for fear of his life. For some time now we have suspected Thompson here of being a member of this group."

"That's all ya can do is suspect," Whitey snarled, "Ya can't prove a damn thing."

"Oh we'll prove it," the Associate Warden said with a cunning smile, "we'll prove it all right, but right now I would like to know about this food riot that is supposed to take place."

A look of surprise crossed Whitey's face; half raising out of his chair, he flared back at him. "Food riot? I know nothing about a food riot."

A sneer appeared on the Associate Warden's face as he removed a slip of paper from the folder, and read, " 'This note is to inform you that Whitey Thompson and Lou Peters are trying to recruit men to incite a food riot.' "

Whitey knew now why the FBI was called in. The Associate Warden had him already condemned and was hoping to place a conspiracy charge to incite a riot on him. This charge would add another ten years to his sentence.

The Associate Warden shouted, "Do you deny this charge Thompson?"

Whitey could feel a wave of anger rising as he yelled back, "Hell yes I deny it—any fool coulda wrote that kite."

" Tell me Thompson, just what *do* you think of our food?"

Whitey could feel a hostile fury building up within himself at the injustice he felt was being dealt out to him. After all, he had just come out of Segregation where he had been cold and hungry for four days, and he shouted, "The food is garbage—stinking garbage." He could control himself no longer; and hurled himself bodily across the table at the Associate Warden.

The Associate quickly pushed his chair back, and as he did so he

15

shouted to the guards, "Get him—get him out of here. Lock him up."

Both guards lunged forward and grabbed hold of him, and held him in a vicelike grip, but Whitey continued to struggle and scream. The guards tightened their grip and dragged him bodily across the floor and out the door. Lou was still sitting on the bench outside. When he saw Whitey being roughed up by the guards, he attempted to rise, but was restrained by another guard.

Whitey looked toward Lou and yelled, "These bastards wouldn't be so brave if I wasn't all chained up."

Whitey was returned to Segregation and ordered to remove his clothes. Completely naked, he was put back into the strip cell. The cold temperature didn't bother him at first, he was too full of hate to feel anything.

A short time later he heard the opening and closing of a cell door. The guards had returned with Lou, but it would be futile for Whitey to try to communicate with him because of the double doors, and the thickness of the walls.

CHAPTER 3.

It was the fifth day after his return to Segregation. Whitey was doing pushups attempting to keep warm, when he was interrupted by the sound of the outer door of his cell being opened. A guard entered, walked up to the inner barred door, and slid a paper tray of food through the bars to him. The guard left him to his meal, as he walked out he left the outer cell door open, and rays of light lit up the interior of Whitey's cell. For the first time in the dark cell, he could see what he was eating. He sat on the floor using the wall as a back-rest; with the plate resting on his lap he began to eat. He had barely taken his first mouthful when he saw a shadow appear across the floor. He quickly looked up just as the Associate Warden stepped up to the inner door of the cell. In the dim light Whitey could see a trace of a sneer on his wax-like face.

"Ah you must really like the food, you seem to be enjoying your dinner," remarked the Associate Warden in a sarcastic tone.

Without a word, Whitey looked down at his tray, and continued eating.

"Come on Thompson, can't you talk? What do you think of the food now?"

Hatred began to show in Whitey's eyes. He didn't answer, but casually got up off the floor, stepped up to the bars with the tray of food in his right hand, and without warning, he slammed it against the bars! The food hit the Associate Warden directly in the face, splattering the contents all over him.

Whitey screamed at him, "Ya son of a bitch, come in here and I'll fuck you and your daughter too!"

He wanted to say something that really hurt, and it must have had the desired effect. Whitey thought the Associate Warden was going to have a heart attack.

Without a word he stormed out, and in a few minutes he returned with two big guards from the Goon Squad. The Cell House Officer opened the inner door, and the two Goons entered the cubicle and approached Whitey with caution. Strapped to their left arms were shields that resembled miniature mattresses, and in their right hands they carried gas-billies that were also used for clubbing their

17

victims.

Like a cornered animal, Whitey moved to the back of the cell and stood ready to protect himself. He knew he was going to take a severe beating, but this was nothing new to him, and he would not go down without a fight. With his back to the wall, he stood there in the nude without anything he could use to defend himself against the gas-billies, and the onslaught of the guards.

"Come on ya bastards!" he taunted, "ya brave lowlife sons-of-bitches. Come and get me, ya won't get no fucking cherry, come on."

When they moved in on him, Whitey immediately commenced to throw punches, but to no avail; he could not get past the protective shields the Goons carried. He was like a madman, screaming, punching and kicking. The guards using their shields were able to block all of Whitey's punches and kicks, and at the same time, struck back with their gas-billies.

Whitey's head exploded with pain from a blow that caught him across the bridge of the nose. He took another blow to the side of the head knocking him to the floor. He was totally helpless as the Goons moved in to finish the job. He could feel nothing now, and was not aware of the blows he was receiving to the head. A few moments before he became unconscious, he experienced flashes of light from the blows. It was like a dream, and he could sense the cruel kicking to his spine.

The beating was over now. The Associate Warden and his two Goons left, while the main guard locked the cell door leaving Whitey where he fell. How long he lay there he would never know. His first sign of consciousness was when he became aware of his uncontrollable shivering on the floor. He was lying on his back, and as he tried to lift his head, an excruciating pain racked his spine, his head fell back with a sickening thud, again blackness engulfed him.

The groans were an echo that got louder and louder, then suddenly they began to fade until he could no longer hear them. He strained his ears listening, but all he could hear was the pounding of a heartbeat. Each beat was thunderous to the eardrums, and he felt they would explode. A piercing cry broke the silence, Whitey grabbed his ears attempting to muff out the sound. It was then he realized that the crying and the groaning were coming from himself. His breathing was laboring and became more painful each time he inhaled, every breath he took seemed as though it was his last. He laid there a long time, not daring to move. Then his body began to feel as if it was floating on a cloud. The agony began to dissipate, his mind drifted as he strained to bring his thoughts together. He thought he could hear a loud slamming sound that seemed to come from far away, it was like the noise of a cell door opening and closing. Maybe it was a guard looking in on him. He didn't know nor did he

18

care, for he felt his life draining with each trickle of blood, but his will to live was strong. He opened his eyes, but he could only see the pitch darkness of his cell. He decided to turn over on his side to ease his tormented body. As he began to move he was jolted by a sharp flash of pain that shot up his spine. Like a bolt of lightening the shock of it made him suddenly roll over onto his stomach, causing him to grind his nose into the rough cement floor. A piercing arrow of pain shot from his nose across his forehead with such intensity, that his eyes felt like they would pop out of their sockets. He managed to roll over onto his back again, and tried to move his right hand up to investigate the damage to his face. His arm felt as if it would not move, and with sheer willpower, he slid his hand up to his nose, and when he touched it another arrow of pain shot through his head. The tip of his nose was torn, and hanging by a thread. He could feel his life's blood running out of him onto the floor.

Let it run, he thought. *Soon it will all be over, and the pain will be gone.*

He discovered his lips were split open when he began to choke and gag. The blood from his lips and nose were running down his throat; he had been choking on his own blood. He also discovered that he had been bleeding from a wound on top of his head. He did not know how bad it was, nor did he really care as he was already in so much pain.

How many days went by since the beating he did not know; at this point he was more dead than alive. But he was alive. On the fifth day, while unconscious Whitey was transferred to the prison hospital.

Two days after he was admitted, he began to regain his senses. It started when he heard the sound of whispering that seemed to come from a distance. He cocked his head slightly as he listened, but could not make out what was being said. The whispering began to get louder and louder, almost a shout, until he realized it was a voice addressing him. He opened his eyes, and when he did, it was like a signal for the pain to return. He quickly closed them again.

The voice was clear now as he heard someone say, "How are you feeling pal?"

Whitey did not reply, and the voice spoke again, "How are you feeling pal?"

Whitey turned to the speaker, and sitting up in the bed next to him was an old convict. Whitey did not know the man, and just laid there staring at him.

"Come on, can't you talk? Say something," the old man pleaded.

"Just dummy up old man. What's it to you how I feel?"

This was like a slap in the face to the old convict; he was

19

surprised at Whitey's hostility and spoke again, "What's wrong young fellow? All I asked was how you feel. Someone beat you up? Who did the job on you?"

A few moments elapsed, and it seemed as if Whitey was not going to answer. Then in harsh a voice, he whispered, "The fucking bulls beat me up, who else?"

"What the hell did you do to make them beat you like that?"

"Hey just dummy up old man, I don't feel like rapping."

"Okay pal, I understand. But let me tells you something, don't let them guards break your spirit, they can kill you, but they can't eat you."

Whitey did not reply; his mind was on the guards who had beaten him, he was obsessed with hatred. He knew the first chance he got, he would take one or both of them to the grave with him.

Lou Peters had no idea what happened to Whitey until one morning when the Segregation Guard stopped in front of his cell with the food cart. While he was dishing up the food, the guard turned his head to speak to Lou, "Well your buddy did it up good this time. Did you hear that ruckus a few days ago?"

"No, I can't hear anything that goes on in a strip cell. What happened?"

"Your friend Whitey is in the hospital."

Grabbing hold of the bars, a worried look crossed Lou's face.

"In the hospital?" he cried, "What happened to him?"

The guard enjoyed recounting the bad news about Whitey, "It was during mealtime about a week ago, he hit the Associate Warden in the face with a tray of food"

"He what? You must be bullshitting, I know Whitey's nuts, but he isn't crazy!" How bad is he hurt?"

The guard came closer to Lou's cell and slid a paper plate of food through the slot.

"He was banged up pretty good, but he'll recover. Tell me something Peters, why are you in Segregation?"

"That's a good question, I'm not sure why I'm here."

"I'll tell you why," the guard said with a cunning look, "it's because of Leon Whitey Thompson, that's why you're in here."

"What are you trying to give me?" Lou was getting mad.

"Just this Peters, for years Thompson has been your cell partner, and every time he had gotten into trouble, they discipline you along with him because you and Whitey are buddies. Why don't you cut him loose?"

Lou looked at the guard, and coldly replied, "You're right, he is a fuckup and a troublemaker, but you forgot one thing, he's also my buddy, and I would never cut a friend loose."

20

"Don't be such a fool Peters, you may consider him a friend, but he's not really, if you didn't hang around with him you would never get into trouble yourself."

"Yeah sure, I know what you are trying to say, but let me tell you something. He was a victim of the times, neglected, starved, beaten, and mistreated so much that he lost trust in everyone. But he accepted my friendship without question, and no matter how right or wrong he may be, I won't turn away from him, he'll always be my friend."

"What about him trying to recruit men to start a food riot?"

Lou laughed, "Are you crazy? That's a big pile of crap, that little bastard Whitey would never recruit anyone. If he wanted to start a food riot, he wouldn't need help."

The guard shrugged his shoulders and walked away.

Whitey's sojourn in the hospital was a comparatively quiet one. On occasions the old convict tried to speak to him, but received no response. In fact, Whitey spoke to no one, he knew as soon as he was well enough, he would be taken back to the Segregation Hole.

Two days later he was awakened by the doctor. "Thompson, Thompson wake up. How are you feeling this morning?"

"Who gives a damn how I feel? Just get the hell away from me you quack."

"Your recovery was fast Thompson, you'll be going back to Segregation this morning."

The doctor turned to leave.

"Up your ass quack, up your fucking ass," Whitey shouted after him.

Immediately after breakfast, a guard came for Whitey, and returned him to Segregation.

Before he was admitted to a cell he was allowed to shower. The water came out of the showerhead with such a terrific force it stung his wounds.

CHAPTER 4

Whitey was placed in a cell directly over Lou on the second tier. His new cubicle was five by ten feet, with a flush toilet, a small sink, face towel, paper cup, and a roll of toilet paper; also there was a bar of soap and a toothbrush sitting on the sink ledge, but no tooth powder. The cell contained no bed or mattress, but it did have a window in the rear wall made out of three-inch thick frosted glass embedded in steel. The door consisted of steel bars, and Whitey could look between them out over the tier to the opposite wall.

"The screws must be getting weak letting me have all this luxury!" he said to himself.

Lou called out from below. "Hey Whitey, how was your stay in the hospital?"

"In the hospital?" Whitey was surprised that Lou knew about it. "How did ya find out I was in there?"

"Hell Whitey I've known about it for the past two weeks. I also know why the Goons knocked your head in."

"Yeah the sorry bastards did a job on me, I also know why they threw you and me in the hole in the first place."

"Go ahead Whitey, tell me, I'm listening,"

"It was that son of a bitch Red, Red Kendrick, he was the bastard who wanted me to put crepe soles on his shoes. Remember him? He's the one who sent the phony kite to the Associate."

"Yeah, I remember him I knew he was a snitch Whitey, but why the hell did he involve me by putting my name on that note?"

"Simple Lou, in order to get me and feel safe, he had to get you too. He knew if I went to the hole, you would be coming after him. He couldn't take a chance on that happening, so he had to get you thrown in the hole too."

"That dirty son of a bitch," Lou shouted.

"Don't worry about it Lou, Red Kendrick's days are numbered."

Three days later, the heavy steel door to the Cell Block opened, and the guard with four inmates entered, carrying buckets and mops. Once a week the cleaning crew came in to tidy up, and as usual the

22

guard sat reading a newspaper. If he had been paying attention as he was supposed to be doing, he would have seen one of his men mopping the floor and edging his way toward Lou's cell. He would also have seen him pause long enough from his work to slip Lou a pack of cigarettes and matches, then nonchalantly continue with his work.

After the cleaning job was completed, the guard departed with his crew.

"Hey Lou—Lou. What's going on down there? Was that the cleaning crew?"

"Yeah Whitey they just got done cleaning the Flats and the empty cells out."

Whitey was standing near his cell bars, and was just about to call down again to Lou when he got a whiff of cigarette smoke. The smell almost drove him wild; it had been over a month since he had a cigarette. There was no smoking allowed in Segregation.

"Hey Lou, ya jive-ass bastard, you're smoking, where did ya get the smokes?"

Laughter sounded from the first tier.

"What are you laughing at you motherfucker? What's so funny?"

"You Whitey, I knew you would smell the cigarette smoke and go crazy!"

"Yeah I smelled it all right, now tell me how ya got the smokes?" Whitey demanded.

"I knew one of the dudes on the cleanup crew," Lou replied, "he slipped me a pack of Pall Malls and matches."

Whitey went right to work on his towel, and very carefully unraveled it, making it into a long string. After compressing some toilet paper into a ball, he dipped it into water, and squeeze out the excess. He tied the wet paper ball to the end of the string to serve as a weight. Carefully Whitey flipped the paper ball out over the edge of the tier; he immediately slacked off the string lowering the wad to the floor below. He gave it plenty of line, and it hit the floor four feet out in front of Lou's cell.

Lou poked his towel between the bars, and at arms' length he flipped one end out. On the third attempt the towel landed on the wad of toilet paper. Lou gently pulled in the towel, dragging the paper ball along with it. In a piece of dry toilet paper he wrapped ten cigarettes and a half book of matches, and tied the small package to the end of the line.

"It's all set Whitey, take it away slowly."

Whitey was excited with anticipation of having a cigarette. He carefully proceeded to pull on the string inch by inch. He felt the weight of the small package as it cleared the floor on Lou's level. Being extra cautious, he carefully pulled the string, and as he did so

23

he was waiting for the small package of cigarettes to appear at the edge of the tier. His anticipation ended when the package got stuck.

"Son of a bitch, it's stuck, the dirty bastard's stuck!" Whitey screamed out.

"Play it cool Whitey, and give it a little slack."

Doing what he was told; Whitey slacked off on the string. Then he tried pulling on it again. This time it came up with no trouble, Whitey was excited about the smokes. "I got 'em Lou—I got 'em."

He was overjoyed as he lit up a cigarette; pulling the smoke into his lungs he inhaled deeply, and the first drag made him dizzy. He quickly sat on the floor, took another drag of the cigarette, and as he sat there he savored this rare moment. He couldn't let the guards find the cigarettes, so he hung them by string down a small air vent. With strict rationing they lasted ten days. On the evening of the tenth day he smoked the last cigarette, then he called down to Lou. "Hey Lou—Lou you know what, I've been thinking."

Laughter sounded from below. "Well hooray for you! You been thinking, that's an accomplishment! What were you thinking about?" Lou continued to laugh.

"Laugh you bum. I'm gonna ask the bull for a cell move."

"You are going to what? Are you crazy? The only way you'll get moved is on a slab."

"Fuck you and your slab! How come the crew never cleaned up here, only down on the Flats where you cell. How come huh, tell me?"

"Maybe it's because you throw all your shit down here, and leave nothing up there for them to clean. What the hell are you going to do man? Answer me."

Whitey did not reply, he stepped over to the sink, picked up a roll of toilet paper, and deliberately dropped it into the toilet bowl. Subsequently barefoot, he stepped up on the bowl, and with his left foot on the edge, and his hands braced against the wall, he put his right foot down on the roll of toilet paper, and using his full body weight he pushed down on it until the toilet bowl was completely plugged up.

He pressed his left knee against the wall flush button. As long as the button was pressed there would be a continuous high-pressure flow of water, and the sound of it was deafening. In seconds the bowl was filled with water, and running over the side. It was extremely cold on Whitey's bare feet, and it was only a blink of the eye before the floor was covered with rushing water. It flowed out of the cell, across the runway, and off the tier, hitting the main floor with a terrific splash. The flow of water came gushing off the tier like a miniature Niagara Falls!

"Goddamn," Lou bellowed, Whiteeeey! You son of a bitch, Where the hell is that fucking water coming from?"

24

Whitey yelled back, "The shitter's plugged up and overflowing!"

"You crazy bastard you're getting me all wet down here!"

"Just hang tough Lou," Whitey shouted, "and let me know when the water reaches the main door."

From Whitey's location he could not see the entrance to the Cell Block, but Lou being on the Flats had a clear view of the heavy steel door.

"Yeah the water is running under it now, you're going to be getting company real soon."

The main door burst open, and an angry guard cussing and swearing rushed in, "Where's all that water coming from?" he shouted.

Over the noise of rushing water Whitey could hear the guard's loud bitching as he ran toward the stairs. He dashed past Lou's cell, and as he did so he caught a glimpse of him hanging on the bars endeavoring to keep his feet out of the water. The guard flew up the stairs, and ran straight to Whitey's cell.

In a fit of rage he yelled, "Thompson have you gone crazy? What the hell are trying to do?"

Innocently Whitey replied, "I'm not doing nothing, the shitter's plugged up and running over!"

" 'Course it's running over, get your goddamn knee off that flush button. What's wrong with you?"

Whitey smiled and removed his knee from the push-button.

The guard took his key out and opened the cell door. He rushed straight to the toilet bowl, and as he did so Whitey stepped aside to let him pass, and then nonchalantly stepped out onto the tier.

The guard was furious when he looked into the toilet bowl. "Hell I guess it is plugged up, anything would be plugged with that roll of toilet paper jammed in there. Damn it Thompson I've a mind to call the Goons in here."

"Hey go ahead and call 'em, who gives a fuck? Fuck you and your Goons too!"

Whitey took a step toward the guard. The officer was going off duty soon, and did not want more trouble with Whitey. He just wanted to get his shift over with, "All right Thompson, just calm down, I'm going to put you in another cell."

Whitey sensed the guard was weakening, "Hey all right, how about putting me in a cell next to Lou?"

"Nothing doing Thompson, I can't do that and you know it. I have to keep you on this tier, so I'm going to put you in the corner cell."

After the guard had Whitey secured in his new cell, he spoke to him in a pleasant voice, "Thompson why did you have to mess up on my shift? True, I go by the book, but I have never mistreated you, or any other inmate."

"Yeah sure," Whitey said sarcastically, "I'm sure you don't mistreat inmates, you just like to fuck over convicts, I'm a convict, not an inmate."

The guard stood there a moment staring at Whitey. Whitey never liked to be called an inmate by anyone; it went against the grain with him because he thought an inmate as someone who was in a psychiatric hospital, or an informer, (commonly known as a snitch in prison). Or any prisoner who butters up to the guards and staff for favors.

Whitey, with hostile eyes stared directly back at the guard, and in a low angry voice he hissed, "Don't ever call me no fucking inmate, or I'll tear this jive-ass cell apart!"

The guard, somewhat taken aback, seemed to be collecting his thoughts on how he should handle this situation. He knew he had to use kid gloves when it came to a confrontation with Thompson.

The expression on the officer's face changed to an understanding look as he said, "Thompson I'm not going to make out a report for plugging up the toilet and flooding the place. I understand your situation somewhat, and I'm going to give you a pass this time. In the meantime I'm going to get a crew in here to clean up the water. But you better understand me—and understand me good, don't ever screw up on my shift again."

The hatred in Whitey was overflowing, "Don't do me any favors, make out all the fucking reports you want, and you know what? Fuck you and your shift too!"

Again the guard was taken aback; he knew it was useless to try to have any further discussion with Thompson. Turning around sharply and after he stormed off the tier and out of Segregation, Lou called out, "Hey Whitey, that bull moved you, where the hell are you at now?"

"I'm locked up you fool, I'm over in the corner cell."

"You're lucky Whitey you're not back in the strip cell with your head caved in."

"Who gives a fuck? I told you I'd get a cell move, and this tier cleaned."

"But you didn't get down on this tier in the cell next me," Lou laughed.

"Yeah well you better watch tomorrow, I'll flood this cell too!"

"Are you crazy?" Lou screamed. "It's already cold in here, without you running water all over the place."

"Okay—okay Lou, don't worry I won't flood it." Whitey laughed. Then he turned his attention to his new cell; giving it the once-over he discovered that it was bigger than his last one. His present cell was ten by ten feet, and it too had a window identical to the one in the other cell. It was frosted, making it impossible to see through.

The cell also had standard equipment, but Whitey found one small addition, he picked up a pencil stub that was lying behind the toilet bowl.

The day seemed as if it would never end. After the evening meal was served, it was a long and tiresome wait for the guard to throw him a blanket at 10:00 P.M.. Quickly Whitey wrapped it around his body for he was shivering, and he lay down on the floor, using the roll of toilet paper as a pillow. As he lay there, he thought about the events of the day. His mind drifted to Lou who was in Segregation just for being his friend, nothing else. Then his mind shifted to —Red Kendrick. Whitey knew that when he returned to the main population he would get Red. Then an afterthought crossed Whitey's mind. Suppose he was not returned to population; suppose he was transferred to another prison, and never gotten to see Red again? Suppose! Suppose! There was only one thing left to do; he had to get word to Blackie or Shorty, to take care of Red. Whitey was smiling as he fell asleep. He knew the contract would be set, and Red Kendrick's days, were numbered.

CHAPTER 5.

Early the next morning after breakfast, Whitey's craving for a cigarette began to increase. He wanted one now more than ever; he was suffering from a nicotine withdrawal; that alone would drive a man crazy!

He knew Lou had no cigarettes but yelled down to him anyway, "Hey Lou, you got a cigarette? "

"Yeah I got a whole carton," Lou replied. "What else do you want?"

"A good piece of ass!"

"Whitey you been locked up too long, you wouldn't know what to do with a piece."

"Yeah maybe not, but it would be fun trying. Hey by the way Lou, what's behind this building we're in?"

"There's a small yard out there between Segregation and the kitchen building."

"Do any cons ever get to go out there?"

"Yes, sometimes the kitchen crew is let out for a breath of air. Why do you ask?"

"How about a guard tower, is there a guard tower out there, or any guards around?"

"No, there's no tower out there, but once in a while there's a bull out there. What the hell do you want to know all this for? Is this another one of your crazy ideas?"

"What's so crazy about wanting to get some smoking tobacco?"

"Nothing, but I know you're going to do something stupid to try and get it, and if you're thinking about your cell window, it's as solid as a rock, and you'll never break it open."

"That's what you think Lou. I'm gonna knock a hole in it just big enough to pull a sack of smoking tobacco through."

"Who's going to tie a sack on the string for you, dummy?"

"I'll put a kite on the end of the string," Whitey replied, "asking anyone out there to tie some tobacco on it. I hope a con sees the note and not a bull."

"You know you're crazy Whitey, first off, what the hell can you use for a tool? You'll need a jack-hammer to get through that window."

28

"Lou, you have no imagination, I have all the tools I need."

Lou started to laugh as he said, "All the tools you'll need? You don't even have a brain, never mind tools!"

"Maybe I don't have a brain, but I have a comb and a toothbrush, and that's all I need. Now shut up and let me go to work."

Whitey turned to face the window, and carefully examined each pane of glass to see if one might be loose. On the bottom, the second one from the right had a little give to it. He raised his leg up in the air, and tried kicking it with the heel of his bare foot. Damn that hurt! The pain shot up his leg, but he tried again.

"I need a cigarette," he kicked the window repeatedly, until he felt his heel getting raw.

"Fuck the pain," he hissed, "I want a smoke." He kicked at the window a few more times. The excruciating pain was more than most humans could bear. But Thompson was so intent in what he was doing, combined with the thought of tobacco, made him oblivious of the pain.

He stopped for a moment to inspect the window to see if he had made any progress. He was excited when he discovered he could move the pane of glass up and down about a quarter of an inch. He stepped over to the sink, and picked up his comb, and tried working the end tooth of the comb into the mortar between the glass and the steel. The steel bar had a ridge on it that prevented the glass from being removed. If he could work some of the mortar out, he would be able to move the glass up and down an inch. This would allow plenty of room to get a sack of smoking tobacco through. It was slow work, and at times he wished he could put his fist right through the pane of glass. As he worked he became frustrated with his slow progress, and he began to cuss out the workmen, whoever they were, for building such a strong structure.

Occasionally a guard would come in to make his rounds. Whitey would hear him coming, and lean against the wall, or drop to the floor and start doing pushups as if nothing was wrong.

On his first day of work at the window, he kicked, scraped, and hacked on it until 10 P.M. He was so engrossed in what he was doing, he did not realize the time until he heard a guard coming with his blanket. He quickly dropped to the floor, and commenced doing pushups as the guard walked up to his cell. For a moment he stood watching Whitey, then he stuffed the blanket between the bars.

"I see you're getting your exercise Thompson, it seems every time I come by your cell you're doing pushups."

At the officer's remark, Whitey stopped in the middle of a pushup, and hissed at the guard, "What the fuck's it to ya? Just do your job and get the hell out of here."

Once the officer was gone Whitey moved to the bars to retrieve his blanket. He was totally exhausted from the day's events, and all the pushups he was compelled to do. He curled up in the threadbare blanket after placing a roll of toilet paper under his head. He was in need of a cigarette, and as he lay there he thought about the beating he had taken, and just before falling asleep, he knew he would retaliate, by taking a guard to the grave with him.

Early the following morning, after the guard retrieved the blanket, Whitey focused his attention on the window. *I'll get through ya today, ya son of a bitch!*

A short while later the guard returned with the usual paper plate of food, and after sliding it into Whitey's cell he departed. No words were exchanged. Whitey was thankful for that, he wanted to be left alone so that he could get back to work on the window. It was an obsession with him, after eating breakfast, he was angry and disturbed when the guard returned to pick up the empty plate and spoon.

Once the guard was gone, Lou called out, "How's it going Whitey?"

"Not bad—not bad at all. I should be fishing before too long"

"I hope you get a bite," Lou called cheerfully.

At the time, Whitey had no idea, nor did he realize it would take him twelve long days to accomplish his project.

Whitey turned to the window with a kick. Again he worked on it all day long; at times his imagination ran away with him, and he thought he smelled cigarette smoke. This inspired him to work even harder. He was so engrossed in what he was doing; he did not notice the red stains appearing on the glass. When he finally did notice, it took a moment before he realized that it was his own blood. It was coming from his fingers—they were raw from the clawing. At the sight of his blood, his anger rose, and he began to work more feverishly. Again he checked the window to see how far it would move, but his hard work caused no change, and he became furious at the lack of results. He stood back glaring at the glass, and he wished that he could charge hurling his body at the window, and burst right through it. But this was impossible, and he knew it.

Once Whitey started something, he would not give up, and the second day's work dragged on into the third, and the third into the fourth. The obsession Whitey had to get through the window was so great that he lost track of time. He didn't realize how many days had gone by, until the twelfth day when he discovered enough mortar had been removed. This was it! He could slide the window pane up a good inch, and the space was large enough for a sack of tobacco to pass through.

Quickly he grabbed his towel, and began to construct a string

30

from it. Next he took the cardboard tube from the center of the roll of toilet paper, and after soaking it in water, he folded and pressed it into a small square. This he would use for weight on the end of the string. With the stub of a pencil he wrote a note on a piece of toilet paper, and attached it to the line. The note read, 'Tie a sack of tobacco, matches, and cigarette papers on this string, and give it a gentle pull. Thanks.'

"Hey Lou, I'm all set, I made a hole in the ice. I dropped my line through it and I'm ready to go fishing,"

"Good luck, I hope you get a bite." For the first time since Whitey started this escapade, Lou's doubts began to change, and he too felt the excitement of the moment.

It was impossible for Whitey to see the ground below from the small aperture. Once he played the string out, all he could do was hope that a prisoner, and not a guard, would see the note. Occasionally he would give the line a gentle jerk to make the note jump up and down, hoping to attract someone's attention. To relax Whitey sat on the floor to wait for a nibble.

As Whitey sat there on the cold floor waiting for a bite, his mind drifted back to his boyhood days. He often sat on a bank at the edge of a stream, fishing for sunfish or whatever he could catch. He was excited at the anticipation of a catch, and it was fun sitting there using a stick for a fishing pole. Never once did he dream that he would one day be in the Federal Penitentiary at McNeil Island; fishing through a hole in a window, for a sack of Stud smoking tobacco.

His thoughts were broken when he heard the day officer open the main door to the Cell Block. He quickly pulled in the line, and wrapped it up in the remains of the towel. Whitey doubted that the guard could see the hole in the window. He would have to come into the cell and check each pane of glass to find it.

Every day without fail the guard would check all unoccupied cells along with Whitey's cell and as he looked in on him Whitey said in a surly voice, "How about a smoke?"

Showing no patience the officer replied, "I'll give you a smoke—I'll give you a club across the head."

With sheer contempt Whitey shouted, "Ya jive-ass-no-class-funny-style-prick, you're good at knocking heads in ya cheap son of a bitch!"

Without another word the officer continued along the walkway, stomping as he went off the tier, down the stairs, and out of the building, slamming the big steel door behind him. For a moment after his departure, the sound of his key locking the main door echoed throughout the Cell House.

"Hey Whitey," Lou yelled. "What the hell did you say to that bull? He sure was pissed off the way he flew by here."

31

"I guess he just didn't like my compliments. I called him a-jive-ass-no-class-funny-style-prick!"

Lou chuckled as he said, "You can't leave it alone can you Whitey?"

When the evening watch officer came on duty, Lou was surprised to see that it was not the regular guard. He was a young guard. At a glance, Lou immediately knew by the cut of his uniform, and the glistening shine of his shoes, that he was new to the Correctional System. He was carrying two trays of food, and as he slid one under the bars of Lou's cell, he smiled and said, "I'm Officer Novak. Officer McKay is home sick, I'm filling in for him."

Lou retrieved his tray, and in a military fashion, the young officer strutted toward the stairwell leading up to the second tier. Whitey was standing up to his cell door anxiously waiting for his food.

"You must be Leon Thompson," he stated in a cheerful voice, "I'm Officer Novack. Are you ready for your dinner?"

"Does a bear shit in the woods? Man I'm starving."

As this was not the regular officer, Whitey thought he would try to con him out of some extra food, and in a coaxing voice he continued, "No kidding officer, I'm starving. There's never enough to eat. I could use a refill, what do ya say?"

The guard glanced at the tray heaped with food. As he handed it to Whitey he said, "I'm sorry Thompson you know I can't do that. You're only allowed one ration."

Being more persuasive with the young guard, Whitey pleaded, "Come on, sure you can. No one will ever know. Come on what do ya say? I'm so hungry I could eat the ass of a skunk!"

"I sure wished I could—honest, but you know I'm new here, I could get myself in a jam."

"Ah come on. Ya know what happens to the extra food when it goes back to the kitchen—they throw it away. So come on man, no one will ever know. What'd you say, I'm starving."

The officer stood there a moment looking into Whitey's pleading eyes, and then slowly shaking his head, he conceded. "Okay I'll do it just this once, but don't foul me up."

"Don't worry about it. Ya got my word on it."

Officer Novack left the tier, he returned shortly with a second tray of food, and as he turned to leave he said, "Enjoy your meal Thompson."

Whitey did not acknowledge the guard's departure, but under his breath he said to himself, "You fucking sucker!"

"Hey Whitey," Lou yelled, "how did you con that fish bull into seconds? He gave me an extra tray too."

"He couldn't resist my personality, just eat up and shut up!"

The following morning immediately after breakfast, Whitey was listening for the sound of the work-call whistle before he played the string and note out of the hole. The reason he waited was that there would be no inmates outside the buildings until after the work whistle blew. Off in the distance, he heard the whistle blow.

"It's about time," he said aloud as he hurriedly played the string out the window.

Whitey sat on the floor holding the end of the string when suddenly it jerked. He jumped up and hurriedly began to pull in the line. As he pulled the string in, he realized there was no tension on it, and he began to cuss as the end came dangling through the hole. The note was gone. After twelve long and arduous days of clawing, banging and hacking at the hole in anticipation of a cigarette, the disappointment was too much for him. He stood there in disbelief. No doubt a guard must have discovered the note, but then again it could have been an inmate. As these thoughts ran rampant through his head, Whitey's blood began boiling with rage. He was furious as he gathered and knotted the string into a ball, then flung it into the toilet, flushing it down the drain. Then he turned to the window, and screamed through the hole, "Ya dirty dick-licking bastard, ya mother-fucking son of a bitch, up your mother's ass!"

"Hey Whitey—Whitey, what's wrong? What're you pissed about?"

If Whitey heard Lou calling, he showed no sign of it as he continued to cuss out the culprit.

"Ya bastard, ya son of a bitch, ya take-it-up-the-ass punk! Some bastard broke the string and took the kite."

"Oh-oh Whitey, that's means you got trouble man, if a screw got that note he'll be coming after you."

"Who gives a fuck? Let the son of a bitch come after me. What the hell can they do? Lock me up? Beat me up? Who gives a fuck?"

There was no reply from Lou because he knew Whitey was furious, and anything he said would just infuriate him more.

A silence settled over the Cell Block. Whitey stood quietly listening and waiting for a telltale sound. He was waiting for the Cell House door to burst open admitting an angry guard, but to his surprise, no one appeared.

The day passed by slowly, and when the evening watch officer came on duty, nothing was mentioned about the note.

After the officer departed Whitey called to Lou, "What 'd you think happened to the kite?"

"Hell I don't know. If a screw got it he probably just tore it up and threw it away, or else someone would of been up here by now. You know Whitey I can't help but laugh at you, all your work was for nothing, you never did get a smoke."

"You're full of shit, it wasn't for nothing. It gave me something to do. It kept my mind busy, and that's worth something."

"Yeah I guess you're right Whitey, that's one way to look at it."

That night when Whitey received his blanket from the guard, nothing was said about the note or the hole in the window. It was still on his mind when he fell asleep, and he wondered who had broken the string and taken the note, a guard or an inmate?

Most inmates didn't know how to occupy their time or use their God-given brains. They have no imagination and become vegetables. What can a prisoner do when he is locked up alone in a cell for days and weeks on end? He has to put his mind to work, and sometimes do things he wouldn't normally do. He does anything short of killing himself to keep occupied. Some men masturbate, others play with their own stool, smearing it on the walls and drawing designs. Most people would think these men were insane, but they were not, they were men who had been in Segregation too long, and used the only means at their disposal to try and save their sanity.

As long as a man kept his mind occupied whether it may be negative or positive thinking, he would survive. But the prisoner who lets himself go on a self-pity trip, winds up bashing his head against the wall, or jumping off a tier.

CHAPTER 6.

Every day in Segregation was the same, the daily routine was identical. Nothing changed, causing each hour, each day, each week, to run into one another, and time stood still, or so it seemed. At an early hour on the morning of Whitey's forty-second day in Segregation, he was surprised when an officer (without warning) unlocked his cell door.

He was ordered out of his cell, and to continue down to the Flats (main floor), and to stop in front of Lou's cell.

Whitey stood there while the guard opened the door for him. At the sight of Whitey, Lou's face lit up with a smile, "Whitey you fucking termite, you look like you just fell off a freight train."

"What're talking about fucker? You look like you just escaped from the Chicago Zoo!"

Both men's hair had grown to a considerable length, their eyes were bloodshot, and there was an insane look about them.

The officer pointed to an anteroom where they were ordered to strip and shower. After the endless days and nights in a cold damp cell, the sting of the scalding water stimulated their tortured bodies, and it was welcomed.

After the two men had dried themselves off, they were issued a pair of socks, underwear, shoes, and a set of new prison blues. After weeks of being barefooted on a concrete floor, it felt good to have shoes and socks on their feet again.

Once they were dressed and ready, they were escorted from Segregation out through the big steel doorway onto the Flats of Cell House Four. As the small convoy of men made their way along, catcalls could be heard issuing from the cell block.

"Hey Whitey—hey Lou, how you guys doing?"

A more familiar voice called, "Whitey, hey Whitey, hang tough, pal."

Whitey shifted his eyes and caught sight of Blackie standing up to the front of his cell.

"Everything's cool Blackie, do you know the name of the game? The game is the red headed woodpecker. Are you hep to the wood-

35

pecker?"

"Hell yes Whitey I'm hep, it's as good as taken care of."

Shorty, who was standing in the cell next to Blackie shouted, "Hey Whitey, Lou, where they taking you guys?"

The convoy of men had reached the corner of the Cell Block, and just before they disappeared through the doorway, Whitey called back, "They're taking us to the Warden's house for dinner, and after dinner he's going to fix us up with his daughter!"

"If you fuck her, you'll fuck anything," Shorty shouted after them.

A chorus of laughter could be heard echoing throughout the block as the small procession disappeared through the doorway, and out the gate, leaving Four House behind them. A duty guard let them pass through into Two Building. There the Segregation guard turned the prisoners over to the Cell House Officer of Two Block, and departed.

In a stern voice the Cell House Officer commanded, "Okay boys, let's go follow me." He quickly walked around the corner of Two Block, and started down the Flats, with Whitey and Lou following. The first three cells they passed were occupied, but the fourth one was empty. Lou was placed in it and locked up. Then Whitey and the guard continued along the Flats. Whitey was locked up eight cells down the tier from Lou, and as soon as he stepped in the cubicle, the door slid shut behind him with an earsplitting bang. Immediately after the door closed, it was locked by remote control by a guard standing at the switch panel at the end of the tier. Once Whitey was secured, the Cell House Officer stepped up to the door, and double locked it by securing the hasp with a heavy bright red padlock. This pound and a half padlock served two purposes. One, not only did it double the locking security of the door. But also at a glance it was a badge of warning to all guards not to unlock this cell door under any circumstances. Once this lock was in use on a door, it could not be opened except on orders from the Captain of Security, or the Warden. (THIS WAS DEADLOCK.)

Whitey's new cell contained a steel bunk and mattress. Setting on a shelf over a small sink were a face towel, bar of soap, toothbrush, tooth powder, and a roll of toilet paper. He continued inspecting the cubicle to make sure nothing was planted in there, such as a shank (knife), or other contraband. He would not put it past a Security Guard to plant something illegal in his cell. Whitey had served much time, and he knew of prisoners that were set up by guards, and as a result they received more time, and in some cases, even death.

While Whitey was inspecting his cell Lou called out to him, "Hey Whitey. What cell are you in?"

"I'm down at the end of the tier, I'm in cell 2-A-12."

"You're in 2-A-12? That should hold you Whitey. I'm in 2-A-4 and I know it'll hold me!"

"Yeah but it won't hold all your bullshit," Whitey chuckled back at him.

"Fuck you Whitey. Hey what's going to happen next?"

"Shit I don't know, I guess they're going let us rot here for a while, you know what that red padlock means."

Lou was surprised to hear Whitey mention the red padlock. "Yeah I know what it means, but I don't have one on my cell door. Do you have one on yours?"

"Yeah, the sons of bitches put one on mine. I guess you know what that means Lou. They're gonna let my ass rot in here for a while, then after a few months of this shit, they'll put me on a set of water-skis to Alcatraz. They might even send your ass there too Lou."

"Bullshit Whitey, you may end up on the Rock, but they're not taking my ass there."

"Your ass belongs to the Feds Lou, if I go to the Rock, you can be sure your going too!"

"Hey the way I feel Whitey, I don't give a shit where they send me as long as I get fed".

At each mealtime an inmate pushed a food cart into the Cell House along with two helpers. While the food cart man filled the trays, the two helpers (called tray runners), passed them out by sliding them through a slot in each cell door. All this was done under the supervision of an escort guard. Breakfast was at 6:00 A.M., Lunch at 11:45 A.M., and dinner at 3:30 P.M. The highlights of each day for the prisoners in Deadlock, were the meals.

Once the food was passed out, and each prisoner received his tray, the escort officer and crew left the building, returning twenty minutes later to collect the dinnerware. The guard then counted the trays, spoons, and forks. The prisoners were never given knives.

Once a week on each Monday an inmate from the library (again escorted by a guard), would bring books to Deadlock. He would make out a list of the name and number of books he left, and on the following Monday he would return to collect them. The old books had to be turned in before he would leave new ones. Each prisoner was allowed two books a week, and after they had been read, they would trade them back and forth.

Clothing Exchange was once a week. Each Friday evening right after the 6:00 P.M. head count, the Deadlock prisoners would disrobe, and were compelled to stand up to the bars stark naked to receive their clean clothes. First he would hand his dirty items between the bars to a trusty. A guard would check each article of clothing, and in exchange the prisoner would receive clean ones.

Each evening at 7:00 P.M. dirty socks were placed on the bars. The trusty, with a guard would walk along the tier pushing his cart, exchanging clean socks for the dirty ones. If a prisoner was asleep, or for some reason did not have his dirty socks on the bars during stocking exchange, then he missed out. By the smell it seemed as if some of them did not change their socks very often!

After weeks of lying on a cold floor Whitey welcomed the luxury of a warm bed, and while lying on it he thought about his childhood days. He knew something was wrong in the family, but did not know it pertained to his mother. Having never met his mother, he began to ask questions about her, but received no answers. There were six other children in the family, but he never felt he was a part of this group. Also he didn't think the man he called "Pop" was his real father. He felt he didn't belong, and at an early age he was always trying to do constructive things to impress the adults. All he ever wanted was a little love and the right attention, but instead it seemed all he received were whippings. Often he would do things hoping to win approval; his intentions were good, but they always backfired, and he was punished. His father would never ask him the why or wherefore of his intentions. One such intentional deed stood out above the rest in Whitey's mind.

CHAPTER 7

It was a cold winter morning in January 1927, and Whitey had just turned four years old. There was a fresh blanket of snow on the ground that had fallen the previous night, and the northern winds were sharp and frigid. Whitey and his brother Edwin, who was three years his senior, was playing out in the back yard with Edwin's puppy. After a while they began to feel cold, and decided to go into the big barn that was located a short distance from the house. They could not get the door open because of the snow that had drifted against it. Whitey made his way to the back porch for a shovel, and finally, with much effort, the boys managed to open the door a few feet.

Their father had over two hundred chickens and due to the severe cold weather all of them were inside the old barn. As the two boys stepped through the doorway they could see them all huddled together on the roosts. Whitey felt sorry for the birds thinking they were freezing. There was no flooring in the barn, only the bare earth. Whitey suggested that they should build a small fire to make it warm for the chickens. Edwin agreed, and accordingly Whitey hurried out of the barn. He took off running toward the house, disappearing into the cellar where he found an old wooden orange crate. With considerable labor he managed to drag it through the snow, and into the barn where Edwin was piling pieces of wood in the center of the earthen floor. Again Whitey dashed out of the barn, and returned with an old car tire. This too was added to the growing pile of wood. Once more he returned to the cellar to retrieve an empty gallon jug. In the corner stood a wooden sawhorse, and mounted on it was a fifty-gallon drum of fuel oil. While Whitey was filling the jug with fuel, Edwin was upstairs in the kitchen after matches. He returned to the barn and waited for Whitey who soon appeared in the doorway with the gallon of fuel oil. Grabbing the jug out of his hands, Edwin quickly poured the contents on the huge pile of wood and the car tire.

Whitey would never forget the terror that followed the moment Edwin lit the match. In a blinding flash the hungry flames shot up to the ceiling of the old barn, reaching out for the dried wood covered with cobwebs and dust. Immediately from the source of the fire, a stream of black smoke began to rise, and in seconds the barn became

39

an inferno.

The chickens were screeching and fluttering trying to escape, and one flying bird, with wings flapping, came sailing at Whitey. He screamed and threw his hands in front of his face to ward off the screeching missile; in doing so, he fell over backwards, knocking the wind out of himself. He was fighting for air now, and in the smoke filled barn he could no longer see his brother, but he could hear him screaming, "The puppy, where is my puppy? Whitey, Whitey get out of the barn." Being the eldest, Edwin tried to take charge of the situation by ordering Whitey out of the barn, and telling him he would follow him right after he found his puppy.

No one will ever know, even Whitey himself, how in the intense heat, and blinding smoke, he found his way to the outside where he fell into the snow, gasping for air.

His sixteen-year-old sister Marge had seen the smoke from the kitchen window, and came running out of the house. Whitey was still lying in the snow gasping for air; his eyes were red, and tears were running down his cheeks.

Marge was shouting as she ran to him, "Edwin, Edwin, my god where is he?"

Whitey was coughing and could barely talk, but he managed to tell her that Edwin was still in the barn. With signs of panic she dashed into the smoke-filled barn, and at the same time Charlie, their older brother, came charging out of the house. By this time the barn was totally engulfed in flames. Charlie ran toward the inferno just as Marge emerged through the doorway, carrying Edwin in her arms. She was totally exhausted and collapsed, falling to the ground. Charlie, frantically, using his hands as scoops, shoveled snow over the victims, endeavoring to extinguish their burning clothes.

Marge had minor burns, and most of her hair was singed off. Fortunately her hair would grow back, and the burns would soon heal without a trace. Edwin was lying motionless next to her in the cold powdered snow. His left leg was badly burned, and charged flesh and skin hung loosely from it.

For Whitey, the next few hours were a nightmare of fear. He was alone in the house while the rest of the family were at the hospital with Marge and Edwin. His father was still at work, and up to this point knew nothing of the burning barn.

It was just after sunset when Whitey had gone upstairs to hide in the attic. He had gone up there immediately after they took Edwin and Marge off in the ambulance. It was nighttime now, and darkness had set in throughout the house. There was no electrical service in the home, and Whitey was too small to reach, or know how to light the gas lamps mounted high on the walls. He came out of the attic and sat down at the head of the stairs.

Whitey had been left alone many times, and for a small boy he had no fear of the dark. But yet he sat there shivering, and a fear began to run through him as he thought about his father. What could he tell him about the barn? Would he realize it was an accident, and hadn't meant for it to burn down? He only wanted to make it warm for the chickens, but now there were no more chickens. The big barn was gone; the only remains were a giant ugly black spot in the snow, and even the puppy was dead. He knew he would not be given a chance to explain the situation, and knew he would be beaten mercilessly when his father came home.

"Oh what am I going to do?" He wailed. "Pop is going to kill me, I know he is going to kill me." He began to cry, but suddenly stopped as he heard the backdoor open and then shut with a slam. He sat there in total horror as the sound of his father's extremely angry voice penetrated the walls of the house.

"What happened to the barn?" he shouted. "Who burned it down? Goddamn it where is everybody? Is anyone home? Answer me damn it."

Whitey was sitting very quietly, afraid to move, he was praying for a miracle. His trembling was beyond control, and he didn't know when he started to stir, but found himself standing up and shaking so violently he lost his balance in the darkness, and fell up against a bedroom door.

His father heard the noise and ran to the hallway. Quickly he struck a match, lighting the hall gas light. The glow of it revealed Whitey standing at the head of the stairs. His father, as if in a trance, stared at him for a moment. Whitey was not sure, but he thought he could see fire coming from his eyes! Suddenly his father charged up stairs. Before Whitey could utter a word, his father grabbed hold of him, and slapped him severely across the face. He tried to scream, but no sound came forth. Again his father slapped his face and he began shaking him violently. What happened to the barn? Answer me you little bastard, you burned it down didn't you? Damn it all I said answer me. Where the hell is everybody?"

Whitey was doubled up with fear, and he tried desperately to speak, but with the violent treatment he was receiving, he was unable to utter a word.

Once again his father slapped him, then slammed him against the wall, and shrieked, "Who burned the barn down? Answer me, where's everybody at?"

"Pop, Pop don't hit me again, please, Edwin is in the hospital, he's in the hospital."

His father stood there a second or two as Whitey's words began to sink in. Without warning, he released his vicelike grip on Whitey causing him to fall over backward down the stairs to the bottom landing. His father like a raging bull, charged down the stairs. He disappeared out the door, leaving Whitey lying there badly bruised, and crying, but there was no one to hear him.

Edwin's recovery was slow, he healed well, and soon he was able to run and play like any normal child. Except for numerous scars, one would never know that he had been seriously hurt, but Whitey's hurt was just beginning. His father never forgave him, and the endless beatings he received turned his fear into hate. He developed such a fear of his father, he felt the only way to escape him was to kill him. Although he never did kill his father the seed was planted.

CHAPTER 8.

Ervin Thompson, Whitey's father, was a hard working man; he was employed by the New York, New Haven, and Hartford Railroad. As an engineer on the New York, New Haven, and Boston run, it left little time for him to spend with his family. Occasionally he would have a layover in New Haven, and had no excuse not to return home, instead, most of the time he chose to get drunk and carouse around. When he did return home, he was always tired; rarely was he sober, and seldom in a good mood.

On these rare occasions when his father came home, Whitey would try to stay out of his way by hiding out. Only after his father would return to work, did he feel safe. This practice did not always work, for at times, when his father was in an extremely foul mood, he would hunt for Whitey until he found him. When he did, he would take out his aggressions on the boy by beating him with a cat-o-nine-tails. The beatings were more than Whitey could endure; his hatred for mankind grew, and he would carry the emotional scars to his grave.

In the eyes of his father, Whitey was a brat, a bad boy who was no good, who continuously needed punishment. Whitey could not understand this, nor could he understand the hatred his father had for him, and most of all, rarely did he know what he was being punished for. As a child Whitey would get into trouble and do things wrong, but these were not deliberate acts, it's just that he did not know any better. It was during this time his father was supposed to be a real father, and take the time to give Whitey love, and understanding, and a chance to learn right from wrong, and the correct way of doing things. Whitey was always trying to impress older people in what he was doing; but in the eyes of the adults, he was just a kid showing off and acting silly. But he wasn't acting silly, for he was always trying to do something constructive to gain recognition. But in the eyes of the adults he was nothing but a pain, and told to shut up, stop what you're doing and get out of here, or I'll slap your face and send you to bed. To the boy this was rejection, total rejection, and that's the way it went for him day after day, rejection, rejection, instead of love and understanding all he ever received was, rejection.

43

There were numerous guns in the house, and at times Whitey would watch his father clean and handle them. Also he would watch him shoot rats out behind the dog houses. At the age of four he didn't really know what a rat was, but he knew his father didn't want them around the place, especially where he kept his hounds. There were eight of these friendly dogs, and now and then one of the bitches would have a litter of pups that were put up for sale. They sold for five or six dollars a piece, which was good money during the depression years.

One day in August, the summer following the tragedy of the barn burning down, Whitey was outside playing. He discovered one of the hound dogs wasn't moving, and he thought she was dead. She was lying on her side with newborn puppies crawling all over her. There were six of them. Never having seen newborn puppies, Whitey thought they were rats chewing on the hound dog's stomach. Without investigating further he quickly ran to the house screaming, "Rats—rats, Pop, there's rats out there eating the dog!"

When he received no response, he didn't quite know what to do. He started to leave the house when he noticed the gun cabinet with three shotguns standing erect behind the glass door. He quickly pulled up a chair and climbed onto it, and found the cabinet door was unlocked. Opening it he took hold of the nearest gun. He didn't know if the weapon was loaded for he was too young to understand such complications. With great difficulty, he dragged the gun out to the backyard, and somehow managed to aim it at the dog. The weapon was heavy for the youngster, and it was a struggle to hold it up. The shotgun was loaded, and it went off with a terrific explosion that knocked Whitey backward to the ground. Luckily he wasn't hurt, but the hound dog and her puppies, were splattered all over the ground!

His father had heard the shot, and in a fit of rage he seemed to appear from nowhere. Angrily he used one hand to literally snatched Whitey off the ground, and with the other he scooped up the twelve gage shotgun. Like a crazed animal, he carried the boy into the house, and as he entered the kitchen he dropped him on the floor. Spinning on his heels, he went straight to the gun cabinet, got two shells, and loaded the double-barreled shotgun.

He was a deranged man as he shouted, "I'm going to kill this little white-headed bastard." Then he turned to Whitey as he lay quivering on the floor, and jammed the double barrel into his stomach. "You little white-headed son of a bitch, you're no-good, you never was any good, you're nothing but a crumb-snatching pain-in-the-ass! You little bastard, you've been nothing but trouble ever since you been in this house, and I'm going to put you out of your misery."

The boy was terrified, "Please Pop, please don't kill me." But his plea was in vain, for the angry man took no notice of his cries, and the excruciating pain from the shotgun jammed into Whitey's stomach, was more than he could bear.

Cringing like a terrified animal in the middle of the floor, Whitey suddenly knocked the shotgun barrel away from his stomach. On hands and knees, he scurried under the kitchen sink where he crouched trembling in fear. But he could not escape the eyes of the shotgun as it was aimed at him. He was going into shock as he looked into the receiving end of the weapon. He began to hear someone screaming and pleading, then he realized it was his own voice as he cried, "Pop, please, please don't hurt me no more."

Marge, who had been visiting a neighbor, came rushing into the kitchen.

"Pop," she screamed, "have you gone crazy? For heaven's sake put that gun down."

Still holding the shotgun over the boy, he turned and looked at Marge. He stared at her for a split second, and with increased rage he jammed the business end of the gun again into Whitey's stomach, and shrieked, "I'm going to kill this useless little bastard, he don't belong to me anyways."

"Pop please don't hurt him, what's wrong with you? He's only a baby."

"I don't give a damn if he is a baby, when your mother ran off, she should of took this little bastard with her."

"Pop, for god sake what're you saying? Don't take it out on him because of the problems you had with Mom. He's just a child, it's not his fault."

For a few interminable seconds, time stood still as his father held the shotgun pressed against the sobbing boy's stomach. Suddenly he slammed the weapon down on the table, and stormed out of the room.

Years later while in the penitentiary serving time, he often thought and wished that his so-called father had pulled the triggers.

In the ensuing years Whitey rarely saw his father when he had not been drinking. On one particular day he had fallen into a drunken stupor on the front room couch. Whitey had been outside playing, and came into the house just as he began to stir. There was a smell about his father that fouled the room. He sat there in disarray, his hair was twisted and matted, and he was in dire need of a shave. He looked up through bloodshot eyes as Whitey entered the room.

"Where the hell have you been?" he yelled .

Whitey froze in his tracks, "I've been outside playing."

45

"You little son of a bitch, did you take a quarter while I was sleeping? If you did I'm going to whip your ass"

"No Pop I didn't take no quarter."

"You took that quarter boy, and if you admit it I won't whip you, all I want is the truth."

Whitey thought it best to tell him what he wanted to hear. Little did he know that no matter what he told him, he would still receive a beating.

The man went crazy, he grabbed his leather cat-o-nine-tails, and proceeded to beat the boy. He was merciless, and the pain was unbearable, but the boy was thirteen years old now, and he was determined to hold back the tears. When he wouldn't cry his father whipped him all the harder. Each time he struck him with the cat-o-nine-tails, his father yelled, "You're a thief, you're nothing but a thief."

The whipping seemed endless, but finally his father ceased the brutal attack, and ordered him up to his room. This was just one of the many unjust beatings he received during his life.

Holding back the tears, Whitey made his way up the stairs to his room, and flopped on his bed. The pain was more than he could endure. He could hold back no longer, and grabbed a pillow to cover his head to muffle out the sound of his crying.

Just a boy of thirteen, and oh how he hated that man. Except for animals, he was developing a deep hatred for anything that walked or crawled on this earth.

Though it wasn't easy, Whitey always managed to conceal his feelings of contempt and hatred. However, later in the day, he could no longer hide how he felt when he saw Edwin sitting on the front porch steps with a large bag of candy. Whitey asked him where the candy came from, and was told it was none of his business. Edwin had beaten up on Whitey a number of times, and he would never put up a fight because he thought he was too small to whip an older boy.

Again Whitey asked him, "Where did you get the candy?"

The same reply, "None of your business."

"It is my business. You stole a quarter from Pop, and I took a licking for it."

Setting the bag of candy aside, Edwin started to get to his feet. "That's too bad crybaby, what do you want to do about it?"

Whitey was standing in front of his brother. His eyes were bloodshot from the crying, and his body was raw from the leather thongs.

"I want some of that candy," he demanded.

Edwin gave him a gentle shove, forcing him to take a backward step. "Why should I give you any candy crybaby?"

Whitey could feel his adrenaline rising, and he no longer feared his older brother. "You stole that quarter from Pop, and I took a licking for it, so you better split that candy with me."

Edwin did not reply, instead he gave Whitey a shove knocking him off the porch to the ground below.

Whitey jumped to his feet, and without a word he ran around to the side of the house. He knew full-well Edwin had taken the quarter, and he really didn't care if he had, for it was not in him to squeal, but when Edwin refused to share the candy, it was more than he could endure. (In the 1930s a quarter would buy at least a pound of penny candy.)

Whitey went directly to the tool shed, and he knew exactly what he was after. Hanging on a peg were three pieces of rope, each one two and a half feet in length. He wrapped each piece of rope one turn around his right hand, and gripped them tightly. Then using them in a whip fashion, he swung, hitting the shed door with a sharp crack. A cunning smile formed on his face, and he quickly returned to the front porch. Edwin was still sitting there eating candy.

"What's the rope for? What do you think you're going to do with it?"

Whitey took a step closer to his brother, and in a chilling whisper he replied, "Never mind the fucking rope, do I get any candy?"

Edwin rose from the chair, and as he did so he said, "Forget it crybaby I'm giving you nothing."

This time Whitey was ready and lunged at Edwin screaming, "You fucking redheaded woodpecker!" And with that retort, he lashed out with the rope, using it like a bullwhip, he caught him around the head. The severity of the stinging rope knocked him back in pain up against the chair. Edwin quickly recovered, and started toward Whitey again, "I'm going to beat you within an inch of. . . ." He never got to finish the sentence, for Whitey lashed out again with the rope cutting his words short as he struck him across the face. Edwin fell over backwards, striking the chair as he fell to the floor, and blood spurted from his lacerated face. He tried to protect himself with his hands, while Whitey swung the rope repeatedly.

Each time the rope swished through the air Whitey yelled, "You lying bastard, you son of a bitch you stole that quarter and Pop beat me for it."

Edwin, in his haste to get away from the striking rope, rolled off the porch, and fell to the ground. He quickly tried to escape, but to no avail, for Whitey leaped to the ground after him. Edwin's face, hands, neck, back and arms were covered with blood. He began to cry, and the crying turned to pleading screams, "Please don't hit me no more, please. You can have the candy Whitey, take it, it's all yours."

In disgust Whitey looked down at his brother, "Keep it, I don't want it. If Pop ever hits me again because of you I'll kill you, you hear me? I'll kill you in your fucking sleep!"

Whitey looked at him scornfully, and walked away bitter, and full of hate.

At an early age in life, Whitey should have been outside participating in sports and games. Instead he was a lonely boy of thirteen, with thoughts of hatred and killing.

CHAPTER 9.

Each day that passed left its mark on Leon Whitey Thompson, not only was he mistreated in the home, but unjust treatment at school made him feel inferior.

One morning while in the fifth grade he was standing in line. They were waiting for the recess bell to sound, and most of the children began to fidget. Whitey, who was standing in the eighth position in line, did not notice the teacher pushing her way toward him. Without any warning whatsoever, she slapped him sharply across the face. The impact of the slap was so sudden and severe it caught him off balance. He couldn't believe what had just happened, and why the teacher had slapped his face.

Miss Rinn, a spinster, was in her early forties, an attractive woman with jet black hair and brown eyes. She was a strict disciplinarian, so strict that at times she was unfair.

Whitey was shocked; he stood there feeling embarrassed as the other children stared at him. He knew he had done nothing wrong, so why did she slap him? His embarrassment turned to anger, and he felt like screaming at his teacher. He had all he could do to control himself; he wanted to get even. All sorts of schemes were flashing through his mind. I'll bust her head open with a chair, no, I'll get one of Pop's shotguns and blow her head off!

Miss Rinn obviously knew that Whitey had done nothing wrong, but this wasn't the first time that an incident like this had occurred. True, there were a number of times she had to reprimand Whitey for fighting, but more often as not, she was very unfair to him. She would never dare to slap any of his classmate who came from well-to-do families, as she knew there would be repercussions from their parents. By most people, Whitey was considered nothing more than white trash who came from a low-class family who couldn't care less for his well-being. Consequently he was used as a scapegoat, and received many unjust punishments. He never told anyone about his mistreatment at home or at school, but he developed a deep hatred for Miss Rinn and all school teachers.

Whitey never cared about the consequences. He became such a bitter boy, that if one of his classmates so much as looked at him wrong, he would haul off and hit him right in the mouth. Most of the school children stayed clear of him, and this satisfied Whitey for he was a loner. His dislike for his classmates was obvious. He was envious of them and the things they had. Whitey never had anything decent, he wore worn out sneakers, and hand-me-down clothes that never fit. He felt like an outcast, and he didn't belong. He was also jealous of the children who had mothers waiting for them when they came home from school. Whitey was starving for attention and a mother's love, and not having this, added fuel to his hatred.

One afternoon Miss Rinn had gotten on to Whitey for fighting, and told him that she was going to have a talk with his father.

Whitey lived on Pine Rock Avenue, a country road. That evening after school he hid out in a ditch across the road from his house. He was waiting for Miss Rinn. He did not have long to wait before he heard the sound of a model T Ford coming down the road. Not wanting to be seen, he crouched low behind the bank as she turned her vehicle into the driveway. As she passed by he saw Miss Rinn propped up behind the steering wheel. The model T canvas top was down and the windshield was folded forward on its hinges. His father heard the vehicle arrive, and shook her hand as she stepped out of the car. Then they both disappeared into the house.

From the moment Whitey heard Miss Rinn's Ford coming down the road, his anger rose. Suddenly he knew what he was going to do, and ran to the pump house for a long length of rope. On either side of the driveway were two big oak trees. He tied the rope from one tree to the other forming a rope barrier across the driveway. After this was accomplished, he quickly vanished into the brush where he had a clear view of the drama that he hoped would take place.

He no sooner hid himself when Miss Rinn, and his father, emerged from the house. His father seemed to be angered. He was pounding his right fist into his left hand, no doubt emphasizing to the teacher, the whipping Whitey was to receive.

From his view point Whitey watched them shake hands and part. Miss Rinn stepped into the car and perched herself behind the steering wheel. Mr. Thompson (acting like a gentleman), walked to the front of the vehicle, reached down, took hold of the crank-handle, and gave it a vicious turn. The Ford came to life with a puttering purr. Smiling after his deed, he stepped aside to allow the vehicle to pass. He took off his hat and gave a courteous bow.

The evening sun was setting in the West, and its brilliant glare seemed to zero in on the approaching car. Miss Rinn's vision was

impaired by the setting sun, and was unable to see the rope stretched across the road in front of her. As she approached it, her speed
was approximately five miles per hour.

From his concealment, Whitey watched with anticipation waiting
for the rope to catch across the front of the car. But to his surprise,
it was tied too high, and the front end of the car went under it. The
rope cleared the windshield catching Miss Rinn under the chin. She
was snatched out of the car by the neck as the vehicle puttered
across the roadway, and stalled in the ditch!

For the next two weeks Miss Rinn wore a neck-brace, while Whitey
did some serious hiding from his father. No one could prove who tied
the rope between the trees, but Miss Rinn always had her suspicions!
She was sure Whitey was the culprit.

By this time the older children in the family were grown and gone.
Marge had gotten married, while Edwin and Charlie joined the C.C.C.
(Civilian Conservation Corps), and were stationed in Meeker,
Colorado. It was shortly after this when Whitey began returning
home from school to an empty house. Half the time there was no food
and nothing in the icebox.

It was hard for a child growing up during the depression years,
and even harder when living from day to day in constant fear of
hunger. There were many times Whitey would come home for lunch,
and having found nothing to eat, he would return to school half
starved. It was not unusual for him to go as long as three or four
days without any nourishing food.

He was a solitary boy and never talked about this problem.
Periodically he would go over to the home of Roy Ely; the one and
only classmate he could tolerate. They were both the same age, but
Roy looked up to Whitey's toughness, and was willing to do anything
for him.

From time to time it was touch and go, and he was just one step
from starving, and during these periods, food became the most
important thing to him. He became desperate, and began to strong-
arm other children while at school. To Whitey it was a necessity to
survive, and his misdeeds took place in the school yard, the library,
and the hallways. He did not steal money, but he would take their
candy, apples, or whatever food they might have.

On occasion the thefts had been reported to the school officials,
but this was all to no avail, for it did not deter him. He did not
consider it stealing when he took food from other children. He was
starving, this was survival. It did not matter to him if it was right or
wrong, and he remembered one day in November of 1936 the hunger
pains were more than he could bear. The weather was very cold, and
it was snowing outside, but he was forced to leave the house in

search of food. He walked down the hill to a little neighborhood grocery store. Out in back of the store he looked to see if he could find something eatable that the grocer may have thrown out.

Whitey's hands were extremely cold as he went from box to box, digging them out of the snow, only to find them empty. He was cold and about to leave when he spotted another mound of snow. He brushed the snow away and discovered a paper bag that contained some green carrot tops. They couldn't have been there too long as they were not frozen yet. Grabbing the bag he ran for home, quite content that he had found something to eat.

He did not keep track of the time they had been cooking. The aroma was quite good, but the first mouthful gagged him! On the kitchen shelf he found a bottle of vinegar, and poured some on the greens hoping to improve the flavor. It helped a little, very little, but his hunger was so great that he devoured half of them, and the next day he finished off the remainder.

During the days of the Great Depression, housewives would phone in their grocery list, and the delivery boy would promptly deliver the order to their homes. If for some reason no one was home when the delivery was being made, the cart boy would leave the groceries on the front porch, and collect for them on the next trip.

It was two days before the Thanksgiving, but to Whitey it was just another day. He knew there would be no turkey on the table or any decent food for that matter. His father didn't seem to care if there was food in the house or not.

Home problems were driving Whitey more frequently into the streets. On this particular day he was walking by the schoolhouse on Helen Street. On the front porch of one of the homes he saw a cardboard box overflowing with groceries.

Before stepping onto the porch, he cautiously glanced around, seeing no one he stepped up onto the porch. He noticed the box contained three paper bags of food. In one bag was a large turkey. Again he furtively looked around, there was no one in sight, he grabbed the bird, and ran home as fast as he could. When he reached his doorway he stood there gasping for air, and as he did so, a feeling of guilt began to engulf him at the thought of what he had just done. Other than ripping kids off for food at school, this was the first time he stole anything. Suddenly he thought about his father, and the feeling of guilt turned to worry. What could he tell him? Where could he say he obtained the turkey? He began to feel apprehensive about the situation, and decided that the best thing to do was to return the bird.

He returned to the house and as he stepped up onto the porch, he noticed the grocery box was empty. The occupants of the house had returned. Should he just leave the turkey and run? Or should he ring the doorbell? Before he realized what he was doing he rang the doorbell. He jumped with a start when the door swung open. An overweight, middle-aged woman appeared in the doorway and said, "Yes little boy, what is it?"

"Is this your turkey, I found it on the sidewalk. Does it belong to you?"

She turned her head and called over her shoulder, "Edward, come here quickly."

A huge pot-bellied man appeared, "What's the problem?" he asked gruffly.

"This boy says he found our turkey."

The huge man moved closer to Whitey, and placed his left hand on his shoulder and said, "Did you find the turkey boy? Or did you steal it?"

Whitey's first impulse was to say he found it, but he wanted to be honest and said, "I took it sir, but decided to bring it back."

"You decided to bring it back you little thief," as he spoke he slapped Whitey on the side of the head. The force of it knocked him off the porch onto the ground.

Dazed, Whitey got up off the ground; his vision was somewhat blurred until he recognized the huge bulk of a man coming down off the porch.

"You damn thief, you dirty little thief," the big man bellowed.

Whitey's head cleared immediately, he took off running, and as he rounded the corner of the school building he could still hear the man shouting, "You thief—you thief!"

Once he was home safely in his bedroom, he thought about the quarter his father accused him of taking, and how he had told him he would not whip him if he told the truth. Whitey lied, and received a whipping. A short period ago, he told an adult stranger the truth about the turkey. Again he was whipped. For a young boy of thirteen he was totally confused by the adult world.

Whitey was puzzled, very, very puzzled by the so-called adult world. Like a terrified animal he suddenly ran out of the house onto the front porch; he started down the steps, then suddenly stopped abruptly. He stood there for a moment, looking westward toward the evening sun. In all it's brilliance it was descending behind the hills, making way for the darkness of night. High in the heavens there were still trickles of light dancing across the soft clouded skies.

Whitey looked up at this spectacular show of lights, and with tears running from his bewildered eyes he began to scream at the top of his voice, "You fucker, you fucker why don't you tell me what to do. Tell me—teeeell meeeeee whaaaat toooo dooooo! Goddamn it, tell me."

53

While he screamed at the heavens, he dropped down to his knees, and with both fists clenched, he began to beat on the wooden steps. Still screaming, he jumped up off the cold ground, and took off running down the hill into a wooded area. At the edge of the woods was a narrow road, known as Brook Street. When he reached the road he had his emotions under control, and he knew exactly what he was going to do. Off in the distance he could see a ray of light flickering through the trees. The light was shining from Roy Ely's house.

Roy wanted to become close friends, but with Whitey's temper it was difficult.

On this particular evening, Whitey wanted to confide in Roy. He quickened his pace, and in no time he covered the short distance to Roy's house. Behind the house was a clubhouse, and Whitey ran straight to it, calling out, "Hey Roy—come out here. Hey Roy."

Instantly the back door swung open casting a warm ray of kitchen light across the yard.

Roy appeared in the doorway, "Who's out there? Is that you Whitey? Come on in."

"I don't wanna come in Roy, I gotta see you a minute, come out here."

Whitey could hear Roy call back into the kitchen, "Hey Mom I'll be right back. Whitey wants to see me a minute, okay?"

"All right," his mother called back, "but you hurry it up, supper will be ready in a minute. Tell Whitey he's welcome to eat with us."

Whitey and Roy went inside the clubhouse which his father had built two years ago. Roy fumbled around in the dark and lit a candle. He was surprised to see Whitey's bloodshot eyes and the trace of tears staining his cheeks, and asked, "What were you crying about?"

"Who said I was crying," Whitey replied angrily, "You never seen me cry, have you?"

Roy took a step back before he answered, "No I have never seen you cry, but your eyes and cheeks look like you have been crying."

"I wasn't crying, it's from the cold, I ran all the way down here from my house, don't ever say I was crying again."

"Okay Whitey I won't, but what do you want? What I mean is why are you here?"

In a whisper Whitey said, "Roy I want to borrow your Pop's twenty-two pistol."

Roy's face turned white, "What! I can't let you take his gun, why don't you get one of your father's guns?"

"I can't, he keeps them locked up. You want to be my closest friend don't you?"

"Well yeah Whitey, you know I've always wanted to be your best

54

friend. Okay I'll get the gun for you, but tell me why you want it."

"Okay I'll tell you." Whitey told Roy about the turkey and how the man slapped his face when he returned it. About his father, how he whipped him for a quarter he never took. He was tired of being accused of wrong doings, punished and humiliated whenever he tried to do right. Now for the first time in his young life he was going out to deliberately do something wrong.

"I'm going to rob Adler's store, and I need a gun. Will you get it for me now?"

"Okay—okay I'll get it, but you'll have to give me some of the candy, all right?"

" I'm not after candy, I want money. Money will buy all the candy and food I want."

As Roy started out the door Whitey called after him, "Make sure the gun is loaded and find out what time it is."

Adler's country grocery store was the only building on a dead-end dirt road just off Helen Street. Adler was an elderly man in his late sixties and closed his store at 9:00 P.M. sharp. There were no street lights outside the store, and across the road there was a vast area of vacant fields, and beyond the fields, lay a forest of rustling trees.

Roy entered the clubhouse, from under his jacket he pulled out a small caliber twenty-two pistol, and as he handed it to him he said, "It's loaded Whitey, the time is eight o'clock, and can I go with you?"

He was not disappointed when Whitey refused to let him go on the robbery, in fact, he was glad he was refused for he didn't really want to go. He was merely trying to give Whitey the impression he was brave enough to accompany him.

Lying under the bunk-bed, Whitey found a black stocking cap, and pulled it over his head. Then he tied a dirty brown rag over his face, and all that remained visible were his boyish blue eyes. From under the bed Whitey retrieved a grimy old black rain coat, which he donned.

"I better get going, Roy. If all goes well, I should be back by nine thirty or so."

Roy was like a soldier waiting for orders, he leaned forward so as not to miss a word.

"At nine fifteen or so you come out here and build a fire in the stove, and sneak me out some food I'll be staying here all night."

Roy's parents were used to the boys spending nights together in the clubhouse. It was a one room affair, ten by fifteen feet. The single door structure had a window at either side, and a solid wall at the back where the bunk-beds were. In one corner was a small potbelly wood stove, and in the center of the floor was a tiny kitchen table with two chairs.

At twenty minutes to nine, Whitey left the cabin, and in the chill of the night, he started up the road. It was a lonely and very dark walk. Seldom did any vehicles travel these roads, and it was a rare occasion to see a person or a car after dark.

The night air was crisp and chilly, but it did not stop Whitey from perspiring as he hurried across the yard of Helen Street school toward the grocery store. As he neared the building, he slipped his right hand into the oversize pocket of the raincoat. When his fingers gripped the cold handle of the gun, a surge of power raced through his veins. He stopped and reached down, using his left hand he fumbled around on the ground for a small pebble. A pebble on the tongue would make one's voice sound different.

Silently making his way up to the storefront window he peeked in and saw Adler alone in the store putting the daily receipts into a leather bag.

Using the dirty rag Whitey concealed the lower half of his face, and at the same time he extracted the gun with his right hand. Gripping the weapon tightly he entered the store. Adler raised his head from the register in time to look down the barrel of the twenty-two. He froze where he stood, his face turned completely white, and he began to tremble causing him to drop the money bag onto the counter.

Quickly, Whitey reached across to retrieve the fallen bag; then he held it out to Mr. Adler.

In a distorted voice he ordered, "Put the rest of the money in the bag."

Still trembling the old man did as he was told. Once the register was empty Whitey grabbed the bag from the old man and began moving sideways as he made his way to the door. Once there he flung it open and dashed out and disappeared in the darkness.

The moment Whitey disappeared out the door the proprietor pulled out a twenty-two rifle.

As he ran across the field, Whitey was pleased how easily the robbery went. But suddenly the crack of gun fire broke the silence. He quickly looked over his shoulder toward the store, and there silhouetted in the light of the doorway, was Adler firing at will.

Whitey knew the old man could not see him out beyond the rays of the store light. He paid no attention to the gun reports and kept on running. Suddenly his right leg went out from under him and he fell to the ground. Holding the bag of money in his left hand, and the gun in his right, he tried to scurry to his feet. It was then he realized he was hit in the leg by a stray bullet. His exploded in a furious rage, and screamed obscenities, in doing so he almost swallowed the pebble! He spat it out and took deliberate aim at the silhouette standing in the doorway.

Whitey opened fire yelling at the same time, "You son of a bitching bastard I'll kill you!"

The distance was too great for accurate shooting, but Whitey's shots had their effect as two of them went bursting through the store window. The old man was terrified and ran back inside the store, hiding behind the counter.

Whitey pulled the rag off his face, rolled it into a makeshift rope, and tied it to serve as a tourniquet. Using his handkerchief as a bandage, he bound it around the wound. He managed to get on his feet, and as he did so he glanced toward the store. There was no sign of movement. But Whitey was sure the police were summoned, but it would take fifteen or twenty minutes before they could respond.

Except for the injury, the darkness was no handicap for Whitey knew the terrain. The pain was severe, but he gritted his teeth, and kept on moving.

The tripping and, falling seemed to last for an eternity before Whitey managed to make it back to the clubhouse. His arrival was shortly after 10:30, long past his scheduled time.

Roy was anxiously waiting for Whitey, and he was shocked when he staggered in. He felt his own body tremble as he helped his injured friend onto the bunk bed.

"What happened to you?" Roy cried. "Your're covered with blood, I better call my Mom."

"Damn it, don't you call anyone! Just calm down and listen to me. The bullet's not in deep. Listen I want you to go into the house and get some clean rags, a bottle of iodine, and a sharp knife."

For a second Roy was disoriented, but at the sharp sound of Whitey's voice, he snapped back to reality, and scurried out of the clubhouse, and in a short time returned with the items.

Whitey took the knife and held the tip of the blade over the burning candle to sterilize it. Subsequently he spilled a drop of iodine on the sharp edge of the knife; then he poured some of it into the raw wound. He held his breath to try to keep from screaming, but even then he could only hold it for a second before he cried out. By gritting his teeth he got himself under control, and began to probe for the bullet. The pain from the probing was not nearly as severe as the sting of the iodine. He poured more medication into the wound. His body was trembling, his leg began to shake violently with waves of pain, and he was forced to cry out again. Again he gritted his teeth and held his breath. He continued probing until finally the bullet was removed.

The pain was excruciating and racked his entire being. Lying on the bunk, he tried to relax allowing Roy to dab the wound with more iodine. Then very gently he spread Cloverine Salve over it, and neatly wrapped the injured leg in clean cloth. Roy was so engrossed in dressing the wound he did not notice that Whitey had passed out.

57

Gently he laid a blanket over the motionless boy, and made him as comfortable as possible. He placed a log in the potbelly stove, and left the club house for his own bedroom.

Early the next morning Whitey woke up. He was still in pain, but managed to count the stolen money—a total of forty-two dollars. Whitey gave Roy two dollars along with strict instructions. He told him to watch how he spent it, and not to buy anything in Adler's Store.

Being young and strong his wound healed in a reasonable time, but during the first week of healing it was painful for him to walk. It was during this period he had to fake it, giving people the impression that he had banged his knee in play.

He had pulled his first successful armed robbery. He was encouraged by the thought he could at any time he chose, walk out of the dark into the light with his hand around the grip of a revolver, or the stock of a shotgun. It gave him a sense of power.

CHAPTER 10.

The next few years were unbearable and were more than Whitey could endure. His hatred and distrust for the human race began to form a shield around his being.

Two weeks after his sixteenth birthday he left home. He decided to hitch his way to Florida. He thought that once he was there, if he could not find a job at least he would be where it was warm. He had visions of being in a tropical climate surrounded by palm, orange and banana trees! Little did he know it was only a dream.

His first day out Whitey hopped a freight train from New Haven, Connecticut to New York City. From New York he got a ride to Philadelphia where he tried to hop another freight train. It was here he had his first encounter with the law. During the 1930s and early '40s, if a person was caught hopping a freight train, or riding the rods or rails, as it was called, he was thrown in jail, or beaten up or both.

Whitey was preparing to make a run for a moving freight train, when a railroad Dick (policeman) with a club, appeared out of nowhere. Whitey jumped aside just in time to avoid being hit by the club. The railroad Bull (as they were sometimes called) didn't get a second chance to swing at Whitey, for he was already running across the tracks. He gave up the idea of hopping a freight train, and went back to hitchhiking.

He arrived in Raleigh, North Carolina just after midnight, and found his way to the Union train station. Whitey selected a bench in the waiting area, and within minutes fell asleep, only to be awakened by an officer of the law poking him with his night-stick.

The policeman spoke with a southern drawl, "Wake up boy Are you lost? Wake up."

Whitey opened his eyes and replied, "I'm not lost, I'm with my Mother."

"Where's your Mamma boy? I don't see her."

Thinking fast Whitey replied, "She's in the toilet."

The lawman looked toward the restrooms, then back to Whitey, "If you're here with your Mamma, then where's your luggage?"

"She's got it in the toilet with her, she is. . . ."

Whitey was interrupted by the ticket agent who was listening to

59

the conversation, and as he came out from behind the ticket window he said, "This boy is with no one, he came in here all alone about a half hour ago. He sat down on that bench and fell asleep, and that's when I called the police."

Turning to Whitey the lawman reached down, took hold of him, and roughly pulled him to his feet, "Boy, are you a Yankee? Where you-all from? How old are you boy?"

"I'm sixteen, I'm from Connecticut, and I'm on my way to Florida to look for work."

"So you *are* a Yankee," the officer's face lit up. "I got just the place for you."

Whitey was taken to the city jail where he was booked on a vagrancy charge. The very next morning he was taken to the municipal court to appear before Judge West. Judge West was prejudiced toward Northerns, a typical southern judge of the early 1930s and '40s. In a heavy southern drawl he said, "Well now, I see we have a Yankee troublemaker heah, we don't take kindly to Yankee troublemaker."

"Yes sir, I'm a Connecticut Yankee, but I'm no troublemaker."

Judge West rose to his feet and struck the bench with his gavel, "Silence, you-all be silent. You-all don't speak unless ordered to. The arresting officer says he offered you-all a job, and you refused."

"That's a lie, I told him I was going to Florida. He never offered me a job."

Again the gavel struck the bench. "Our Officers never lie. We have good working accommodations here. I'm going to provide some for you for six months on the gang."

This was Whitey's first experience in a Kangaroo Court. He would never forget Judge West as long as he lived.

After sentencing Whitey was remanded to the county jail. On the morning of the fifteenth day along with two other prisoners he was loaded into an enclosed truck that was called the Dog Wagon, and transferred to the Durham prison camp. Whitey had heard stories about the southern chain gangs, and how young boys were molested and raped. He tried to conceal his fear from the other two prisoners by sitting with his head bowed.

"Hey Cotton hold your head up, this isn't the end of the world."

The voice was thunderous and startled Whitey. He looked up at the big man. "Are—are you talking to me?"

"Yeah you're the only person with blond hair, so I must be talking to you. Like I said, this isn't the end of the world. I can see this is your first trip out to the gang. What's your name?"

"Leon Thompson, Leon Whitey Thompson."

Big Jim held out his hand, "Glad to know you Whitey. You got the blondest hair I ever seen, I'm just going to call you Cotton, okay?"

60

Shrugging his shoulders Whitey replied, "Call me whatever, it don't matter to me."

Smiling, Jim turned to the other prisoner. "How about you youngster, what's your name?"

The young man was surprised when Jim spoke to him, "My name is Richie Gene Smith, but everybody calls me RG."

Jim looked from one to the other, "How old are you guys? How much time are ya doing?"

"I'm eighteen," RG replied, "I got six months for vag."

"I'm sixteen," Whitey said, "I got six months for vag too."

"Sixteen! You're just a baby," Big Jim said. "You don't belong on no chain gang. I bet it was Judge West who sentenced you. "

"You're right. He didn't like me because I'm a Connecticut Yankee from New Haven"

"New Haven," RG yelled excitedly, "I come from East Haven, East Haven, Connecticut."

Both boys were excited about this unexpected meeting, and both coming from Connecticut, they felt a kinship.

"See Cotton, I told you this wasn't the end of the world," Jim said with a smile.

Whitey was beginning to relax, and was feeling better because of the new friendships.

"Look Cotton," Big Jim said, "You got some real hard-cores on the gang. Some of them are pretty good old country boys, but the majority of them are no good and will never change their lifestyle. You're just a young kid Cotton, it may get a little rough for you out there, but I tell you what, if any of them bastards try to mess with you, just let me know. That goes for you too, RG. Hell, you're just a couple of kids, you only got six months and I know how ya feel on your first trip to the gang. You boys got a short time to do and. . . ."

"Short time!" Whitey interrupted. "Are you nuts, six months is a long time."

Jim laughed, "Yeah I guess it is a long time to you boys, but what I was trying to say was, when you guys get out you should hightail it back home, or wherever you come from, before it's too late."

"What do you mean?" RG asked. "What do you mean before it's too late?"

"Just this," Big Jim continued, "the first time I was sentenced to the gang I was seventeen years old. I did five years for robbery, served my time, got out and come back with a brand new ten years. I did my time again, but here I am going back, only this time, it's for life. I got into a fight one night with a bartender, and I just upped and shot him. You see he was hitched to my kid sister, she has a couple of kids by him. While I was pulling time on the gang, my kid sis and her kids were starving while this son of a bitch was tending bar, he

61

thought he was a big-shot. He seldom went home and when he did, he never brought home any food or money. Sue, that's my sister's name and the kids were starving, and whenever she asked him for money to buy food, he would give her maybe a buck or two, but most times he would just whip her and tell her to find a job. I didn't know how he was treating her until two months ago when I was released from the chain gang. I shot the son of a bitch. No man's going to whip my kid sister."

"Goddamn!" RG exclaimed. "Life! That's a hell of a jolt."

Big Jim was a tough-looking blue-eyed man of thirty-two with premature streaks of gray in his thick brown hair. He stood six foot four and weighed two hundred and fifteen pounds. He was a powerful man with ham-like hands, so powerful he looked as though he could squeeze a person's head and pop it open like a grape.

"I don't blame ya for killing that son of a bitch, but if you're doing life, why do you give a shit what happens to a kid like me?"

"That's just it, because you are a kid I care what happens to you. You have about as much chance as a snowball in hell on the gang if someone don't watch over you. I know because I went through that shit when I first went to prison. I don't understand that judge giving you kids six months for vag. That judge should have slapped your hands and sent ya back home."

CHAPTER 11.

The prison gang labored from sunrise to sunset, each day literally took its toll for the road work was hard and tedious. They worked six days a week with Sunday as their day of rest. The quality of the food was unpalatable, and the quantity was minute, scarcely enough to keep a man alive. Each day the meals were identical, for breakfast they received a small bowl of unflavored hominy grits, and a cup of black chicory coffee. For lunch they received one slice of corn bread, a cup of chicory. Before eating the corn bread one had to virtually pick the cooked cockroaches out of it! At supper a bowl of plain boiled navy beans, a slice of corn bread, and the customary cup of chicory coffee.

Sunday afternoons they were allowed to lie on the grass. The first Sunday after Whitey's arrival he was lying on the grass with RG beside him. Whitey felt someone pull gently on his right ear. He was afraid to say anything or open his eyes. He lay there hoping and praying the ear pulling would cease. Someone whispered, "Hi there, you-all want to be my boy?"

Whitey knew what the man had in mind, but was too nervous to reply.

The voice whispered again, "I'm going to give you time to think this over. I'll be out here next Sunday, we'll talk, but no matter what, you're going to be my boy."

As the man walked away, he glanced over his shoulder. Whitey got a look at his face. He was mean-looking with beady mouse eyes, medium build, and had a foul smell about him.

"What was that guy whispering about? What did he want?" RG asked.

"You know damn well what he wanted," Whitey replied in a nervous voice.

"Why don't you tell Big Jim? He told us to tell him if anyone messes with you or I."

Later that evening, Whitey told Jim of his predicament.

"Look Cotton," Jim said, "next Sunday go back out there and lay on the grass, if he starts any shit with you again don't say a word, just get on your feet and punch him dead in the teeth. Just do as I

63

say, if he tries to hurt you I'll break his fucking head."

"Whose head you going to break?" The question came from a man who just walked up to the group.

"Hey if it ain't Yank Stewart," Jim said with a smile, "shake hands with Cotton and RG Yank. Boys this is an old pal of mine, Yank Stewart."

While shaking hands Yank Stewart said, "Any friend of Big Jim's is a friend of mine."

Jim related to Yank what had occurred with Whitey out on the grass earlier that day.

Yank Stewart was disgusted, "Yeah I know that crummy bastard, that's Elmer Twist. He's doing time for child molesting. You do what Jim tells you Whitey, don't worry."

The following Sunday afternoon Whitey, and RG were lying on the grass. Whitey lay there feigning sleep. A few minutes passed before he sensed someone lying down next to him. Elmer started to play with Whitey's ear and whisper obscenities, as he did so Whitey slowly rose to his feet, and simultaneously, with a smile on his face, Elmer came to a sitting position. The man was eagerly stretching his head forward in anticipation of a kiss, but instead he received a vicious blow directly between the eyes. Whitey had caught him off guard, and Elmer's first reaction was to cover his face. The element of surprise was in Whitey's favor, he threw another punch to Elmer's head, and then slammed him a sharp blow directly between the eyes.

Whitey was slim, but he was fast with his fists, each punch carried his hundred and ten pounds. He was like a machine-gun, his punches were connecting fast and furious.

A circle of convicts had formed around the combatants; they were cheering for the boy.

"Give it to him Cotton, lay it on the bastard."

"Stick it to him kid, that's what he wanted to do to you!"

Above the noise of the crowd, Jim, Yank, and RG were also yelling, "Ya got him Cotton, put it to him. Beat his fucking head in!"

Whitey didn't see the guard making his way through the mob until he felt strong arms clamping around him.

Big Jim yelled at the guard, "Take it easy with that kid, he did what he had to do."

The guard took Whitey inside to the grilled gate that led to the dormitories.

"All right now, you-all tell me what the ruckus was over," the guard demanded. He was a tall country-boy past forty dressed in bib overalls, and looked as though water had never touched his face or hands in weeks! While waiting for Whitey to answer, he let a huge wad of chewing tobacco go flying across the wooden floor.

"Answer me Yankee boy, what was the ruckus over?"

"Nothing," Whitey replied, "nothing."

"Now that's a crock, you don't fight for just nothing. I've been a guard going nigh on to twenty years. So ya ain't got to tell me what the ruckus was about, I *know* what it was about. Where ya-all come from boy?"

"New Haven Connecticut."

"Well I'll be damned, I spent three years in New Haven, in the U.S. Cavalry. I liked that country, had some good times. Lookie here boy, next time you get into a ruckus, do it where you can't be seen. I know why ya had the ruckus so I gonna forget about it, now go."

The guard opened the gate, and without a word of thanks Whitey walked out.

A few weeks after the fight, Whitey, Big Jim, RG and Yank Stewart, were on the grass engaged in a friendly discussion.

Jim was saying, "Go ahead Cotton, you can climb that pole."

"Hell I can't shimmy up there. Are you crazy or something? Fuck that flag."

The pole and flag in question stood in the middle of the lawn, the flag had gotten stuck, and hadn't been lowered in three days. The base of the steel pole was embedded in concrete, there was no way to remove it. Nor were there any pegs to enable anyone to climb it. A number of prisoners had tried, but were unable to get more than halfway.

Again Big Jim spoke, "Go ahead Cotton, you're the lightest, let's see you climb it."

A few of the guards joined in, "Come on Thompson, I bet you can do it."

They were all cheering Whitey on and he felt like a hero. He was thrilled to hear the many voices shouting encouragement. He removed his shoes and socks and stepped up to the pole. He wiped his hands on his pants' legs, then rubbed them in some sand to help him get a better grip. As he reached to grab hold of the flag pole, Jim gave him a boost, and he began to shimmy up the pole. Progress was easy until he passed the halfway mark. The higher he climbed, the pole was getting thinner, making it difficult to grip. As he neared the top, the pole began to sway, and he thought it would snap off, and he would fall.

Fuck it, he thought to himself, *if I fall and be killed, I'll still be a hero.*

On he went struggling up the pole. He was nearing the top now with only a foot to go, and he could feel his arm and leg muscles giving out.

"What have I got myself into?" He asked himself, "I can't hang on much longer."

From below prisoners and guards began to yell in earnest, "Go on Cotton, you're almost there. You can do it kid—you can do it."

Whitey looked down to the ground, all he could see were cheering faces looking up at him. With his second wind he found new strength, and his muscles seemed to be screaming with the crowd, "We can make it—we can make it."

All he had left for strength was his determination. He gripped the pole with his left hand, and using his free hand, he managed to get the rope back on the track. The flag was lowered amid loud applause from below.

Whitey was thirty-five feet off the ground. He moved down a few feet at a time, took a rest, then moved on again. It was touch and go as he continued down the pole in this fashion.

He was below the halfway point with seventeen feet to go, he felt his muscles begin to tighten up. He clung desperately to the pole. He was afraid to release his grip for fear of losing it altogether. A moment passed, and very slowly he tried to release his hold. Gradually he began to slide down, faster and faster his speed increased. But luckily, Big Jim was there to break his fall, catching him in his arms. If it had not been for the big man, he may have broken some bones.

A guard took Whitey into the infirmary to medicate his skin burns. After being treated he went back to receive congratulations from the waiting group. It was his moment of triumph. A guard ordered everyone to step aside to make room for the Captain who was coming through. It was a trim figured man of forty-five who strode forward in military fashion. In his neatly pressed uniform, the Captain's stride was long and precise. He came to a snappy halt three feet in front of Whitey. The Captain had obviously been a military man, and his actions seemed out of place in a prison camp of this nature.

"Leon Thompson?"

"Cap, yes sir Captain," Whitey was beaming.

"I think you deserve a reward for your performance. It took a man of courage to go up that pole, so this is for you." He handed Whitey a dollar bill.

Whitey was standing like a soldier. His chest expanded an inch as the Captain presented him with the money. This was a high point for the young man, to be rewarded for his success. Not like the past, when his good deeds backfired, he was severely punished for his failures. At five foot eight, Whitey stood seven feet tall as he extended his hand for the dollar bill.

"Thank you sir, thanks very much."

The Captain turned sharply, and marched away.

Big Jim who was standing nearby put his arm around Whitey. "Cotton, if I hadn't seen it with my own eyes I would never believe it. The only thing anyone ever received from the Cap, was work and punishment no matter what they did. Come on let's spend that buck."

At the canteen store Whitey bought four packs of Camel cigarettes, (12 cents a pack), seven penny postcards, four bottles of Coca Cola (5 cents a bottle), and five, 5 cent candy bars. Whitey gave Big Jim, Yank Stewart, and RG each a pack of Camels, one bottle of coke, and a candy bar. The three men gave Whitey a pat on the back in their way of thanks.

Again the four friends were seated on the grass, enjoying the treats.

As Jim lit a cigarette Whitey said to him, "Here Jim, these are for you." He handed him the seven penny postcards.

"I don't have no one to write to Jim, I got these cards for you so you can write to your sister Sue."

Jim hesitated a second as Whitey held out the cards, then reaching for them he said, "You're a good little dude Cotton, you're okay."

"Fuck you, Jim, and don't call me Cotton."

CHAPTER 12.

O n the morning of July 5, 1939, Whitey and RG received forty-two days' good-time, and were released. After saying goodbye to Jim, and Yank Stewart, the two boys decided to team up together and head for California.

The boys were penniless, as they headed south on Highway 1.

"How far is it to the state line?" RG asked Whitey.

"Hell I don't know, what difference does it make as long as we're out of this state by tomorrow morning."

The boys walked along the highway, and each time a car or truck passed, they tried to hitch a ride. Two hours later they were still walking. They were tired and hungry, and had given up hopes of a ride, when a semi-trailer truck stopped and picked them up. There was a sigh of relief when they crossed the state line. They were dropped off just outside the little town of Cheraw, South Carolina.

Their next ride was with an elderly man in his late sixties, who was driving a battered 1935 Ford. The man asked the boys where they came from, and was not surprised when they told him Connecticut. He said he could tell by their accent they were from the North. He was surprised at their age, and being so young he felt sorry for them. As they neared Camden he introduced himself as Ed Blue.

"This is as far as I go boys, this is where I live. Do you young'uns think you can stand a bite of vittles?"

"Does a bear shit in the woods?"

Old Mr. Blue laughed, "Hey that's a good'un boy. I take it you-all are hungry. Well don't fret, my misses, that's my better half, she'll fix you boys up with some vittles."

Mrs. Blue, set a nice plate of chicken and dumplings in front of each boy. When dinner was finished they thanked Mrs. Blue, and Whitey insisted on washing the dishes. She said she wouldn't hear of it, but Whitey washed them regardless. RG did the drying.

After a pleasant evening of conversation, Whitey realized the hour was late, and suggested they should be on their way. The kindly old couple invited them to stay the night, and get a fresh start in the morning. Whitey politely refused and said they must be going.

"You-all keep your noses clean," the old man said as they walked out the door. "Don't take any wooden nickels!"

For the better part of the night, the boys walked down the highway, and not a word was spoken between them.

RG broke the silence, "I don't wanna walk all the fucking way to California. I got a hole in my goddamn shoe. Hey here comes another car—stick out your thumb."

Whitey turned, and using his left hand to shield his eyes from the blinding headlights, he stuck out his thumb and shouted, "We've got a live one, it's stopping."

The following morning just outside the little Georgia town of Washington, Whitey and RG, stretching and yawning, walked out of an old barn.

"Boy I'm starving, and I need a cigarette," RG said.

"Yeah me too," Whitey agreed. "Let's see if we can bum a smoke off that guy over there." Whitey pointed across the highway at a young man in his middle twenties walking in the same direction as the two boys.

"Hey buddy—hey buddy, can you spare a smoke?" Whitey shouted across to him.

The stranger called back, "Yeah I got some smokes, come on over."

The two boys crossed the road, and the stranger held out a pack of Camels. Whitey and RG each took one, and without a thank-you they lit up.

The young man held out his hand to the boys, "Hi I'm Jell Paris."

RG reached for his hand and shook it. "RG is the name, this is my buddy Whitey."

Jell reached out for his hand, but Whitey pulled back, and said, "Jell Paris, what kind of a name is that?"

Jell laughed, "It's just a good old rebel name. Where you-all headed?"

"West to California."

Whitey remained silent, but was beginning to show anger toward RG. "Hey don't be telling this guy our business, we don't know him from Adam."

Jell spoke in a condescending voice, "you're the strangers not me, I live here."

Jell pointed down the highway, "See that clump of trees? Well I live in that little house out beyond them, and if you boys are hungry I'll fix you up with a meal, how's that sound?"

"That sounds great," RG was beaming, and at a fast walk he hurried down the road with Paris a few steps behind him.

Whitey took his time walking toward the grove. He was trying to

69

figure Jell Paris out. There was something false about him. He was surprised when he walked around a bend and saw Paris sitting on a stump, off in the distance RG was hurrying on toward the house.

"What's up Paris? Why you sitting here? Where's my buddy going?"

"Everything's okay. I have a bad leg that's killing me. I told your buddy to go on to the house and help himself to some food, and bring it back here—you know, like a picnic."

Whitey glanced toward the house, he couldn't see RG anymore; turning back to Jell he said, "I don't trust you, where are your folks?"

"You're a suspicious fucker! Look beyond the house, see my Ma and Pa working?"

Whitey looked past the house and sure enough, off in the distance was what appeared to be an elderly couple working the land, they seemed to be hoeing something.

"See, I told you everything's okay, here comes RG now."

RG was making his way across the field, and as he drew near he shouted, "Give me a hand with this stuff, don't just sit there."

Whitey dashed to meet him and grabbed hold of a pot, it contained ham hocks and beans. RG also had a wicker basket filled with corn bread, three plates, silverware, and a large jar of buttermilk. The three hungry men dove into the food. The beans were not quite done, and the ham was a little on the raw side, but it all disappeared in record time. They finished off the meal by wiping their plates clean with corn bread, and chasing it down with buttermilk.

Jell offered the boys a cigarette. Everyone lit up, and as Whitey took a drag he stared at Paris. Paris could sense his burning eyes, "What's wrong with you Whitey? Why you looking at me that way?"

"I'll tell you why, them are some expensive shoes you have on, and your clothes are real nice. Are you sure you're a farm boy and live in that house?"

Jell Paris became angry, "I set you up with a nice meal and you don't even appreciate it. You don't like me do you?"

"You said it, I don't like you, and I don't believe that's your house. You used my buddy. He stole that fucking food, and he didn't even know he was stealing it."

"No, that's not true," Paris protested, "I really live there. Hell I wouldn't send RG into that house if I didn't live there."

"Well prove it then," Whitey said with a cynical smile, "prove it by taking the pot and dirty dishes back to the house."

Paris gathered up the dirty dishes, and placed them in the wicker basket. The boys watched him, and just as he reached the back door, the old farmer came running around the corner of the house swinging a hoe. The hoe barely missed Jell's head. He dropped the basket, and made a hasty retreat running back toward the grove of

70

trees with the farmer right on his heels.

The farmer's voice carried across the plowed field, "You stole my vittles you tramp! I'll kill you, you city slicker!"

From their vantage point among the trees, Whitey and RG watched the drama until they realized Paris was leading the farmer their way.

Whitey shouted, "Come on let's get out of here, I don't want that crazy farmer after me!"

Both boys ran down the highway, and just as they rounded a turn Whitey looked back over his shoulder. Jell Paris was beginning to put distance between himself and the farmer.

After rounding the bend, the two friends hid in some heavy undergrowth just to the left of the highway. In a few seconds Jell Paris came dashing around the bend, and disappeared down the highway. With disgust the farmer had given up the chase, and after a few minutes elapsed the boys came out of hiding; they too made their way down the road.

Four days later just outside Jackson, Mississippi, Whitey and RG were washing their faces beside a river bank.

RG nudged Whitey and said, "Look, I think I see something just over that rise."

RG walked closer to get a better view. He called to Whitey, "Come hear, it's Jell Paris, he's over there on the ground sleeping."

Whitey began to look around. He walked a few steps and picked up a broken limb the size of a baseball bat. Slowly he crept up to the sleeping man. Paris had removed his shoes and had put his coat under his head for a pillow. He was sleeping soundly.

Whitey swung the limb like a golf club hitting Paris in the head. It was a sickening thud. Paris let out a faint grown, his body quivered for a second, then went limp.

"Whitey for Christ sake you killed him," RG shrieked.

"Shut up damnit and get his shoes—get his shoes."

Whitey went through the man's pockets. In his coat he found two and a half packs of Camel cigarettes, a book of matches, and four dollars and thirty cents. Whitey jammed the contents into his own pocket. RG was standing by with the newly acquired shoes.

"Come on Whitey let's go," he shouted.

"Wait a minute," Whitey picked up the club and raised it to strike, "I'm gonna kill this son of a bitch."

RG charged, and using his shoulder he caught Whitey in the midsection knocking him over into the sand. He started to scramble to his feet, but RG put a bear-hug on him, pinning his arms to his sides.

"Turn me loose you mother-fucker—turn me loose."

RG had all he could do to hang on, and he knew he could not

71

continue for much longer. Whitey was wiry as a bobcat, and as strong as a bull.

RG pleaded, "Please don't kill him Whitey. Let's just get the hell out of here."

"All right—all right, let go of me."

They ran across a field, and fifteen minutes later they reached a set of railroad tracks. They were just in time to hop a slow-moving freight train. In turn they grabbed hold of a steel bar grip on one of the passing cars, and scrambled up the ladder to the top; where they sat to catch their breath.

"Look Whitey, look, coming across that field."

Jell Paris was making a desperate run for the train. Barefooted he charged across the field. At the speed he was traveling he had a great chance of catching the last boxcar.

Whitey quickly sprang to his feet and ran jumping from one car to the next toward the rear of the train. Both Whitey and Paris reached the last car at the same time. Paris was running alongside it and was ready to fall from exhaustion; he made a desperate lunge and was able to grab hold of the bottom rung. Breathing heavily he pulled himself up the ladder.

Whitey made a wild leap to the same car; he scrambled to the edge and looked down just in time to see Paris clinging desperately to the ladder. The train was picking up speed, Paris didn't see Whitey coming down after him. Just as he looked up, he received a terrific kick to the face. Paris let out a scream as he hit the ground in a cloud of dust and skidded over an embankment. The clatter of the iron wheels drowned out his final scream.

Sprawled out, Whitey was resting with his eyes closed on top of the moving car when RG touched him, and yelled in his ear, "I don't understand you, not too long ago you were just a scared kid, and now I don't think you're scared of nothing, even killing."

"That's right," Whitey shouted, "All my life I've been afraid of being beat up by my father, or someone older than me. But Big Jim taught me not to be afraid of any bastard, no matter how big or small they are. I'm not afraid no more, I'll kill any son of a bitch who fucks with me, and that goes for you too, don't ever put your hands on me again."

"Hey Whitey, I don't give a fuck about Paris. The only reason I grabbed you, I didn't want you to kill him, because you—you're my friend,"

Whitey gave RG a sharp look that slowly turned into a smile as he glanced down at his feet. "Hey them are some nice-looking kicks you have on, do they fit okay?"

"They fit perfect pal, do you think Mr. Paris will miss 'em?"

CHAPTER 13.

Whitey and RG made their way out to California. For the next two years they worked at various jobs. Whitey was a born leader, and with his natural abilities he could have gone far. But he began to use drugs and alcohol, and never stayed long in one place. He would do good work, receive a paycheck, and be on his way. This was one of those times, Whitey and RG had just received their paychecks, and were preparing to leave for Los Angeles.

"You know Whitey we're in no real rush, let's go out for a hamburger, have a few beers; then I know where we can get laid for three dollars each."

Whitey was shocked, "Three dollars! Are you crazy? No ass is worth three whole bucks!"

"Come on Whitey, it's not the money, you're afraid because you never screwed a gal in your life."

Whitey blushed, and answered without his usual self-confidence. "You're nuts man, I laid a lot of girls, I don't tell you everything."

"Bullshit Whitey, you and I been together for two years now. There's not much I don't know about you. You want to get fucked or not?"

"Hell yes I wanna get fucked."

"Good, you know the girl already, she's Ann the waitress, where we worked"

"Ah shit man, she's old, she must be at least twenty-five or thirty!"

RG laughed, "Boy Whitey you sure got a lot to learn. She may be a few years older than us, but she's pretty and built like a shit-house. Now do you want to screw her?"

"You crazy RG? She never said more than ten words to me."

"Today I told her we're quitting our jobs, and heading for L.A. She said if we want a little fun for three dollars a piece, drop by her place tonight."

"Well okay, but let's have a few beers first."

"It's a deal, tomorrow's Sunday, we can sleep in. Monday we'll take off for L.A."

They went to the corner grocery and bought four bottles of beer. The proprietor knew the boys were under age, but sold them the beverage anyway, for they had been buying their groceries in his store.

Once the boys had consumed the beer they went to Ann's house. She welcomed them with open arms.

During the depression years a dollar was hard to come by. Her waitress job was hard work, and the tips were very small, if any at all. The only men she ever sold her body to were former workers in the restaurant.

The few beers left the boys feeling good, and Whitey no longer felt shy.

"Okay Whitey I'll take you first," Ann said cheerfully, and led him into the bedroom.

After closing the door she said, "Not that I don't trust you Whitey, but would you give me the three dollars first."

"Yeah sure," he said as he fumbled with his wallet, and managed to pull out three dollars.

His eyes were wide open when she started to undress. Ann chuckled when she noticed the bulge in his pants. "Come on," she laughed, "get undressed."

Ann removed her clothes, and helped him with his. Then she guided him to the bed, and made herself ready to receive him, but he did not move.

"Are you afraid?" she asked, "What's wrong?"

Whitey tried to respond, but the words would not come forth.

"Well I'll be darned you're a virgin! Well don't be afraid, I'll take care of you!"

After his first sexual encounter was over, Ann put her arms around him, and speaking softly she said, "Whitey I feel honored to be the first woman you had. I hope it was as beautiful for you as it was for me."

He answered, "It was great Ann, real good, but don't tell RG this was my first lay."

"Don't worry, I won't tell him, but you know something? I wish you weren't going to L.A."

Whitey did not reply; instead he walked out of the bedroom closing the door behind him.

RG was sitting in the kitchen. He smiled when Whitey entered the room. "Well how was it?" he asked excitedly.

Whitey lit a cigarette, and like an old pro he replied, "She wasn't bad, but to be truthful, I've had better."

With a knowing smile, RG opened the bedroom door, and

74

entered.

The next morning, Sunday, Whitey was awakened by RG pounding on his bedroom door.

"Whitey wake up, we're at war! The Japs have attacked Pearl Harbor."

"RG you son of a bitch, if you don't get away from my door, I'll be attacking you."

"Don't you understand?" RG yelled, "Our country is going to war."

Whitey was awake now, and unlocked the door. RG rushed in all excited, "Do you know what this means Whitey? We'll have to go into the Service. Do you understand what I'm saying?"

"Yeah, yeah I understand, but where the hell 's Pearl Harbor?"

"It's in the Hawaii Islands. I guess we won't be going to L.A. now. Uncle Sam will be giving us a steady job! By the way Whitey, what's today's date?"

"It's December 7, 1941."

"Well I guess this is it Whitey, I'm going back to Connecticut to see my parents before enlisting in the Marine Corps."

"Join the Marines! Why don't you join the Navy?" Whitey asked.

"Because, I want to enlist in the Marines, and I'm going home to do it."

"Well go ahead stupid, I'm tired of your company anyways."

RG made a phone call to his mother, and told her he was coming home to join the Marines. She wired him the money for a bus ticket.

The time had come at the Bus Terminal for the two friends to say goodbye.

"What are ya gonna do Whitey? Ya gonna join the Navy or wait to be drafted?"

"Na why wait? I'm just going to enlist."

"Well it looks like I got to go Whitey, the bus is getting ready to pull out."

"Okay Richie Gene Smith, I'll be seeing you."

Before RG boarded the bus, he gave Whitey a warm embrace, and as he turned away he said, "We had some great times, goodbye Whitey."

"We sure did pal, you take care now."

From the doorway of the bus RG called back, "I sure will—hey pal, I'm gonna miss ya."

The door closed, and he never heard Whitey's last words, "So long pal, I'll miss you too."

Little did Whitey know this would be the last time he would ever see RG. Richie Gene Smith was killed in the South Pacific during the invasion of Iwo Jima. At the moment it happened, Whitey was a half mile offshore, on THE USS *Wrangell*, AE 12.

As the Greyhound bus pulled out of the depot, Whitey gave a final wave. He felt lonely and lost, and decided to go see Ann. She was understanding and invited him to stay with her.

On the morning of the fourth day, he informed her that he was enlisting in the Navy, and going back to Connecticut to join up.

"Why not join up here?" she asked. "Why go all the way back there to enlist?"

"I want to join the Navy from the state I was born in."

"I guess I know how you feel Whitey, and I'm proud of you."

He enlisted in the Regular US Navy in New Haven, Connecticut. When he was sworn in, it was the proudest moment of his young life. He loved his uniform. It was the first time he felt he was as good as the next person, his uniform proved it; they were all dressed alike—sailors in the United States Navy. He no longer had to feel inferior; he was equal, and if need be he felt he would gladly die for his country. At last he had obtained the feeling of belonging.

Whitey was assigned to the USS *Bunch* D.E. 694 (Destroyer Escort). He served in the European Theater of War, and sailed the North Atlantic during the days of the notorious German Wolf Packs. His ship made eighteen voyages across the Atlantic, escorting convoys to European destinations, and to North Africa.

In 1944, right after the invasion of France, Whitey was transferred back to the United States, and returned to Newport, Rhode Island Naval Base. Here he was reassigned to the USS *Wrangell* . (Ammunition Explosive). The *Wrangell* was tied up at Earl, New Jersey, Ammunition Dump. She was loaded with ten thousand tons of high explosives. Then set sail for the Pacific Theater of War by way of the Panama Canal, to join the 58th Task Force.

The *Wrangell* participated in the invasion of Iwo Jima, Okinawa, and during the months of June and July 1945 she laid off the coast of Japan. During this period she was one of the main source of ammunition supplies for the bombing and bombarding of the Japanese Empire.

Toward the end of July the *USS Wrangell* was ordered back to the Philippines where she was to rearm and prepare for the forthcoming invasion. It was there, while anchored in Leyte Gulf that the atomic bomb was dropped on Hiroshima—the war was over.

Not long after, the Wrangell received orders to set sail for home by way of the Panama Canal. She tied up at the Navy docks in Balboa. The crew was anxious for the chance to celebrate the war's end, and it was their first shore leave in many months.

Whitey loved the Navy; he had the impression all sailors had to be tough, and live up to their reputation. Consequently he had gotten drunk, and into many fights during the war years. When his ship docked in the Canal Zone, he considered this his last change to raise hell, and celebrate the war's end. When he returned to the US, he would settle down to a peacetime Navy, and make a career of it. But this was never to be.

Whitey went on liberty in Balboa with a shipmate named Todd. They had no plans for trouble; all they wanted was to enjoy the victory of a long hard-fought war. The Navy Shore Patrol picked the boys up for drunkenness and returned them to their ship. The S.P.s knew that the two sailors had just returned from the war, and didn't want to report them to the Officer of the Deck. With a warning not to return to town, and a promise to board ship, the S.P.s left them on the pier. But the sailors were not ready to board ship, and after the S.P.s left they staggered toward the main gate. The Marine on duty would not let them pass.

"Sorry sailors," the Marine told them, "the S.P.s left word not to let you guys go ashore. Best you return to your ship and sleep it off."

The two sailors retraced their steps, and as they walked on past the Marine barracks, they noticed a 1941 Marine pickup truck parked at the curb. Todd immediately jumped into the pickup, and in a few minutes he had it hot-wired. Whitey hopped into the truck. Todd kicked it in gear and with motor roaring and wheels spinning, they took off. The Marine sentry heard the roar of the motor moments before he saw the truck. With headlights out the pickup plunged out of the darkness, and the Marine attempted to wave it down. Todd's foot went to the floorboard, and the truck jumped into high speed. The Marine barely escaped with his life as he threw himself aside to avoid being hit. Before the vehicle disappeared down the road, the alert Marine was back on his feet and commenced firing his .45.

Three miles down the road, the truck accelerated into a hairpin turn at such a speed, it rolled over with a grinding crash. Luckily, except for minor cuts and bruises, the two young sailors were unhurt. They crawled out of the overtured vehicle. Undetected, they were able to slip back to the base, and board their ship. That night they went to sleep thinking all was well.

Early the following morning, the local authorities and the Military Police came aboard ship for Whitey. They had found one of his Navy dog-tags in the wreck.

The Marine posted at the gate, told the authorities there were two sailors in the truck. The Military Police questioned Whitey to to identify the other sailor, but he never divulged his name. The following day the *USS Wrangell* set sail for home, minus Whitey who was confined in the Navy Base Brig.

Two weeks later on November 18, 1945, Whitey received a Summary Court Martial. He stood before a panel of five, a commander, two lieutenants, and two lieutenant J.Gs. He was charged with stealing a government vehicle, drunk and disorderly on a military base. In a military court of law a serviceman is guilty until proven innocent.

The officers he stood in front of were all in the Naval Reserves. There had always been animosity between the Regulars and the Reserves, and he knew that he would not stand a chance before this panel. He remembered another time when he stood before Judge West, and was sentenced to six months on the chain gang. It was a Kangaroo Court and he felt the sentence was unjust. To Whitey this was another Kangaroo Court, and he knew he did not stand a chance before this panel.

"As Supreme Commander of this Summary Court Martial, it is my duty to inform you Seaman First Class, Leon W. Thompson, that you are guilty before the eyes of this court, and your punishment is, you are to receive a B.C.D. (Bad Conduct Discharge) from the United States Navy."

"Wait a fucking minute! I have some rights," Whitey burst out. "I demand a record hearing. I seen a lot of combat in this war. You chicken bastards spent the whole war safe and sound. Now the war is over, you don't need guys like me anymore, so you kick me out of your Navy like a surplus reject."

The two Marine guards were ordered to usher Whitey out of the room. It is almost impossible to describe the disheartening despair Whitey felt. He couldn't hold back the tears for he genuinely loved the Navy, and now they were forcing him to suffer another rejection.

After the court martial Whitey was placed aboard an A.P.D. (Attack Personnel Destroyer), and returned to the U.S.A. He never had a chance to really celebrate the war's end. There was no ticker-tape parade for him, or a warm welcome for a man returning from the war in irons. In Brooklyn, N.Y. Navy Yards at the Flushing Avenue Receiving Barracks, on February 4, 1946, Whitey received a Bad Conduct Discharge from the U.S. Navy.

Whitey returned to his home state of Connecticut. As the train pulled slowly into the station, a sick feeling engulfed him. There was no greeting for this returning Vet. From this very station a little over four years ago, he experienced the same feeling; for there had been no one to wish him well, and a safe return from the war.

"New Haven, New Haven, Connecticut. Next stop, Wallingford, New Britton, and Hartford." The conductor shouted as the train

78

came to a grinding halt.

Whitey's thoughts were of the South Pacific, he wished he had died there. He felt no one would have cared, just as no one cared now upon his return.

With his sea bag over his shoulder, he walked through the station and on out to the familiar streets of his hometown. The sidewalk was crowded with people pushing and shoving. Whitey, who was in a foul mood, stopped short to avoid bumping into a woman who had suddenly stopped in front of him. His reaction caused a man behind to jar into him.

He spun around to face the stranger, "You want to keep your teeth fucker, watch where're you're walking," he growled. The man stared for a moment before he realized Whitey was addressing him. One look at his angry eyes was enough; the stranger apologized and proceeded to walk around him.

People were beginning to stare, Whitey was at the exploding point, and he yelled, "What are you staring at you old bats? Fuck you, fuck the whole world and every son of a bitch in it!"

With that outburst Whitey caught everyone's attention! A few people in the crowd were embarrassed at the language, while others shrugged their shoulders and walked away.

Whitey started to move on when he heard someone shout, "Hey you with the sea bag on your shoulder, hold it right there."

Whitey stopped in his tracks. Standing at the edge of the sidewalk, next to a light pole, was a red-faced cop.

"All right son, I want to know just what that outburst was all about. Come on now, tell me or I'll be running you in. I don't take to cussing in public now."

"I'm not you're son," Whitey scowled, "ya want to run me in, have at it."

"Hold on, I don't like to be arresting a young man such as you until I know what the trouble might be. Would you be having some identification now?"

All Whitey had for an ID was his B.C.D. from the Navy. He handed it to the policeman. The officer read the document. "'Tis a shame son, today's February fourth, you just received the discharge today. Where did you serve? What theater of war?"

"What difference does it make? It was all for nothing," Whitey spoke coldly, "but if you must know, I was in the Pacific."

The policeman was understanding and sympathetic. "Don't take it so a hard son, you fought in the war, you're a veteran no matter what. I see you were in the Regular Navy. But you're young lad, so don't be going off half cocked. You be on your way now, tomorrow is another day."

"Yeah," Whitey said with a sigh, "tomorrow, tomorrow is another day."

The next morning Whitey went to apply for his state bonus of $200 that all veterans were receiving for their service in the war. Also the unemployed veterans were to receive $20 a week for 52 weeks. Whitey was informed only veterans with an honorable discharge could qualify.

He was furious, "You dirty bastards!" He screamed. "That discharge don't change the fact that I fought honorably in that whole stinking war. Don't that count for something?"

"I'm sorry," the woman said, "but that's the rule."

"You know what you can do with that rule, shove it up your big fat ass." Whitey stormed out of the building.

That night he got very drunk. *I should get myself a Reisen machine-gun,* he thought, *and go back to that State building and blow everyone away.*

CHAPTER 14.

Since his court-martial Whitey had a bitter taste in his mouth, and he knew it would always be there. He felt he should receive a bonus like any other veteran returning from the war. But the rejection of a state bonus was more than he could bear. He made a decision to collect his bonus in his own way. But first he decided that it was best to leave Connecticut.

He purchased a 1941 seventy-four Harley-Davison, and before leaving town he thought he would look up his old buddy, Richie Gene Smith. He found his parent's address in the phone book, and started to go to his home, but then decided it was best to call first. He was glad that he did, for it was from RG's mother that he learned that he had been killed on Iwo Jima. Whitey was saddened by the news. He packed his sea bag, and after tying it across the bars of his motorcycle, he rode out of town.

It was a long and lonely ride as he headed west, and occasionally he would find an old barn or shed where he would rest. He had no intention of spending more money than necessary, and when the opportunity occurred, he would connive or steal, rather than pay.

From Connecticut to Idaho he left a long chain of robberies, and occasionally he broke into motels for a good night sleep. He would wait until the early hours of morning, and as he rode down the highway he would be on the lookout for a remote motel. He would pick the lock of a vacant unit, open the door and push his motorcycle inside out of sight. He would set his alarm clock, and go to sleep. Before daybreak he would be on the road again.

During his travels Whitey seldom bought gasoline. He carried a quart can and a small hose from a hot water-bottle that he used to siphon gas. Before siphoning any gasoline he would place a note along with two dollars under the windshield wiper of the car. The note read,

> 'Sir, I'm a passing motorist, I ran
> out of gasoline. I syphoned some
> gas out of your car. I hope the two

dollars will cover the cost.
Thank you.'

Late one night, just outside Logansport, Indiana, Whitey was caught by a State Trooper while in the progress of siphoning gas out of a car alongside the highway.

"I'm not stealing officer," Whitey said innocently. "I ran out of gas. If you look under the windshield wiper of this car you'll see I left a note along with two dollars."

Looking at the windshield the officer was surprised, "Young fellow, looks like I misjudged you. I wish all motorist were as honest as you. Go ahead and get your gas."

Whitey syphoned a few gallons of gas, and when he was ready to leave he thanked the officer, and with a wave of the hand he rode off down the highway.

Approximately a half hour later Whitey returned to the car, grabbed the note and two dollars off the windshield, and quickly rode away.

After leaving Logansport Whitey headed north west for Seattle, Washington. In early spring he hired out to Military Sea Transport Service, previously known as Army Transport Service. Three weeks after being employed, Whitey signed aboard the transport *Private Joe. P. Martinex,* and one week later she set sail with a load of army troops for Japan.

The *Martinez* eased its way across Puget Sound to the open sea. Her course was set for Yokohama, Japan. After the troops disembarked, the *Martinez* was ordered to Sasabo. She was to go on a shuttle run carrying troops and supplies between Pusan, Korea, and Sasabo, Japan.

During one of these shuttle runs she had just returned from Korea, and was tied up to a dock in Sasabo. Except for Whitey and a few others who were on duty, the ship's crew was permitted to go ashore. That same evening a crew member's locker had been broken into, and a large sum of money was stolen.

Two days after the incident, the *Private Joe. P. Martinez* received her sailing orders. With a load of troops, she was bound for the United States.

On the second day at sea, Whitey was ordered to the First Mate's cabin.

"Thompson, you were on duty the night Harris's locker was broken into. I want to know if you heard any pounding or unusual noise. If so, about what time was it?"

"I didn't hear nothing. When I came off duty," Whitey replied, "I went straight to my bunk and fell asleep.

There was no more questioning until the transport pulled into the port of Seattle.

Whitey was on duty at the bow helping to tie up the forward lines to secure the ship, when the Second Mate approached him, and said, "Thompson, just as soon as the lines are secured, report to your quarters, there are two CID agents there wanting to talk to you."

Whitey had no idea what the Criminal Investigation Department wanted with him. He returned to his quarters to find them waiting for him. He was told he was a prime suspect for the theft.

"Why me?" Whitey shouted in anger. "There was at least ten men aboard ship that night."There was no reply, instead the agents shook Whitey down, and then searched his quarters. Finding no stolen money, he was escorted off the ship in handcuffs. Whitey relived the feeling he had when he returned from the war in irons.

George Harris was a married man, and like most of the ship's crew he spent most of his earnings while on shore leave. When he returned home what could he tell his wife? He had to cover up the loss, what better way than to say the money was stolen from his locker? He could have easily made his locker look like it was broken into; then report it to the First Mate. This would make a more convincing story to tell his wife. The only problem was he had no thought or cared that an innocent person may go to jail.

That's just where Whitey was taken—to the city jail, and booked on suspicion of robbery.

One hour later, another member of the ship's crew, Bob Brown, was also booked on the same charge, and placed in jail.

"I'll be damned Whitey, what're you doing here?"

"You heard about Harris's locker; they think I broke into it."

"Me too, that's what they got me charged with. I've been busted once or twice, but I never robbed Harris. Do you have a record Whitey?"

"Nothing to speak of but I guess that's why they grabbed you and I. We're the only ones with a record, and mine ain't shit."

That afternoon, Whitey and Bob went to court for arraignment; bail was set for both men at $2,000. each. Whitey had most of his earnings, and made bail. Bob did the same.

On Wednesday, a Federal judge, dismissed the charges for lack of evidence.

Whitey left the courthouse, and went to the 2nd Avenue garage to pick up his stored motorcycle. After paying storage he rode down to the docks. He went aboard the *Martinez* to retrieve his personal belongings. As he was leaving the ship carrying his sea bag, he bumped into George Harris coming down the passageway.

Whitey dropped his sea bag on the deck. Reaching for his buck-knife he said, "You fat son of a bitch you had me arrested I'm gonna cut you up!"

Harris was a large man, six foot two, weighing two hundred and sixty pounds. He was twenty-nine years old.

"I never had anyone arrested. They asked who I thought robbed my money. I told them I had no idea. I never mentioned your name or anyone else, and that's the truth."

Whitey put his buck knife away and retrieved his sea bag. Tossing it over his shoulder, he proceeded along the passageway. "Just get the fuck out of my way, and stay out of my way."

The big man stepped aside permitting Whitey to pass, and as he did so he said, "I'm sorry for what happened Whitey, don't be mad at me for it."

Whitey stopped in his tracks, and turned around to face Harris, "Let's get one thing straight big man, I don't like you, and if you ever get in my way again, I'll cut you to ribbons."

Harris shook his head and walked away.

As Whitey left the ship, he bumped into Bob Brown.

"Hey Whitey what's happening? Why the sea bag? Are you leaving us?"

"The Coast Guard pulled my seaman papers. On my application I never mentioned my B.C.D. I guess this is the end of my shipping career, piss on it," Whitey laughed.

Following Whitey's discharge, he rented an apartment on Ninth and Pike Street in Seattle. Each evening he would go to the Stadium Cafe to eat. After having dinner he would go to the nearest bar, drink until closing time, then get on his motorcycle and ride to his apartment.

It was in the Stadium Cafe where Whitey met Rose. She was a lovely slender girl of eighteen, with a radiant smile, electrifying brown eyes, and flamboyant red hair. She had an outgoing personality, very good understanding and Whitey loved talking to her.

One night after the bars closed; Whitey staggered into the Stadium cafe for a cup of coffee. Rose was just going off duty, and sat down beside him. She was concerned about him riding a motorcycle in his drunken condition. She persuaded him into leaving the cycle parked outside the cafe. Whitey agreed on one condition that she walk home with him.

The two soon became very close, and shortly after Whitey moved in with her. She asked him what he did for a living, and he told her he was a Merchant Seaman between ships.

Whitey became deeply involved with Rose, and showered her with gifts. They were rather expensive, and she was concerned where the money was coming from.

Rose questioned him about it, "Whitey it's been quite a while since you last shipped out. I'm worried about where you are getting all this money from."

"Hey there's nothing to worry about, I had some money saved up, okay?"

"I'm sorry Whitey, but I don't believe you. Please tell me the truth?"

"I'm telling you the truth—no kidding—don't worry about a thing."

No matter how convincing Whitey sounded; Rose continued to worry. One evening she came home from work, and on the nightstand was a gift-wrapped present. It was an expensive watch, and Rose brought it to Whitey's attention.

"Whitey don't take me for a fool. This watch is very expensive. You can't afford presents like this. All I want is the truth. If you can't be honest with me, we're finished."

"Damn it, okay here it is. I've been pulling robberies. You wanted to know the truth, well now you know."

A tense moment passed before she spoke, and when she did it was in a pleading voice, "Why Whitey? Just tell me why you had to steal."

"It has nothing to do with you Rose, absolutely nothing."

"Nothing to do with me!" she cried, "It has everything in the world to do with me; don't you realize that I love you, I don't want them taking you away."

"Ah come on Rose," Whitey pleaded, "I'm not gonna get caught."

"Don't be so stupid Whitey, if you stay here long enough, you're bound to get caught. Our only chance is to leave the state."

" You mean you'll go with me if I split?"

"If you go, then I go too, but first you have to promise me you'll never steal again, promise me Whitey, promise."

"Okay—okay, you got it, I promise."

Whitey had given Rose his promise, but he soon broke it. The night before they left for California, he held up the 2nd Avenue tavern. He parked his motorcycle behind a billboard two blocks away. Just before entering the establishment, he pulled a Navy watch cap over his head, covering his blond hair. Then looking quickly up and down the deserted street, he opened the door and was met with a blast of music and laughter. On his left there was a jukebox, and it was playing, "I'm Looking Over a Four-Leaf Clover."

Except for the bartender there were five patrons, two women, and three men seated at the bar. No one took any notice of Whitey as he sat down next to the jukebox at the end of the bar.

The bartender was a florid faced, heavyset middle aged man. He was ringing up a sale when Whitey slipped his right hand inside his shirt front, and gripped the handle of a .45 semiautomatic. After making change for a customer, and filling several beer glasses, the bartender asked Whitey what he would like.

"I'd like the contents of the cash register please," Whitey ordered in a cold voice.

Above the blare of the jukebox, the bartender did not understand what Whitey had said, nor did he notice the half-concealed gun in his hand. "Sorry sir, what did you order?"

Sliding off the stool, Whitey reached down and grabbed hold of the electric cord to the jukebox. With force he snatched it out of the wall socket.

"What the hell are you do. . . ." the bartender started to shout; the words froze in his mouth when he saw the automatic staring him in the eyes.

When the cord was pulled, the customers simultaneously turned their heads toward the jukebox. It was then they noticed the gun in Whitey's hand, as he rested it on the bar for all to see.

At the sound of Whitey's voice a chilling silence engulfed the room. "This is a holdup. Get your hands on the bar." And to the bartender he hissed, "Empty the register in this bag." He handed the startled man a pillowcase.

To keep control of the situation Whitey eased his way behind the bar. A customer nearest to him evidently had too much to drink, and using poor judgment, he started loud-talking, "Don't give him your money, he's a coward, a two-bit coward, he won't shoot."

Under the influence of alcohol the instigator felt brave, and started to stand up. Whitey knew he had to shut this guy up immediately, or lose control of the holdup, and that would mean trouble for him.

The revved up drunk stood up and leaned on the bar. Then he turned to the other customers for support, "Let's jump him, he won't shoo. . . ."

Whitey had taken a step forward toward the inebriated man, and struck out with the automatic, inflicting a sharp sickening blow to the side of the head, dropping him to the floor. The impact was so fierce it sent blood splattering, some of it landing on the woman seated next to the fallen man.

Whitey now had control, and hissed, "The next person that moves is dead."

The room was silent except for the sound of the nervous bartender stuffing the money into the pillowcase. The job completed, he handed it to Whitey, who quickly held it open ordering everyone to put their wallets, purses, and the contents from their pockets into it.

With the gun still trained, Whitey stepped out from behind the bar. "Don't anyone move for five minutes, or I'll blow your fucking heads off!"

He disappeared out the door, and jumped over a fence, and made his way around to the back of the tavern, into an alley. Running down the alley he was running parallel with 2nd Avenue, jumping over trash cans and empty boxes, and made his way back to his motorcycle.

He proceeded to remove the money from the wallets and purses, and just as he was doing so, he heard the sudden wail of sirens. He peeked through a crack in the billboard just in time to see two police cars zoom by.

He quickly dropped the money back into the pillowcase along with the rest of the loot; then he stuffed the pillowcase into his saddlebags. Next he quietly pushed his motorcycle toward the alley, parking it behind a trash dumpster. Suddenly the morning's silence was broken with a loud wailing of a siren as another police car dashed down 2nd Avenue.

Under the noise of the police siren, Whitey fired up his motorcycle. He rode out of the alley toward Pike Street and home; seven hundred dollars richer.

Later that day, Whitey and Rose, were on the road heading south for California.

CHAPTER 15.

Whitey had no trouble finding work in Los Angles; three days after their arrival, he went to work for Braswell Freight Lines. He was driving turnaround between Los Angles and Phoenix, Arizona. Rose also went to work as a waitress, and the next few months were pleasant ones. It gave Rose a chance to get to know and understand Whitey better. He told her about his childhood, and how he ran away from home, the chain gang, and the injustice he felt the Navy dealt out to him. The rejection from his home state, and the discharge from M.S.T.S. because of a crime he had not committed.

"I'm so sorry," Rose sympathized. "I understand things better now, but I still worry. Every time there's a knock on the door, I think it's the law after you."

It was twelve o'clock midnight three weeks later. Whitey had returned to the Los Angles terminal from Phoenix, Arizona. He had just turned in his log, as he turned to leave the driver's room, Pete, the dispatcher, called to him from the outer office. "Hey Thompson, come here a moment I want a word with you."

Whitey stepped into the office and said, "Yeah Pete what's on your mind?"

"Today a couple of detectives were here inquiring about you."

"What did you tell them?"

"I told them you should be pulling in from Arizona about four in the morning."

Whitey looked at his watch; it was now 12:20 A.M. He was grateful for the head-start, and he thanked Pete for tipping him off.

Whitey parked his motorcycle two blocks from where he lived. He walked the rest of the way home, but before entering the building he listened for voices from within the house. The building was quiet, so he entered by the back door.

He found Rose asleep, and awakened her with a gentle shake.

In a sleepy voice she asked, "Hi honey, just getting home from work?"

"Be quiet and listen, the law's on to me and I have to split."

Rose shot upright in bed, "The law? Oh my God."

Whitey hurried to pack his seabag, and in doing so he dropped a package wrapped in a rag to the floor. The bundle contained a sawed-off double barreled shotgun, and a .45 semiautomatic. Whitey quickly picked it up, and in his haste to stuff it into the seabag, one end unraveled, exposing the stock of the shotgun.

Rose was horrified. "That's a gun!" She shouted. "What are you doing with it? You promised me, you promised."

"That was in Seattle Rose, I've done nothing down here."

"Then why are the cops looking for you?"

"That's a good question girl. No one knows we left Seattle, unless you told someone."

"Oh God, my girl friend Diane at work. She wanted to know why I was quitting. I told her we were going to Los Angles. She promised not to tell anyone, do you think she did?"

"Does a bear shit in the woods? Of course she did, I'm sure of it."

Whitey finished packing his seabag. "Come on Rose, get your clothes together, we got to get out of here."

"I'm not coming with you this time Whitey."

"What! Come on, I don't have time to argue with you. Let's go girl."

"Please don't be mad at me Whitey, I love you, but I'm not going to run again.

Whitey took her in his arms, "I'm not mad at you Rose, I'm mad at myself, I guess there's nothing more to say. I do know I got to get out of here right away."

He held her tightly, and after a quick kiss, he grabbed his seabag and was gone.

In the silent room, Rose sat on the edge of the bed brushing away her tears. A few moments passed, then suddenly she cocked her ear to the sound of a motorcycle off in the distance.

CHAPTER 16.

It was 2:30 A.M. when Whitey rode off the Ridge Route on Highway 99 heading north to Sacramento. After his arrival, he would make daily trips to the Bay Area. These were not pleasure trips, for he would spend each day carefully casing out a bank.

One Monday morning at 5:30. Whitey hot-wired a 1945 Ford Coup, and drove to San Francisco. He steered toward Fisherman's Wharf, where he parked the vehicle. The time was now 7:10 A.M., traffic was beginning to pick up, and businesses were starting to open their doors.

From a street vendor Whitey bought a container of coffee and two donuts. After he finished the refreshments, he lit a cigarette, and tried to relax, but relax he could not. The plans of the day were spinning through his mind. Lying on the seat next to him was the shotgun wrapped in a rag. The cut-down version of the weapon appeared more deadly than it did in its original form. The full length from stock to barrel was fourteen inches, giving it the appearance of a double barrel shotgun pistol. Both barrels were loaded, and in his jacket pocket were ten more shells. From his rear pants' pocket he pulled out a pair of light weight leather gloves, putting them on. Then with the cloth he proceeded to wipe the steering wheel and the interior of the car for fingerprints.

He lit another cigarette, took a deep drag, held it in a moment, then exhaled. He sat there watching the smoke drift gently against the windshield. His eyes focused to the water's edge, and shifted to a red and white ferry boat that was edging its way to the dock. Looking beyond the dock off in the distance, he saw lying there looking like a monstrous battleship, Alcatraz Island—commonly known as the Rock. To the prisoners it was "Hellcatraz," island of the living dead. Alcatraz, the most notorious, most feared prison this country has ever known. It was the ultimate in maximum security for the worst troublemaker, and they were all there at one time or another—the toughest of the tough. Al "Scarface" Capone,

George "Machine-Gun" Kelly, "Creepy" Alvin Carpis, Frankie Carbo, Mickey Cohen, the legendary Birdman of Alcatraz, Robert Stroud, and many more.

As Whitey Thompson looked at the island across the Bay, little did he know that within ten years his name would be added to this select list.

Bringing his attention back to the business at hand, he glanced at his wrist watch. From his jacket pocket, he pulled out a can of black shoe polish and opened it; took his comb and began to work shoe polish through his hair. Once this was done he looked into the rear view mirror to inspect his handiwork. Next he took out a small bottle of rubbing alcohol and cleaned his comb. He dropped the dirty rag and the remains of the shoe polish out the window, then returned the bottle of alcohol to his inside jacket pocket.

Again he checked out his equipment; the sawed-off he carried inside his jacket under his left arm. The two outside jacket pockets each contained five extra shells. His left rear pocket held his comb, while the right rear one carried a tightly rolled up duffel bag, and in his shirt pocket was a neatly folded paper bag.

Again he glanced at his wrist watch, "Nine thirty," he said aloud, "I better get moving."

He lit another cigarette and started the car. Leaving San Francisco, he drove back over the Oakland Bay Bridge to the city of Oakland. He parked the car one block over from Telegraph and Broadway. Before getting out of the car he made one final check of his equipment, and made one change. He placed the folded brown bag into the palm of his left hand. He was now ready.

The time was exactly three minutes after ten when he walked into the Bank of America, and precisely two minutes later he came out the door, and casually walked away.

Before walking out of the bank, he left strict instructions that if anyone came near the door to follow, or summons help, within the next three minutes, he or she would be gunned down by his accomplice who was concealed across the street from the bank.

Whitey turned the first corner, and without drawing attention as he walked along, he pulled the duffel bag out of his pocket. Opening it up he slipped the half-full paper bag inside it, and pulled the strings tight while he continued walking. Just as he rounded the next corner, he heard the sound of sirens. He paused long enough to light a cigarette, and then blended in with the crowd. He made his way back to Telegraph Avenue, crossing over at a crosswalk to the opposite side. He continued up Telegraph a short distance, and then disappeared into Capwells Department Store where he took the elevator to the third floor. He immediately went into the men's room. Once inside he stepped into a toilet stall. He was relieved to find no one else in the restroom. Very quickly, with the alcohol and the use of toilet paper, he removed the polish from his hair. Then he stepped out of the stall to inspect his image in the mirror, and was satisfied at what he saw. He then quickly pulled out the sawed-off shotgun, and buried it under the dirty paper towels in a large trash can. Following this, he removed the extra shells from his jacket pocket, and these too were buried in the trash can.

With the duffel bag in hand, Whitey left the restroom, and made his way back to the men's clothing department, where he bought a brown corduroy jacket. He asked the clerk if she would be kind enough to wrap up his old one as he was going to wear the new one. He returned to the restroom where he retrieved his shotgun and shells. Then after disposing his old jacket in the trash can, he made his way to the cafeteria where he had coffee and donuts.

The clock behind the counter showed the time, 11:15 A.M.. The cafeteria was teeming with people coming and going. Over his coffee and cigarettes Whitey sat there watching the activity. Again he glanced at the clock. It was now 11:30. He sat there a moment longer adjusting himself. Then he picked up the duffel bag, and walked out of the store to San Pablo Avenue, stopping occasionally to window-shop, check his watch and move on. It was 11:45 when Whitey flagged down an approaching Greyhound bus displaying a sign over the windshield, "SACRAMENTO."

If he had attempted to board the bus at the Greyhound Depot, there might have been police there to check out the travelers.

The rhythm of the bus rolling down the highway was a satisfying feeling for Whitey, as he reclined comfortably with a little over eight thousand dollars in the duffel bag.

CHAPTER 17.

Two weeks after the robbery, Whitey was employed by Golden West Lines as a long-line truck driver. The job was a cover for him as he was working under the name of Leonard Johnston. His crimes continued as he pulled numerous armed robberies. He was living high, foolishly spending money on drugs, alcohol, and women. This way of life continued on into the summer of 1947.

It was shortly after the first of July that he teamed up with William Shaw, a co-driver, commonly known as Bill. He was a medium built man of five foot nine, with an olive complexion. A good-looking fellow, thirty years of age, married with two children. His wife Shirley was a lovely woman of twenty-six.

Bill had many problems, and while driving over the road with Whitey, he would continuously be recounting his troubles. He was deep in debt, his wife was very unhappy, the children were in need of clothes, and he was behind with his rent.

Whitey was always an outspoken person, harsh in his ways, and said what was on his mind. He was tired of hearing Bill's problems and told him so. "You know Bill, your problems are becoming a pain in the ass. I'm tired of listening to your troubles."

"Hey man," Bill shouted, "I'm just making conversation, I didn't mean to offend you."

"Goddamn it," Whitey shouted, "if you need money go rob a bank!"

Whitey sat behind the wheel, and as he drove along he could feel Bill's eyes staring at him.

Turning his head, he glanced at Bill, "What the fuck you staring at?"

"Nothing Whitey, it's what you just said, "I've thought about robbing a bank. A few grand would set me straight."

Whitey had been casing a place out, but changed his mind about it because it required two men to pull it off. He always worked alone, and had trust for no one. This particular robbery was worth approximately thirty grand, and Whitey hated to pass it up.

"A few grand could put you in prison too, have you thought

93

about that Bill?"

"If I'm busted, the state will take care of my wife and kids. What've I got to lose?"

"Just your freedom, but it takes more than talk to pull a bank job."

"You sound like you pulled a job or two."

Whitey gave Bill an icy stare, and in a cold voice he said, "If you're serious about pulling a job, let me know, but if you're just a lot of talk, then you better forget this conversation ever took place."

Whitey had an apartment on 29th Street, and one evening Bill and his wife dropped by for a visit. Bill knew Whitey only as Leonard, and he introduced him to his wife as such.

Shirley knew that Whitey was struck by her beauty. She had blue-eyes, and a perfect figure, thirty-six, twenty-two, thirty-six. Like a queen on a throne she held her hand out to Whitey. He accepted it, and as he did so, her head bowed slightly, and the weight of her blonde hair swung gently forward. Suddenly Whitey knew what she reminded him of, a French Poodle that he had seen in heat this last spring. The Poodle was trotting along in front of a German Shepherd. She had an alert and springy movement, tail curled high, and every second or two, she turned to see if the German Shepherd was following. Her tongue lolled out, and she had a doggy grin as she anticipated what was to come. A very lively quick French Poodle, Whitey thought, as he shook Shirley's hand.

Whitey went into the kitchen, returning with three cans of beer. The evening consisted mostly of small talk. Shirley sat directly across from Whitey, and it was all he could do to keep his eyes off her. She was like a small child sucking on a lollipop, the way she ran her tongue over and around her can of beer with her eyes focused on him. From her actions she seemed oblivious of her husband sitting next to her.

Shirley excused herself to go to the bathroom. Turning quickly to Whitey Bill whispered, "I was thinking over what you said the other day, I'm ready anytime you say."

"You better be sure, once the job is underway there's no pulling out. If you try, I'll cut you down in your tracks, understand?"

Both men were shaking hands on the new partnership when Shirley returned.

"What's the handshaking for?" she asked.

"Nothing," Bill replied, "I just invited Leonard over for dinner tomorrow."

Shirley smiled, "That's great, love to have you for dinner that is!" She laughed at her own joke, and giggled and smiled at Whitey.

"We better be going," Bill said, "we have to pick up the kids from my mother's house. See you tomorrow night Leonard, dinner at six.

Come on Shirley let's go."

As they walked out the door Shirley called back, "You can come earlier if you like."

Two weeks previously he had purchased a 1941 Chevrolet for transportation. He was punctual for his six o'clock dinner engagement.

When dinner was over, while Shirley washed dishes the two men had a chance to talk. Whitey told him his real name, and how he held up a number of banks.

"I can't believe it, by yourself you actually pulled some bank jobs. I'm ready for the next one Whitey, you can count on me, but I have to get a gun."

"Don't worry about it, I have a shotgun for ya. I already altered it. Tomorrow morning pick me up around eight, and we'll test it out by the American River."

Shirley had finished the dishes and returned to the front room.

"Bring us another beer," Bill demanded. The conversation about bank robberies excited him so much that he was drinking one beer after another. At eleven o'clock he dozed off.

"Looks like your husband fell asleep. I guess I better be heading home," Whitey said.

"You don't have to rush off," Shirley cooed. "I'll tell you what, let's you and I go get a pizza. At the same time we can pick up the kids from Bill's mother, we're supposed to pick them up at eleven thirty." Pointing at her husband, "Look at stupid, he's too drunk to drive. Come on let's go, he'll still be asleep by the time we get back."

They drove to the pizza parlor first, and then went to pick up the children. On the way Shirley asked, "How much money have you got? When you paid for the pizza I seen a good lump of green in your wallet."

"I don't know how much I got, a grand and a half, two grand maybe, why?"

"Oh I was just wondering, with that kind of money, maybe you'd like to run off with me. Bill is a bore, always broke, and I'm a beautiful girl."

Whitey couldn't believe what he was hearing, then again—yes, he realized he could believe it, for he already had her pegged for a tramp, a good-looking French Poodle tramp!

"Answer me Leonard, don't toy with me, I seen the way you looked at me. I'm sure you'd jump at the chance to have me. There's lots of guys who'd love what I'm offering you."

Whitey looked at her for a second; then his attention went back to the road.

"Tell me Leonard, before we get to my mother-in-law's house, do you want me or not?"

"I don't want nothing from you Poodle, you understand, *nothing*. Now let's go get your kids"

The force of his voice frightened her, and she sat there staring at him.

Next morning Bill picked Whitey up and drove to the American River. After Bill parked the car, Whitey got out with the shotgun, and started to walk toward the river. He realized Bill had stayed in the car, and yelled to him, "Ain't you coming Bill?"

"No, go ahead I'll wait here in the car."

This seemed strange to Whitey; but he shrugged his shoulders, and proceeded to the water's edge. He put a shell into the shotgun, aimed it at the water and pulled the trigger. Whitey put in another shell, and fired it again. He had done a perfect job in hacksawing off the stock and barrel. Again he loaded the weapon and started back to the car.

Bill saw him coming and hastily started up the engine. Just as Whitey walked behind the car, he slammed it into reverse, and at the same time jamming down on the accelerator. The motor revved up, and like an angry monster the automobile came alive. An earsplitting roar bellowed from the exhaust pipes; the wheels spun for a second as they dug for traction. Dust and gravel flew; then the car shot backwards just as Whitey flung himself out of the path of the charging vehicle.

Bill immediately slammed on the brakes to avoid backing into a huge pine tree that he had hoped to pin Whitey to.

The moment he jammed on the brakes, Whitey was back on his feet, and in one bound he was at the side of the car with the shotgun pressed against Bill's head.

"You son of a bitch! You tried to kill me!" Whitey was furious and shouted in rage. "You crawling bastard, you lowlife prick get out of that car." With his left-hand Whitey grabbed the handle of the door and swung it open. Bill climbed out of the car trembling with fright. Whitey made him drop to his knees by jamming the gun barrel into the left side of his neck. Whitey's rage was at the boiling point, "Why did you try to kill me?"

"You—you know why," Bill blurted out. "Because—because you tried—you tried to get my wife to run off with you."

"What the hell are you saying?" Whitey pressed the gun barrel sharply into his neck.

"Last night, when—when you and Shirley went to pick up the kids, she told me how you propositioned her, how you asked her to run off with you."

"Run off with her! Me run off with that French Poodle slut! I should blow that pussy-full sewer pipe's brains out."

Bill's body shook with fear as Whitey poked him harder with the shotgun. Finally he ordered Bill back behind the wheel of the car. "Just drive me home bastard, then get out of my sight before I blast a hole in you. Run off with your wife? She's nothing but a slob who thinks every man she sees wants to fuck her! I rejected the bitch, and she can't stand rejection."

For a while there Bill thought he was going to be killed. He didn't like the things Whitey said about his wife, but he knew there was nothing he could do about it. He also knew his wife was a flirt, and had caused him trouble before, but nothing like this.

Bill pulled up in front the apartment, but before Whitey got out of the car he said, "The job's off. I can't trust a guy who is hung up on a broad, even if the broad is your wife. There is nothing worse than a lying bitch, except a stupid bastard who lives with one. The deal is off, and from now on you better stay the hell away from me."

That night while in bed, he was still feeling the anger over the episode with Bill and Shirley, and he had the feeling it was not over with. But what could Bill do? There was nothing he could do, and the next time he wouldn't be so lucky; he'd blow the bastard away.

Whitey was very restless, and it wasn't until after 1:00 A.M., when finally, a troubled sleep rested on him, and he heard the thunderous blast of the big five-inch thirty-eights going off. He was back in the Navy during the invasion of Iwo Jima. He bolted upright in bed, and it took a few moments for his head to clear before he realized that someone was knocking on the door.

"Wait a minute—wait a minute damn it."

Whitey, with sleepy eyes unlatched the door, and two big burly detectives rushed through with drawn   guns. Whitey was subdued before he realized what happened.

"Hey get your paws off me. What the hell's the beef anyways?"

"We got a warrant for your arrest. The charges are suspected bank robber, and possession of illegal weapons, namely sawed-off shotguns."

Whitey, with all his careful planning couldn't believe this was happening, he made one mistake—William and Shirley Shaw.

"That lowlife bastard, I should have killed him and his bitch," he mumbled to himself.

William Shaw wanted revenge, so he informed on Whitey, and in doing so, little did he realize he too would be charged with possession of a sawed-off shotgun, and receive a five-year prison term.

Whitey received a sentence of fifteen years, and while waiting in the county jail to be transferred to the McNeil Island Penitentiary, unexpectedly Rose came to visit him.

"When I heard what happened Whitey I just had to come see

97

you."

"Look Rose, I don't want you wasting your life on me, so beat it. If you ever try to see me again I'll refuse the visit."

With tears clouding her eyes Rose turned to leave, and just before the door closed behind her she said softly, "I'll always love you Whitey."

When the door shut, Whitey whispered, "You too Rose, I'll always love you."

CHAPTER 18.

It had been two weeks since Whitey and Lou were transferred to Deadlock, and Monday morning a black prisoner by the name of Wyatt was placed in a cell next to Whitey. Shortly after he was locked up he called out "Hey Whitey Thompson, you remember me?"

"Yeah Wyatt, I know ya, you worked in the BCR."

"Listen Whitey I have some news for you. It's all over the joint how Red bum-beefed you. Someone threw a blanket over him and flipped him off the tier, and he landed on his head, He's in the hospital now all fucked up, they don't believe he'll make it."

"Hey man, do they know who did the job on Red?" Whitey asked.

"Yeah, the word is out that a couple of your friends did the job. Whoever did it did a good one. Red's head is bashed in, he's nothing but a vegetable."

The news about Red Kendrick really made Whitey's day. Smiling, he lay down on his bunk to think about it. Good old Blackie and Shorty, he knew he could count on them.

Whitey shouted to the other end of the tier. "Hey Lou, did ya hear about Red?"

"Yes Whitey, I heard he slipped on a banana peel, and fell on his head!"

A few chuckles sounded from the second tier. Whitey was about to yell back to Lou, but was interrupted by the sound of the main Cell House door as it swung open with a loud bang, followed by the shouts of a guard, "Chow, chow down, get ready for chow."

As if on a signal the prisoners started to yell. "Chow down all you sweet things get ready for your slop!"

Another voice, "That's exactly what it is—slop, slop for the hogs!"

Someone else yelled, "I got your slop, right here between my legs, come and get it."

There was more laughter and catcall throughout the Block.

The food cart was pushed in, coming to a halt in front of Whitey's cell. Ross, the cart-man started to fill trays, while the runners carried them to the cells.

99

Whitey was acquainted with Ross, and called to him in a whisper, "Ross, hey Ross push your cart a little closer, I want to talk to you."

Ross waited until the guard wasn't looking, and pushed the cart nearer to his cell and said, "What can I do for you Whitey?"

"Do me a favor Ross, your cell partner works in the front office, ask him to find out if I'm on any transfers."

The guard looked down the tier and saw Ross ending his conversation with Whitey.

"Get away from that cell, what the hell do you think you're doing?"

Ross yelled back at him, "Hey what're you getting on me for? He was just telling me I forgot to put bread on his tray."

The angered guard walked up to Whitey's cell door, "When something's missing on your tray, you tell me about it, not the cart-man—understand?"

"Fuck you screw, I'll tell you nothing."

"I'm too smart for you Thompson, you can't rile me up."

Whitey was seated on his bunk with his food tray on his lap. He got up and stepped up to the bars of his cell and hissed at the officer, "Yeah you're one smart fucker copper, shove your food up your ass, and stick the cart up there with it!"

Whitey slammed his food tray up against the cell bars. The guard jumped back, but not in time. The main contents of food splattered his face and uniform.

He was furious, "You little bastard, I ought to come in there and beat your head soft."

Like a monkey he leaped up onto the cell bars. As he hung there by his hands, he was hissing and spitting at the guard. Then suddenly at the top of his voice he let out a bloodcurdling scream. Everyone in the Cell House was frozen in their tracks. There was absolutely no movement or noise except for the scream that echoed throughout the Block.

In amazement—almost fear, Ross and the food-runners were looking at him as the screams penetrated their eardrums.

The guard was astonished at Whitey's actions, and stood there transfixed not quite knowing what to do. Suddenly the screaming turned into shouting, "Come in here you big son of a bitch, you brave mother-fucker, I'll flush you down the shitter!"

The guard turned his attention to Ross and the food-runners. "All right, the show's over. Let's get those food trays passed out." Then turning back to Whitey he said, "You get no second tray Thompson, you pull another stunt like that, and I'll write a shot (report) on you. You keep it up, Thompson, and I'll be forced to come in there."

100

The guard knew he couldn't enter Whitey's cell because of the red padlock on the door, and he was glad of it.

The hatred that had built up in Whitey was ready to explode. He was so enraged he felt he could pull the cell bars apart with his bare hands. He had the feelings of a crazy man, and he didn't care. All he wanted was for the guard to come into his cell. He had no fear, even of death, and when a man begins to feel this way, he is dangerous.

The guard moved nearer to Whitey's cell. He wanted to try and calm him down before it got out of hand. If he let him get away with this type of tantrum, then the other prisoners would think him weak, and unable to handle his job. He had to get the upper hand.

"Look Thompson," he whispered, "calm down now, I'm going to forget this incident ever happened, but if it happens again, I'll have to make out a report."

Like a mad badger Whitey hissed at the guard, "Get away from in front of my cell, I can't stand the stink!"

Laughter broke out, and the convicts started catcalling to harass the guard. The officer, on cue, rounded up his crew, and immediately made a hasty retreat from the Cell Block.

For the ensuing five days it was peaceful in the Cell Block. Ross had no news about transfers. Whitey asked him what had happened to the young guard, and was told his name was Price, and he was working on another shift, but would be back the day after tomorrow.

"Shit, I thought he was gone for good."

CHAPTER 19.

As usual, Monday morning in Deadlock started off like any other day. Five-thirty A.M. the thunderous blast of the wake-up horn, the bellow of the Cell House Officer calling out, "Rise and shine, rise and shine. Let's hit it, get ready for count."

There is a shuffling sound of movement in the Block. A hundred and fifty prisoners with grunts and groans shove and push their way out of bed. The chattering begins as they call out to one another; toilets flush with the sound of running water blending in with the vibrating pulse of the Cell Block as it once again comes alive.

Ross came in pushing the food cart, with excellent skill he maneuvered it within a few feet of Whitey's cell. Ross began dishing up the food, as the eager runners went right to work.

Officer Price was back on duty. He walked up to Whitey's cell and said, "I received word that you have been cooperative for the last week. If you keep on improving, I believe you will be sent back to the main line, and get your job back in the shoe shop. Also, Thompson. . . ."

Cutting him off Whitey shouted, "I heard enough of your shit. You come in here and feed all this crap to me about going back to population, and getting my old job back. You're just trying to get my hopes up, that's when they slap leg irons on me and ship me to the Rock. You'll never have the pleasure of telling me I'm going to the Rock."

Basically Whitey was wiry tough, and would not back down from anyone. He was well liked for his courage by his fellow prisoners, including some of the guards, particularly the ones who beat him up, for they too respected his courage. Whitey would always fight back to the last ounce of strength. They could not break his spirit, and if not for anything else, they had to respect him for that.

The deep gashes from the beating had healed over now, but the scars were still there. They would remain there, and serve as a reminder for the rest of his life.

The next morning he was awakened when the guard shouted, "Chow—chow down, get ready for chow."

Whitey rolled out of his bunk, and reached for his mirror. Going to the front of his cell, he held it through the bars at an angle that

102

enabled him to see down the runway. He was looking to see which guard was on duty. Whitey was disappointed to see it was Officer Price.

Ross stopped the food cart in front of Whitey's cell, and went straight to work filling trays while the runners hurried off to deliver them. Ross pulled a pack of Camel cigarettes out of his pocket. A quick glance told him that the guard was not looking, and in a shuffleboard motion he slid the pack on the floor. It went under the bars into Whitey's cell who was ready for the missile, and as it slid into his hands he nodded his head in thanks. Ross went about his business filling trays.

When the meal was over Whitey lit a cigarette. Then he reached up on his shelf for a book, titled "*Knock on Any Door.*" He had read it earlier in the week, but right now he wanted it for another purpose. He opened it to the center, placed ten cigarettes between the pages, then closed the book. He stood up to the bars and yelled down to the other end of the tier, "Hey Lou, I have something for you, its coming down."

Whitey reached between the bars and laid the book flat on the floor. Again, just like shuffleboard, he slid it with force and precision; it came to a stop right in front of Lou's cell.

"Nice shot Whitey. You must have hit it rich. Where did you get the Camels?"

"Never mind where I got 'em, I'm just a rich kid that gets all the breaks!"

"Okay rich kid! Thanks for the smokes."

The next morning Ross once again parked his food cart a few feet from Whitey's cell and hastened to fill the trays. While the food runners passed them out, Ross began to fill another tray. While doing so he kept his eye on Officer Price who was at the far end of the tier. He loaded the tray with extra bacon and hot-cakes. He quickly handed it to Whitey and as he sat down to enjoy the meal he nodded a thank-you to Ross.

In record time Whitey finished the meal, drank his coffee, and topped it off with a cigarette. He lay down on his bunk, and was deep in thought blowing smoke rings, when Officer Price approach his cell and said, "Getting enough to eat Thompson?"

Whitey turned his head to see who was speaking. At the sight of Price he looked at him with disgust and replied, "Does it make any difference to you how much I get to eat?"

"If it were up to me Thompson, this would be your last meal."

"You know something Price, you're such a miserable bastard I bet you go home from work every night, and beat up your wife, kick the dog out, and lock your kids in the bedroom!" Not waiting for the guard to reply Whitey yelled, "Hey Lou, you know what, someone shit right in front of my cell, there's a big pile of it standing here, what a stink!"

103

"So that's where it's coming from! I can smell it down here!" Lou yelled back.

On that note the food cart crew left the Cell Block with Officer Price mumbling to himself.

The evening wore on, it was getting near time for lights out. Whitey was tired and went to bed, but sleep would not come. The events of the day were whirling through his mind with thoughts of Alcatraz. He reached for a cigarette and matches, and after lighting up he tried to relax; he was unsuccessful and called out, "Hey Lou, is tomorrow the day for our water-ski ride?"

"Fuck you and your water-skis Whitey."

From the second tier someone shouted, "Shut up down there and go to sleep."

Whitey bounced out of bed and jumped to the front of his cell. He was fuming, and as he grabbed hold of the bars he yelled, "Who's the loud-mouth? Who told me to shut up?"

The unknown voice sounded again, "I did, just shut up, or I'll fuck both you water-ski freaks."

Whitey began to churn inside; his blood was boiling as he tightly gripped the bars, and shook them violently. "Lou—Lou," he yelled, "did you hear what that bastard just said?"

"Yeah Whitey, sounds like we got a wise-guy in the house. Hey wise-guy, how would you like to try and shut us up?"

A silence fell over the Cell House as everyone listened.

"You wait until next time these doors open up, I'll shut you up," yelled the voice from the second tier.

"Hey Lou," Whitey called, "do you know who that punk is? Do you recognize the voice?"

"No, I don't Whitey, that's why the ugly fucker is so brave."

The talkative prisoner on the second tier thought all the cells on the Flats were Deadlock cells, and was not worried about being discovered. But this was not the case for only inmates considered the most troublesome had a red padlock on their cells. For instance, Lou had no extra lock, and was privileged to take a shower each evening along with the other tiers. The showers were on the main floor on the opposite side of the Cell House.

"Whitey—hey Whitey," Wyatt called in a whisper, "put your head near the bars I have something to tell you."

Whitey complied, and Wyatt whispered to him, "Hey I know who that wise-guy is."

Whitey's adrenaline began to rise; he was excited, "Who is he Wyatt?"

"His name is Tod Baker, you know who he is, he used to cell over in 4 House."

"Did he used to work in the Furniture Factory?" Whitey asked.

"Yeah that's him Whitey, I recognize his voice, that's Tod Baker."

"Okay Wyatt, thanks for the tip."

Quickly Whitey picked up a pencil and paper, and wrote, 'The loud-mouth on the second tier is Tod Baker. He showers the same time you do. Need I say more?' He placed the note between the pages of a paperback book.

"Hey Lou," Whitey called out, "I'm shooting a book down to you." He slid the book down the tier, but it stopped just wide of the mark.

Lou flipped his blanket out over the book, and managed to drag it in close enough to reach it.

"Hey Lou," Whitey yelled again, "what's happening, did you get it?"

"Yeah I have it now, but I had to do a little fishing for it."

"Well shake the pages, I put a kite in there."

"I found it Whitey, relax, everything is cool."

Whitey smiled as he lit a cigarette and lay down on his bunk. After a few drags he put it out, turned over, and went to sleep.

The following morning in its usual manner, the Cell Block came alive. The bellow of the wake-up horn, the slam of the main Cell House door, the voice of a guard shouting, "Rise and shine, rise and shine!" The bitching of convicts, water running, toilets flushing. It was the usual madhouse, horns blowing, buzzers sounding, bells ringing. Each one had a specific meaning; the wake-up horn, the count buzzer, and the chow bell. Every day seemed like total madness.

Whitey was at the sink splashing water on his face when the count buzzer sounded.

"Count time—count time," a guard shouted.

He barely had time to stand up to the bars when an officer scurried by counting as he passed.

Ten minutes later the all clear bell sounded.

"Count's clear—count's clear," the guard shouted.

If the count had not checked out with the total, then a re-count would immediately be made, and the prisoners would have to stand up to the bars again. If the re-count still did not tally, then the escape horn would sound. Every cell and prisoner would be checked out by a guard. The officer would ask each inmate his name and number that was compared to an identification card. There were over fifteen hundred prisoners, and in approximately ten minutes they would be able to identify the inmate who was trying to escape, or had escaped.

There were occasions when an inmate working outside his cell would go into hiding in a vent shaft or cubbyhole. There had been incidents when an inmate had hidden out successfully for a few hours before he was caught. For his effort, he was charged with attempted escape, and usually received more time.

One man did escape from Cell House 1, and somehow he made his way to the prison boat landing, where he knocked out the guard who ran the prison boat. But before he could get the motor started, he was recaptured. No one knew how he managed to get out of the Cell House, through the locked doors and gates, and past the guard towers. It was a mystery, and Custody could never get the escapee to talk.

On this particular morning the count was clear. "Chow, get ready for chow," the guard shouted.

Ross pushed the food cart along the Flats, stopping a few feet from Whitey's cell. The cart man hastened to fill the trays while the food runners proceeded to pass them out. Ross began to fill another tray, and while doing so he kept his eye on Officer Price who was at the far end of the tier. He loaded the tray with extra bacon, and hot-cakes, and quickly handed it to Whitey who retrieved it through the door slot.

Whitey looked at the loaded tray, and nodded his thanks to Ross. He sat down on his bunk to enjoy the extra food. A moment later Ross stepped up to his cell door, "Coffee Whitey?" He asked.

"Yes," Whitey stuck his cup through the bars, and held it while Ross poured the coffee.

"My celly will check again," he whispered to Whitey, "I'll see you later." Without waiting for a reply he went back to his job.

The morning seemed interminable until 11:15 A.M. when Ross and his gang came in with lunch, but he didn't have any news for Whitey.

He returned again at 3:30 P.M. this time with news of a transfer to Leavenworth that was leaving in the morning. Whitey's name was not on the list.

"How about Lou? Is he on it?" Whitey asked.

"I don't know if he's on it or not," Ross replied.

Before the cart man left, he slipped Whitey another pack of Camels. Again Whitey sent ten cigarettes down to Lou by way of the shuffle-board.

"Hey Whitey," Lou called out. "Where're you getting all these smokes from?"

"What the hell's it to you? You enjoy smoking them don't you?"

"Not if you're pimping for them," Lou laughed.

"Are you calling me a jailhouse pimp? If you are mother-fucker, you got your last cigarette."

"Heeey Whitey, just kidding. These are the best cigarettes ever, no matter where they come from."

Both men chuckled. The two men often kidded back and forth in this fashion, and one never knew if they were serious or not.

Whitey called to Wyatt, and handed him a couple of cigarettes; then called out again to Lou, "Hey Lou, I just got the word a chain is leaving in the morning for Leavenworth."

"Hey Whitey, if you happen to get a chance would you. . . ." Lou did not finish for he was interrupted by shower call.

"Showers," a guard shouted. " All you able-bodied men get ready for your showers."

"Hey Whitey," Lou called again, "it's shower time, I'll talk to you later."

"Okay man, take care of business."

Cell doors began to open and close with the usual noise, and from the inmates the usual shouting, catcalls, and horseplay. Whitey went to his sink, and began filling it with water. He stripped off his clothes, and using his T-shirt as a wash cloth, he gave himself a cell bath. When this was completed, he scrubbed his T-shirt, and hung it over a makeshift line, hoping it would be dry by morning.

When his chores were finished, he dressed himself, and lay down on his bunk to enjoy a cigarette. As he inhaled deeply, he could hear the showers running, and the inmates yelling on the other side of the Cell Block. Suddenly everything went quiet. The noise ceased; not a sound could be heard except for the running of water.

When Lou had come out of his cell at shower call, he went around to the other side of the Block. After taking off his clothes, he placed them on a bench; then he stepped into one of five shower stalls. Each stall contained four showerheads. Lou quickly washed, and hurried out of the shower to dry himself. After dressing he went to the clothing room window to turn in his wet towel, and received a dry one. While doing this, he was continuously taking note of each man who came into the shower area. Just as he turned from the towel window, he saw his man go into No. 4. shower stall. Lou edged his way up to the rail in front of the showers, and standing on the other side, waiting his turn, was a tall slim-looking man in his thirties. The noise of the showers was deafening, and Lou had to shout to make himself heard, "Hey Tod, Tod."

The slim man looked around, when he saw Lou, his legs went limp.

"Well, well, Tod Baker, the man who told me and my buddy to shut up. You even called us freaks. You said you'd fuck us both. W-ell—well," Lou said derisively as he walked around the rail simultaneously looking to see where the guard was. The officer was at the far end of the area, and did not see Lou come around the rail. Tod began to panic, looking in all directions for a place to run, but he could go nowhere. His path behind was blocked by a line of men waiting to shower, and on either side of him was the pipe rail. He had no choice but to face Lou.

"Hey—hey Lou, I was only kidding, I was . . . ."

He never got to finish his pleading, Lou hit him flush on the chin,

107

dropping him to the floor like a ball of lead. The sharp impact of Lou's fist against Tod's jaw, was so loud that it echoed throughout the shower area. A split second after Tod's body hit the floor there was only the sound of running water, a heavy silence had settled.

The silence was broken by the shrill of a guard's whistle as he ran toward the fallen man. Three more guards appeared on the scene. The shower room officer immediately took control of the situation by ordering all inmates to stay right where they were. Then turning his attention to Tod, he lifted his head and placed a folded bath towel under it.

"All right," he said, "I don't suppose anyone saw what happened."

"Yeah I saw what happened."

The guard looked at the speaker and recognized him, "All right Mark, tell me what happened."

Mark was a pleasant-faced old man in his seventies. He was an international bank robber, born before the turn of the century. He was an old-timer whom even the guards respected.

"Not much to tell," the old man went on.

"Just tell me what you saw Mark, that's all."

Mark was about to speak just as Tod began to stir; everyone's attention turned to the man on the floor.

"Just take it easy now," the guard ordered.

Tod looked up at the many faces looking down at him, and when he saw Lou's face, his features turned white.

Again the guard asked Mark to tell what he had seen.

"Well let's see now," the old man continued, "I was standing here in line waiting my turn to shower when this here youngster (he pointed at Tod) pushed his way toward the front of the line, and in his haste to get ahead of everyone, he slipped on the wet floor, and as he was falling his head hit the rail, and he knocked himself out, and that's exactly what happened."

"That's right," another prisoner spoke up, "it's just like the old-timer said, he fell and hit his head."

The other inmates also agreed, stating in unison that was exactly how it happened.

Tod was lying there wide eyed, and he too agreed with the old-timer. To the guard he said, "Yes, yes sir, I slipped and fell like he said, but I'm okay now sir."

"All right then," the guard ordered, "get up and take your shower, don't ever try jumping the line again, understand?"

"Yes sir, I'll never do it again sir."

Lou was smiling as he returned to his cell.

At the precise moment the Cell House became quiet, Whitey knew that Lou had taken care of Baker. In between cigarette puffs he laughed to himself, and wished that he could have seen Tod when he got it. He lay down on his bunk to await the return of Lou. A few moments elapsed before he heard the opening and closing of cell doors; then Lou called out to him, "Hey Whitey—Whitey."

"Yeah Lou, how'd it go?"

"Why don't you ask him yourself?"

"Okay I will. Hey you on the second tier, hey Baker."

There was no reply, and Whitey called again, "Hey Baker—cat's got your tongue? Come on loud mouth answer me."

Whitey heard a weak whisper from the second tier, "What—what do you want?"

"What happened to you loud mouth? I heard something happened to you over in the shower."

There was a moment of silence before Tod answered, "Ah, nothing much happened, I just slipped on the wet floor and hit my head."

A loud chuckle issued from Whitey's cell. "Okay Baker, you punk, let that be a warning to you. Next time you loud mouth my conversation, you'll dress out in a pine box."

Everyone was waiting for Baker's reply, but there was none.

Whitey undressed, and crawled into bed. Before falling asleep he chuckled as he thought about Tod Baker.

Early the following morning, Whitey was rudely awakened. Someone called out his name, "Hey Whitey, wake up man, it's me Lou, wake up."

In the dim light Whitey opened his eyes, and was surprised to see Lou standing in front of his cell. "How the hell did you get out there? Where's the bull?"

"Never mind the bull, just dummy up and listen. I'm being transferred to Leavenworth. The bull let me wake you up to say goodbye. I wish you were going with me Whitey."

"Me too Lou, if I was then I wouldn't be going to the Rock."

The two men looked at each other, and for a brief moment their eyes locked. They shook hands, and Lou said, "So long partner I'll catch up with you."

Whitey was thankful for the semi-darkness of his cell; it hid his emotions.

"Come on Peters, get a move on," a guard shouted, "let's go,"

Lou turned to leave, and as he walked away, Whitey called after him, "So long pal."

At 3:30 P.M., Ross pushed in the evening meal cart, and again spoke to Whitey "I seen a list of transfers for Alcatraz. Your name is not only on it Whitey, it heads the list, and you'll be shipping out early tomorrow morning. I'm sorry pal."

109

"Thanks Ross, you been a pal, a real pal, I'll never forget ya."

"Likewise Whitey. I won't see you again, so we better say goodbye now, just in case."

"Yeah sure Ross, oh by the way if you get a chance, tell Blackie and Shorty I'm on my way to the Rock, tell them to play it cool."

The two men shook hands; then Ross turned his attention to his job, and continued to fill trays. When Officer Price wasn't looking, he slipped Whitey another pack of cigarettes.

Well, this is it, Whitey thought as he finished off his meal, *I'm on my way to Alcatraz, I guess I have to pay the piper.*

Whitey lay on his bunk to finish his smoke, and concentrate. He thought about the day he arrived at McNeil Island. It was hard to believe it was ten years ago. On the second day after his arrival, he was summoned to the counselor's office. He had some forms for Whitey to fill out.

"What the hell are these for?" Whitey asked.

"One is for your correspondence list, and the other is for visitors."

"I don't want no goddamn visitors, or anyone writing me. Besides I don't have no one in the free world anyways. Just stick your list up your ass," he shouted at the counselor.

Whitey, never having a visit or letter was completely cut off from the outside world. As the years passed by it seemed as if the world outside had never existed for Whitey, it was only a dream, he had never been there.

CHAPTER 20.

At 5:00 A.M. the following morning Whitey was abruptly awakened by a guard, "Okay Thompson, up and out of there," he ordered.

Whitey slowly moved out from under the blanket, and as he did so, he heard the padlock being removed from the cell door. He slid his feet over the edge of the bunk, and placed them on the cold concrete floor. His eyes were not yet accustomed to the darkness of the cell, and he couldn't see a thing as he fumbled for his clothes.

The guard yelled at him, "Never mind your clothes. Don't touch anything, just come out of there the way you are."

Whitey paid no attention to the guard's orders. He continued to fumble in the darkness for his clothes.

"Goddamit, I told you not to touch your clothes. Come out as you are," the guard shouted.

Whitey was cold and his body was shivering. "What the fuck is wrong with you screw? It's an iceberg in here, give me time to put clothes and shoes on."

"Come out of there Thompson like I told you, leave everything behind."

Whitey stepped out on the tier dressed in a pair of boxer shorts. The early morning hours on McNeil Island were always cold, and this morning was no exception.

There were two guards, one fell in behind Whitey, and the other in front; they started down the tier. Half the Cell House was now awake, and shouting encouragement to Whitey.

"So long Whitey, hang tough man, be cool."

"Be cool," Whitey shouted out loud, "be cool shit, I'm freezing!" And he suddenly spun around on his heels, knocking the rear guard to one side as he dashed by him. He caught the officer off guard, and it took him a few seconds to collect himself together.

Whitey streaked down the tier like a naked jack rabbit straight to his cell. He charged in and made a grab for his pant's before the guards reached the doorway. He had one foot in his pants' leg and was about to slip in the other, when one of the guards yelled at him.

"Come out of there Thompson, or we will drag you out."

Whitey made a grab for the wooden stool, and held it over his head as he screamed at the guards, "Come on in and get me fuckers! I'll cave your goddamn heads in!"

"This is your last warning Thompson, put that stool down and come out of there, or we'll drag you out—*now*."

The whole Cell House was now wide awake. Cussing, shouting and catcalls could be heard from one end to the other. Voices sounded from all directions.

"Hey you fucking Hacks let the man get dressed."

The shouting continued getting louder and louder.

"Put that stool down Thompson and come out of there," the guard ordered again.

The second officer intervened and spoke for the first time, "Ah hell, let him put his clothes on, what's the big deal anyway?"

Whitey still held the stool. The first guard could see that he was not getting anywhere with him, so he grudgingly conceded, "All right Thompson, put on your clothes, hurry up about it."

It seemed as if everyone in the Cell House was calling well-wishes to Whitey.

"Good luck Whitey, take care."

The shouting increased; the guards did not attempt to quiet them. From experiences of this type of situation, they had learned to leave well enough alone, and it would simmer down on its own accord.

The heavy Cell House door opened, allowing Whitey and the two guards to walk through. Then the door slammed shut behind them, sealing off the shouting prisoners.

Whitey, under escort of the guards, was led to the shower room. In the room there was a long line of five-man shower stalls. On the floor in front of each shower head was a large flat steel disc, and when stepped on, the water shot out with terrific force. The temperature was preset behind a locked door, and usually set very high. Midway down the walkway stood three guards watching over five prisoners already in the showers.

The nearest guard to the approaching column spoke first, "Who you got there? Is this Thompson?"

"Yes this is him, he's all yours Robinson."

The two officers turned Whitey over to Robinson, and promptly left the area.

"Take your clothes off Thompson, and grab a shower." Robinson ordered.

Whitey obeyed, and stepped into the nearest shower stall. There was a prisoner still showering, and when Whitey entered the stall he nodded his head. Ignoring the greeting, Whitey stepped onto the steel disc. The water shot out icy cold, and he immediately jumped off the plate yelling, "You mother-fuckers!"

The prisoner burst out laughing.

Whitey was furious and shouted, "What're you laughing at fucker?"

The big man's laughter turned into a smile, and he said, "The name's Johnny House."

"Yeah I know who you are, I've seen you around. My name's Whitey Thompson."

"Yeah Whitey, I know who you are."

Again Whitey moved toward the disc. He stood to one side as he stretched his right foot out and cautiously pressed down on it. Again the water shot out, but he was well to one side of the main flow. Testing with his hand he waited until the water was hot, then he took his shower.

The other five prisoners were already getting dressed.

After drying off Whitey was told to stand with his arms extended in the air and his legs spread apart. He obeyed and the guard ran his hand through his hair and beard. It had been three and a half months since he had a shave and hair cut. The guard went over Whitey inspecting between his fingers, under his armpits, and then ordered to lift his testicles. After this was done, he was told to lift one foot at a time to inspect between his toes.

"Okay Thompson, bend over and spread your cheeks."

While holding his buttocks, Whitey bent over allowing the officer to look up his rectum. With the shakedown completed he was handed a safety razor and ordered to shave. Once this was accomplished he received a set of clean prison blues, underwear, socks and shoes.

When the six prisoners were dressed and ready, the first guard spoke to them, "All right let me have your attention. My name is Jones, and this here is Officer Murray, and Officer Robinson. I'm in hopes when we arrive on Alcatraz I will be able to put in a good report for each one of you men. So it's up to you, you can make this trip as easy or as hard as you want. So shoot your best stick, any questions?"

"Yeah I have one," Whitey replied with a smirk, "what's a stick?"

Jones replied, "Like I just said, you can make this trip as easy or as hard as you want."

Officer Murray ordered the men to line up single file starting with Whitey, followed by Johnny House, Freddie Steinburg, Lieto, Williams, and then Chili.

Officers Murray and Robinson secured the prisoners. Each man was handcuffed, chained and shackled to each other, and they wore leg-irons that allowed a twelve-inch step.

The prisoners were now ready for the long march to the boat dock.

Officer Jones gave the command, "Start moving slowly out that door."

Whitey growled, "How the hell else can we move but slow, all chained up like this."

"Goddamn it Williams get in step," Lieto said angrily.

"I am in step fucker, you're the one that's out of step," Williams scowled.

Johnny yelled, "Hey ass-holes, you have to walk in locked step when you're wearing chains. You know that."

Johnny was a huge two hundred and twenty-five-pound man; he was an easygoing person unless he was rubbed the wrong way. He was annoyed at Williams and Lieto for causing the chain to jerk his ankle. Being chained together with a lock step of twelve inches could be very painful on the ankles. They tended to get raw and swollen when a man got out of step, and caused a sudden jerk on the chain.

The six prisoners started their shuffling walk toward the doorway, through several more doors and gates that were unlocked in front of them, and re-locked after the procession passed through. The small group made their way toward the main entrance to the prison. Up in the high tower a lonely guard with rifle at the ready observed their every move. When they reached the main entrance, the high towered guard pressed an electrical button, and the big gate slid open, allowing the three guards and their prisoners to pass through. Still under watchful eyes, the column moved slowly down the hill toward the boat landing, where the prison boat was tied up. A few trusty inmates who worked the dock were also giving the prisoners a shifty eye until Whitey yelled out, "What you staring at mother fuckers! I'm no goddamn Egyptian!"

114

PART 2.

TRANSFER, THE

TRAIN TO ALCATRAZ

1958

CHAPTER 21.

Still under the eye of the high towered guard Officers Murray and Robinson assisted each prisoner onto the gangway. The six inmates and their guards were the only passengers aboard the prison boat. The vessel was manned by two inmate trusties, and one Correctional Officer who was the skipper.

"Cast off the bow and stern line," the skipper called out. The vessel began to tremble into a violent vibration as the twenty-four-hundred horsepower engine came alive.

They were underway, and as the boat turned her bow toward the mainland and the coastal town of Steilacoom. Whitey eyes drifted back to the island. His features were hard, and his expression was cold—cold as the prison he was leaving behind. He came to McNeil Island on this very boat, and now ten years later, this same boat was taking him away. He looked across the water at the prison fading in the distance. For a fleeting second a ray of sadness seemed to glisten in his eyes. He quickly erased the feeling, and his thoughts returned to the present. His features were the same but there was a change in his eyes. For a fleeting moment, they had shown a sign of sadness, now they were cold—extremely cold. Tomorrow he would board another prison boat, to an island out in the bay—Alcatraz. The end of the line for the living dead, the Island of no return.

Johnny House was going to Alcatraz with a natural life sentence. Earlier that year he had received the sentence in an Alaskan court for a shotgun killing. He had shot another man who was trying to establish power in Johnny's underworld business. At the time of the killing Alaska was still a territory. Born in Texas, Johnny House was a handsome-looking man of fifty. His good looks had fooled many people who didn't think he was tough, there

117

was nothing weak about him—he was tough, *very* tough.

Whitey had had nothing to eat since the night before, and was experiencing hunger pains. The other five inmates had been in the main prison population. This morning they were awakened at 4:00 A.M., and escorted to the Dining Hall and fed an early breakfast. But Whitey who wasn't officially informed about his transfer received no breakfast. According to rules and regulations, every prisoner, including those in Deadlock, were supposed to be fed before leaving on a transfer. The guards disliked Whitey, and felt they could safely get away without feeding him.

Whitey addressed Officer Jones in a gruff voice, "How about something to eat?"

"What's wrong with you Thompson? You had a good breakfast this morning."

"Bullshit, no one fed me you lying bastard."

"Hold your tongue Thompson, you'll get fed on the train."

"You're sorry you know that Jones? I bet you feel good beating a man out of his food, you lousy bastard."

"All right that's enough Thompson, just cool off."

"Fuck you copper, I want a cigarette you son of a bitch."

Whitey's outburst startled Jones, and he came to his feet. He could hide his anger no longer. He was furious and shouted at Whitey, "Thompson that's the last outburst I want to hear from you. When you have something to say, say it in a normal voice. You may get some results, and for your information, there's no smoking on this boat."

"Hey fuck your results," Whitey shouted, "I didn't ask if I could smoke, I asked for a damn cigarette."

Johnny House sat on Whitey's right, he was irritated and shouted, "Give him a cigarette for Christ sakes. There is also another rule that states whenever a Federal prisoner is in transit, he is to receive one pack of cigarettes each day he is in transit."

"I know the rules House," Jones inferred, "you'll receive your cigarettes in due time." Then turning to Whitey he continued, "You're nothing but a troublemaker Thompson."

"Hey thanks for the compliment, at least that makes me something, but I still want my goddamn cigarettes," Whitey said.

"Yeah let's have the cigarettes." Johnny protested.

Whitey turned his head slightly, and glanced at Johnny House and the rest of the prisoners. He didn't really know these men. He had seen all of them at one time or another, and if it came to a showdown he might be able to trust Johnny, Freddie, and Chili, but he was not sure of Lieto or Williams.

The other prisoners joined in the protest, "He's right, how about our smokes? We want our cigarettes."

118

"All right—all right, quiet down," Jones was mad, and he hated to give in. The only way to quiet them was to give them their cigarettes. On the seat next to him was a duffel bag. Jones extracted five packs of Camel cigarettes out of the bag. Starting with Chili, Jones put a pack into each man's shirt pocket, until he reached Johnny.

"Hold it I don't smoke cigarettes," he said, "I smoke cigars."

To everyone's surprise, Jones retrieved three cigars from the duffel bag, and stuck them in the pocket of Johnny's shirt.

"Well I'll be damned, will wonders never cease?" Johnny said with a laugh.

With a voice of authority Jones said, "When the boat ties up at Steilacoom, I will give each man a book of matches, but not until then. There is no smoking allowed on the boat."

Jones stood there a second. He was challenging Whitey or any of the prisoners to dare make a reply. No one spoke, a triumphant smile appeared on Jones' face as he returned to his seat. Feigning a hard look, he sat down facing the prisoners giving the impression he was tough. He sat there, straight up in his seat with his shoulders back, his chest puffed out, and his arms folded. He thought to himself, I've gotten them back under control, and I'll keep them that way! Damn that Thompson, look at him sitting there—just a wise punk. If I had him alone for five minutes, I'd break his spirit, he just thinks he's tough!

Whitey couldn't help chuckling to himself as he stared across at Jones, look at the bastard, he thinks he's tough! The truth of it is he's afraid he'll have trouble, that's why he gave us the cigarettes now.

Whitey's thoughts were disrupted by a loud blast from the boat's horn, and realized they were pulling up to the pier at Steilacoom. There was another short blast from the horn—ALL STOP—and the engine ceased with the signal.

In one movement the prisoners rose from the bench, Officers Murray, and Robinson helped the prisoners disembark. They shuffled their way off the pier, across a set of railroad tracks to the Steilacoom station.

Steilacoom was a whistle-stop, a customary wooden building and platform with two benches. Jones told the prisoner to be seated as it would be a while before the train pulled in.

Once settled the men immediately with some difficulty, because of the handcuffs, extracted the cigarettes from their pockets. Johnny had less trouble with his cigars.

Jones gave each man a light, then placed a book of matches in their shirt pockets.

Johnny began to smile after inhaling a few satisfying puffs.

119

Whitey showed no emotion as he smoked his cigarette. He enjoyed the smoke immensely, but from his expression no one would know it.

For a period of time the prisoners were contented to talk and joke. But as time wore on, the seating became uncomfortable and in the morning's heat, tempers began to flare.

Jones could sense tension beginning to build. He quickly opened the duffel bag, took out six Hershey bars, and passed them out. Then he walked over to a Coca Cola machine, and purchased each man a bottle of coke (Coca Cola cost ten cents a bottle.)

Whitey hungrily ate the candy bar, and unlike the other prisoners he accepted the bottle of coke without a thank you.

"Why thank him? He's just trying to butter us up with candy and coke."

"No, I'm not Thompson," Jones spoke up, "I'm just trying to make this wait a little more bearable."

Whitey looked coldly at the guard, "Look screw, if you want to make it more bearable, then take these fucking leg-irons off."

Whitey carried too much bitterness to let anyone butter him up with candy and Coke. He was sure the other prisoners felt the same way. Any one of them would cave a guard's head in at a chance to escape, and would enjoy doing it. All of them would kill for their freedom.

Since the beating from the guards, Whitey was like a wild animal who would kill at the slightest provocation. No one knew what was going on in his head. He would always have the element of surprise in his favor. They could imprison his body, but they could never lock up his mind. He was deep in concentration when the sound of a train whistle brought him back to reality. At last, the train was pulling in and they would soon be on their way.

As the Canadian Pacific came to a grinding halt, the men rose from the bench, and tried to stretch their muscles the best they could under the circumstances. The only person to step off the train was the conductor who placed a step-stool in front of the Pullman compartment.

Officer Murray and the conductor assisted the prisoners in boarding the train. Once aboard the Pullman, the conductor led the way to their compartment which contained a stationary table with six chairs around it. There were four single beds folded to the wall, and a long cushioned bench that would accommodate the six prisoners. In one corner a door opened to a small toilet. Because of the cuffs, shackles, restraining belts, and chains that held the men together, the toilet became a problem to use. As for the beds, they were unable to use them at all.

After the procession entered the compartment, they seated

themselves on the bench. Whitey, who was at the head of the line, was seated just a foot from the corridor door. As soon as the men were seated, Officer Robinson quickly closed the door and locked it from the outside, and stationed himself in the corridor. No one could get in or out of the compartment unless Robinson unlocked the door. Officers' Jones and Murray remained inside with the prisoners. This compartment, was reserved by the Federal Bureau of Prisons.

Jones, was the officer in charge. He stood up to make an announcement, "You men, I don't want any trouble out of you, and when we arrive at Alcatraz, I'll put in a good report on each one of you. But if I receive the least bit of static from any one of you, I'll turn in the worst report I can possibly make out."

"Ah go fuck yourself," Whitey hissed. "Who the hell do you think you're talking to, a bunch of kids? Piss on your reports, who cares?"

"Who cares? You'll care when you get to Alcatraz Thompson."

Officer Murray, who was standing by the door, was well aware of the situation. He felt Officer Jones was handling these prisoners the wrong way, especially Thompson. These men had been termed incorrigible, and were on their way to Alcatraz. Because they were wearing shackles and leg-irons, don't for one minute underestimate their abilities. Jones may not have realized it, but you had to handle these men with kid gloves, or a touchy situation could occur. There was a right and wrong time to lay down rules, and he believed Jones' timing was off when he delivered his speech just after boarding the train. He would have been better off if he had waited until the prisoners had been fed. It was easier to talk to a man who had a full stomach. But even so, one should use a choice of words when speaking to Thompson. Thompson had an unrelenting frigidity in his heart and arteries. This made him a very dangerous man to fool with, and Murray knew it. But there was nothing he could say, Jones was the senior officer in charge.

Jones sat there expressionless, while Whitey stared at him with hostile eyes. Murray was aware of similar looks from the other prisoners. The atmosphere became tense; except for the clackerty-clack of the train wheels, a quietness settled over the compartment.

Excluding Whitey, Jones spoke to the others in a sarcastic voice, "You can thank Thompson here for the report I'm going to put in on all of you just as. . . ."

"What the hell you trying to pull?" Johnny interrupted "You trying to turn us against Whitey? Well forget it. I don't give a fuck about you or your report either!"

Before Jones could respond the other prisoners joined in.

"Fuck your report," they yelled.

"Fock re-port," Chili shouted in broken English. "You think bunch kids we are?"

"All right that's just about enough of your. . . ." Jones didn't finish as there was a loud knock on the door.

Murray called through the door, "Yes Robinson, what is it?"

"There's a porter out here wanting to know if you want lunch served,"

"What about it Jones?" Murray asked, "Do you want lunch now?"

"It's rather early isn't it?"

Whitey made a lunge from his seat, but was pulled up short by the chains. He yelled, "What the hell you mean too early? I haven't eaten since last night."

"All right—all right, quiet down," Jones shouted at Whitey.

"Well what's it going to be? Do we feed now or not?" Robinson called.

"Ok Robinson," Jones replied, "open the door, let's get it over with."

Robinson opened the door, and standing beside him was a black porter. He was a gray-haired man of sixty with a cheerful smile on his wrinkled face. He was six feet tall though he stooped over a bit, no doubt from a life of hard work.

"Yes sir," the porter said addressing Jones and Murray. "What would you gentlemen like?"

"Okay," Jones said, "you can bring sandwiches all around, take the prisoners orders first."

The old porter turned his attention to the seated prisoners, and with an extra cheerful smile he said, "All right boys, I know you all are hungry and thirsty, what'll it be?"

Jokingly Johnny said, "I am thirsty, bring me a scotch and soda."

"Okay," Officer Jones said, "let's cut the clowning and give the man your orders."

Whitey spoke up first, "Do you have any ham? If so bring me a thick ham and cheese on rye, with a dab of mustard, a glass of cold milk, and a cup of black coffee. You got that?"

The porter took the order and replied, "Yes sir I got it, and how about you other boys?"

They all agreed on the same order except Freddie, who ordered a roast beef sandwich.

All three guards ordered ham and cheese sandwiches.

The porter smiled at the prisoners. It was a warm understanding smile; he knew there would be no tip from this compartment.

122

After a short interval, the porter returned balancing a huge tray over his shoulder. Officer Robinson unlocked the door letting him in; he was greeted with a cheer.

"Here's our food," Freddie exclaimed. "Three cheers for the porter, hip-hip-hurray."

The porter set a pot of coffee on the table, along with a pitcher of milk, sandwiches, potato chips and pickles.

The chain of prisoners stood up, made their way around the table, and with some difficulty they managed to be seated. The kindly old porter placed a sandwich and napkin in front of each man. Then he filled all the glasses with milk, and was about to reach for the coffee pot when Jones stopped him.

"Never mind that, I'll do the pouring for them, thank you."

"Yes sir," Turning to the prisoners he said, "If you boys want anything, just have your boss man ring the buzzer." Smiling and with a wave of the hand he left the compartment. He was a kind old man, and all he could see were six human beings shackled and chained together. It didn't matter to him who or what they were, or why they were prisoners. He was just a warmhearted person wanting to show kindness to his fellow man.

The prisoners had an extremely hard time trying to eat or drink. The cuffs, restraining belts, and chains made it practically impossible. Every so often one of them would cuss out the guards as he endeavored to eat, but they finally managed.

After finishing lunch, the prisoners made their way back to the bench, and while enjoying their cigarettes the old porter returned, "Was everything all right boys?" he asked. "Did you enjoy your lunch?"

"The food and service was excellent, and you my friend are perfect. I wished I could give you a tip, but I'm sure you understand my situation," Johnny remarked with a smile.

The old man looked at Johnny, "Long as you boys enjoyed the service, that's all the tip I need, thank you."

He picked up the tray of dishes, and turned toward the door. As he passed by Whitey he smiled at him.

Damn it Whitey thought, why did he have to smile at me? Why does he have to be so fucking polite? Why couldn't he come in here, slammed the food on the table, and go without all that polite shit? I hate all mankind, and here comes this old man, who treats all of us like brothers or something. If I start thanking him the bulls will think I'm getting weak!

Chili interrupted Whitey's thoughts.

"Off-cer Jone, I use toilet now? I go now, okay?" Chili asked.

"All right," Jones replied, "I can't take the manacles off. All of you will have to get up."

Officer Murray opened the door to the toilet. As the men stood up Whitey was mad as he didn't have to go. Chili, being the first man in line had the first crack at the toilet. He was in front of the toilet bowl fumbling with the zipper on his fly. He began to do a little dance jumping up and down. He had to go badly, and he couldn't hold it much longer as he tried to unzip his pants. With the handcuffs locked to the restraining belt, it was almost impossible.

"Damn fock! Damn fock hondkuff, you unzip, I piss quick!" Chili yelled.

It was hard to keep from laughing, and everyone except Whitey laughed. Chili finally made it. The laughter stopped as quickly as it started; it was not amusing anymore, it became serious business; except for Whitey they all had to relieve themselves. Chili stepped back, and as he did, Williams took his place at the bowl. After Williams had relieved himself, Chili was able to squeeze out of the toilet, leaving Williams jammed to the wall, while Lieto had his turn. Now Chili and Williams were just outside the doorway, leaving Lieto pinned to the wall, while Freddie had his turn. When the pissing party first started, Whitey didn't have to go, but after Lieto relieved himself, he realized that now he too had to go. He was worried if he was going to make it to the toilet bowl in time; he had all he could do to hold it back!

At last Freddie was jammed to the wall, while Johnny was going.

"I'm next," Whitey announced, "Jesus Christ am I going to make it? Hurry up House, or I'll piss all over ya!"

"I'm going as fast as I can Whitey, just hang on, I'm almost done."

At last Johnny was through. He jammed himself to the wall pushing Freddie out the door; leaving Whitey standing near the toilet bowl fumbling with his fly. The handcuffs were making it difficult for him.

"Oh Christ," he yelled, "let me unzip this fucking fly before I piss my pants!"

Just as he got it unzipped, the first three men on the chain started to shift away from the door pulling Johnny and Whitey with them.

"Stop moving you sons of bitches," Whitey shouted, "you're pulling me away from the bowl." Whitey had been pulled about a foot away. He had his penis in his hand, and could hold back no longer; he was compelled to take a side angle shot! He let go, and the first gush of the stream missed the bowl, hitting Johnny's left pants' leg.

"Watch it man!" Johnny yelled. "You're pissing on my leg."

124

Whitey quickly got the range, and was hitting directly into the bowl, when suddenly he was pulled away from it again.

"Stand still you mother-fuckers," he yelled, "you're making me piss all over the place!"

"Give him some slack you bastards, he's pissing on me again," Johnny shouted.

Whitey twisted around as far as he could, and his aim was hitting the bowl again. What a relief! He got himself zipped up just as Johnny squeezed out of the toilet, enabling Whitey to step out behind him.

When they were once more seated on the bench, Johnny said, "Man! I never went through so much bullshit in my entire life just to get pissed on!"

Whitey spun his head around to face Johnny, "Are you referring to me?"

Johnny was smiling, "Yeah, I guess I am Whitey, but hell don't get uptight, it wasn't your fault. I can't blame you because I got pissed on!"

At first Whitey was angry at Johnny's remark, but when he saw the smile on his face, he knew he was joking. They looked at each other, and their eyes locked for a second. For the first time there was a rare trace of a smile on Whitey's face.

Whitey began to like the big Texan, and the pissing party was the beginning of a bond between them. For the first time since the journey began, Whitey's guard relaxed somewhat as he joined in conversation with Johnny. It seemed as if everyone was talking to each other now, even the guards were chitchatting back and forth.

As the day wore on there was less talking to be heard, and soon it stopped altogether. Lieto and Williams had their eyes closed. As they snoozed, their heads were bobbing in a loose motion up and down, like a cork floating on an angry stream of water. A laziness had drifted over the compartment. Whitey, along with Johnny and Freddie, were looking out the window at the sights. Up in the sky were pillows of white clouds. In the distance were soft hills of rolling green, an occasional house dotted here and there, and in the foreground the continuous row of telephone poles as they flashed by the window.

Inside the compartment there was a vibrating sound, a rhythm of music from the clackerty-clack of the steel wheels, and the movement of the train. Whitey and Freddie both had a cigarette going, and Johnny was puffing away on a cigar. The compartment was filling up with smoke, and it was becoming noticeably warm.

"Hey it's getting hot in here, how about opening up the window," Johnny suggested.

"The window won't open," Jones informed him.

"Ain't there no air-conditioning on this train?" Whitey asked.

"The vent is already open. There's nothing more we can do."

"Bullshit, I'm burning up man. I need some air, "If you can't open the window, then open the fucking door." Whitey yelled.

"The door stays locked," Jones was angry. "I have orders to keep it closed."

"Hell we can't go any place," Johnny shouted, "you got cops all over the fucking train."

Looking toward the other guard Whitey shouted, "Hey how about it Murray? Tell this fool to open the fucking door. Shit you got a guard sitting outside, so what's the problem?"

Murray turned to Jones, "It is getting kind of warm and stuffy in here. Under the circumstances, I think it would be wise to open the door, don't you agree?"

"Yes, I believe you're right Murray, under the circumstances I think it would be wise."

Jones called out to Robinson who complied, and swung the door wide open, and at once they could feel a cool breeze come in from the passageway. Jones cautioned the men about any outburst while the door was open.

Now and then a passenger would walk by. They would stop long enough to take a look in at the prisoners, then move on. As time went on there seemed to be increasingly more people walking by. A number of them would peek in and smile, while others would give cold hard stares. Of course there were those who would look sad, and show sympathy for the prisoners. But most of them were just curious, and you couldn't blame them, how often does one see six notorious convicts on a train being transferred to Alcatraz.

Whitey paid no attention to the passengers, he despised all of them, and closed his eyes to shut them out. Suddenly he heard the voice of child. He opened his eyes, and standing beside him in the doorway was a little girl—a very pretty child of seven years old. As she stood there a ray of sunlight reflected on her from the window, her soft brown hair glistened with streaks of gold, her blue eyes were full of excitement and wonder as she looked up at him. Whitey stared at her, he was surprised to see her standing so close. It had been ten years since he had any contact with anyone from the free world, and he felt uncomfortable with the presence of this young girl.

"Did you speak to me?" He asked.

"Yes, I asked what did you do?"

Whitey sat there trying to think of what to say. He had many answers, but how could he tell this innocent girl of the things he had done?

"Well," the little girl insisted, "aren't you going to tell me?"

126

Whitey always had a snotty answer for anyone who spoke to him. But this simple question from a little girl took him by surprise; it floored him.

"Say little girl," Williams called out, "I'll tell you what Whitey done, he tore off a little girl's arm and beat her to death with it!"

The child was shocked, she looked into Whitey's eyes, and he could see she was terrified. He was about to speak to her when she suddenly bolted from the doorway, and ran down the corridor as fast as she could go.

The moment she disappeared from the doorway, Whitey turned his attention to Williams. His hostile eyes flamed, and in a cold whisper he said, "You son of a bitch, you're a dead man, you're a walking dead man."

Like an enraged bull Whitey jumped up from the bench dragging Johnny with him, and literally hurled himself at Williams.

As Whitey flung himself at Williams, Jones shouted to Robinson, "Get the door—get the door quick."

From the outside, Robinson immediately closed and locked the door. Both Jones and Murray shouted at the prisoners to break it up. All of them were tangled in their shackles and chains, and as they struggled there was cussing and shouting. Because of the cuffs being locked to the restraining belts it was impossible for any of them to use their hands. But Whitey did manage to use the back of his head, and in swinging fashion he struck Williams a sickening blow to the bridge of his nose.

The two guards charged to the entangled men, and after quite a complication, Jones pulled Whitey back to his seat; while Murray helped reseat the other men.

Once everything was back to normal, Jones told Murray to get a wet towel and attend to Williams' nose, for it was bleeding profusely from both nostrils.

Williams looked at Whitey, and beneath the blood on his face was a trace of a smile, and he said, "Hey, hey Whitey I was only kidding man."

Officer Murray began to wipe and clean Williams face as Whitey hissed back, "I don't kid, you're a walking dead man."

"All of you are quiet," Jones ordered, "I don't want any more trouble, understand?"

A silence settled over the compartment. A moment later it was broken by the sound of the train's whistle; then a screech of the wheels as the locomotive began to slow down.

"I don't like what happened a moment ago," Jones said, "and right now we're pulling into a station, the door will remain closed. Once the train is underway again, I will have Robinson open the door, but if there is another incident or outburst like the one we

127

just had, I will have the door closed, and locked for the remainder of the trip, is that clear?" But there was no response, and Jones repeated again, "I said is that clear?"

"Hey does a boar have tits! You know damn well we understand. Hey look," Johnny shouted, "this station is loaded with cops."

Everyone turned their head toward the window just as the train came to a grinding halt.

"Wow, can you believe it? Look at all those cops lined up out there; you'd think Dillenger was aboard this train!" Freddie said with a laugh.

"I wonder why all the cops, something must be going down," Lieto remarked.

"Don't you guys know why all that heat is out there?" Freddie said. "Hell anyone can figure it out, it's because of us you fools, what other reason would they be out there?"

This was true, The Federal Bureau of Prisons, had notified all cities and towns the train was to stop in, that there were six dangerous convicts aboard on their way to Alcatraz. It was up to the local authorities to use their discretion in extra security precautions at their train stations.

While everyone was looking at the activity outside the window, Williams tried to get Whitey's attention.

"Hey Whitey, I'm sorry man, I was only kidding—honest." Williams waited for a reply, but none came. "All I can say is I'm sorry Whitey, can't we just forget the whole thing?"

The activity outside the window was being ignored as everyone had their attention focused on Whitey. Both guards sat there watching and waiting for the outcome, and a suspense hovered over the compartment.

Whitey focused his eyes on Williams. "Okay I'll forget it this time on one condition. If that little girl comes back, I want you to apologize and tell her you lied, but if she doesn't come back, you better stay out of my way and don't ever get in my face again."

"You got it Whitey, you got my word."

The tension was broken, and from the platform came the sound of the conductor's voice, "Board—all aboard."

The train had been in the station for twenty minutes with the door closed. The compartment became warm, stuffy, and extremely uncomfortable for the men. Their shackles, chains, and handcuffs, became an added irritation for them. Their ankles and wrists had been chaffed raw from movement.

Again they were underway, and Jones called for Robinson to open the door. The cool breeze from the corridor was a godsend for the prisoners. It seemed as if there were more people than ever walking up and down looking in at them. Some looked familiar,

128

they were people who had already been by, and were now getting a second look.

Whitey was happy to see the little girl appear in the doorway. Their eyes met, and as Whitey looked at her he thought he could detect a trace of fear. Yes, he could see it now, in her eyes he could see that she was afraid of him. Why should she come back and stand a foot away from someone she feared? Children were often afraid of lions, tigers, and apes, yet they will go to see them time and again at the zoo. Is that it? Or is her curiosity stronger than her fear? At that moment, looking at this little girl Whitey wished he could put his arms around her and tell her not to be afraid.

With his eyes still on the girl, Whitey said to Williams, "You got something to say pal?"

"Yeah sure Whitey," he said, "Little girl I want to apologize. What I said earlier about Whitey was not true, I was just joking."

Her eyes lit up showing relief, "I'm so glad that wasn't true, but what did you do?"

Not quite knowing what to say to this young girl, Whitey pointed at his chains and shackles, and replied, "This is what happens when you're a bad boy, they take you to jail."

The answer seemed to satisfy the little girl, and she skipped away. Moments later she returned, and said, "Your name is Whitey, my name is Sandra, but they call me Sandy."

After the introductions Whitey suggested that she had better return to her parents.

During the day Sandy dropped by numerous times to talk with Whitey, and they became friends. On one occasion Sandy asked Whitey if he would ever steal again, and he told her no.

Jones thought to himself, look at that lying bastard, lying to that little girl. The son of a bitch would steal the teeth right out of her head.

"Okay Sandy run along now," Whitey said.

Smiling cheerfully she disappeared from the doorway.

While he had been talking to her everyone sat quietly listening to the conversation, and now that she was gone Johnny was the first to speak.

"That sure is a sweet little kid, isn't she?"

Whitey started to answer, but Jones cut him off, "Well, well, well, the tough Whitey Thompson has a soft spot after all."

"What the hell is wrong with that?" Johnny flared back. "So he has a soft spot for a little girl, so what? There are not many adults who don't have a soft spot for a little kid, except maybe a moron like you."

Whitey chuckled at the remark, and nodded his head at Johnny.

129

Jones was angry, "Another remark like that House, and the door closes."

House sat staring at Jones. Tension began to rise, but was suddenly broken by Williams.

"Hey fellows, I hate to do this, but I have to go again."

"Damn, another pissing party! Please don't piss on me again Whitey," Johnny laughed.

Robinson closed the compartment door, while Murray opened the one to the toilet. The prisoners stood up, and the shuffling ordeal began again.

CHAPTER 22.

The train made two more stops, and in each station there was extra security. Again the locomotive was moving south on its journey. The time was late afternoon, and it seemed as though every passenger had walked by at least once to take a peek at the prisoners. The corridor traffic was thinning out somewhat, not as many people were walking by, and most of them could be recognized as having passed by before. Some of them, like old friends, would smile at the prisoners, but Whitey would never return it.

The train ride was tedious for the prisoners not being able to move about or stretch their muscles. Johnny and Whitey had their heads together in a quiet conversation. The guards were surprised to see this, because both of these men never had much to do with anyone. As for Whitey, it seemed the only time he ever talked to anyone was to cuss them out. These two men apparently were becoming friends. Their conversation was interrupted when a porter came down the corridor striking a set of dinner chimes.

"Dinner is being served in the Dining Car," he called out.

The old black porter appeared in the doorway and said, "Okay boys, I'll take your orders now. On the menu we have, chicken-fried steak, round steak, New York and T-bone steaks, vegetable soup or salad, and for the desert, we have chocolate cake, or vanilla ice cream, or both."

Turning to Whitey the porter said, "All right sir, what would you like for dinner?"

"I want a thick T-bone with a load of French fried potatoes, skip the soup, and just give me more potatoes, and I'll have ice cream for desert."

"Yes sir—yes sir." Turning to Johnny, he asked, "and yours sir?"

"His order sounds good to me, how about you guys, you want the same?"

They all agreed on the same order. And in turn the guards ordered sandwiches for themselves.

After the porter had left, the prisoners stood up to make their

131

way to the wash basin. Like the toilet party, they went through the same routine. Chili was first; Murray held the faucet open for him while he struggled to wash his hands, with his handcuffs attached to the restraining belt, it was barely possible. After his hands were washed, Murray handed him a paper towel. The next man in line, Williams, went through the same procedure. To the prisoners it seemed as though they were always in line waiting for something. The shackles, cuffs and chains made simple things hard to cope with. Things that most people take for granted, was hard for the prisoners—such as going to the toilet, washing their hands, lighting or smoking a cigarette, eating, or just trying to sit comfortably.

After the washing party, they made their way around the sturdy table. Before the men could be seated, Murray had to place a chair behind each man, and with some difficulty the prisoners simultaneously sat down. Chili who was at the end of the chain, was seated directly across from Whitey.

"Hey here's the food!" Williams cried.

Two waiters entered, and each one carried a large tray. The porter directed them in setting up the table. Six wooden platters containing steaks and fries were set in front of each man. Also, along with the entree, they set all the condiments on the table.

Chili was wide-eyed, "By Got, what feast. I no got feast so good before!"

At one side of the compartment Officers Jones and Murray were seated at a small table with their coffee and sandwiches in front of them. Once the waiters had everything in order they retreated from the compartment. The porter made one final check to be sure everyone was satisfied.

Whitey reached for his fork and steak knife, but his fingers barely reached to the edge of the table. Each prisoner had the same difficulty, because of the handcuffs attached to the belt.

All eyes focused on the guards who were drinking coffee, and eating sandwiches quite impervious to the prisoner's predicament. It was too much for them when they saw the guards eating with so much ease.

"How the hell we supposed to eat?" Whitey blurted out.

In a surly voice Jones said, "That's your problem. I was given strict orders to keep you men secured until we reach Alcatraz."

"But we can't eat if we can't reach the food. Just release one hand so we can eat."

Whitey let out a chilling scream. The door was open, and a number of people in the passageway froze in horror as the sound of the scream echoed throughout the corridor.

Jones shouted to Robinson, "Get the door—get the door shut."

132

Anticipating the order, Robinson was already in the process of locking the door.

At the precise second of Whitey's outburst, he pushed back his chair, and shot his feet up to the edge of the table jerking Johnny's feet off the floor by the chain that held them together. Then with all the mad strength he could muster, and using the table as a brace for his feet, he pushed himself over backwards, pulling Johnny and his chair along with him. This created a chain reaction all the way around the table, and as each prisoner went over backwards he shouted out obscenities.

"You jive-ass bastard," Whitey raged, "you lowlife son of a bitch!"

The compartment was in a complete turmoil as the prisoners lay on the floor tangled, twisting, turning, shouting and lashing out with their feet. They were calling Jones every foul name they could think of.

"All right," Jones shouted. "Okay I'll release one hand."

The prisoners quieted down when they realized Jones had given in. It took some maneuvering, and with the help of Jones and Murray, the prisoners were back on their feet. The guards righted the chairs, and placed one behind each man. Again they sat down and the guards pushed them up to the table.

Starting with Whitey, Jones freed his right hand. Then turning his back to him, he proceeded to unlock Johnny's cuffs. Jones put himself in a precarious position exposing his back to Whitey who developed a personal hatred for him. His right hand flashed out, he grabbed the steak knife, and his first impulse was to plunge it deeply into Jones' back. Whitey held the knife no longer than a second, but to him it seemed like an hour. Go ahead sink it in, he thought, what're you waiting for? Do it now while you got the chance, go ahead kill him, do it quick before it's too late. Kill the dirty bastard, kill him. Whitey's mind was running at random with visions of Sandy interrupting his thoughts. How can I kill this guard? This little girl has made friends with me, she trusts me. What effect will it have on her life if I kill this guard? Put the knife down fool, don't do it.

It was too late now, the moment had passed; Officer Jones would never know how close he came to dying.

Beads of perspiration had formed on Whitey's forehead, quickly he returned the knife to the table; he sat there staring at it. You went soft, you didn't kill him because of the little girl.

"What's wrong Whitey?" Johnny asked. "Aren't you going to eat?"

"Yeah, I'm going to eat." With his napkin he wiped the perspiration from his face.

The feelings he was experiencing were strange to him, and he

133

couldn't quite understand his actions, for he had always hated, and distrusted everyone except for RG, Rose, and a few friends in prison. The opportunity was there to kill the guard, but that little girl was on his mind. He was unable to plunge the knife into the officer's back.

CHAPTER 23.

With the meal over, The prisoners returned to the bench. Robinson opened the door, and the cool air was refreshing as the men relaxed with their after dinner smokes.

Johnny retrieved a cigar from his pocket, and just before he lit it, he held it up to admire its structure. Then gently placed the cigar between his lips and took a long drag on it inhaling the smoke deep into his lungs. As he exhaled, he leaned his head sideways and whispered, "You were going to waste that bull."

Turning his head slightly toward Johnny he whispered, "What are ya talking about?"

"I saw you pick up the knife. What stopped you? Never mind, I don't really care to know, I'm just glad you didn't do it. You only got five years left Whitey, why turn it into life?'

Jones glanced at the two men, "What are you two whispering about?"

"I was just telling Johnny here what a kind face you have," Whitey replied.

"That's right," Johnny added with a smile, "you do have a kind face—the kind I like to throw shit at!"

Laughter filled the compartment. Jones was saved from further embarrassment when the porter entered accompanied by a bus boy. The laughter ceased.

While Whitey was enjoying his cigarette, Sandy walked up to the doorway and said hello.

"Hello Sandy, look little girl, you shouldn't be hanging around here, you better beat it."

She was disappointed, and sad as she turned away.

After she left Whitey thought, why was I so cold to her and sent her away? You know why, you figure there is no future for yourself, so why make friends with anyone from the free world. At McNeil Island you closed yourself off from the outside, and prison became your way of life to the point where no one existed beyond

135

the limits of your world. But right now you are outside your limits, and meeting people you never knew existed, the old porter, and Sandy, who only want to be friends. So just relax and enjoy the train ride. What have you got to lose?

Whitey glanced at Jones who misinterpreted his look, "When you get to Alcatraz Thompson, you're going to start off with a bang after I submit my report on you."

"Go ahead submit your report you son of a bitch!"

"Shut up Thompson, if you can't talk civilly, I'll be forced to close the door. You're always trying to start something, so just shut up."

Johnny intervened. "Whitey was sitting right there saying nothing, and you opened up on him about your report."

"All right House, that's enough talk out of you too," Jones warned.

"Thanks Johnny, but I don't need anyone to stand up for me," Whitey said.

"I know you don't Whitey, I'm just fed up with this bull's crap. He can make out all the reports he wants, then stick 'em up the Warden's ass!"

"All right House, I'm warning you, I don't want to hear any more out of you, understand? And that goes for you too Thompson."

"Hey that's fine," Whitey replied, "Anything you got to say to me, save your breath and put it in your fucking report."

The remark brought a chuckle from Johnny, and Whitey was not certain, but he thought he saw a trace of a smile on Murray's face.

Jones sat there staring, he thought it best not to reply to Whitey's last remark, and maybe, just maybe he would shut up! The compartment became silent.

Damn Jones, look at him sitting over there staring at me. I hate that son of a bitch. The hollow sound of the train whistle interrupted Whitey's thoughts. He could feel the train's forward motion slack off as it rolled into another station.

Out in the corridor the conductor was calling out, "Portland, Portland, Oregon. Next stop Salem, Salem next stop."

This particular Canadian Pacific was primarily a tourist train, and very few passengers would embark or disembark. Most of the people came from Washington, and as far away as Canada; they were on their way to visit the great city of San Francisco. Technically the prisoners were on their way to San Francisco too, but not as tourists, for San Francisco was their last stepping-stone to the Island in the Bay.

After the customary stop, the silence of night was broken as the big locomotive came alive, and continued her journey south.

136

CHAPTER 24.

The train ride was tedious, and the prisoners showed signs of fatigue; one by one they dozed off. Soon all of them were asleep, including the two guards.

Suddenly Whitey came awake, there was panic in his eyes. He couldn't breathe and was desperately fighting for air. Calm down Whitey, relax, breathe easy, that's good, everything is all right now. Whitey let out a sigh of relief. It's horrible to wake up fighting for air, but he was fine now and wide awake. He took a quick look around to see if anyone else was awake; they were asleep, and the compartment was very quiet except for the sound of wheels running on steel rails.

The train was humming right along, she seemed to be flying now. Whitey looked toward the window and in the distance he could see lights from a lonely house. He wondered what the people who lived there were doing at this moment. It was the wee hours of morning; were they getting ready for bed? Or were they arising for work? Could they hear the rumble of this train, and the mournful sound of its whistle? He wished there was some way he could let those people know he was on this train, and that he existed.

Whitey awakened to reality at the sound of a bell ringing. Looking toward the window he caught a glimpse of a flashing red light as the train shot across an intersection of a quiet country road. At times there would be a car or two at a crossing waiting for the train to pass. For a split second as the train zipped by, all he could see were the headlights of a car, and in a flash they were gone. He began to wonder who was in the car. Perhaps it was some young lad taking his date home from a dance.

As for the opposite sex, Whitey missed having a woman as much as any man in prison. Rose was his first real love affair, but he knew he had to put her out of his mind as well as the thoughts of all women. As it was, big time was hard enough on a man without thoughts of women on his mind.

A bell clanging at a railroad crossing snapped Whitey out of it. He fumbled for a cigarette, the pack was empty, and he called out to Jones, "Hey Jones wake up."

There was no response, but Johnny stirred, "Did you say something?" He whispered.

"Yeah, I tried to wake that flatfoot over there, I'm out of smokes."

Johnny yelled at Jones, "Hey Jones wake up for Christ sakes, wake up."

Jones woke with a start, "What—what's wrong?" His face was pale.

"I need some cigarettes, that's what's wrong," Whitey bellowed.

To everyone's surprise, Jones opened the duffel bag, pulled out a pack of Camels and gave them to Whitey who received them without acknowledgment.

He was just about to light up a cigarette, when Robinson called into Jones, "The porter is out here, he wants to know if anyone would like some coffee."

"Yes, send him in."

Robinson opened the door admitting the porter who set a pot of coffee and cups on the table, "I thought you might like a little coffee. This is the end of my run as I get off at Roseburg. So long boys." He backed out the door, and was gone.

Whitey had a cigarette with a cup of coffee, and as enjoyed the luxury, rays of morning light appeared through the window, a new day began. Whitey felt as though he had been on the train for weeks. His body was stiff from sitting for so long. His ankles and wrists were raw from the chains and irons.

The morning sun was rising with the promise of a beautiful day, and it was just a matter of hours before the prisoners would be locked up in a cell on Alcatraz.

"What's the date Johnny?" Whitey asked.

"It's July 20, 1958," Johnny replied, "what difference does it make?"

"I don't know, I guess I just kinda lost track of time."

Jones took six candy bars out of the duffel bag, and handed one to each prisoner along with more cigarettes, and three cigars for Johnny.

"Well looky here, another candy bar for breakfast! Can you spare it?" Whitey said in a sarcastic voice.

It was fruitless to say anything to Thompson. Ignoring him Jones continued passing out the treats.

The train was highballing right along. She had left Oregon during the early morning hours, and was now traveling through northern California. While Whitey enjoyed his candy, he focused his attention out the window watching the landscape go by. He was hoping to see a landmark that he might recognize. Instead, through the window pane, he saw visions of Rose. He had pushed his memory of her out of his mind, but now it was back. Was it back because of his return to California? Whitey had no control over his return to California, just like he had no control over his memory. He had done well in keeping the past out of his mind for the last ten years, but he realized he couldn't rid his mind of the past forever. It would always remain in his memory-bank at the ready, waiting to flash across the screen of his mind.

Out in the corridor the conductor's voice sounded, "Next stop Oakland, California."

Whitey felt tension building within him, and this tense feeling was turning to anger. He could feel the anger flow through his body, and it gave him strength. He felt protected behind his shield of hate, he had no fear, and he could cope with anything, even Alcatraz. After all, he knew what prison life was all about—he had the scars to prove it!

There was tension in the compartment as the train drew nearer to its destination. The rhythm of the wheels was getting louder and louder, and it had an erie quality to it, "Clackerty-clack—clackerty-clack—Al-ca-traz—Al-ca-traz—Al-ca-traz."

Whitey's thoughts were broken when Johnny said, "Well it won't be long now."

"Yeah," Whitey agreed, "but do you realize how long it took for me to get where I am today? It took thirty-five years of scheming and careful planning to get me where I am!"

"Yeah Whitey, but how many years of planning will it take you to get off the Rock?"

Jones interrupted, "Thompson don't have a brain to plan with."

Whitey looked sharply at the guard, "But at least I have one. That's more than you've got. If you had half a brain you'd be dangerous."

Just as Jones was about to reply, the conductor called out, "Oakland—Oakland, California. All off that's getting off."

The prisoners stood up to stretch themselves, and while doing so the train started to slow down causing the men to rock unsteadily on their feet. It almost caused them to fall. Being shackled together, it was hard for them to keep their balance when the motion of the train was erratic. The locomotive began to run slower and slower, until it was barely moving along. It seemed they would never reach their destination; then suddenly it began to pick up speed; then it slacked off again, and came to a long grinding halt.

From the corridor came the loud commanding voice of Robinson, "Please, all you passengers stay on the train until these prisoners have been removed."

Johnny whispered to Whitey, "Did you hear that? I guess he thinks of us as trash that has to be removed."

139

Lined up on the platform there were twelve Oakland policemen, and two more who boarded the train to assist the Federal guards. The prisoners made their way out of the compartment, and commenced to move slowly through the passageway.

"Stand back, please, let these prisoners through, please," one of the policemen shouted.

Behind him, Whitey heard someone complaining, "Stop that pushing, quit shoving little girl, wait your turn."

The prisoners were moving forward slowly when someone grabbed hold of Whitey's arm.

Angrily he turned his head, "Who the hell. . . ." A smile replaced his angry look when he saw it was Sandy.

"I wanted to say goodbye Whitey," there was sadness in her voice.

Looking down at her, their eyes held for a fleeting moment, "Goodbye Sandy."

Sandy released Whitey's arm and stood to one side as the prisoners moved toward the exit. As Whitey neared the end of the passageway, he looked over his shoulder hoping to get a glimpse of Sandy, but all he could see was a crowd of people. The chain moved out of the corridor, and just as Whitey stepped onto the platform, he heard her voice call out, "Whitey I like you, goodbye Whitey."

Without replying he moved forward, and under his breath he whispered to himself, "I like you too Sandy. What the hell is wrong with me, getting sentimental over a little girl."

The prisoners had to be assisted as they stepped off the train, and made their way to a carryall bus. Waiting for them in the bus were two Alcatraz guards. After leaving the station, the small carryall snaked its way through the slow-moving traffic toward the Oakland Bay Bridge.

One of the Alcatraz guards shouted to the prisoners, "You men better enjoy your cigarettes now, because they will be taken away from you before we board the boat."

The prisoners immediately lit up a cigarette, and they continued to smoke them one after the other, while Johnny enjoyed the flavor of his cigar. He loved his cigars, and this could very well be the last one he would ever have.

It took a few minutes for the bus to cross the Oakland Bay Bridge. As it traveled down the off-ramp, it made slow progress into the city of San Francisco. Through the busy streets the carryall moved along at a snail's pace. The traffic was very heavy. It seemed to the prisoners that they were zigzagging up and down every street in the city on their way to the Fort Mason Dock.

140

CHAPTER 25.

The Warden Johnston, the prison ferry boat to Alcatraz, scraped against the landing at the Fort Mason Dock as she rose up and down on the gentle swells. She was fifteen minutes late casting off for the one o'clock trip to the Island. The skipper glanced at his watch, then looked back at the gateway to the pier. He was waiting for nine extra passengers coming from the state of Washington. At length, the carryall bus rolled through the gate and came to a halt. The prisoners were helped and escorted to the boat dock. But before they were allowed to board the boat, a guard shook each one down, taking away the remainder of their cigarettes, cigars and matches.

The skipper of the boat, who was also a Correctional Officer, checked the new arrival's names as they boarded *The Warden Johnston.*

"Well Whitey," Johnny said, "here we are at last."

"Yeah they're finally going to get me on those water-skis."

"I bet your old friend Lou would laugh if he could see you now," Johnny chuckled.

"Yeah I bet he would, I sure miss him and all his bullshit. By the way how did you know Lou Peters was my buddy?"

"I worked with him in the Furniture Factory at McNeil."

"No kidding," Whitey was surprised to learn that Johnny knew Lou.

"Yeah I like Lou, he's good people, and he told me a lot about you. That's how I knew you were his buddy."

The chain of prisoners was led to the passenger deck where they were seated on a long wooden bench.

THE *Warden Johnston* sailed out into the bay. The riptides were eminently treacherous as the boat steered a wide turn to starboard. It then made a direct approach to the wharf on the southeastern side of the Island.

Whitey sat there while the easing grip of exhaustion overwhelmed him. His mind began to drift; they say just before a man dies his life flashes in front of him. Various incidents of Whitey's life seemed to be flashing by now. He was sure he heard someone speak to him, "Hey

Whitey are you going to the show today?" It was his boyhood friend, Roy Ely. "Are you going to the movies? There's a good picture playing, `ALCATRAZ,' staring George Raft."

Whitey went to see the movie that day, and George Raft became his instant hero. At the time he was too young to know much about the prison in San Francisco Bay. He never dreamed that one day he would become a resident of the Rock.

PART 3.

ALCATRAZ

"THE ROCK"

1958 TO 1962

CHAPTER 26.

The sound of *The Warden Johnston's* horn broke Whitey's thoughts, and there, right in front of the launch, was Alcatraz.
A big sign on a cliff caught the attention of the prisoners.

KEEP OFF! ONLY GOVERNMENT BOATS PERMITTED WITHIN 200 YARDS. PERSONS ENTERING CLOSER WITHOUT AUTHORIZATION DO SO AT THEIR OWN RISK.

The Warden Johnston edged cautiously into the slip, and was made fast. Then the skipper performed a habitual security rite; he locked the wheel of the boat. He then went ashore where he attached the boat's ignition key to a line, and signaled a guard in a bullet proof gun tower. The guard came out, stepped over to the tower rail, and hauled the key up by a pulley. The key would stay there until the next scheduled trip when the guard would lower it.

There were four men standing on the dock. Two guards, and the other two were civilians. One of the men was a rather pocked-faced man, whom Whitey learned later was Mr. Dollison who was in charge of prison industry. Later on in 1961 he became the Associate Warden of Alcatraz. The other man was the doctor waiting to return to San Francisco after his daily visit.

The prisoners stood up, and made their way off the boat onto the dock where a small bus was waiting. The warm July afternoon was quiet except for the clink of the chains around their ankles, as they slowly climbed into the bus.

Whitey, being first on the chain, was able to sit by a window, and view the area where cargo supplies were sifted, and then passed through a metal detector that resembled a door frame with a humped sill. This was dubbed "The Snitch-Box" by the convicts. The cargo was then hauled into the prison at the top of the hill. Another such detector, kept there for visitors, stood beneath a shelter at the far side.

Addressing no one in particular Freddie said, "Boy I don't think this crate will make it."

A few of the men chuckled, and Whitey also had his doubts, the way the bus was laboring up the narrow and tortuous road. It was a twisting route carved into the south east facade of the rock. As the bus made its slow progress up the hill a guard in the high tower had

145

it under his eye. At the beige-color prison entrance on the crest, a grim reception committee waited—guards in charcoal uniforms with maroon ties, and rifles at the ready.

The prisoners, still hobbled, found it difficult to shuffle up a short flight of concrete steps, through a granite archway to a grated door. On the right were the offices, including the Warden's office. The turnkey recognizing the party opened the gate; they stepped into a vestibule, and turned left into the Visitor's Room. The room had no windows, a reddish rug, and a few chairs, with lamps and standup ash trays for visitors. There were seldom more than two or three visitors during an entire year.

The guards, Jones, Murray and Robinson, were checking in the transfer papers on the prisoners, and no doubt giving a favorable account of their behavior!

No guard was armed now, except for the sentry at the door, who carried a gas-billy, a combination metal club and tear gas gun.

The six inmates were lined up; a guard began to remove the handcuffs, midriff restraining belts, chains and leg-irons. There was a feeling of relief on the faces of each man after the burden was removed, and they were able to stretch their arms over their heads. The men discovered even more bruises and raw spots on their bodies, but this would pass.

A guard ordered them to strip to the skin for the ritual known as "Dress-In." The same way a guard had done before their departure from McNeil Island, an M.T.A. (Medical Technical Assistant) now conducted an orifice search ear, nose, mouth, rectum. He was probing for contraband such as dope, a coded message, even a tiny tool useful in an attempt to escape. An article such as a jeweler's chain, or a watch spring to file through a bar would do the job. This would take time, but they had plenty of that!

Whitey was still number one in line, so he was the first to get the finger wave. The M.T.A. put on a surgical glove, greased his finger, and inserted it up his rectum. Whitey shouted, "Hey goddamn it, watch what you're doing."

The M.T.A. did not reply as he coldly continued probing. Finishing with Whitey, he put on another surgical glove, and started to insert his finger up Johnny's rectum. Johnny jumped three feet in the air and yelled, "Goddamn your finger's cold!"

This brought on laughter from the other men, but Johnny was not laughing, "You freak bastard! You sure love to degrade a man."

"He's a juice-fruit Johnny," Whitey bellowed, "he gets his kicks out of it."

"All right boys, let's hold it down so we can get this over with," a guard said.

After the ritual was accomplished, each man was handed a pair of

146

backless canvas slippers. These were known as "Scooters" by the convicts. The prisoners, still naked, were led back in the vestibule. Directly opposite the vestibule was the command post of the most important man while on duty—the Armorer. His station was the nerve center of the prison, and was only accessible from the exterior.

There was just one guard on duty in the command post, and only he alone could open the door. On the inner side, he was sealed off by a steel plate pierced with gun-slots, and a narrow vision panel of bulletproof glass.

The two guards with the prisoners, began the complex progression into the Cell House. They approached a barred gate, but the turnkey couldn't open it. It had a metal shield covering the lock hole on both sides. The turnkey nodded his head, and the guard in the Nerve Center glanced into his mirrors set at an angle, and checked the chamber beyond the gate. He then touched a button that released the shield; the turnkey then inserted his key and opened the gate, and once inside, he closed and locked it. The metal plate slid back into place covering the keyhole. They were now confronted by a solid steel door; the turnkey peeked through an eye-level slit, scanned the interior, then opened the door. They passed through, and he relocked it. They faced still a third door, barred and crossed barred, the last barrier to the Cell House.

As they walked through the last door, the prisoner stared in surprise. With its high windows and skylights, and it's tripled-tiered Cell Blocks, their nostrils caught a distinct odor, and a familiar one. It was the mingled scent of disinfectant, and of men closely packed together. Their surprise came in the splash of color, bright even in the murky daylight. The Cell Blocks were painted a shocking pink, trimmed in barn red. The naked newcomers scuffed along in their canvas slippers down a wide aisle between two cell blocks; a corridor called Broadway. Their Custodial Guides directed them to turn right at the far end. The group walked along a lateral corridor to a stairway that took them to a large basement room the size of a tennis court containing thirty-five showers.

The guard on duty there noticed Whitey's tattoos, an electric chair on his back.

"You must be superstitious. Have any more?"

Whitey turned to face the guard, revealing naked girls; one tattooed on each thigh. On his chest were two blue birds, and various other Navy tattoos up and down his arms. On the right shin a rooster, and on the left shin, a pig. A pig and a rooster are a Navy superstition, and once they are tattooed on the legs, it signifies that the sailor would never drown at sea.

"All right, let's shower up," the guard said.

Whitey saw a single knob at each shower, indicating a single cold stream. He had heard about the cold water showers on Alcatraz. He braced himself under the showerhead, and turned it on full force for a quick soaking to get the shock over with as fast as he could. He was shocked, but not by a chilling impact, the water was warm; it was premixed by a guard at the end of the row.

After the shower, each prisoner received an issue of shoes and clothing. Then the convoy of men walked toward a section called Broadway. They had to be careful not to slip on the cement floor that was waxed and polished to the gloss of a bowling alley. They walked along Broadway to the west end of C Block. The guard instructed them to hold it up. Then he placed Chili into an empty cell, the next cubicle was for Williams, then Freddie, Lieto, Johnny, and finally Whitey who was put into C-113. These cells were in the quarantine section of the prison, and the new arrivals would remain there until assigned jobs.

Whitey stood at the cell front staring at the lustrous corridor floor. This was it, he would serve out the remainder of his sentence at this super-maximum security prison, and super-maximum security it was. From the moment he stepped off the boat at the wharf, until he reached his cell, everywhere he looked there stood a guard. He had never seen so many Custodial Guards.

He turned his attention back to his cell. His new home was five feet wide by nine feet long. The rear and side walls were made of concrete and steel. The only light and air admitted was from the barred front. The short uprights between the stout crossbars had cores of cable embedded in the toughest alloy steel that could resist the most persistent saw or file. The fixtures in the cell were a steel bed that could fold against the wall. Bolted into the opposite wall were two steel folding shelves at separate levels, for use as a seat and table. On the right rear wall was a toilet, and next to it was a wash bowl with a single cold water faucet. Over the wash bowl ran two wooden shelves for personal effects, and beneath them, wooden pegs to hang clothes.

Whitey turned his attention back to the corridor, and across from C Block was the inside of B Block. This section was for blacks only. When a black man came to Alcatraz, he automatically went into the segregated colored section.

The Cell House itself was a huge building resembling a warehouse, with tall double barred windows and skylights. Inside this building were three gigantic cell blocks—A, B, C, and the isolated D Block, or Treatment Unit, and the library behind a grated partition.

The Block A was in disuse for prisoners, and was now reserved for storage. This block is where the army had its solitary confinement cells on the side facing the south east windows. It was mainly used in the old days as isolation quarters after the dreaded dungeon was abolished, and while the old D Block was being modernized.

The other blocks, B and C, contained a total number of 336 cells in double banks of triple tiers. Each block had two banks; each bank, three tiers, and each tier had 28 cells. Along the center of each block between the banks, ran a utility corridor, commonly known as the "tunnel." It was a narrow dark passage cluttered with sewer pipes, water mains, and electrical conduits that served the cells. The solid steel doors at either end of this corridor, on all the tiers were locked, and the tunnel was inaccessible to convicts.

Broadway ran between the two big Blocks, B and C. The Dining Room was at the south east section. The library, across the outside bank of C Block occupied half the area against the west wall. The other section in the south west corner held D Block, the Isolation Quarter, the Special Treatment Unit, known to the inmates as TU. This small Block, sealed off by concrete walls and two solid steel doors, had 42 cells in three tiers. Six of them on the bottom row were set aside as dark cells for Solitary Confinement. Each cell was double doored.

This was the general setup of the Cell Houses when Whitey first arrived on Alcatraz. After his survey of the cell and the area around him, Whitey immediately lay down on the bunk and fell asleep. It had been over twenty-four hours since his departure from McNeil, and he was extremely tired. But as tired as he was, he did not let his guard down for a minute. Even as he slept he could sense something was wrong, or someone's presence. He quickly opened his eyes, and not a moment too soon, for a man was standing in front of his cell. Whitey turned his head and looked toward the man; he was dressed in a dark blue business suit.

"Thompson," he said, "Why were you sent here to Alcatraz?"

"It was a bum-beef," Whitey replied, "just a plain old bum-beef."

"Okay Thompson, you are here now, and I really don't give a damn what you did at McNeil. I don't even care about your train ride report. You are here now and your record is clean on Alcatraz. In other words, you are starting here with a clean slate. Just do your own number and stay out of trouble, but if you get out of line we'll bury you." Not waiting for a reply, he left.

"Hey Whitey," Johnny called from the next cell. "Do you know who that guy was you were just talking to? He's Blackwell, the Associate Warden."

"Who gives a fuck. Don't bother me Johnny, I'm going to sleep."

Again Whitey lay down on his bunk, and had scarcely fallen asleep, when he was awakened by the sound of his cell door opening. He looked up from his bed, and saw that there was a guard standing in front of his cell. Christ what now damn it!

The guard was looking at a list of names on a clip board. Whitey got off his bunk and stood in the open doorway rubbing sleep from his eyes. He was in a bad mood, and spoke out to the guard, "What the hell is it man? What do you want?"

The guard sounded cheerful. "You can't become a resident of Alcatraz until you are numbered and your picture is taken, so let's go now."

Whitey reluctantly came out of his cell, and together with the Custodial guard walked down Broadway to a grilled gate leading into the Dining Room. Before entering, the Custodial officer nodded his head to a guard up on the south east gun gallery, who lowered a key down to him on the end of a string. He unlocked the gate to the Dining Room, and just to the left behind a meshed screen door was a small stairwell room, the photo lab.

Once the meshed screen door was unlocked, the officer nodded to the guard on the gallery, who quickly pulled the key back up.

The gun gallery was a long caged-in cat-walk that ran the length of the south east-south west wall, and was approximately fifteen feet up from the main floor. All along the walk, at five foot intervals, there were portholes used for firing rifles or tear gas through. At the north end of the Cell House, there was an identical cat-walk that ran the length of the north east-north west wall. Both these gun galleries were manned twenty-four hours a day, and from these posts a guard had clear vision of all the tiers and corridors between the Cell Blocks.

Whitey stepped into the small photo room, not much larger than a single cell. The officer handed Whitey a safety razor, and turned him toward a sink, telling him to shave. To Whitey's surprise the blade was sharp, and his overdue growth of beard came off easily.

A picture of Whitey's left and right profiles was taken, and then he was told to face the camera. The guard hung a four by seven inch name plate around his neck. Printed on the plate was:

U.S. PENITENTIARY
Alcatraz
1465
7 19 58

Smiling at Whitey the guard said, "Congratulations Thompson, you are now officially a resident of the Rock."

He was ordered to stand outside the Dining Room gate under the watchful eye of the gun gallery guard, while the Custodial officer made the returned to Broadway for the next man. Whitey could hear the loud clang of a cell door opening and closing, and a moment later the officer reappeared with Johnny House, who immediately started to laugh.

150

"What's so fucking funny?" Whitey asked.

"I didn't recognize you with your beard cut off. You don't look like a goat anymore."

"How'd you think you'd look with a black eye?"

Johnny continued laughing as he entered the photo lab.

To the right was the Cell House Officer's desk, and directly across from it, under the stairwell of B Block, on the wall, was a tobacco rack. Whitey started to move toward it. The Cell House Officer who was sitting behind his desk looked up from his paper work and saw Whitey walking across the corridor.

He called out to him, "Where do you think you're going?"

"I'm going to get some tobacco." He didn't wait for the guard's reply; he had made up his mind that he was going to get some tobacco regardless, and continued toward the rack.

From the rack Whitey retrieved a sack of Stud rolling tobacco, matches, papers, and immediately proceeded to roll a cigarette. In seconds the task was accomplished, and after placing it between his lips he lit a match. He took a long drag inhaling the smoke deeply into his lungs. His face turned purple, and his eyes rolled in their sockets as he quickly bent over. In one gigantic cough, like an exhaust pipe, smoke shot out of his mouth! He coughed again and cussed loudly, "Damn, this tobacco is rotten! It tastes like mildewed shit!"

All the tobacco was mildewed from dampness due to long storage on the Island.

Whitey took another puff on the cigarette, this time he was ready for the horrible taste. The second drag was not as bad, and the consecutive ones seem to improve. But not to the point where one could fully enjoy the cigarette, but to Whitey it was better than nothing.

He was still smoking the cigarette when Johnny approached from the photo lab, while the guard went for the next man.

"Where did you get the smoke?" Johnny asked.

Pointing to the rack, Whitey replied, "Over there on the wall."

Johnny walked over to the rack, retrieved the makings, and as he walked back to Whitey, he rolled a cigarette. Striking a match, he lit up, took a drag, and like Whitey before him, he immediately blew the smoke from his tortured lungs.

Gasping for breath he said, "Wow, that tastes like hell! I sure wished I had a good cigar."

"Cheer up House, in just five months, I hear we get a choice of cigarettes or cigars for Christmas. No kidding, you have your choice."

"Is that right, you're bullshitting me Whitey?"

"No that's true House, honest."

The Custodial guard had finished taking pictures of all the new

151

arrivals.

"Okay men," he said, "we're going below for the rest of your clothing and toilet issue."

The prisoners in single file, proceeded down a flight of studded metal steps to the Shower and Clothing Room. A guard at the foot of the stairs ordered the inmates to walk over to a screened-in section that served as the Clothing Room. Behind the screen, at the ready, was the Clothing Room Officer, and a convict, waiting to hand out the new issue.

"All right men, line up at the counter by numbers. Low number first."

Whitey, who had received his number first stepped up to the counter.

"What size pants and shirt do you wear?" The convict asked.

"Thirty-thirty, and fifteen shirt."

The prisoner behind the counter immediately disappeared behind the clothing racks, and reappeared with a new pair of pants and shirt. The colors of the denim trousers were a blue-grey, flecked with white, and the shirt, a blue cambric. The Clothing Room convict stamped Whitey's number into the pants and shirt, then he placed them into a small wooden bin that had Whitey's number stamped on it.

"You're wearing one issue now," the inmate said to Whitey, "this Saturday morning when you come down for a shower, turn in your dirty clothes; come to this window, give me your bin number, and your clean set will be given to you."

Along with the issue Whitey received two pairs of boxer-type cotton drawers, five pairs of socks, a large red and blue railroad handkerchief, a safety razor holder, and shaving mug. A tin cup, a nail clip, a small mirror, a face towel, toothbrush and dental powder; a mattress and cover, two sheets, and one pillow case. He was told to rotate his bed sheets and turn in one at a time along with his pillow case on Tuesday shower day.

Once the men received their issue, they were escorted back up the stairs. After the last man passed through the doorway, the guard slammed the heavy steel door shut and locked it. As the group of men walked by the Cell House desk their Custodial guide said to a coworker, "They're all yours Mack, I'm done with them."

The Custodial guide disappeared around the south east corner of B Block, while the prisoners headed back down Broadway. Whitey stopped in front of his cell, C-113, while the rest of the column continued on to their respective cubicles.

The Cell House Officer rose from his desk, and signal up to the gun gallery guard to lower down the key.

At the control box the officer called out to the inmates, "What are

152

your cell numbers?"

In turn they called back, with Whitey calling his number last, "113."

All cells were opened and closed singly or in units up to fifteen by guards at the manual control boxes located at either end of the tier.

The instant Whitey stepped into his cell, the door slid shut and locked. He dropped his mattress on the bed, and commenced to put away the rest of his issue. Just as he finished his chores, an inmate pushed two old army blankets between the bars. By the looks of them they could have been leftovers from WW I; they were very thin and threadbare.

Whitey quickly made up his bed and lay down; it was very warm and he looked toward the rear of his cell where he hoped to see a ventilator. In the back wall just a few inches above the floor to the right of the toilet bowl, was a metal ventilation grill, six by ten inches, but there was no air coming through it. The prisoners used to call these ventilators the "Telephone." All cells were built back to back, with the electrical and plumbing tunnel in between. The prisoners would sit on the toilet bowl, and yell through the ventilator to the inmate in the cell behind him.

Whitey felt exhausted, and had barely closed his eyes when another inmate came up to his door. He handed Whitey a worn out bath robe, and an old navy pea coat.

"When you go to shower, wear the robe and carry your laundry with you," he told Whitey.

"Yeah, yeah I know."

"You just came in from McNeil, right?"

"So—what about it," Whitey was in a mood.

"Did you happened to know Ben Sipes?"

"Hey look man, I'm tired, I don't feel like rapping, shove the fuck off!"

Without another word the inmate moved along the tier to pass out the remaining garments. Again Whitey flopped down on his bed, and was about to close his eyes when Johnny called out to him, "Whitey, hey Whitey."

"Yeah, yeah Johnny, what the fuck is it now?"

"You're not going to make many friends talking to that convict the way you did."

"Hey who gives a shit? I wasn't sent here for winning any popularity contests."

A chuckle sounded from Johnny's cell. Again Whitey closed his eyes endeavoring to get some sleep; instead he heard a loud outburst of yelling. It was explosive to the ears, the shouting voices, the shuffling of feet, the earsplitting banging of cell doors. The noise became louder as the convicts returning from the mills filed into the

Cell House. Everyone was getting into the noisy act; even the guards on the control boxes joined in the mad chorus.

"Get into your holes," shouted a guard. "Lock up—lock up—get into your holes."

Once the inmates were safely locked in their cells, guards, one on each tier, would shout to the Lieutenant that their tier was secure.

"B One is secure Lieutenant."

"B Two all secured Lieutenant." And so on.

Next a loud horn would sound, indicating that the Cell Blocks were locked down. Subsequently a loud bell would ring; it was the signal for all guards on the tiers to start their head count. It was also a signal for the prisoners to stand up to the bars in front of their cells. Each inmate was required to be in this position when the guard hurried by making his count.

Whitey stood up to his cell door waiting for his first count on Alcatraz. He looked across the glittering floor of Broadway to the cells of B Block. This was the first time he realized that all the inmates in the cells across the way were black.

The majority of the two hundred and eighty-five man population on Alcatraz were white, including Mexicans and Indians; a mere twenty-seven of this count was black. Strict segregation rules were enforced. All blacks celled on one tier. Whites, Mexicans, and Indians could cell next to one another, and the majority showered first on Saturday mornings, and on Tuesday afternoons. The blacks were first; each week they would alternate. It was the same in the Dining Hall, the blacks and the majority had their own tables, and each week the tiers would alternate as to who would eat first. After the count had been made, the all clear bell sounded, and immediately after the bell, a guard shouted, "Chow, chow down, chow."

From the Lieutenant's desk the duty officer shouted out his orders to the guards manning the control boxes. "Release B One."

A loud bang echoed throughout the Cell House, as the guard swung the metal control box door open on B One. He reached into the box with both hands and gripped the long control handle. With all his body-weight he pulled down on it. As he did so there was the sound of sliding doors, followed by a thunderous clang of steel as they slammed open. This was followed by the shuffling of many feet.

"Hey Whitey," Johnny called, "are you ready for chow?"

"Does a bear shit in the woods?"

Whitey was sitting on his bunk, and was about to say something further to Johnny, when suddenly his cell door shot open with a terrific bang. He had not expected to be released so soon for chow. He stepped through the doorway simultaneously with the rest of the tier, and was greeted with a smile from Johnny.

"What are you smiling at?" Whitey asked.

154

"I'm smiling at you fucker, come on let's go to chow."

They fell into step with the other inmates walking down Broadway. The Lieutenant was sitting at the Cell House Officer's desk, and behind him, bolted to the wall, was a huge windup clock with a long slow moving pendulum. During the evening when the lights were out and the Cell House was quiet, you could hear the haunting sound of the clock, "Tick-tock, tick-tock." It was so loud, if one did not know better, he would think it was on the wall in his cell.

Whitey and Johnny proceeded along with the line of men flowing into the Dining Room. Their eyes scanned the area for familiar faces. On either side of the room was a row of tables, each table accommodated ten men, with five sitting on each side. The Dining Room was large, airy, and plenty of light from the barred windows along the south wall overlooking the Bay. On the south wall was a large photo of Alcatraz. The light from the North was less intense where an outside balcony ran the length of the Mess Hall. This balcony was constantly patrolled during meal time by armed guards. About midway along the north wall, a guard sat inside a gun cage constructed of steel bars and mesh wire, dimly lit to provide better vision of the Dining Room. Above on the ceiling there were silvery ornaments, but they were not for decoration; their only purpose was to release tear gas bombs. The Dining Room was known as "The Gas Chamber," as it was the focal point for most riots. Just the touch of a button by a guard, and tear gas would explode into clouds of blinding, choking fumes.

The food line was moving right along. Whitey and Johnny followed the inmates in front of them through the center aisle of the Mess Hall.

"Hey Johnny—Johnny," someone yelled.

Johnny turned his head to see who was addressing him; sitting at the third table, was an inmate called the Grasshopper.

Recognizing him Johnny called back, "Hey Grasshopper, you wino fucker, how are you?"

"Okay Johnny, I'm doing okay, I'll see you in the yard this weekend."

Grasshopper was a harmless little skid row wino. A few years earlier in Sacramento, the Grasshopper, while under the influence of wine, walked into a bank and handed the teller a note demanding two hundred dollars. The note stated he was armed, and if she did not cooperate he would shoot. The lady teller smiled at the Grasshopper and whispered, "I'll cooperate."

The Wino, as he was sometimes called, handed the teller a paper bag. She very politely counted out ten twenty-dollar bills, put them in the bag and handed it back to him. The Grasshopper thanked her and started for the door. The teller caught the eye of a security guard

155

who apprehended the Grasshopper without a struggle, he was not even armed.

Johnny knew the Wino from McNeil; he had been transferred to Alcatraz a few months earlier.

As they began to recognize familiar faces, there was a chorus of voices calling to both men. "Hey Whitey, ya did it at last, how ya doing Johnny?" And so on.

It was a comforting feeling to know you had friends, even here on the Rock, though Whitey didn't consider them as friends, he thought of them merely as acquaintances. Just the same, it was a warm feeling to see a familiar face in a prison such as Alcatraz, and you knew you were not entirely alone.

In cafeteria style Whitey moved along in front of the steam table. Beyond the grilled gate, he observed inmate cooks at the huge steam pots in the kitchen. Following Johnny he picked up a tray, a plastic bowl, a compartmented plastic plate, metal fork and spoon. No knife was issued except on infrequent occasions when a steak was served.

"Hey Whitey, I'll be damned, hey Whitey."

Turning his attention from his food tray, Whitey looked toward the barred grilled gate, and standing there leaning against the bars was a powerfully built Mexican, known as Chino.

"Whitey you fucker, what brings you to the Rock?"

"Same thing that brought you here Wet-Back!"

Like the Grasshopper, Chino was transferred from McNeil a few months earlier. While at McNeil, Whitey, Blackie, Shorty, and Chino used to work out together lifting weights. Chino was a good-looking man, six feet tall, two hundred and twenty-five pounds; black hair, dark eyes, olive skin, and strong as a mule.

"I'll see you in the yard Whitey."

"Yeah we'll see," Whitey said as he continued his way through the steam line. His tray was loaded. His first meal on Alcatraz consisted of a tasty soup made from leftovers, Polish sausage, mashed potatoes, fresh sweet peas, bread, coffee, and cake for desert. Together with Johnny, he turned from the steam tables, and a guard pointed to a designated table. There were eight men already seated at the table, and Johnny and Whitey filled the last two spots.

Whitey was extremely hungry, and he dove into his food. Old habits were still with him, as he kept his eyes on his plate while he ate. Johnny had developed similar habits.

Sitting directly across the table was a stocky middle-aged man, who was watching Whitey with much interest. A few minutes passed, and not once did Whitey look up from his plate.

Finally the man said, "Damn it all, can't you take your face out of that plate long enough to say hello."

Whitey immediately stopped eating; he raised his head slowly, and

156

focused his eyes on the speaker. When he saw who it was his face lit up with one of his rare smiles.

"Hey old-timer," Whitey reached across the table, and they shook hands.

"I seen you standing there Whitey, with my bad eyesight I wasn't sure it was you."

"I'd forgotten you were here Archie, haven't seen you since '54. Say I want you to meet a pal of mine, Johnny House. Johnny, this is Archie."

"I take it you knew Whitey at McNeil Island," Johnny said.

"Yeah, that's right," Archie replied. "Say, this guy on my right is Mondoza, next to him is Warren, and the big lug sitting next to you Johnny, is Big Longo."

Both Whitey and Johnny shook hands with the new acquaintances, while shaking Mondoza's hand Whitey remarked, "You look familiar, where did I see you before? Now I remember, you were working on the docks today with a couple of other cons when we pulled in."

"Yeah, that's right, I work there every day."

"How did you get a bonarue job like that? A little ass-kissing I suspect!" Whitey joked.

Mondoza was a happy-go-lucky Mexican; a medium built man of thirty who was liked by all. He loved to laugh and had a great sense of humor. He was serving thirty years on a bogus charge.

Mondoza came from the Los Angeles area, and during the early '50s the FBI suspected him of smuggling drugs across the Mexican border. They were suspicious of him, but not once could they catch him carrying any drugs. It seemed every time Mondoza turned around, he was being stopped and searched, but was always clean. The FBI was becoming annoyed at their failure to apprehend him on a drug charge. Mondoza had to be on his toes at all times.

One day while driving down Wiltshire Boulevard, he discovered he was out of cigarettes. He pulled over to the curb stopping in front of a Ma and Pa's grocery store. In his haste he left the motor running, and the car door open as he hurried into the store. A few moments later he returned to his vehicle, and found two FBI agents standing by his car. Mondoza immediately realized his mistake, but it was too late now. They forced him to place his hands over the hood of the car, and spread eagle. One agent shook him down, while the other kept him covered.

"He's clean," the first agent said, "maybe we had better check out his car. You do it Louis while I watch this guy."

Entering the car on the passenger's side, agent Louis opened the glove compartment, and removed a pound of marijuana wrapped in a brown bag with a Mexico label on it.

Mondoza knew he was had. They were actually going to arrest him for marijuana that they themselves had planted in the glove compartment. Mondoza was charged with possession of illegal drugs, and also charged with smuggling drugs across the border into the U.S.

He was framed, but good, and was sentenced to thirty years in Federal Prison.

Warren was also a product of the Los Angeles area. A very quiet spoken man in his middle thirties, a light complexion, brown hair, hazel eyes, with a medium build. His job on Alcatraz was maintaining the sewing machines in the Clothing Factory. There was not much to be said about the man, except he was well liked by the other prisoners. He kept to himself most of the time. He had been on Alcatraz ten years now, and was serving a fifty-year sentence for kidnapping.

Big Longo was exactly what his name signified—big. He was born in Texas, and stood on a six-foot four frame, all two hundred and twenty pounds of him! He had a medium dark complexion, dark brown eyes and hair, he was thirty-two years old, and he too was well-liked by his fellow inmates. Big Longo was an extrovert, always ready for a laugh, and had a great sense of humor. He seemed to constantly wear a smile on his face. How did a good-natured man such as Longo wind up on Alcatraz?

He had joined the Army at 18, and had fought in the Korean War. Shortly before he was to return to the U.S., he was given a shore pass in Sasabo, Japan. Longo who had just returned from the war zone, was ready for a good night on the town. He was a young man feeling his oats, but didn't know how to handle his liquor. While under the influence of alcohol, he hired a cab driver to drive him back to the Army Base. When it came time to pay his cab fare, he felt the driver was overcharging him. The cabby being Japanese didn't understand English, and Longo did not understand Japanese. Both men were arguing with each other in their native tongues. Longo, who towered over the little oriental, was leaning over him shouting, and at the same time the cabby was looking straight up and screaming in Longo's face. At the moment, in his drunken mind, all Longo could see was a North Korean soldier. He clamped both hands around the cab driver's neck, and lifted him clean off the ground. Longo was so powerful he didn't realize his own strength, especially when he was under the influence of alcohol. Finally he released his grip, and when he did, the driver's legs doubled up under him, and he rolled over backwards down a bank, and splashed into an irrigation canal. He was dead before he hit the water. Longo left the scene not realizing he had just killed a man.

The Army Court Martial found him guilty of murder, and sentenced him to death by hanging. They confined Longo to the Big Eight Disciplinary Barracks to await his execution. But the day before he

158

was scheduled to hang, his sentenced was commuted to one hundred and fifty years. One week later, in the early spring of 1951, he was shipped off to Leavenworth, Kansas. Shortly after his arrival there, he was transferred to Alcatraz.

Archie—Archie Lyons was a stocky, average middle-aged man, who had lived in Washington, D.C. During his prime in the late '20s and the early '30s he had been a welterweight boxer, who fought his way up the ladder and became a contender in the top ten. He was a starving fighter, and money was hard to come by during the depression era. Before he knew it, he was over the hump, and became an unemployed boxer without a trade. So like many down-and-outers of the times, he turned to crime. In the late '40s he was arrested for armed robbery in the District of Columbia. This was a Federal crime. Archie was sentenced to thirty years in Federal Prison, and sent to Atlanta, Georgia. In the early '50s he was sent to McNeil Island for a short stay, and then transferred to Alcatraz.

In his younger days Archie Lyons was quite a man. Now he appeared even older than his years, with thick lens glasses he wore to aid his extremely poor vision. Like Mondoza, Warren, and Longo, he was liked by the inmate population. Even with his ailing health, he had a great sense of humor, and was always ready for a joke.

"What happened Whitey?" Archie asked. "What brings you to the Rock?"

"Ah, you know how I am Arch, I always head south for the winter."

"Yeah, but this is middle of summer Whitey." This brought a chuckle from the group of men. "No bullshit though, what happened at McNeil to bring you here?"

Whitey had been taken up with the moment and was smiling, but Archie's question brought a grim expression to his face.

"I was bum-beefed, and I don't care to discuss it, okay Arch?"

"Sure Whitey I understand."

"Say you guys," referring to Johnny and Whitey, "when you get out of quarantine, try to get a cell over in. . . . " Longo did not get a chance to finish what he was saying. He was interrupted when a doughy wad of bread bounced off Johnny's shoulder, landing on the table in front of him. Johnny looked around to see who might have thrown the wad of dough, and just as he turned another missile came flying through the air. It glanced off the back of Whitey's head, who came to his feet with the quickness of a cat.

"You bastard," he shouted as he spun around looking for his assailant; he was furious and looked as though he was ready to take on the whole Dining Room! Johnny came to his feet also, he too was ready to fight, when he noticed the Grasshopper laughing, he was the guilty one—the culprit who threw the missiles.

Johnny yelled at him, "Grasshopper you little fucking wino, I'll

159

break both your arms."

For a moment, Whitey and Johnny were furious until they saw other prisoners throwing wads of bread at each other. Again they sat down to finish their meal.

"Don't let that upset you guys," Archie told them, "they are like a bunch of kids always throwing wads of dough at each other. Hell it's their recreation period," Archie laughed.

There was not too much the guards could do about the playful act, because the Hole (Special Treatment Unit) wasn't large enough to hold every one of the missile throwers! They could pop the tear gas from the ceiling, but they didn't, as that would surely set off a terrifying, murderous riot. The guards didn't pay much attention to the playful acts.

If an inmate did go to TU for some minor infraction, it would be for five to thirty days. For a more serious offense, a prisoner might be in TU for six months or a year. Fighting was considered a minor offense, unless the inmate was unpopular with the guards, then he might be kept there indefinitely.

It took approximately twenty minutes to eat, then the guard would look carefully down both sides of the table to check the flatware. Next he would have the inmates pass their silverware to the head of the table so he could count the spoons and forks. Once he was satisfied with the count he then would raise both hands in a gesture for the inmates to rise from the table. Simultaneously the prisoners would stand up with such force it would send the long bench hurling over backwards. Another hand signal from the guard and the prisoners would march out of the Dining Room single file. The meal schedule was so precisely clocked that the last man in the first unit would be marching out of the Dining Room just as the first man in the line of the next unit was marching in.

After dinner was over, and the population safely locked up, the inmates lined up at their cell doors for the last stand up count of the day. The time was 6:00 P.M., and they would remain locked in their cells until breakfast, some thirteen hours later.

After the last standing count they had three and a half hours until lights out, three and a half precious hours to do as they pleased within the limited confines of their cells. Each cubicle was separated by a six-inch cement wall, with one man to a cell.

After count cleared, Whitey lay on his bunk smoking a cigarette, and to kill time he began to leaf through a library catalog provided in each cell. The Library was off limits to the general population, except for a few inmates who worked there. To received books from the Library all one had to do was to pick out the selection of your choice from the catalog. Each inmate was issued blank library cards. Using one card at a time, the inmate would write his name, prison number, and cell number; then in the spaces provided he would list up to twenty selections. On the Lieutenant's desk there was a box marked, "Library Cards," and on the way to the Mess Hall in the morning, the inmate would drop the card into the box. Later on that day, a convict Library worker would deliver the books to the cells. Whenever an inmate finished a book it would be dropped into the same library box.

He replaced the catalog on the wooden shelf, and began to build himself another cigarette. He was just putting a match to the finished product, when a bell sounded. It was the 6:30 signal to all instrument players. This was the music hour, which lasted until 7:30. There were a few men who played such instruments as the guitar, banjos, trumpet, and harmonica.

From the second tier Whitey could hear someone strumming on a guitar. Two Negroes were in conversation on the bottom tier across the way, and soon other men were calling back and forth. Whitey just sat there on his bunk looking across at the inner side of the bank tiers. It reminded him of a huge beehive as the inmates puttered about in their cells. The chatter was getting louder, and an argument was developing. The pitch was rising, but above all the confusion, floating in from the south east side of C Block, were the soft musical note of a harmonica. As Whitey listened to the sweet mournful sounds, he observed an officer on the floor as he patrolled Broadway. The officer walked along at a very slow pace as he glanced at the cells on either side. He reminded Whitey of a school teacher as he strolled along indifferently looking for cheaters during a classroom exam. The guard felt secure in his patrol, and why not? He was safe from the reach of these dangerous men who were known to the outside world as unredeemably evil—murderers, kidnappers, robbers, and thugs. He was the zoo keeper, and the convicts behind bars were the tigers in the cage. Whitey observed every movement of the guard until he could no longer see him. Then he held his mirror through the bars of his cell at such an angle to see the departing guard disappear around the corner of C Block. He glanced in his mirror at the clock on the wall above the Lieutenant's desk—7: 29 P.M.

At precisely 7:30 P.M. the bell sounded announcing to all musical instrument players the "Happy Hour," (as the convicts called it) was over.

After the bell had sounded, the noise and chatter in the Cell House seem to quiet down. Whitey rolled and lit another cigarette and lay back down on his bunk.

He finished his cigarette, and dozed off. He was sound asleep when the bright lights abruptly blacked out; the house lights were still on and shed a ghostly twilight over the Cell Blocks and corridors. As Whitey slept, he wasn't aware of the fact that every fifteen minutes all night long, an officer made a count.

161

A new prisoner to Alcatraz is totally exhausted on his first night. He has heard all kinds of stories about the place; some of them exaggerated. He builds up such an anxiety on the tedious train ride, that even the noise of the Cell Block, or vibrant fog horn from the Coast Guard lighthouse on the North west end of the Island, had no effect against the sedation of fatigue.

CHAPTER 27.

Whitey was sleeping soundly when a raucous blast of the rise and shine horn yanked him out of his slumber. Six-thirty A.M., twenty minutes until count time. Twenty minutes for personal and housekeeping chores.

Each new arrival was informed of regulations. Whitey quickly hopped out of bed, brushed his teeth, washed his face and hands, got dressed and cinched his belt-buckle that was made of leather in place of metal to keep the electronic eye detector of the snitch-box from buzzing. He made his bed, straightened up his cell; and at the sound of the count bell, he took his position at the front of the cell. A moment or two later, a guard came dashing by counting the occupants as he passed. This was the first of twelve official counts of the day.

The Lieutenant called out his command, "Ring in outside C!"

The trek by units to breakfast began.

When the meal was over and the prisoners were leaving the Dining Room, they had to file through the electronic eye, (commonly known as the snitch-box). It could be rolled on its wheels to wherever it was needed. But it would be predominately in front of the Dining Room, or the doorway to the showers, or the door leading to and from the yard.

The inmates marched back to their cells; again they were counted. Count cleared, then a bell sounded ringing them out to the shops. From his quarantine cell Whitey watched the men walk by. Everyone who was assigned to the mills went to work, but there were a few inmates who refused to work at all, so they were compelled to stay in their cells. They were allowed no privileges; they couldn't write the usual two letters a week. They were given nothing to smoke, but they always managed to get some smoking materials. There were very few privileges to take away from a man. The way Whitey looked at it, everything they did get was a necessity, not a privilege.

With nothing to do he stretched out on his bunk for a nap, but was awakened by a slopping sound from the corridor. He turned his head to peek though the bars, and saw a muscular little man

163

swinging a mop. He was cleaning up Broadway; he noticed Whitey watching him, so he dropped the mop handle, and walked over. Johnny had also seen him.

As the inmate neared the cells he spoke to Whitey, "Hi there, my name is McCoy, Shorty McCoy, you guys just come in yesterday from McNeil, right?"

"Whitey Thompson's the name, this is my buddy Johnny in the next cell, yeah we just came in yesterday."

"Hello Johnny, glad to meet you."

"Same here Shorty. Boy you sure keep that corridor shining."

Shorty McCoy was a cheerful little guy of five foot five, with brown hair and eyes, and a fair complexion. He was a very powerful man, and a likable person. Shorty was born and raised in Kentucky; he was a descendant of the feuding Hatfields and McCoys. He had originally been sentenced to three years in Federal Prison for operating a moonshine still, and sent to Louisville. During his incarceration there he was continuously harassed by another prisoner—a much larger man who was a bully. Shorty, a country boy, was very quiet. He had told the bully numerous times to quit messing with him, as he was not looking for trouble; he just wanted to mind his own business, serve his time and get out.

Shorty was serving the last six months of his sentence, soon he would be going home, but the bully did not let up; he did everything to harass Shorty. The reason he picked on him was that he felt he could get away with it. He thought McCoy was too afraid to do anything about it, so the harassment became worse as time went by.

One day, while working on a road job, the bully started throwing pebbles at Shorty while he was digging in a ditch.

"Will you quit that before you hit me in the eye with one of those stones."

The bully paid no attention to Shorty's complaints. If he had listened to the tone of Shorty's voice, he would have realized he was at the breaking point and was dangerous. He threw another stone, and Shorty McCoy, the quiet little man, could take it no longer. With the edge of his shovel he split the bully's head wide-open killing him instantly.

Shorty was tried, found guilty, and received a new sentence. His three-year term was parlayed into life imprisonment, and was sent to Alcatraz.

In the world of concrete and steel, when a prisoner has a problem with another inmate, he has to take care of it himself. There is no one he can turn to, and if he tells an officer—once he does, he becomes a snitch.

Shorty McCoy said that cleaning Broadway corridor was his regular job. He enjoyed doing it because he worked alone with no one to answer to except the Cell House Lieutenant, or guard. On his corridor job he worked seven days a week. His only duty was to sweep, mop, and polish Broadway. This took him approximately one and a half hours each morning; the rest of the day he could read or sleep. He also told Whitey and Johnny that all work in the Industrial Shops were paying jobs; they could make from $20.00 to $60.00 a month depending on the job and their skill. The money they earned would go on record, or they could have it sent home. Many of the prisoners had no homes. The majority of the inmates on Alcatraz were forgotten men. Some who did have families, were disowned by them. On the first of each month the mill workers would receive a receipt stating how much they had earned the previous month. Some old-timers had as much as five or ten-grand on the books.

Shorty also said if there was anything he could do for them, to let him know. He lived on the Flats on the south east side of B Block, in cell B-102.

Whitey was just rolling a cigarette, when a tall man wearing a business suit, stopped in front of his cell. He had the position of Classification Councilor—the man who assessed the newcomer's abilities and probable behavior pattern. Also all request for visitors and correspondence had to go through this man before being approved by the Bureau of Prisons.

"Leon W. Thompson 1465?" He asked. "According to your record you have been at McNeil for ten years; during this time you have had no visitors or letters, is that right?"

"If that's what the record says, I guess so."

"Ordinarily there is a three-month waiting period here on Alcatraz before a newcomer can have a visit. In your case you don't have to wait the three-month period, and we're allowing you two visits a month. They cannot be a former inmate, do you have two people for your list, like members of your immediate family?"

"I don't want no visits nor do I want to write to anyone."

"Don't you have any relatives you would like to keep in touch with, or visit you?"

"I told you I don't want no fucking visits, nor write to anyone."

"You have a girl friend, Rose Orth, she tried to write to you at McNeil Island. You can have her put on your correspondence list if you like."

"Look, I didn't want anyone writing to me ten years ago, and I still don't. I don't want any visitors or correspondents, understand?"

"Suit yourself Thompson, if you change your mind, just fill out a request slip. Now then, about work, there are five different places you can work, the Brush Shop, Pallet Shop, Tailor Shop, Glove Shop, or the Kitchen Culinary. But three of them have a waiting list, the Glove

165

Shop needs men right now, so does the Culinary."

"Fuck the Culinary, I'll work in the Glove Shop?"

"Okay Thompson, you start work Monday, I'll have you moved to a new cell this afternoon. Normally new prisoners remain in quarantine for two weeks, but at the present time they need men in the Glove Shop."

The Councilor jotted notes on his clip board; then moved onto the next cell, "Johnny House 1466?"

As soon as the Councilor departed, Johnny called to Whitey, "I'm going to work in the Culinary Whitey, where did they assign you?"

"The Glove Shop, I'll talk to ya later."

The remainder of the morning was uneventful. During this time Whitey dozed off, only to be rudely awakened by the noise of the returning mill workers for lunch.

On each work day right after lunch sick call was held. As Whitey and Johnny walked out of the Mess Hall they saw a line of inmates near the Lieutenant's desk. Whitey walked over and took his place in the growing line.

The M.T.A. (Medical Technical Assistant) was in charge of sick call. He would dispense aspirins, cough medicine, and such, and listen to the symptoms of the inmates. If he decided an illness required a more professional diagnosis, he would write the inmate's name and number on a list to see the doctor on his two-hour daily visit.

When Whitey's turn came up the M.T.A. gave him a hard look, and in a somewhat snotty voice said, "You just transferred in, there's nothing wrong with you."

"Hey you don't even know my fucking name."

"I don't need to know it. Just return to your cell."

At the M.T.A.'s last remark Whitey got hot under the collar. "What the fuck's wrong with you? My nose was plugged up all last night, all I want is some Mentholatum."

Raising his voice to a high pitch, the M.T.A. said, "Just blow your nose! Now get out of here, and let me take care of the sick men in this line."

That did it for Whitey! His eyes turned cold as he shouted, "You lowlife son of a bitch; the only sick person here is you! Now give me something for my fucking nose."

As Whitey moved around the medicine cart toward the M.T.A., he didn't see the Lieutenant walk up.

"Hold it right there Thompson," the Lieutenant ordered in a commanding voice.

Whitey spun around to face the intruder. He was furious, and like an overheating radiator, he was ready to explode.

"Is this a fucking sick line or not?" He yelled at the Lieutenant. "I want something for my nose so I can breathe when I sleep, and this

166

fucker tells me to blow it."

The Lieutenant had handled many a situation in his day. He could see that this one might easily get out of hand with all these convicts milling around, and he knew he had to cool down this hard-core convict as quickly as he could.

"All right Thompson, hold it down," the Lieutenant said in a normal but commanding voice, "just quiet down and tell me what's the problem."

"All I want is some Mentholatum for my nose, and this quack tells me no because I just came in on a transfer. My nose plugs up at night, and he tells me to blow it."

The Lieutenant turned to the M.T.A., "You have some Mentholatum. just give him some."

With a wooden tongue depressor, the M.T.A. transferred a dab of Mentholatum from a large container to a small half ounce paper cup. With a hard stare he handed it to Whitey who took it without a word of thanks, and walked back down Broadway.

While Whitey waited for the guard to pull the cell bar, Johnny caught up to him.

"I sure thought you were busted back there Whitey."

"Ah fuck that M.T.A. bastard! Next time he gets in my face I'll just go alongside his fucking head."

Johnny tried to cool him down, "Forget it Whitey, let's get ready for our cell move, okay?"

After the noon count cleared, and work call sounded, the Lieutenant with clip board in hand, call out a list of names, "Leon Thompson, Johnny House, Freddie Steinburg, Alvato Lieto, Holt Williams, Amando Silta. You men are going to make a cell move. I want you to walk around B and C Block to find an empty cell of your choice. Then report immediately to the Cell House desk, and give me the cell number."

The Lieutenant signaled the guard at the control box to open their cells.

"Let's look on the south side of B Block Whitey," Johnny suggested.

Both men walked down Broadway, made a right turn at the corner of B Block walking past the entrance to the Dining Room and the Cell House desk. This section was known as "Times Square." They continued along the east wall of the Block, and turned right on what was called "Michigan Avenue," the south east side of B Block. They continued along the Flats of Michigan Avenue to the south west end of B Block. On the second tier they found two empty adjoining cells. Whitey picked B-252, while Johnny took B-250. The west gun gallery was approximately twenty feet from their new cells, and directly across the corridor was A Block, not in use at this time.

167

They returned to the Lieutenant's desk to give him the new cell numbers, and were ordered to get their personal gear ready. The Lieutenant informed them that he had to get all moves completed in time to be put on the daily movement sheet. Regular cell moves were usually made on Saturday morning right after showers and clothing exchange, but the Lieutenant told them that this was an emergency move to get them out of quarantine in time to report for work on Monday morning. He also gave them permission to go to the yard on Saturday and Sunday. Then he informed them that there would be a movie this weekend (there was a movie shown twice a month).

Freddie found an empty cell on the east side of B Block, while Lieto, Williams and Chili moved onto the North west side of C Block.

Whitey and Johnny carried their meager belongings to the new cells; then stood waiting in front of the cubicles for the guard to appear and pull the control bar.

"Where the hell is that son of a bitch?" Johnny complained.

Before Whitey answered, the guard pulled the bar, and they stepped into their new cells; the doors slid shut behind them with a loud bang.

All cells were alike, but these had just been freshly painted a tan color, and did not look as dreary as the ones they had vacated.

Whitey set about making up his bunk, hung up his clothes, and put his toilet articles and mirror on the wooden shelf. Once this was accomplished he stepped up to the front of his cell, and looked across the corridor at the deserted A Block. It appeared so cold, dark and dirty. The black emptiness of the place gave one the impression of utter loneliness and desolation. He stood there pondering at the empty cells, and wondering about the prisoners who had served time in them, and what they might have been like.

"You dumb son of a bitch," he said out loud, "they were just like you—a stupid bastard locked up in a cage!"

"Who you talking to Whitey?" Johnny asked from the confines of his cell.

"No one, I'm just bitching to myself."

"Well as long as you don't bitch back, you're okay," Johnny laughed.

"Ah shut the fuck up House." Still grumbling to himself Whitey said, "Look at this fucking place, there's nothing but concrete, and bars all around, not a goddamn window in sight. Why the hell I picked this end of the Block I'll never know."

That evening, immediately after the 6:30 count, an officer went from cell to cell passing out Wings cigarettes. This duty was performed three times a week, Monday, Wednesday, and Friday evenings.

In desperate need of nicotine, Whitey tore open the pack, pulled

168

out a cigarette, lit up, and took a deep drag filling his lungs with the much needed smoke. He held it for a moment or two, then casually let it flow through his nostrils. It had a stale taste, but it was infinitely better than the Stud tobacco he had been smoking, and if he rationed them, they would last him until Monday night.

He took another drag, "Hey House," he called, "what do ya think of these tailor-mades?"

"I'd rather have a cigar, but they're better than that dust we've been smoking."

"You said that right. Say House how come you want to work in the Culinary?"

"Because I don't want to work in any of the sweat shops."

"That's good enough reason, but you know what? I think the Lieutenant screwed up when he let you move here to outside B. I don't think he knew you were going to work in the kitchen."

"What has that got to do with it, what difference does it make?"

"I don't know," Whitey replied, "but I noticed on the Flats of Broadway, that all the south cells of C Block were filled with white Culinary workers, across the way from them on the south side of B Block I seen nothing but black kitchen workers. So I figured the south end of Broadway must be Kitchen Row. If that's the case, I bet you'll have to move again. I can't say for sure, but I've done enough time elsewhere to know they always keep the kitchen help in the same section, they call it Kitchen Row."

"Damn, I wish I had known that before, I don't like Broadway."

"Well you don't have to accept the job man," Whitey yelled.

"Ah hell! I want to work in the kitchen; to heck with it, if I have to cell on Broadway, then I have to cell on Broadway, fuck it!"

Whitey pulled another cigarette out of the pack, lit it and lay back on his bunk to relax, and as he did so, his thoughts were of Johnny. He had begun to really like the big Texan, and he had hoped he wouldn't accept the Culinary job. Whitey liked having someone he trusted in the cell next to him. Of course he would never tell Johnny that.

Whitey took another drag and listened to the background noises. He could hear a splashing sound like a beaver slapping water with its tail. Someone was washing his face. Occasionally a toilet flushed and the sound of it would drown out the murmuring voices.

Sometimes the murmuring turned into shouting, "Shut the fuck up, you're interrupting my conversation."

"Hey man, screw you and your conversation."

"Who said that? Was that you Art?"

Convicts would yell to each other clear to the opposite end of the Cell Block. They had to shout at the top of their voices to get above the other noise.

169

"Was that you Art? You mother-fucker," the voice shouted again.

"Yeah it's me you bastard, what about it?" The friendly argument continued.

"What about it? I'll tell you what about it skinhead, when the doors open in the morning, come out swinging mother-fucker!"

Someone else shouted, "Both you girls shut up! Or come Saturday I'll see both of you in the yard."

"If you see me in the yard screwball, you better bring your stuff (knife)."

Above the chatter and noise, the strumming of guitars could be heard, and from a distance drifted a sweet but mournful sound of a harmonica. Whitey wished everyone would be quiet so that he could fully enjoy the beautiful sounds as they floated gently throughout the Cell House.

A few weeks later he would become acquainted with Gus Lazinsky, the talented player.

After the music ceased, and with nothing to amuse himself with, Whitey again leafed through the library catalogue. Alongside some of the titles listed, someone had written his opinion of the books, "This book is fantastic." "This book stinks." "Good book," and so on. Whitey fell asleep with the catalog in his hand.

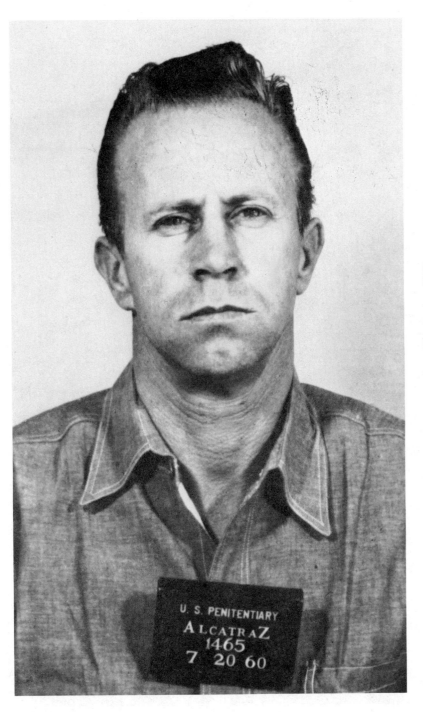

U. S. PENITENTIARY
ALCATRAZ
1465
7 20 60

Mugshot of Whitey Thompson 1960

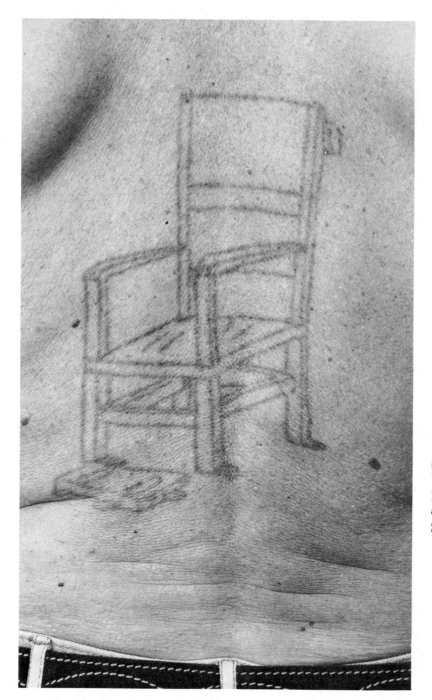

Unfinished Electric Chair on Whitey's back. Courtesy Jim Chapman.

Westside View of Industrial Building. Courtesy Golden Gate National Recreation Area.

Clothing Shop.   Courtesy GGNRA.

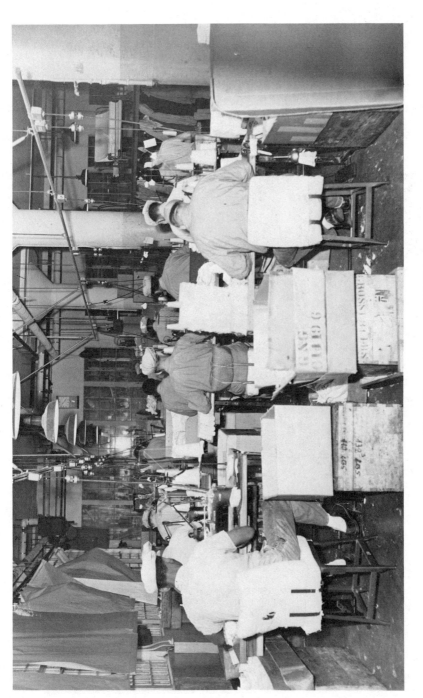

Glove Shop. Courtesy GGNRA.

Michigan Avenue as it is today.

Prison Morgue as it is today.

Shower Room as it is today.

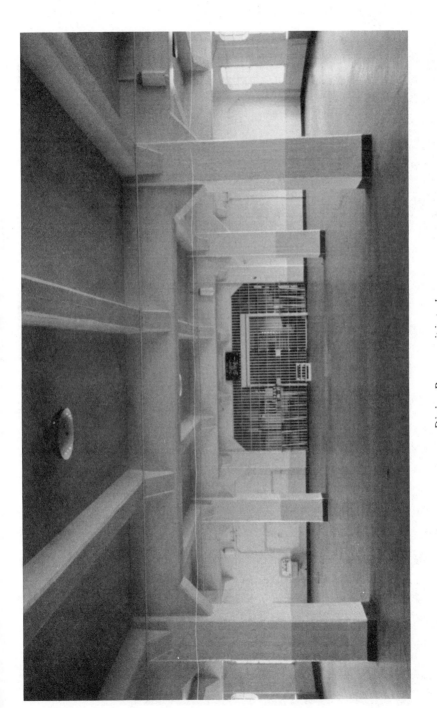

Dining Room as it is today.

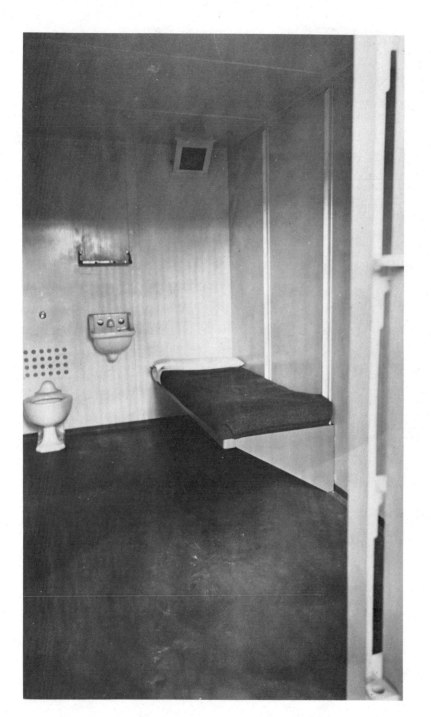

Cell in the "Treatment Unit".   Courtesy GGNRA

South End of Island including Light House and Warden's House . Courtesy GGNRA

Aerial View of the Rock. Courtesy GGNRA

CHAPTER 28.

Saturday morning wake up on Alcatraz came at the same time as any other morning, 6:30 A.M.. Whitey was out of bed at the first blast of the horn. He quickly brushed his teeth, washed his face and hands, made his bed, and took his place in front of his cell for standing count. As he stood there he suddenly had the urge to go to the toilet. Could he hold it until after count? Hell no, he could not wait! He quickly pulled down his trousers and undershorts and sat on the toilet bowl. He was still sitting there when the count buzzer sounded.

"Goddamn," he growled, "to hell with it, he'll just have to count me on the throne."

"What's wrong Whitey?" Johnny called.

"It's count time and I'm taking a crap."

Whitey received no sympathy from Johnny who said, "Crap or no crap, you better get up to the bars Whitey."

It was too late, the second tier count officer came charging around the corner of B Block, hurrying by Whitey's cell. He slid to a halt, spun around, and dashed back.

"What the hell are you doing? Get your ass up to the bars," the guard was furious. "If you don't get up to the bars right now, I'll write a shot (report) on you, you'll end up in TU."

"Up your ass with TU," Whitey bellowed at him. "Can't you see I'm taking a shit?"

The officer left in a fit of rage, and went on counting, and Whitey just went on. . . .!!!

Johnny called, "Hey Whitey, that fool is going to get you put into TU. "

"Big deal, they won't be getting a cherry."

"I don't like to see you get screwed up over nothing. You could have said, 'Hey I'm sorry officer, it won't happen again.' "

"What? Are you crazy? Me say I'm sorry to a hack! Fuck TU, they can bury me in there before I would ever say I'm sorry to any bull."

"They'll probably just do that Whitey."

"Yeah, well I don't give a shit; when I have to take a crap, I'll take

171

it, count time or no count time! Piss on their rules! Hey when nature calls there is but just one rule—shit!"

A chuckle sounded from Johnny's cell, at the same time the all clear sounded, and the prisoners were released for breakfast.

After breakfast Whitey and Johnny were leaving the Dining Hall, when the Lieutenant called Whitey aside.

"Thompson, the count officer told me you weren't standing up to the bars at count time. From now on during count time you be up to the bars. Going to the toilet is no excuse. You're new here so I'm going to give you a pass this time. I don't want to start you off in TU."

"Hey Lieutenant," Whitey sneered, "I don't give a damn about your TU, if you want to put me there—have at it."

"Just go back to your cell Thompson, stand up to the bars for count, then get ready for clothing exchange and showers."

Immediately after count was cleared, Whitey removed his clothes, put on his bathrobe, canvas slippers, and gathered up his dirty clothes for exchange.

As he stood there waiting for his cell door to open a bitter memory flashed through his mind. He was thinking about all the good time he had lost before his transfer. While at McNeil he had built up over six hundred good days, and they were all forfeited. All his good time was lost, and he knew it would never be returned to him. He still had five years to go, and there were times he doubted if he would ever make it. He was like a time-bomb—a bomb that had a malfunctioning timer mechanism in it that could be triggered off by the slightest provocation, and he didn't really care. He felt he had nothing to look forward to—nothing—but did he? He didn't realize what was happening to him; he was beginning to experience mixed feelings. The self-made barrier round his frame of mind was beginning to disintegrate, and emotional feelings were entering the forbidden territory. This can't be true, it can't be, for he had developed a hatred for all living things, but how about the little girl on the train? You liked her, and the old black porter, and now Johnny House who was fast becoming your friend; you like him. That's what is happening, you are showing emotion—showing emotion for other people, and if it keeps up, you might even show a little feeling for yourself. Ah I'm thinking crazy!

His thoughts were broken when his cell door slid open. He grabbed his dirty clothes, and quickly stepped out on the tier before the door shut behind him. He quickly fell into step behind Johnny, and the single line of prisoners made their way along the tier. They turned at the corner, down the stairs to Times Square, across the Flats, to the solid steel door that led down to the Basement.

The officer on duty at the head of the stairs held up his hand for Whitey to stop, cutting off the line between him and Johnny. Whitey and the rest of the inmates had to wait until fifteen men, on the return trip, came up the stairs; thus never overcrowding the Shower Room.

Coming down the stairway into the Basement, directly to the left, was a row of huge wooden bins where dirty clothes were disposed. The line moved along slowly while they deposited each item of laundry into the correct bin. Then from a carefully stacked pile of clean towels, each man picked up one, and waited his turn for an empty shower. The wait was short for Whitey, and as soon as one man moved out, he moved in.

The Shower Room scene was like a recreational period in a school yard. The only difference was, instead of children, these were grown men playing childish pranks such as snapping a towel at some unsuspecting person's bare behind, or slipping up to someone in the shower, and dousing him with a bucket of cold water. The various noises were devastating, and a fog bank of steam hung overhead like a heavy curtain over a huge stage, waiting to close down after the final act.

Whitey enjoyed the shower, but with all the pandemonium going on one couldn't relax under the hot water. This was the only time one could get warm through and through on this desolated Island. The sting of the water's flow was exhilarating to Whitey, and he was enjoying it to the fullest extent, when someone yelled at him.

"Hey hurry up Whitey, get outa there, too much water's bad for you."

Standing next to a bench, waiting for an empty shower, was Archie. Whitey smiled when he saw it was the old man.

"Hi Arch how's it going?"

"Okay Whitey. Hey you better get out of that shower before you drowned."

"I get to shower twice a week; I want to enjoy it. You only shower once a year, so what's your hurry?"

"Piss on you Whitey, you never knew what a shower was until you came to prison."

Whitey stepped out of the shower, dried himself off, and after donning his bathrobe, he took his place in line to pick up his clean clothes. When his turn came he gave the counter man his number. The worker went directly to Whitey's clothing bin, and return with trousers and shirt.

"What about shorts, T-shirt and socks?" Whitey asked.

"You pick them up on Tuesdays only."

Without another word, Whitey turned away from the counter, and took his place in the household supply line. There he picked up a roll of toilet paper, three books of matches, two envelopes, two sheets of writing paper, and a bar of soap. Whitey asked about tooth powder.

"When you're all out, bring the empty can to me on any shower

173

day," the officer said.

"How about a smoking pipe?" Whitey asked. Each inmate was entitled to one pipe a year. The officer handed one to Whitey after writing his name, number, and the date in a record book.

Johnny was waiting in front of his cell when Whitey returned. "Are you going to the yard Whitey?" He asked.

"Yeah I guess I'll give it the once-over. How about you, are you going?"

"Yes," Johnny said as the guard pulled the bar allowing the prisoners to enter their cells. Whitey immediately got dressed, put away his household supplies, tidied up his cell, and then waited for the next count before going to the yard.

The count bell sounded, and after count was cleared, the Cell House Officer called out, "Yard call, release outside B-One and C-One, release B-Two and C-Two, and. . . ."

Mocking the guards, some prisoners called out, "Yard call, released outside B-One."

At each control box a guard was standing at the ready. When the signal sounded, simultaneously they pulled the bars, and in groups of fifteen, the doors opened.

Whitey and Johnny came out of their respective cells, and blended in with the flow of traffic, down the stairs onto the Flats. Every ten feet or so there was a guard on duty to keep the line moving. In front of the yard door entrance was the portable electronic snitch-box. The buzzer sounded when Whitey started through; he froze in his tracks, he knew he had no metal or contraband on his person, so why did it go off? The guard took him to one side and began to shake him down. He removed a pack of Wings cigarettes from Whitey's shirt pocket, and told him to go through the electronic eye again. He obeyed, and this time the buzzer was silent. The guard handed him back his cigarettes, and informed him, to always slide the pack down the side of the electronic box, and to retrieve them after he had walked through. The aluminum foil on the package is what set off the buzzer. No one could walk through the snitch-box with so much as a safety-pin.

There was one old convict who had a metal pin in his left knee joint, every time he went through the electronic box, the buzzer would sound. If the guard on duty was in a good mood, he would wave the old convict on, but on most occasions he would make him strip off all his clothes, including his shoes and socks. After his belongings were cleared, then the old man would walk through the snitch-box in the nude, of course the metal pin would set off the buzzer. He had to endure this unfortunate situation often.

Once you cleared the yard door you went down a flight of concrete steps to the first landing; on the landing was a stationary electronic eye. The inmates were compelled to walk through the box coming and going to the yard. Across the yard to the west wall, was the Sally Port (heavy steel door). Midway down a steep flight of steps, was another electronic eye that one must go through on his journey to and from the mills. The old inmate was obliged to strip naked in all types of weather.

Both Whitey and Johnny made their way to the yard, and as they walked down the concrete steps they were greeted by a chilling wind. It was the middle of July, but no matter, this was Alcatraz, the Rock, and it was cold everywhere on the Island. This did not deter the convicts, for the highlight of the week were the Saturday and Sunday recreational periods. (That is if the weather permitted.) Blustery weather was something to dread, for it meant confinement to a cell with little to do, from 5:00 P.M. Friday, until 6:30 A.M.. Monday. The stretch of monotony was broken only by treks to the Mess Hall, and an hour in the Chapel for churchgoers.

The recreation yard was a trifle smaller than a football field, extending from the angle of the T shape prison looking toward San Francisco and the Golden Gate. There were twelve huge concrete steps serving as bleachers that rose against the Mess Hall. These high steps conveyed a view that was spectacular, especially if rains or high winds whipping through the Gate during the night, had swept the atmosphere clean.

Looking to the West an inmate could see the majestic sweep of the Golden Gate Bridge with its towers orange-red against the sky. Beyond it rose the green patch of the Presidio of San Francisco. The apartment skyscrapers on Russian Hill, the street-like rows in a hillside vineyard; Coit Tower on Telegraph Hill, the fingered piers spreading out from the Embarcadero—also startling close. A cable car could be visible climbing up the Hyde Street Hill. All this was only a mile and a quarter away—so close it seemed you could toss a stone and hit it, yet it was so very far away.

After repeated trips to the yard, it seemed to get smaller and smaller—enclosing you. Along the top of its twenty-foot wall, ran a gun-way with a parapet, and at the three corners, squat gun boxes. A cat-walk linked the wall to the south gun tower on top of the Industry Building.

It was just a twelve minute boat ride for the convict to come over from San Francisco, but a ten or twenty-year trip to get back—perhaps never. There was no truth that the Spanish explorers, or Mexicans ever set foot on Alcatraz, nor Indians before either of them. Indians had a special reason to shun the Island; they considered it a dwelling place of evil spirits.

Johnny House walked off leaving Whitey standing on the high bleacher steps overlooking the yard. A number of inmates were

175

sitting at one end of the yard playing chess or dominoes on portable card tables. Some prisoners were playing bridge with dominoes that had playing card markings instead of dots. You could put in an order for dominoes playing cards, chess sets, or regular dominoes. These cost anywhere from two or three dollars up into the hundreds. The good sets were made of ivory. No regular playing cards were allowed because they were made with a celluloid content that could be ground up and used as an explosive.

The main portion of the yard was being used for a softball game, while others were playing handball off a section of the wall that had markings on it. There was no safe place in the yard with balls flying from all directions!

Over in another section a few prisoners were working out weight-lifting. Whitey decided to walk over and watch. Archie was at the iron yard, and Whitey stopped to talk to him a while about old acquaintances. Then he made his way over to watch Johnny who had sat in at a dominoes' game. The coldness began to chill his bones; but no matter what part of the yard he was in he could not escape the wind. He made his way back up to the top bleacher where he could see a magnificent view out beyond the wall.

Off in the distance across the Bay, standing in all her splendor was the beautiful Golden Gate Bridge. If one looked closely you could see the sun's reflection on the moving cars.

Lucky bastards, Whitey thought. Then he glanced toward the Bay itself, he could see sailing craft, and motorboats with people who were enjoying life. He quickly turned his eyes away, and drew his attention to the prison yard. He noticed a diagonal red line painted in each corner, with the words, "KEEP CLEAR." The corner sections of the yard were a no-man's-land. If an inmate stepped over one of the lines, he would automatically draw gunfire from one of the towers.

Whitey sat there in the cold listening to the howl of the wind above the shouts of the convicts playing in the yard. Again his vision took in the sights of the Golden Gate Bridge, and the insect-like cars that crawled down its back at a snail's pace; the boats in the Bay, sea gulls soaring high on angry turbulent winds, and in the yard, inmates at play. At a glance he took all of this into view. It reminded him of a stage play, and he was in the bleachers seated in the best seat in the house, watching the show.

In reality there were two different plays going on at the same time, and from his viewpoint he could see them both. One was beyond the prison walls where he could see the activity of cars moving on the Bridge, and the birds flying overhead. In the Bay, there were the people in their boats. They were all part of the caste; to Whitey, the greatest acting in the world was behind the walls of the Rock. The props were a stage of concrete, with a backdrop of steel. The guards were actors too, they stood in their high towers waiting to play their biggest role—waiting to shoot and kill some unfortunate convict who strayed over the line. The whole ordeal was a play with no rehearsals. Fate was the playwright, so God help the ones who muffed their lines.

Whitey's thoughts were broken, he snapped back to reality when the recall horn sounded, yard was over, they must return to their cages.

The convicts gradually formed a line in front of the electronic box at the first landing. The huge heavy steel door to the Cell House was slowly opened. The officer at the head of the stairs motioned the convicts to start forward. The inmates moved at a leisurely pace up the stairs, through the doorway and the portable snitch-box. After coming through the box the single line of prisoners became a double line, as the convicts shuffled off to B and C Blocks.

Whitey was standing in front of his cell when Johnny came walking down the tier.

"There is a movie this afternoon Whitey, I'm going, how about you?"

"No, my name ain't on the list. I'll be going tomorrow."

The guard pulled the bar locking them up; immediately followed by a standing count, and then the trek to the Dining Room for lunch. Again they returned to their cells for another count, and as soon as it was cleared, a buzzer sounded followed by the ringing of a bell.

A guard called out, "Movie call. Only those on the list need come out. Movie call."

The doors opened with one loud bang after another, but Whitey's remained closed. He watched the men as they passed his cell, one or two spoke to him as they hurried by.

"Hi Whitey, how ya doing?" Both Big Longo and Warren shouted as they passed his cell. They were out of sight before Whitey could answer.

"See you later Whitey," Johnny said as he dashed by.

After the last man had gone by, Whitey sat on his bunk, and reached for the top of the steel table that folded down from the wall. To occupy his time he began to tear a sheet of writing paper, along with some wrappers from Wings cigarettes into neat oblong strips. Out of the strips he began to construct a small picture frame. He was busy with his project and didn't hear someone approaching his cell until a shadow crossed his table. He looked up, standing in front of his cell was a black inmate.

"You breaking rules," the inmate said. "You not to be making picture frames."

Whitey's expression turned to a cold hostile stare, and he hissed at the man, "What the fuck business is it of yours what I do? Get out

177

from in front of my cell."

"I'm going to tell man—I'm going straight down and tell the Cell House officer."

The informer hurried down the tier. The moment he was gone Whitey tore up the unfinished frame, and flushed it down the toilet along with the unused strips of paper.

A few minutes later he heard footsteps coming down the tier; he sat motionless on his bunk waiting for the officer to appear. The officer stopped in front of his cell, and signaled to a guard at the control box.

"Open 252," he ordered. The door slid open. "All right Thompson out of there."

Whitey stepped out onto the tier and leaned his back against the rail. He watched the officer enter his cell, and immediately he began to pull the bed clothing apart, throwing the blankets, sheets, and pillow on the floor. In his haste he stepped on the bed clothes as he made a grab for Whitey's clean T-shirt, undershorts, and socks. These too were thrown to the floor along with a mirror, toothbrush, tooth powder, comb, shaving brush and tin cup.

In a surly voice Whitey shouted, "You forgot to throw my coat and towel on the floor!"

The officer stormed out of the cell making a grab for Whitey who quickly sidestepped.

"Stand still," the officer ordered, "I want to shake you down."

"If you want to shake me down just say so, don't make no sudden grabs at me."

Whitey turned around, and held his hands over his head while the guard shook him down.

Finding nothing the officer snarled, "Get into your hole."

Whitey stepped into his cell, and none too soon, for the guard at the control box deliberately pulled the bar with haste. The steel door slammed shut, barely missing his leg.

"You mother-fucker!" Whitey shouted.

If for some reason a guard had it in for a convict, it was not beyond him to try to jam the prisoner in the cell door. In this fashion, there have been a number of cases where a prisoner has been badly hurt. The guards always claim it was an accident, no one could prove otherwise.

When the guard had departed, Whitey began to straighten up his cell; as he went about tidying up, a madness was rising in him.

"That black snitching bastard," he growled out loud. "That son of a bitch, his days are numbered. He put the finger on the wrong man, he's a walking dead man."

Whitey sat down on his bunk, but sprung right back up, he was unable to sit still. He was building up steam, and began to pace back

178

and forth, and as he did so, he rolled a cigarette in an attempt to calm himself down.

He was still pacing the floor, and full of rage when the movie was over. Johnny returned and stopped in front of Whitey's cell. Whitey's, concentration was so deep toward the black man, that he didn't notice Johnny standing there.

"Hey Whitey, what are you beefing about, what's wrong?"

"Does something have to be wrong?" Whitey flared back at him.

"No nothing has to be wrong. But the look on your face tells me something's not right. You look like you're ready to take on a wildcat. What happened?"

Whitey told Johnny about the picture frame, and how the black informed on him; how the guard tore up his cell. He also told Johnny he was going make the black pay for it.

"If I were you Whitey I'd forget it, he isn't worth the time."

"Man I don't understand you Johnny, you're doing life for blowing some dude away, now you stand there telling me to forget about a snitch. I don't get it man—I just don't get it."

"That was different Whitey, that punk was out of his territory trying to move in on my rackets. I had no choice but to waste him."

"You wasted the bastard all right, now you're doing life for it. Seems to me you wasted yourself along with him."

"But that was different Whitey, you don't understand."

"The hell I don't. Tell me—if you had it to do over again, would you blow that dude away?"

"Damn right I would! No son of a bitch can move into my territory and get away with it! I'd blow that bastard away again—right now if I could."

"All right Johnny, you don't know it but you proved my point. The bastard was out of his territory when he stepped on my toes, I can't let him get away with it, you know that's true."

"Yeah I guess you're right Whitey. But I don't like to see you mess up. You only have five years left, forget that dude. Why not serve the time and get the hell out of here."

"Don't you think I want to?" Whitey was hot under the collar. "Course I want to get out, but let me tell you something, if I was getting out tomorrow morning and some fool stepped on my toes, I'd just have to give up my freedom."

"Look Whitey," Johnny spoke in a whisper, "I know how you feel pal, but give yourself time to think it over carefully. Then if you feel you must get that snitch—I guess you have to get him. Fate calls the play you know, all we can do is follow the script, so do what you have to do Whitey. I'll always back you up, that goes without saying."

"Thanks pal, that goes both ways."

After lock up the count bell sounded. Once count was cleared, the convicts made the trek to the Dining Room, and back again to their cells for the last standing count of the day. When this was done, an officer stopped in front of Whitey's cell.

"Here are two razor blades Thompson," the guard said as he placed them on the door ledge. "They have to last you until a week from tonight. Then you'll receive two new ones, but you must have the old blades lying right here on the bars in exchange. Do you understand?"

"Mind repeating that?" Whitey asked with a snicker.

The officer shrugged his shoulders and moved onto the next cell.

To pass the time, Whitey leafed through the library catalog until 9:30—lights out, so ending his first Saturday on Alcatraz Island.

CHAPTER 29.

Sunday on Alcatraz started with the 6:30 wake-up blast. On this morning for breakfast, the customary bacon and eggs were well received. After breakfast the inmates could go to the yard or attend the nine o'clock Mass.

Whitey remained in his cell and watched a dozen or so Catholic convicts trek past on their escorted march to the Chapel. At the North west end of the Cell House, the prisoners traveled through a gateway, up a flight of stairs to the Chapel, a large room of thirty by forty feet. At one end of the room there was a movie screen that had been rolled up revealing an altar. At the opposite end of the room was a projection booth. A guard stood by the door, and of course there was one in the gun gallery manned for the movie or church service. The guard was up at the second level of the cage where he kept a good watch on the convicts.

After church call, yards was sounded. Whitey decided to go out for some much needed air. It was a clear crisp day, and as he stood on the top step of the bleachers, the view of the Golden Gate was spectacular. In the yard the activity was much the same as the day before. A few inmates were jogging around, while other prisoners bounced about at handball. A softball game was in progress with big league intensity. In the south western end of the yard, a handful of convicts were pumping iron. A few cliques stood apart chattering amongst themselves; while seated at the card tables, bridge, chess and dominoes' experts were playing their hands.

For the best part of the morning there had been a soft breeze drifting in through the Golden Gate, but in a matter of seconds the complexion changed into a cold snappy wind, blowing in off the ocean. There was no weather like the weather on Alcatraz! There were only two seasons—good and bad, or summer and winter! Only at the end of September on into October, was the weather uniform—golden warm days, the sky picture blue. Winter and summer were variable—rain, wind or fog, on occasions a day of sunshine. The only difference between summer and winter was the absence of rain. But every day on schedule, the trade winds would whip through the

Gate, and on most days, especially in summer, they brought in a thick wet fog. July was one of the coldest months of the year, and as the winds stirred up. Whitey was happy to hear the yard recall.

The routine noon count had been made, and after lunch Whitey, along with Johnny, was exiting from the Dining Room. The Lieutenant was standing at the entrance inspecting each man as he passed. He beckoned Whitey over to one side.

"This guy is a nut," Whitey whispered to Johnny, "I wonder what the fool wants."

"Just be cool Whitey, don't blow it. I'll see you up on the tier."

"Thompson you're to get a hair cut," the Lieutenant ordered. "You're not allowed to have your hair more than an inch long."

"How about the hair on my balls, how long can that be?" Whitey asked sarcastically.

With a stern look the Lieutenant spoke sharply, "Thompson you keep forcing my hand, I'll have no alternative but to have you put in D Block."

"Hey I don't give a shit where you put me. Time is time no matter where I'm at."

"You receive no privileges in TU, no tobacco, no blankets during the day, no mattress, and no earphones. In other words Thompson, you receive nothing at all except two meals a day. Is that what you want?"

"Earphones? Hell I don't have any now."

"You don't? Well I'll have a pair up to your cell as soon as possible. But in the meantime, you come out of your cell right after count, go to the screen cage by A Block, an officer will be there with a barber to cut your hair."

"Damn Lieutenant, what about the movie? If I have to get a stinking hair cut, I'll miss the show."

"Sorry Thompson, you'll just have to miss it, do you understand?"

"Yeah, yeah, does a bear shit in the woods?"

Whitey returned to his cell, and none too soon for the guard had just pulled the bar. Whitey flopped on his bunk; he was so furious he didn't hear Johnny calling his name.

"Whitey, hey Whitey, what happened with the Lieutenant?"

"Ah the fucker wants me to get a hair cut."

"Why get uptight over a hair cut?"

"I'm not uptight over the haircut, I just wanted to go to the fucking movies that's why."

"The movie stinks Whitey, you're not missing anything. Besides you can come to the yard right after your hair cut."

"Fuck that windy yard!"

"Well I don't know what to tell you."

"Don't tell me nothing, you know all my life people have been

182

telling me what I can or can't do, I'm fed up with it, and you can bet your sweet ass no one is giving me a hair cut."

"Don't be crazy Whitey, how the hell are you going to get out of it?"

"Let me worry about that okay?"

The count bell sounded. As soon as the movie goers were gone, all doors opened.

"Yard call. Last call for yard call," a guard shouted.

Whitey's door opened with a bang, but he remained in his cell. Johnny appeared in front of his doorway.

"Come on Whitey, don't foul up, go get the hair cut over with."

"No, they're not cutting my fucking hair."

"Well there's nothing more I can say, I'm heading for the yard. I'll see you later."

Whitey did not reply; instead he reached up onto the shelf, and retrieved a razor blade. With his left hand he grabbed a handful of hair, and commenced to hack it off. He hacked repeatedly, and in his haste he cut the top of his head. He didn't realize what he had done until blood appeared running down his forehead. It didn't deter him, for he continued cutting until he had taken off all he could. Then he put the blade into a safety razor, and picked up the tin cup containing a bar of shaving soap. With brush and water, he whipped up a thick lather, and applied it to his scalp. He shaved off the remainder of his hair, stroke by stroke, until he was completely bald. He rinsed his head thoroughly, and dried it with his towel. It was then he discovered he was still bleeding. To stop the flow, he quickly placed a piece of toilet tissue on the superficial wound. It helped, or at least until the tissue became saturated with blood, and then it flowed freely again.

Whitey cussed as he scraped the bloody paper off his head. He placed another piece of tissue over the wound, and held it there. At that moment a guard who was approaching his cell, called out to an officer at the control box.

"Collins, Officer Collins open two-five-two."

He reached Whitey's cell just as the door opened, and looked in. Whitey was sitting on the toilet bowl holding his head over the sink.

"Come on Thompson, let's get a hair cut, come on. . . ." His face went white when he saw blood streaming down the side of Whitey's face and dripping off his chin! The guard spun on his heels and ran down the tier, shouting to his coworker to close 252.

"Lieutenant—Lieutenant, we got a man down!"

Accompanied by the Lieutenant, with the M.T.A. close on his heels, the guard rushed back to Whitey's cell.

When the door opened the M.T.A. was the first one into the cell. The first impression was a gruesome sight. Whitey was still sitting on the toilet bowl with blood trickling from his scalp, down over his

183

forehead, dripping off the bridge of his nose onto the floor. At a closer inspection his appearance was deceiving. The M.T.A. removed the toilet tissue from his scalp, and discovered a small superficial wound.

"It's no more than a scratch Lieutenant," the M.T.A. said as he cleaned the cut.

"Thompson, my patience with you is growing thin," the Lieutenant barked.

"It was an accident."

"Accident hell Thompson, I bet you did it on purpose."

"Hell no Lieutenant, if I wanted to cut myself, I would have slashed my throat!"

"Well one thing for certain, you definitely don't need a hair cut!"

"That's right," Whitey said sarcastically, "You bastards, you put a man in a cell, take away his rights, and don't even let him have control of his own hair. If I ever get out of prison, I'll let it grow down to my ass-hole, and no bastard will make me cut it off!"

"Okay, lock his door," the Lieutenant ordered.

"Hey, how about the goddamn earphones?" Whitey shouted.

The guard and the M.T.A. had already started to walk away. The Lieutenant stood there for a moment, and just before he left he said, "Thompson, do me a favor, next time you're going cut yourself, cut your throat instead!"

"If I do," Whitey called after him, "it won't be *my* throat."

A short time later a guard brought Whitey a set of earphones. In the wall of each cell there were two plug-ins for the earphones; one station for music, and the other for sports. These stations were censored, and they were never permitted to listen to a newscast.

That evening after the last standing count, an officer approached Whitey's cell.

"Thompson 1465, tomorrow morning at work call, you report to the Glove Shop detail that forms out in the yard."

He turned his attention to Johnny's cell and said, "House, you have been assigned to the Culinary Department. You will be awakened at 5:00 in the morning for work, but right after main line work call, you report to the Lieutenant's desk for a cell move to Broadway."

Johnny didn't like the moving part, but he knew he had to if he wanted to work in the kitchen.

"How about you Whitey, are you going to work in the Glove Shop?"

"Yeah I'm starting in the morning on 4th grade. It pays $20 a month, $240 a year. I wonder if they take out income tax and old age pension."

"I'm sure they do," Johnny laughed. "By the way Whitey, what happened to your hair?"

"Hey Johnny, go fuck a rolling donut!"

184

On Monday morning when work call sounded, Whitey came out of his cell and fell in behind the other prisoners. In a shuffling walk they traveled the length of the tier, and as they turned the corner toward the stairs, a guard was counting each convict as he passed. They continued down the stairs, across Times Square, through the electronic snitch box, and counted by another guard. The line of inmates made their way through the heavy steel doorway leading to the yard, and down the concrete steps to the first landing. There they were counted again before walking through the second metal detector, and counted once more as they exited. Down the last flight of steps to the yard where they were counted again.

"Hey Whitey," someone yelled.

He turned around just as Big Longo caught up to him. "How ya doing Whitey, where you going to work?"

"Glove Shop, where do they line up at, do you know?"

"Yeah," Longo replied. Pointing to the eastern side of the yard, "Over there—I'll catch you later."

Whitey continued across the yard to a group of men milling around. One of them was Chili who saw him approaching. He informed Whitey that he was assigned to the Glove Shop.

"That's great Chili, so am I. Which one of these yellow lines is for the Glove Shop."

There was a youthful-looking convict standing a few feet away who had overheard Whitey and Chili. He turned around to face them.

"If you guys are going to work in the Glove Shop," he said, "stay right where you are, this is where the Glove Shop crew forms it's line." Holding out his hand to Whitey he continued, "My name's Russell. What do you call yourself?"

Shaking his hand Whitey replied, "Name's Whitey, and this is Chili."

"Hel-lo, you Us-el," Chili said. Whitey explained to Russell that Chili didn't speak English very fluently, but enough to get by.

At that moment a whistle blew, and Russell informed them that it was the lineup signal. Two lines were formed, with fifteen men in a line. The Industry Officer, with clipboard in hand, walked along checking each man off the list. He stopped in front of Chili.

"Amando Silta?" He asked.

"Ho-kay, 1470," returned Chili.

The officer, with a smile on his face said, "Welcome to my crew."

Chili's face lit up as he answered, "Tank you, tank you sir."

The Industry Officer turned to Whitey, "Leon W. Thompson?"

"Fourteen-sixty-five," Whitey replied.

Smiling again the officer said, "Welcome to my crew."

Once the crews had been checked off, the list was turned over to the Lieutenant who was stationed at the Sally Port. Then a horn sounded, and the heavy steel door embedded in the wall was opened.

The Pallet Factory crew went through the Sally Port first, followed by the Brush Shop, and then the Glove Shop. The Lieutenant checked each inmate's name and number as he passed through.

Whitey followed the line of inmates through the Sally Port, and immediately descended a steep flight of steps carved in the cliff side. Midway down he had to wait his turn to pass through a small six by ten foot building. At the entrance of the structure he was detained by a guard, and after a moment's wait, the officer told him to move on through. It was then Whitey realized it was the third electronic metal detector. The small building had two doorways enabling the traffic to move through uninterrupted. At each outlet a guard was counting the prisoners as they walked in and out; while another officer operated the controls of the electronic box.

Immediately after exiting the building they descended another sheer flight of stairs. Halfway down, a path veered off to the right leading to the Tailor Shop. The Glove Shop crew continued straight down the treacherous steps to a roadway boarded by a double cyclone fence on the west side of the Island. There were armed guards in the gun towers, and on the walls watching them. And from the moment they emerged from the yard, descending the steep cliff side steps, until they reached the road and into the building, other eyes watched their progress—from the lofty gun tower back up the road, to the tower on the factory roof.

Upon entrance to the Glove Shop, the inmates were counted again as they filed past the Industry Officer standing at the doorway. In all, the convicts were counted ten times between the Cell House and the Shops.

The Glove Shop itself contained barred windows on either side running the length of the building. The windows on the east side had a tunnel-like cat-walk outside that ran the length of the building. Inside this cat-walk was an armed guard who kept his eye on the prisoners, and counted them on schedule, every fifteen minutes as they worked.

Whitey looked the shop over and was impressed with the many different types of sewing machines. On the east side of the shop there was an eight by thirty-foot cutting table. To one side of the table, standing like a miniature city, were large bolts of material.

Whitey was assigned to a machine at the far end of the shop. He liked this location because his back was protected by the wall, and he had clear vision of everyone in front of him. He felt paranoid if he knew anyone had the opportunity to come up from behind him.

Just a few feet to his right was Russell's machine, his job was closing gloves—sewing the top side to the bottom half; it took skill for this operation.

186

Whitey's job was comparatively easy, sewing leather tips on the palm side of the gloves. This was a new experience for him, and he rather enjoyed it—time flew.

A work day was scheduled for six hours, but seldom did they manage to get in five. There were many mornings the Bay would be in dense fog, and the inmates were not allowed out of their cells. On occasions the fog hung on until late in the afternoon, of course there would be no work call that day. This type of weather was not welcome, for the convicts would rather be at work than confined all day in a cell; though there were a few who didn't care either way.

The first morning on the job flew for Whitey. A buzzer sounded ending the first period of work; it was time to quit for lunch. The inmates secured their machines, and when this was accomplished they congregated at the shop entrance.

Whitey was lighting a cigarette when Chili and Russell came up beside him.

"Hey Whitey how'd the job go for you?" Russell inquired.

"Okay, it's something to do."

"How about you Chili, how did it go for you?"

"It go fine, me like job. Boss make me jan-tor, keep floor clean. I like push broom, no like work ma-chines, push broom ho-kay."

"What the hell is the hold up?" Whitey asked Russell. "What are we waiting for?"

"We're waiting for the Brush and Pallet crews to go by. Each week a different shop is first. We're last this week, but we'll be first next week."

Directly after the Pallet crew passed by, the Glove Shop officer unlocked and opened the door. Like a trail of ants the convicts made their trek down the road, up the cliff side steps, on the reverse trip back to the Cell House.

The line was moving at a snail's pace, and Whitey thought they would never make it to the Sally Port. Finally they arrived with Russell entering the yard first, followed by Chili and Whitey. Just inside the Sally Port were five guards shaking prisoners down at random.

The officers allowed Russell and Chili to pass, but one of them blocked Whitey's path.

"Strip," the guard ordered.

"Ah shit it's cold man are you crazy?"

"I said strip."

"Ain't this the shits?" Whitey sighed.

He commenced to take off his clothes, as he peeled off each garment he handed it to the guard who checked each item carefully before dropping it to the ground. The same procedure was repeated with his shoes and socks. The guard was deliberately taking his time while Whitey stood naked shivering in the chilly wind.

"Come on man, come on hurry up, I'm freezing my balls off!"

The guard paid no attention to Whitey's plea; he was in no hurry. Then with a sardonic smile he gave Whitey a degrading order to turn around and bend over spreading his buttocks. He was shivering uncontrollably as the cold wind penetrated his naked body.

This fucker is getting his jollies off, Whitey thought as he bent over.

The humiliating period was over, and with the completion of the shakedown he was told to put on his clothes.

Russell and Chili were walking slowly; Whitey dressed hurriedly, and rushed across the yard to catch up to them.

"Did you see them mother-fuckers? They made me strip. How often does that happen Russell?"

"Not too often, but then again it could happen this evening when we return from work, or tomorrow or the next day. The best thing to do is to go along with it, don't say a word if they shake you down again."

"What'd you mean don't say a word? I'm not going to stand bare-ass in that cold wind too many times!"

"That's just what they want you to do Whitey, they want you to blow up, then they'll continuously harass you. Just be quiet when they shake you down, after a while they hardly bother with you. Hell, it's been months since they made me strip."

The three convicts entered the Cell House, and as they did, Russell and Chili veered off toward C Block.

"See you at chow," Russell called to Whitey.

Whitey made no reply as he crossed Times Square on his way to B Block.

After the noon count cleared, the trek to the Dining Room began. As Whitey entered the Dining Hall, he spotted Johnny behind the Steam line dishing up potatoes.

"Whitey, hey Whitey how'd the job go?"

"It's a snap House. I'm doing a job that takes a hell of a lot of skill. I bet I earned at least thirty or forty cents this morning."

"No kidding, I can't wait to tell the kids down at the Malt Shop about your success. By the way my job's great, can't you see what I'm doing?"

"Yeah, I can see they don't trust you on the meat, or you wouldn't be passing out potatoes. Hey by the way what cell did you move into?"

"I moved to Broadway—cell 103."

"103—that should hold ya."

"Fuck you Whitey! I'll see you in the yard Saturday after showers,

188

okay?"

"Okay pal," Whitey said as the held out his tray, "Give me a dab of them pearlies."

With his tray filled, he made his way to a table and began to eat.

Whitey finished his meal; along with the other men at the table, he sat patiently waiting for the guard to give the up and out signal. At last he made the sign; the prisoners jumped up knocking the benches over in their haste to depart the Dining Room.

Standing at the entrance in civilian clothes, was Mr. Dollison, the man Whitey had seen on the dock on the day of his arrival. As he walked by Dollison smiled at him, but Whitey did not reciprocate. Standing next to Dollison was the Lieutenant—Lieutenant Ordway.

"How you doing Thompson?" He asked.

Whitey gave him a sharp cold look, and continued walking back to his cell.

Once count was clear, work call sounded, and the remainder of the day passed by uneventfully. That evening, just after lights out, Whitey was having his final cigarette before going to sleep. As he lay on his bunk, he began to think back on the events of the day. He was surprised when he realized he had gone all day long without getting into any type of trouble. Of course he got mad a number of times, but kept it to himself. No arguments, a perfect day with no trouble. *Damn, they should give me a parole!*

For the first time in years Whitey's spirits seemed to have picked up. It was because of his new job, it was his first day at work in a long time, and he enjoyed the challenge of running a machine. Working in the Glove Shop was better than being locked up in a cell all day. His feelings were riding high and he was in a cheerful mood. But it did not last, suddenly he flashed back to yesterday, to the picture frame, and the black man who had informed on him. It wasn't that easy to terminate someone on Alcatraz; security was tight with one guard to every three prisoners, so you really had to plan things carefully. It wasn't as if he saw the black man a dozen times a day; when he did see him it was by chance meeting, and that was the problem. He had to plan it so he would know ahead time just where the black man would be. It might take weeks, months, or even a year or more to set it up. But Whitey was a true convict with the patience of a cat, and he knew eventually he would even the score, the black man didn't know his days were numbered.

189

CHAPTER 30.

The first few weeks in the Glove Shop passed by swiftly, Whitey was developing speed and skill, and was proud of the job he was doing. As time wore on he was feeling much better about himself, and the people around him. Though now and then when he would think of the mistreatment he had endured; bitterness and resentment would return.

One Saturday morning toward the end of August, Whitey was out in the yard during recreation period. He was sitting on the top step of the bleachers, and had just finished rolling a cigarette, when Johnny greeted him.

"Hi Whitey, what're doing sitting up here all by yourself?"

"Just relaxing. What's wrong with you Johnny? Your voice sounds like you're mad at something."

"Yeah I am mad, it's this bully who works in the kitchen. He tries to push his weight around. He got in my face a while ago, so I had to punch the fucker out."

"How come the guard didn't see you?" Whitey asked.

"It happened in the Tray Room, the guard was out in the kitchen somewhere. He didn't hear or see a thing. You know there's a lot of noise in the Tray Room. You know the dude Whitey; you knew him at McNeil, he's that big Mexican they call Chino. If he's a friend of yours, you better tell him to get his act together or they'll be dressing him out in the Carpenter Shop."

"Hey, he's no friend of mine, I just know the guy, that's all. He's not a bad sort, I know he acts like a bully, but that's his way. When you get to know the guy he isn't all that bad."

"Hey I don't give a shit what kind of a guy he is, just do me a favor will you Whitey? Tell him to stay out of my face, or he's going to get hurt—I mean hurt."

"Sure Johnny I'll talk to him now. I see him over at the dominos tables."

Johnny headed toward the north end of the yard to watch a handball game in progress, while Whitey sauntered toward the dominoes' tables. Chino, with a smile on his face and a bruise on his chin, looked up from his game as Whitey approached.

190

"Whitey, how ya doing? You want to play some dominoes? You can take on the winner."

"No, I don't wanna play, I just want a word with you when your game is over."

"Come on Chino," one of the players said, "it's your turn to play."

"Hold your piss, punk, I'll play when I'm ready."

Having been acquainted with Chino for a number of years, Whitey had gotten to know him for what he was—a bully; a harmless bully, all his action was with his tongue! He loved to loud-talk people, and because of his size and strength, the moment he opened his mouth most people would back down. He never actually put his hands on anyone to physically shove them around. Whitey had warned him on occasions that one day his mouth would get him in trouble.

As for Johnny, Whitey really liked the big Texan, and felt he had enough of a problem with his life sentence without Chino giving him more problems.

Whitey didn't have anything against the big Mexican, but he was going to warn him to back off and to keep his mouth to himself if he wanted to stay healthy. Whitey knew Chino was no killer, but Johnny House was.

Whitey returned to his usual seat at the top of the bleachers, and was looking toward the Golden Gate Bridge when Chino came climbing up the steps, and took a seat next to him.

"I hear you got into it in the Tray Room this morning, is that right." Whitey asked.

Chino's face flushed, "Yeah that's right, the bastard hit me when I wasn't looking."

"Bullshit Chino, you saw the punch coming, you're so goddamn muscle-bound you couldn't duck in time. I don't give a shit if you can duck or not, but if you're going to keep shooting off your big mouth, then you better learn to duck. You're nothing but a bully."

Chino jumped to his feet, and stood looking down at Whitey in a threatening manner, "Just what the hell is on your mind? Spit it out Whitey."

Whitey was also getting mad, "Just sit down and shut up Chino. You don't scare me and you know it. Now just shut the fuck up and listen. We both know it was Johnny House you got into it with, right?"

Chino nodded his head.

"Look, Johnny is solid people, he's not the type of person you loud-talk or push around, because if you do, you are going to get hurt, and hurt bad."

"What do you mean?" Chino cut in, "who's strong enough to hurt me?"

"Just dummy up," Whitey bellowed back at him, "you know damn

191

well what I'm talking about. All I'm trying to tell you Chino is to cut out the wise remarks with your big mouth. I know you're a big strong guy, but that don't mean shit when someone slips up behind you and sticks one in your back, or pipes you over the head. You been pushing the wrong people, and you should know by now that when you start to bully someone in this joint, you better be able to back yourself up, or you gonna get yourself wasted. Your size and strength don't make you tough Chino, you've done enough time to know that. So I'm telling you for your own good to quit bullying people, especially Johnny House, or you may live to regret it."

Chino sat there a moment thinking over what Whitey had said; finally he stood up, and before he walked away he said, "Okay Whitey, thanks for the warning."

Chino left Whitey sitting there with his own thoughts. Shit, here I am telling Chino about screwing up, and that's what I've been doing all my life. Whitey's thoughts were interrupted when he noticed a black man sitting on the bottom steps of the bleachers. It was the inmate who had informed on him about the picture frame. Whitey was about to get up when someone called his name.

"Hey Whitey—Whitey." Moving along the top walkway was Archie. "Hey Whitey," he said again, "How come you're not down there playing ball?"

Shaking his head no, Whitey replied, "Not for me Arch—not for me. By the way, do you happen to know that dude's name?" Whitey pointed to the black prisoner sitting below, "That dude right there."

"Yeah sure, that's LeRoy Jackson, he lives over on Broadway, B Block, 105."

"Okay Arch, thanks a lot, I'll see ya later."

Whitey stood up and started down the steps leaving Archie behind. The black man heard him descending and looked around to see who it was. When Whitey reached the bottom step he leaped to the ground landing in front of LeRoy. He stood there a moment or so staring coldly at him.

"What you looking at?" LeRoy asked.

"What am I looking at? I'm looking at a black jive-ass-no-class-funny-style prick snitch son of a bitch! That's what I'm looking at."

"What's wrong with you man, what're you talking about?"

"You know what I'm talking about snitch."

"Look man, I should never of snitched you off, it won't happen again," LeRoy was pleading.

"That's right fucker, when the right time comes, they'll dress you out in the Carpenter Shop."

"What—what? Hey man, what you talking about?" LeRoy was trembling. "What you mean Carpenter Shop?"

"A pine box, you're gonna dress out in a pine box bastard. Your days are numbered."

Whitey nonchalantly retreated back to the top step and sat down. While he was sitting there, he could feel a cold bitterness returning to his body as he stared down at LeRoy. Out of the corner of his eye LeRoy watched Whitey sit down. The moment he did, LeRoy quickly jumped to his feet, and hastened across the yard to the dominoes' tables. There he sat down a few feet away from a guard who was standing near the tables.

Whitey watched his every move, as he did so he began to chuckle at the paradox; here he had taken the time to talk some sense into Chino, and at the same time in the back of his mind, he was setting up plans to murder a black man!

The recall horn interrupted his thoughts. Again like ants, the convicts formed a long line, and moved slowly to the Cell Blocks and their holes.

CHAPTER 31.

One morning several months later, Whitey was in the Glove Shop busy at his machine. He had just finished his fourth lot of gloves, and glanced up at the wall clock. It was 11:25—almost quitting time. He turned off the switch; picked up an oil can, and commenced lubricating. Every morning without fail he would oil and clean his machine in preparation for the afternoon's work. He had just finished wiping dust, oil, and lint off the motor, when Russell spoke to him.

"Whitey listen, this afternoon after lunch, don't come out of your cell for work call. We're going on strike for commissary, we want commissary just like all the other Federal prisons."

"Shit man, we'll never get commissary here and you know it Russell."

"We'll never get it if we don't try, I know that. But listen, by noon time everyone will get the word to stay in their cells. We're going on strike."

It was true, commissary was never allowed on Alcatraz. The convicts never had the luxury of buying cigarettes, candy, or toilet articles. The lack of grooming supplies caused the majority of prisoners to shave their heads clean. A great number of these men suffered dry scabby scalps, which was caused by continuous use of very harsh soap.

A convict would give anything for a decent bar of soap, toothpaste, or a bottle of shampoo. Items such as these helped a man to feel that he was still a human being. Taking away their freedom was one thing, and perhaps they deserved to be behind bars, but not permitting them to purchase such items, was like taking away their dignity, and their right to be human.

That afternoon during the lunch period the news of the strike was spread all over the Dining Room. The word was out.

As Whitey departed from the Dining Room, he thought he better stack up on tobacco. He went straight to the tobacco rack, and found only four sacks of Stud left; he quickly stuffed these into his pocket.

The prisoners were preparing for a long lock down. Whenever the tobacco rack became empty, you could be sure something was going

194

down. The guards could feel an uncertainty in the air; yet they were not sure what it could be. They knew something was wrong because it was so quiet, the prison had become a tomb. There was no noise whatsoever, no laughing, or the usual chatter amongst the convicts, tension was rising, you could hear a pin drop.

Whitey climbed the stairs of B Block, and as he walked around the corner of the tier, Big Longo was standing at the rail in front of his cell.

"Hi Whitey," Longo greeted. "I guess you got the word about the strike."

"Yeah I got the word, what'd you think I got all this tobacco for?" Whitey pointed to the sacks in his pocket.

"Say you know Whitey, I been meaning to ask you, why don't you try to get a cell at this end of the tier? It's better here, down where you're at you can't see nothing but the bars of A Block. At least down here you got a window and you can see the Berkeley coast line across the Bay."

"I might just do that Longo, let me know when there's an empty cell down this end. Well I gotta go now, I'm gonna go. . . ." He never finished what he was saying as Archie slapped him on the back.

"Hi Whitey, you ready for the lock down?"

"Sure am old man, I'm all ready for it."

"Lock up—lock up, get in your holes, lock up time," a guard shouted.

"I gotta go," Whitey said as he took off running down the tier. He made it back to his cell just in time to jump through the doorway as the steel barred door shut behind him. Once inside, he spun around and yell through the bars at the top of his lungs, "You mother-fucking screw, you fucking hack, jam that door up your ass!"

After getting that off his chest, he turned to his light bulb, carefully unscrewed it, thoroughly checked it over, screwed it back in, and then pulled the string turning on the light. One could never be too cautious while in prison.

During Whitey's years in prison, survival was the name of the game, each day was a challenge, and when night time rolled around, he knew he had survived another day. In order to succeed, a prisoner had to see all, but appear to see nothing. Keep his eyes open for anyone who may try to hurt him. Never let his guard down for one moment. If a fight breaks out, or if a man is about to be stabbed, or if any trouble occurs just keep on walking, and don't stop and stare. Go about your business as if nothing is happening. Always be on the alert, listen to everything that is going on around you, but keep your nose out of it. Don't start rumors; keep your mouth closed at all times on anything you might see or hear. Never hang a false jacket

195

on any man. (A false jacket is something that is not true), and it could get a person killed, it also could get yourself killed! The most important thing, never, under any circumstances, inform (snitch or rat) on anyone, and if you are lucky, you may make it through the day.

Whitey was cautious—extremely cautious, and each time he returned to his cell, he would reach up and unscrew the light bulb. After carefully inspecting it, and finding it untampered with, he would screw it back in the socket, then safely pull the cord. During the daytime when a prisoner is on his job assignment, the Cell House Officer may open his cell door a dozen or more times while letting non-working inmates in or out of their cells. When the guard pulls the bar, all doors open and it is easy for someone to step into another man's cell. Then it would only take him a second to remove the light bulb, screw a different one into the socket, and then quickly be out of the cell before the door closes. The tiers were very long and the guard usually did not pay attention to who was going in or out of what cell. The culprit would take the good bulb, and replace it into the light socket of his own cell. The bulb he left in the other person's cell was all set to explode over its victim when the light string was pulled.

To prepare such a light bulb, all one had to do was to take a paper clip, and work the end of it into the solder on the contact end of a bulb. Then with his fingers he turns the paper clip in a drill-like fashion until he has made a minute hole to the inside of the bulb. Next he fills the light bulb with lighter fluid, turpentine, paint thinner, or any other explosive liquids he can obtain. When the unsuspecting inmate pulls the string, the light bulb will explode overhead, showering the victim with flaming fluid. Before the guard, or guards realize what has happened, the inmate would have been badly burned, and sometimes fatally.

On returning to his cell, to play it safe, Whitey always checked his light bulb. On numerous occasions, before he left his cell for work, he would replace his own light bulb with an explosive one! Whitey was not only cautious about the light bulb, he was cautious about anything that may have been planted in his cell, he would give it a thorough search for weapons or contraband.

When evening came, and the last standing count of the day had been made, and every prisoner was locked up in their cells then you could relax somewhat until the next morning's dawn. With each new day, the name of the game was survival. You had to stay on your toes and if you let your guard down for only a moment, it might be your last.

One thing a man learns while serving time; you never ask another prisoner what his crime is. If he wants to tell you, fine, that's his

196

prerogative, but you never ask.

Whitey had served time with many men and known quite a few of them personally; but the majority of them, he didn't know what their crimes were, he never asked, and could care less. He knew men in prison from all walks of life. Some were big time racketeers and gangsters who came up from the streets. He also knew men who came from well-to-do families. Some were doctors, dentists, airline pilots, and many other professional men. Most of them were outcast people like Whitey, who came from the wrong side of the tracks. There were hoboes, tramps, and even winos from skid row, but all of them were human beings, and had one thing in common—they were victims of the times.

In prison, it is not unusual to have an enemy or two. Whitey had a few enemies during his prison years, but they never worried him as he knew how to take care of them. It was the unknown enemies you had to watch out for—the nuts, quacks, and loonies, who for no apparent reason, except that they are crazy, strike without warning. You had to live day to day with your back to the wall, or have a good friend behind you. Whitey learned long ago, to always know who the people are around you, and be careful whom you trust.

Staring is a no-no, and one thing a prisoner should never do while incarcerated, is stare at anyone. Numerous incidents have occurred behind one inmate staring at another. Men have been stabbed, while others have had their heads bashed in who didn't even realize they had been staring. One case in particular happened in the dining room during lunch time. An inmate was seated at a table eating, and he had his eyes on a culinary worker who was the coffee-pourer. The culinary worker noticed this inmate staring at him while he was pouring coffee. Suddenly, without a word of warning he walked over to the staring man, and emptied five gallons of boiling hot coffee right over his head! The coffee man was taken straight to Segregation, while the other prisoner was rushed to the hospital. He was treated for shock and second and third degree burns. His face was disfigured for life, and he suffered from loss of hair. He had learned a lesson the hard way—convicts don't stare.

The majority of people don't like being stared at. In most cases when a person sees someone staring at them, they merely turn their heads the other way. This is not so in prison, for most convicts are different from ordinary people. Not only does he get uptight when he catches someone looking at him, he may be paranoid, and become extremely dangerous. It seems that the most common place for staring, is in the dining hall. For some reason or other people like to watch others consume their food. In society this is considered rude, nothing more, or nothing less. But in prison, it is not only rude, it is hazardous. When a prisoner is eating, the only way to play safe is for

197

the inmate to keep his eyes on his own food. When he is finished eating, he should just sit there and stare at his empty food tray. Also if he is talking to someone seated at the same table, he should always look directly at the person he is speaking to; never let his eyes wander about, someone might think he is talking about him, and that's when trouble may start.

The bell sounded; Whitey took his place at the front of his cell. As he stood there he could hear the officers scurrying around the tiers making their head count. When a guard reached the end of the tier, he would yell his count down to the Lieutenant. Then the Lieutenant would telephone it into the Armorer, who would send a direct teletype report to the Federal Bureau of Prisons in Washington, D.C. If the count report was a minute late, the wire would get hot from the Bureau wanting to know why the delay. If no report was sent in, or if the wire had gone dead, the Bureau would immediately know that something was wrong on Alcatraz, and the Coast Guard and the Marines were notified.

On this particular day the noon count cleared, followed by work call, and immediately after the bell sounded, the cell doors opened with their usual noise. What followed next was not normal, for there was no movement of feet. There was absolute quiet in B and C Blocks, it was a frightening quietness with an eerie feeling in the air. Through open windows the silence was broken occasionally by the sound of squawking sea gulls protesting in the unique way they complain. Then silence again, no movementit was dead quiet except for the birds.

A guard shouted, "Work call—work call, work call."

Again no movement—just silence.

Once more a guard shouted, "Work call. Those of you who want to work, come out *now*."

Still no movement—silence reigned.

A guard appeared in front of Whitey's cell, "Last chance to come out Thompson."

Whitey just sat there on his bunk staring at the ceiling as if he had heard nothing. But he was listening, his ears were trained on any movement of convicts coming out of their cells. He heard no movement—not a whisper of a sound, like the lull before the storm.

Suddenly the silence was broken by a loud commanding voice of the Lieutenant, "Lock 'er dow—lock 'er down!"

The guards obeyed, and closed all cell doors—Alcatraz was locked down tight as a drum.

Whitey remained sitting on his bunk with his ear cocked, listening. When you have been in prison long enough, you become familiar with every sound, you know exactly what is going on in the Cell House without actually seeing it.

Now and again a single cell door could be heard opening. Then a scuffle could be heard as a number of guards dragged off a prisoner and worked him over before locking him up in TU. The guards, to justify their act, would tag the convict as an agitator of the strike, but in most cases this was not true.

Up to now, Whitey Thompson had not been in any serious trouble on Alcatraz, but with his previous record he knew Custody would be coming after him soon. This sort of thing wasn't new to him; for in past years he had been dragged out of his cell on numerous occasions.

If they did come after Whitey, he felt they wouldn't be getting a cherry, and they wouldn't get him out of his cell without a fight. He reached on the shelf for a pair of stockings, and inserted one of the socks inside the other, then he dropped in a bar of soap. This made a handy weapon to be used like a blackjack.

Whitey thought he heard movement on the tier, and quickly stuck his mirror through the bars, and glanced along the runway. Mid way down the tier he saw a guard talking to an unseen prisoner.

Suddenly the guard shouted to a coworker on the control box, "Open 240."

The single door clanged open, and it could be heard throughout the Cell House. Through his mirror Whitey saw another guard hurry along the tier ready to assist his coworker. Voices could be heard.

"Okay Wilson, why didn't you come out for work call?"

"Fuck work," Wilson exclaimed, "no commissary no work."

From the view in his mirror, Whitey saw the two guards disappear into Wilson's cell, a shuffle and shouting could be heard, and a cry from Wilson, "You bastards, you sons of . . ." The cry was cut off by a dull thud, like the sound of a ball bat hitting a sack of potatoes! A moment later the unconscious victim was dragged out of his cell. Whitey watched the guards carry Wilson down the runway, and vanish around the corner of B Block.

Whitey sat down on his bunk just as an officer walked up to his door. The guard just stood there looking in his cell. Whitey was con-wise and knew that the cat and mouse game had just begun. He knew better than to say anything, so he remained silent, merely sitting there waiting for the officer to speak first. He was well aware of the guards, and what they would do if he spoke out of turn, or said the wrong thing. He also knew that if his door started to open, he would grab his sock-weapon from under his pillow and commence swinging.

Finally the guard spoke, "Why didn't you come out for work call Thompson?"

A few tense moments elapsed, Whitey knew he had to come up

with the right answer or they would snatch him out of his cell.

"I'm a convict," Whitey replied.

"Just what the hell do you mean by that?" The guard was angry. "Are you trying to get smart with me?"

"No, I told you I was a convict, and that's what I am. When the cons in this joint don't work, then I don't work. When they work, then I work."

"Is that the reason you didn't come out for work, because the other men didn't?" The guard asked cunningly.

"That's right, when they work, I work, that's it."

The officer stood there momentarily glaring at him; then without another word he moved onto the next cell. As he worked his way down the tier, he asked each inmate a similar question, and received much the same answer.

If Whitey had come up with the wrong answer and told the officer that he was on strike, he would have been in trouble. Simply to mention the word *strike* was all the guard wanted to hear, and he would have tagged him as an agitator or ringleader.

To pass time Whitey had half dozen library books to read. Or if he wished he could just simply lie on his bunk, and for entertainment, count the steel bars across the way in the deserted A Block! He had the makings for cigarettes; a pipe and pipe tobacco on the shelf, along with nine books of matches, and plenty of rolling paper.

He decided to roll a cigarette, and while doing so, he heard the lonesome sound of a cargo ship's horn as the huge vessel slipped its way across the Bay. It was heading westward toward the Golden Gate, and the high seas. It reminded Whitey of his Navy days. He would feel depressed whenever he heard the lonely sound of a ship's horn carried in on the ocean breeze.

"Thompson," a voice called, "do you want to go to chow? If so come out now."

Whitey jumped off his bunk, dashed out of his cell, and headed down the tier. Except for the sound of feet, there was no other noise, the prison was quiet.

Along the Flats of Michigan Avenue there was a guard posted every ten feet. The column of prisoners made a turn at the end of the tier, and started down the steel steps to Time Square. Up on the gallery there were five armed guards watching the convicts every move; ordinarily, there was one guard on duty in the gun gallery.

The line of inmates slowly made their way across Times Square, and before entering the Dining Room they were compelled to go through the metal detector. Once in the Mess Hall, the inmates formed a line in front of the steam tables. Whitey stood waiting; when his turn came, he picked up a tray and fell in behind the last man. The silence was deafening; when someone spoke, it was in a hushed whisper that sounded like someone was shouting. The outside gallery had armed guards standing the length of it—they were waiting for an inmate to make a wrong move.

Instead of convict kitchen workers, there were guards serving at the steam tables. Whitey moved along slowly, and as the food was placed on his tray he looked toward the kitchen, but saw no inmates working there—just officers preparing food. The Culinary convicts were also on strike. This would be the prisoners last hot meal for some time to come.

Whitey sat down at a table with the other men. There were ten prisoners at one table, and five at the other, a total of fifteen men being fed at a time—only half a tier. They ate in silence, and when they were finished with their meal, a guard gave the signal, they came to their feet at once. In single file, they marched out of the Dining Room, through the metal detector and back to their cells.

As soon as they were locked up, fifteen more convicts were released, until the whole population had been fed.

After the final count of the day, an eerie silence hung over Alcatraz. Absolutely nothing was moving, it was like the inside of a tomb. Usually one could see or hear a fly fluttering around, or a mouse sneaking about for a crumb, but not even the dust could settle down, it seemed to be suspended in midair, causing the air to look like dingy, yellow fog, thick and unmoving. If it were not for the musical surf splashing against the rocks, or an occasional sound of a toilet being flushed, and now and then, the lonely blast of a ship's foghorn, one could truly believe he was in a tomb of the dead.

CHAPTER 32.

Six A.M. lights on, the rise and shine routine started out like any other morning, with grumbling grunts of grouchy men as they brushed "winks" out of their eyes. The cussing and yelling, the sound of running water, and the flushing of toilets; this was the morning ritual that started off a new day.

On this morning Whitey did not respond to the rise and shine horn, he stayed in bed until the count alarm sounded. He casually got out of bed, and moved to the front of his cell—not a moment too soon as the guard charged by making his count. Shortly after this, the all clear sounded. Whitey washed and slowly dressed as he was in no hurry; with the strike on where could he go?

With the new morning, Alcatraz came alive, men were shouting from one cell to another.

"Hey Pete, you awake numb-head?"

"No, I'm still asleep stupid!"

"Kiss my ass Pete, you mother-fucker!"

"Yeah I'll kiss it, I'll even marry it and learn to love it, and raise rattlesnakes!"

"Hey Joe—Joe, what've you got to read?" Another voice called.

"Bob, send down your string so I can tie this tobacco on it."

"Art, hey Art, you got any extra toilet paper? I'm all out."

"Tough shit man, use your finger!"

"Okay Art, wait until you want something, you bastard."

The yelling was getting in gear now—the new day had begun, but there would be no breakfast served in the Dining Room this morning.

Whitey went about making his bed and tidying up his cell. He had just finished when he heard a sliding sound coming from the tier, it sounded as if someone was dragging a heavy object along the floor. With his mirror held out he glanced down the tier, and at the far end he saw two guards. One was dragging a huge cardboard box full of sandwiches, while the other guard was passing them out to the inmates.

"Ah, at last, here comes our steak and eggs!" Whitey exclaimed aloud, and pulled in his spy-mirror.

202

A few minutes elapsed before the guards appeared in front of his cell. One of the officers placed two sandwiches on the bars. Each one was wrapped separately in wax paper. Whitey opened one and found it to be peanut butter between two slices of stale bread. He opened the second one and discovered it to be the same—peanut butter. Instead of eating the sandwiches, he re-wrapped them and placed them on the small table. He looked at them in disgust. He started to reach in his shirt pocket for his cigarette makings, when he heard a slapping sound, then another, and another. Again he held out his mirror, this time to investigate the mysterious noise. He had a clear vision of the runway, but couldn't see anything amiss. Suddenly, from a cell mid way down the tier, a missile shot out over the runway rail, falling to the main floor below, and hitting with a slap. Another one flew out, and further along the tier, more missiles began to sail over the rail—another and another! The sound of slaps were coming from the numerous peanut butter sandwiches hitting the cement floor! They came flying off the tiers like a rain of bombs falling from an air raid sortie over Berlin during WW II!

Again Whitey reached into his shirt pocket for the makings, and began to construct a cigarette. The Cell House was hitting a new pitch with a mixture of diversified sounds, and above it all Whitey heard someone yell.

"Hey Gus did you throw your sandwiches out?"

"Yeah man, I threw them off the tier."

"I don't believe you Gus, you son of a bitch you ate them!"

"Hey no kidding," Gus yelled back, "I threw them off the tier, look down on the Flat, you can see them laying there."

"How the hells do you expect me to know what ones are yours, they all look alike."

Sandwiches were lying all over the place, like an aftermath of a ticker-tape parade.

A loud voice started to cheer the staff, another voice joined in, and soon there was a chorus of convicts shouting.

"Three cheers for J.V. Bennett. Shit—shit—shit!"

"Three cheers for Warden Madigan. Shit—shit—shit!"

"Three cheers for Lieutenant Ordway. Shit—shit—shit!"

"Three cheers for Blackwell. Shit—shit—shit!"

So it went on until they had cussed out every staff member from Director of Prisons, to the Warden of Alcatraz, on down to the lowest man on the totem pole—the guard!

The days were passing by slowly; each one seemed an eternity. On the fourth day of the strike, Whitey broke down and ate one of the growing pile of sandwiches. Three days later he ate one more, and started to unwrap a third, when all of a sudden he yelled, "Fuck it!," and one at a time he threw forty-two peanut butter sandwiches off the tier! *Slap-slap-slap!* He was to eat two more sandwiches before the strike came to an end.

During the past eighteen days of the strike, a small number of inmates were rounded up and taken to TU as ringleaders, though it was never substantially proven. While the strike was in full progress, there were seventeen prisoners in TU who sliced their Achilles tendons. Most of these men slashed just the one tendon on their heel, and had to hop on one leg while a guard unlocked and relocked the doors on the painful trip to the hospital. A few convicts that had slashed the tendons on both heels, were compelled to drag themselves to the hospital for treatment. There they were sutured; their legs put in casts, and returned to TU. No one would inform how the razor blades got into TU. A number of convicts were beaten mercilessly in an endeavor to make them tell where the blades had come from—no one talked.

On the evening before the strike ended, convicts passed the word from cell to cell that all good-time would be forfeited. Whitey was lying on his bunk enjoying a cigarette, when he heard someone call his cell number.

"Hey two-five-two, hey two-five-two, are you there?"

"Yeah I'm here Pete, where the hell did ya think I'd be?"

"Look Whitey," Pete called back, "pass the word along that the strike is over. We got the word that all good-time would be forfeited if we didn't end the strike. We don't want the old-timers to lose their good-time. So pass the word along that the strike has ended."

"Yeah, I figured that would happen. Okay I'll pass the word."

"Hey Whitey—hey Whitey," Pete called again, "you know Big Longo, right? Well he sends word to you that the cell next to him, B-204 is going to be empty if you want to move down to his end of the tier."

"Yeah sure, send word to him, first chance I get I'll put in for a cell move."

Whitey lay back down on his bunk and thought to himself, good-time, hell I don't have any to lose, they snatched all mine at McNeil.

There were a few old-timers who might one day go free, but had their good-time been forfeited, they would never make it out—so the strike ended. It was all to no avail, as the prisoners of Alcatraz never did receive commissary. Whitey was teed off the way it had ended; nothing was gained by it, nothing except starving for eighteen days. The instigators of the strike should have known that the officials would never agree to commissary. So the convicts lost—but had they? Perhaps not, maybe all they really wanted was to break the monotony of the daily routine.

The following morning commenced as if there had never been a strike. Up at 6:30 A.M., wash up, make your bed, stand up for count, and make the trek to the Dining Room.

When Whitey's cell door slid open, he walked onto the tier, and looked over the rail down to the Flats. There, lying everywhere, were piles and piles of stale sandwiches; the rats and mice had plenty to eat; it must have been like Thanksgiving to them! Whitey fell in behind the line of men, and shuffled along the tier, down the stairs to Times Square. As he walked toward the Dining Room, he glanced up Broadway. The whole length of the corridor was covered with trash, and thousands of stale sandwiches were lying all over as far as the eye could see!

"Boy, if Shorty McCoy is still the Cell House janitor, he has one hell of a cleaning up job," Whitey said out loud.

The column of convicts marched into the Dining Room where they greeted each other like long-lost friends. Everyone was trying to talk at once. Whitey couldn't hear what Johnny House was saying to him from behind the kitchen gate. All he could do was wave hello to him.

After breakfast, the prisoners returned to their cells to await work call. When count had cleared the cell doors slid wide open with the usual slam bangs, and the long line of prisoners made their way to the yard where they stood around chattering while waiting for the guard's signal to line up in their respective spots.

CHAPTER 33.

The monotony of the daily routine was again in play. The blast of the wake up horn at 6:30 A.M. Twenty minutes until head count, you wash up, brush your teeth, put on your blue-gray shirt and trousers, heavy shoes and socks. You make your bed, tidy up your cell, then stand up to the bars. After the stand up count, you hear the Cell House Officer shout.

"Let go outside B."

Fifteen cell doors slide open, you step out, march along the tier, descend the steel stairway, and into the Dining Room. You file past the steam table. Your food is served to you by convicts—the morning menu calls for sweet rolls, dry cereal, milk, toast, butter, and coffee, and twenty minutes to eat. At the guard's command you stand up, you turn, you check in your flatware, march out, up the stairway along the tier, into your cell. Another count, then work call.

"Work call—work call. Let go B."

Cell doors open, you march along the tier, down the stairs, through a metal detector into the yard, you stand on a yellow line according to your shop.

The Lieutenant calls, "Brush Shop, Glove Shop, Clothing Shop, Pallet Shop."

You are checked off as you go through the Sally Port and down the cliff side steps to the first landing. Through another metal detector and down another flight of steps and along the road to the shops.

At 11:30 A.M. you come back up the road, back up the stairs, through the yard, up the steel steps, along the tier, and back into your cell for another head count.

The Lieutenant's command, "Let go outside B."

You come out of your cell, go along the tier, down the stairs, into the Dining Room, eat, and march back to your cell for another count. This is followed by work call; you walk along the tier, descend the stairs, back through the metal detector, into the yard and stand on the painted yellow line. File through the gate, down the flight of stairs, along the road back to the shops.

At 4:30 P.M. you return up the road, back up the flight of stairs, through the snitch box, cross the yard, back up the stairway, along the tier, into your cell, and another head count.

The Cell House Officer's command, "Chow call." You file into the Dining Room, eat, stand, turn, march back to your cell. The door shuts with a slam, at 9:30 P.M. your lights go out, night time, you stay in your cell for thirteen hours.

At 6:30 A.M. the blast of the rise and shine horn, and another day has begun, or has it? Maybe it is still yesterday, or yet—maybe it's tomorrow. What difference does it make? All days are the same on Alcatraz. An hour is a day, a day is a week, a week is a month, and a month is a year, and your prison term seems endless. Prisoners can slowly go insane under the exquisite torture of routine. Life on the Rock is so monotonous you feel like bucking the rules just to break the monotony of the routine. You feel like charging out of your cell when the door opens, and take a nose-dive off the tier. Some men have done this very thing.

The strike had been a break in their daily living, but everything the prisoners did, or didn't do, seemed to take on a routine within a routine.

"Yard call—yard call."

It was the first Sunday after the strike ended, and Whitey could not escape the confines of his cell fast enough. He pushed his way along the tier, shoving a few men aside who were in front of him, and hurried past. A few con-wise men who saw Whitey coming, understood his urgency, and stepped aside, giving him room as he went out the door. The cool air of the ocean breeze was welcomed as he inhaled deeply. He made his way up to his favorite seat at the top of the bleachers, and as he sat down, he was panting and gasping for air like a man who had just come off a twenty-mile run. His body was trembling and shaking as if in great pain, his lungs felt as though they would burst. Calm down Whitey, he told himself, it's all in your mind, just calm down, breathe deeply—breathe slowly. That's it—just relax, and breathe deeply.

Claustrophobia—prison cells have caused many a man to experience this mental illness. Claustrophobia gave Whitey the feeling of a noose around his neck, that was tightening slowly, until his throat began to burn, and his eyes bulged; his brains seem to fry as his body screamed with excruciating pain.

During his first month on McNeil Island, Whitey experienced his first sign of claustrophobia, but he would not allow it to get out of hand. He had a strong mind in such matters, and he felt it was a case of mind over matter. His first time in the dark Segregation Hole at McNeil Island, he had a number of bouts with claustrophobia, but managed to get it under control with sheer willpower and positive thinking. But he had no control over his mind while asleep. It was during his sleep when he had a few terrifying bouts with claustrophobia. He would wake up clutching his throat gasping for oxygen. But once awake, with his quick thinking, he would get it under control. It's all in your mind he would tell himself, breathe deeply—relax.

He would conquer his claustrophobia with positive thinking, but on this particular Sunday, he could not get it under control until he was out of his cell and into the fresh air. His breathing was normal now, and as he sat there, he wondered if perhaps he was going crazy—stir crazy.

A voice interrupted his thoughts, "Hi Whitey, I seen you sitting here. I want to tell you that there's an empty cell on the third tier just over me, cell 304."

"B-304? I thought it was 204."

"No it's 304 Whitey, those fools told you the wrong number. The guy in 204 next to me is transferring back to Atlanta, but I don't know when. In the meantime why don't you take 304?"

"Okay Longo, thanks a lot I appreciate it, I'll put in a cop out (request), thanks."

The following Saturday on his way to shower and clothing exchange, the Cell House Officer spoke to Whitey.

"Thompson, right after yard call, you are to move into cell B-304."

When yard call sounded, Whitey was in his cell with his gear ready to move.

You never have much property until it comes time to move, and then you realize how much stuff you have accumulated. He would have to make two trips. The distance to his new cell was not that far, but to make a move like that sometimes took a half hour to an hour or even longer while waiting for a guard to unlock the doors. First you have to wait until the door of the cell you are moving out of is unlocked. Then you carry your belongings to the cell you are moving

208

into, and of course the chances are you'll find the door locked! Again you stand and wait, and wait, you never know how long. If you have to go back to your previous cell for things you could not carry on your first trip, you will find it locked also, and you must wait again. Prison is a long waiting game, no matter what you do, you have to learn to be patient.

Whitey was lucky this morning; Longo was standing outside his cell.

The guard on the control box called to Whitey, "Let's go Thompson, Longo is going to give you a hand with your things, so make it snappy."

Longo pitched right in and grabbed hold of the mattress and folded it in half along with the rest of the bed clothing. While Whitey gathered up the remainder of his things.

B-304 was painted a light blue, the atmosphere seemed pleasant in comparison to his previous cell; this was contributed to the natural light from the windows in the outer wall. The officer pulled the bar, and Longo dropped the mattress and bed clothes on the bunk.

"I'll see you in the yard," he said as he started to leave.

Whitey quickly put his belongings on the bunk, and caught up to Longo. Together they walked out to the yard. Longo went straight to the iron pile to lift weights.

After leaving Longo, he edged his way around the yard, stopping once to talk to Archie and Mondoza, who were engrossed in a checkers game. While he was watching the game Johnny House walked up to him.

"What's new Whitey?" Johnny asked as they shook hands.

"Same old thing, how's it going with you and Chino?"

"Your talk did some good. He don't screw with me anymore. I'll see ya later Whitey"

"Okay House," Whitey said as he turned toward the bleachers. He glanced across the yard and saw LeRoy Jackson talking to the yard officer. Whitey sauntered along to the bleachers, and at the same time he kept his eye on LeRoy who had seen him approaching. When he got within twenty feet of Jackson and the guard, Whitey stopped, took the makings out of his shirt pocket. He began to roll a cigarette while keeping his prey under surveillance. Just as he was lighting up, the guard started toward the dominoes' tables, leaving LeRoy sitting alone on the step.

"Snitching someone off LeRoy?"

209

Whitey's voice startled him "What you want man? Why you sneak up on me?"

"That's the only way to get near a rat—sneak up on 'em!"

"What you want anyway? You stay away, you hear?"

"What do I want LeRoy? I want to know how tall you are, and how much you weigh."

"What for you ask that?"

"I need your measurements," Whitey replied coldly.

"Why, why for you need my measurements?"

"To send to the Carpenter Shop fool, they need to know the size for your pine box."

LeRoy's eyes bulged, and he jumped to his feet. He stood there for a moment wide eyed and trembling; then, with short backward steps, he slowly retreated. Whitey moved forward matching him step for step. LeRoy was frightened and as he stepped backwards he tripped over his own feet, landing on his buttocks.

Whitey, out of the corner of his eye saw the yard officer walking toward them. He stood his ground while LeRoy scrambled to his feet. The guard was just a few feet away when he said, "What happened LeRoy? What were you doing on the ground?"

Staring at Whitey LeRoy hesitated a second, then he replied, "I tripped and fell down."

"You better watch where you're walking," the guard told him, and turned and left.

Whitey moved a step nearer to LeRoy, "That goes for me too LeRoy, from now on you better watch where you walk; time is running out!" Not waiting for a reply he walked away.

Yes, time was running out for LeRoy; Whitey had it all set up, a week from Sunday.

The following afternoon, Monday after lunch, Whitey had returned to his cell, and was waiting for count, when the Cell House Officer appeared in front of his door.

"Leon Thompson," the officer said, when work call sounds I want you to remain in your cell, the Classification Counselor wants to talk to you."

After count cleared, work call sounded. Whitey remained in his cell as ordered, and in a few minutes the Classification Officer came by.

The officer held a clipboard in his hand, and was leafing through some papers.

"According to our records Thompson, you were acquainted with a Rose Orth."

Whitey was taken aback; he was totally surprised at the mention of her name.

"I'm sorry Thompson, I have some bad news, I don't exactly know how to approach you with it."

"It's about Rose, you're trying to tell me she's dead," Whitey finished for him.

"I'm afraid so, you see I received notice she was involved in a motorcycle accident."

Whitey took out the makings and started to roll a cigarette; his hands were shaking, and he spilled half the tobacco. Angrily he crushed the unfinished cigarette between his fingers, and slammed it to the floor.

"Are you going to be all right?" the officer asked.

"Yeah sure. Just get the hell out of here."

"I'm sorry Thompson, I truly am." The officer turned and walked away, leaving Whitey alone with his grief.

He made another attempt at rolling a cigarette, and once this was accomplished he inhaled a deep drag and began to pace back and forth in his cell. He was endeavoring to hold himself together, and was thankful no one could see the tears.

Slowly the week went by, and Whitey's grief developed into a bitter mood. There was nothing he could do about Rose's death, and no one realized this more than him. There was no person anyone could blame for the accident, except Rose herself, but he felt if he had never met her she would be alive today. He was so angry with himself he wanted to strike out at something or someone, and the more he thought about it, the more he wanted to take it out on LeRoy. He pushed everything out of his mind except the black man, and how he was going to kill him. Whitey found out that LeRoy never went to the yard on Sunday afternoons; he always remained in his cell. With the help of a fellow inmate, Whitey obtained a quart bottle of turpentine.

This coming Sunday afternoon during yard recall when the main population was returning from the yard there is always some confusion in the Cell House. Inmates standing or walking about the tiers waiting for the guard to pull the lock up bar. During this period Whitey could pull out the bottle of turpentine, smash it inside LeRoy's cell, and throw a lighted match, engulfing LeRoy in flames.

On Saturday morning Whitey was on his way down to the basement for the usual shower and clothing exchange. The guard held up the line a moment to the basement stairs, and Whitey was surprised to see blacks coming up. Ordinarily blacks were never permitted in the shower room at the same time as whites. An officer had jumped the gun; he had released some whites while there were still blacks in the shower and clothing area.

Finally, Whitey went down to the basement room and found it in the same confusion it was always in on shower days. The noise of running water and the prisoners yelling back and forth with the blanket of steam overhead engulfing the bathers.

Whitey walked around to the dirty clothes bin and disposed of his laundry, he picked up a clean towel off the rack, and just as he turned to the showers he heard it! It was a sharp pop-slap sound, and precisely at the same time of the pop-slap, he heard a loud abrupt grunt. There was no mistaking the sound; Whitey was familiar with it. He knew someone had just gotten it—stabbed! He continued to walk toward the showers as if nothing had occurred, and as he did so, he let his eyes drift to the victim. Under the spray and steam of a shower lay a black man with a knife protruding from his spine. Whitey could not get a good look at the man on the floor, but he could see blood running by his feet, and for a moment he watched it mixing with the water before it swirled down the drain.

It was unbelievable how quiet the shower room became immediately after the stabbing; except for the running of water, there was absolutely no noise whatsoever. There were five guards on the scene, two of them milling about the fallen man.

As Whitey walked over to an empty shower he was able to get a good look at the man on the floor—it was LeRoy Jackson. To the left of the victim two guards had a small blond-headed convict up against the wall. A moment later the guards turned him toward the stairs, they were taking him to TU. Whitey didn't know the inmate, but he learned later that his name was Jerry. He was accused of the stabbing.

Whitey took his place under the showerhead, and began soaking himself just as the M.T.A. arrived dashing to the victim's side. The Medical Technical Assistant shouted at the guards.

"Don't anyone touch the knife."

With the shower water flowing over him, Whitey stood there observing the scene, and to himself he was laughing at the M.T.A.. Look at the fool running around giving orders as if he knew what he was doing.

One of the officers brought a stretcher, and the injured man was placed on it. Two guards climbed the stairs carrying the victim with the M.T.A. leading the way. The inmates continued to shower and exchange their dirty clothes as if nothing had happened.

After LeRoy was admitted to the prison hospital, they had difficulty removing the knife. The blade was embedded so deeply in his spine the M.T.A. could not pull it out. But with the help of vice grips clamped onto the handle of the weapon, and bracing a knee against the victim's back, the M.T.A. was able to remove the knife. LeRoy's condition was critical.

That evening after lights out, Whitey lay in his bunk, but sleep evaded him. He was restless, tossing and turning, nothing seemed to go right, and with the news of Rose's death, past memories he had safely tucked away, came back to haunt him. Now this deal with LeRoy, it was a twist of fate; just one more day and he would have died a burning death.

A strange feeling came over Whitey, what it was—who it was, he could not grasp the clarity of it. Suddenly Red Kendrick came to mind; at a time like this why should he think of him? Like a blow from a hammer, he realized why. His thoughts flashed back to the days when he was in the Segregation Hole at McNeil. He thought of the nights he lay on the cold concrete floor, planning and scheming on how he would kill Red. Kendrick was punished when he was thrown off a tier, but not by Whitey's hand. Officer Jones on the train to Alcatraz; he had the opportunity and inclination to kill him, but at the last crucial moment, Sandy's face appeared in his mind, and now LeRoy Jackson. It was like a magnet, and unknown power, preventing him from performing these tragedies.

Two days after the incident occurred LeRoy was transferred to the Federal Medical Center at Springfield, Missouri. With no control over the lower half of his body he was paralyzed from the waist down.

The morning after the stabbing, Whitey was sitting in his favorite spot high up on the bleachers.

"Hi Whitey, I've been looking all over the yard for you, I should have known you were up here."

Johnny House sat down beside Whitey, and placed his arm over his shoulders in a grip of affection.

"Hey what the hell you doing?" Whitey asked as he pushed Johnny's arm off his shoulders. "You want to give these fools the impression I'm gay or something, what's wrong with you?"

Johnny laughed heartily, and replied, "Nothing's wrong with me Whitey, I'm just happy to see you that's all."

213

With a strange expression Whitey looked at Johnny, then started to laugh and said, "You know what House? You been locked up too long, your turning fruit! Why would you be happy to see me, you see me every fucking day."

"I know Whitey, but yesterday when I heard LeRoy got it in the shower. I just knew you did the shank job, I'm just happy it wasn't you."

Whitey sat there speechless, this was a rare moment when he found himself at a loss for words. The feeling of warmth that flowed through him was indescribable, for he had never experience the true feeling of friendship—of belonging. It was ironic that he had to come all the way to this infamous penitentiary to experience this feeling that only Johnny House could give.

Two months later, Jerry (the accused) went on trial in Federal Court in San Francisco, charged with the stabbing attack on LeRoy Jackson. For four consecutive weeks, each morning, under heavy guard, Jerry, along with a number of convict witnesses on his behalf, were taken to court. Before the court sessions began, LeRoy was brought back from Springfield to attend the trial.

Jerry pleaded not guilty, the reason, self defense. It was explained to the jury that a man in prison such as Alcatraz had to defend himself. LeRoy Jackson had threatened Jerry by telling him if he ever gets a chance he will overpower and fuck him. If he went to Custody and informed on LeRoy's threat to him, Jerry would have been tagged as a rat. A rat did not live long on Alcatraz. A number of guards testified that this was true, and although they couldn't condone Jerry's actions, under the circumstances of prison life, they couldn't blame him.

When the trial ended, Jerry, with the help of convict witnesses who testified for him, and the excellent defense attorney he had along with a sympathetic jury; was found not guilty. When the news reached Alcatraz, enthusiastic cheers of congratulation could be heard throughout the Cell House.

The prison population was happy for him, but the happiness was short lived. That very afternoon when he was returned to Alcatraz, he was placed in TU, and the prison population never saw Jerry again.

By the courts of law Jerry won the case, but the staff of Alcatraz, had him marked guilty.

LeRoy Jackson was transferred back to Springfield, where he died two months later.

214

CHAPTER 34.

For Whitey the days seemed to move slower than ever if that were possible, but even so the months fell by the wayside, and two years had gone by. When he was first assigned to the Glove Shop the job was new to him, and he enjoyed the work, until it became, a boring routine. Two years later it was a drag, and the thought of going to the same job each day became very depressing.

On this particular morning Whitey sat at his machine waiting for the shop whistle to blow, ending another half day of work.

The door to the shop had been left open, and the inmates were congregating outside on the walkway. They were waiting to make the lunch time trek back to the Cell House.

Chili was standing to the left of Whitey, and Russell was on his right; they were enjoying their cigarettes while waiting for the Brush Shop crew to pass. As they walked by the Glove Shop crew, there was catcalling between the prisoners. A big Mexican, as he walked by, spat at Chili hitting him in the face.

The sudden movement of the Mexican, caused Chili to jump backwards to avoid him, and in doing so some of the saliva landed on Whitey. He was caught by the element of surprise, and before he realized what happened the Mexican was too far away for him to reciprocate.

Whitey was astounded, and turned to Chili, "What the hell was that all about? Do you know that son of a bitch?"

"Yes, him So-So," Chili said in broken English. "Him crazy, I bother him no, him pick with me all time already. I do nothing him. So-So spit, him crazy."

"Yeah that's right Whitey," Russell volunteered. "Soda has been picking on Chili here for some time now. Why, I don't know, I guess the fucker don't like people from Chile,"

"He no like me, for why, me not know, him crazy Mex-can, I no do not-thing to him."

215

Whitey couldn't understand why anyone would want to pick on Chili. He was a quiet person, and kept to himself. He was a small man, five foot three, one hundred and twenty pounds.

While Chili was at McNeil Island, Caryl Chessman, (who was commonly known as the infamous red light bandit), was over in San Quentin sitting on Death Row where he had been for the last ten years. He was hoping to receive another stay of execution. Each time he received a date and was scheduled to die; through loophole in the law, he would receive a stay of execution. On this particular day at McNeil there were some convict laundry workers making bets on whether Chessman would receive another stay of execution.

"I'll bet you five packs of smokes he gets another stay," one inmate said.

"I'll take that bet, that fucker is going down the tubes today."

Chili was also working in the laundry that day. He didn't approve of this type of betting.

He overheard a convict say, "I hope they top that son of a bitch."

"Yeah me too, I hope he gets it," another one agreed.

Chili had heard enough betting on a man's life. He picked up a hammer, and screamed, "I don't like man die. You all crazy bet on man die." And as Chili screamed he swung the hammer hitting a convict over the head. Luckily the blow did not kill the inmate, but he was hospitalized for several weeks. For his assault Chili was transferred to Alcatraz.

"I don't know what Soda's problem with Chili is," Whitey said to Russell, "but I got a score to settle now."

"Forget it Whitey, he's just a wet-back bully. He ain't worth catching a beef."

"Hey the bastard spit on me too. No jive-ass-low-class wet-back is going to spit on me and get away with it."

After lunch, Whitey was out in the yard with Russell and Chili waiting to return to work, when he saw Soda standing at the edge of the bleachers.

Soda was a large heavyset Mexican, who appeared to be on some kind of ego trip. No one could understand him, and he seemed to enjoy picking on smaller people, especially if he thought he could get away with it.

Whitey walked over to the big man, and stopped a few feet behind him.

"Hey wet-back," he said in a quiet angry voice.

Soda spun around to face Whitey, "What'd you say?"

216

"You heard me wet-back!"

"Look Gringo, I didn't mean to spit on you, I was spitting at Chili."

"I don't give a fuck who you spat at, some of your slime hit me."

"Look Gringo, you better back off, I'll break you in two you sawed-off punk!"

He hardly got the words out of his mouth before Whitey hit him with a terrific blow to the jaw. As the Mexican fell backwards, Whitey caught him again flush on the nose knocking him up against the bleachers. Like a madman, he was all over him, hammering with one fist after the other. Soda never had a chance to defend himself; the blows were coming fast and furious. Whitey was like an insane person; he was not satisfied with just giving the Mexican a licking, he was virtually beating the man to death. He was so engrossed in what he was doing he never heard the shrill of the officer's whistle, or saw the guards running across the yard. It took three guards to overpower Whitey and drag him away from Soda.

"You mother-fucker, you wet-back bastard, you jive-ass-no-class-funny-style-wet-back, bean-eating-prick!" He screamed as the guards dragged him across the yard toward TU. Whitey was still yelling until the big steel door of TU cut off the sound.

Two guards carried Soda directly to the prison hospital. He had been badly beaten up, both eyes were swollen completely shut, nose broken, his lips swollen and split wide open.

Once inside TU the guards quickly ushered Whitey into a solitary cell. The guard closed the door leaving him alone in the darkness.

As he lay there on the concrete floor, Whitey thought, why did I get mixed up with Soda? He didn't deliberately spit on me. It would have been wise to have overlooked the whole thing. But if I did, how long would I have lasted? I would of been pegged as weak. I guess I could have accepted Soda's apology instead of pressing it into a fight, but if I had, he would have thought me weak. I had to fight him, and besides I like a good fight.

At 10:00 A.M. the next morning, Whitey was taken before the Captain for disciplinary action. Sitting on the committee were the Captain, Lieutenant, and the Classification Counselor. The Captain conducted most of the questioning.

"Let's see," he said as he leafed through Whitey's record, "Thompson 1465. You've been here a little over two years now, this is the first disciplinary report on you, it says that for no apparent reason, you attacked another inmate, but I'm sure you had a reason, do you

217

care to tell me what it was?"

Whitey remained silent as if he had not heard the Captain.

"I'm losing my patience Thompson. Now tell me what the fight with Soda was about."

"How can I tell you? I don't even know myself."

The Captain exploded, "Do you mean to tell me you got into a fight and don't know why? I can hardly believe that, unless you just love to fight."

Matching the Captain's tone of anger, Whitey replied, "I don't care what you believe, I told you I don't know what the fight was about."

"Did Soda provoke you into a fight?"

"No one can provoke me into doing anything."

The Captain asked the Lieutenant if they had any questions.

The Lieutenant said yes, and turning to Whitey he asked, "Tell me Thompson, is there something bothering you? No one gets into a fight and doesn't know the reason why. So what's troubling you?"

"Ah blow it out your ear Lieutenant! Nothing's bothering me."

"All right Thompson," the Captain shouted, "I've heard enough, I'm sending you back to TU for ten days. During that time you figure out why you fought.

Whitey understood why he had received ten days in TU instead of two or three months. Soda was a known troublemaker, and disliked by the guards and staff. In the majority of cases when a fight broke out, and if it was in the yard area, a guard on the wall would generally open fire with a rifle. Taking careful aim he would shoot close to the assailants in an attempt to break up the fight, occasionally they were hit by shrapnel.

No shots had been fired at Whitey and Soda; the guards in the yard could have stopped the fight a lot sooner if they had wanted to. But they saw Soda was taking a beating, and though it appeared the guards charged through the crowd of onlookers in haste to get to the fighting, they still didn't stop the fight as quickly as they could have. In a sense, Whitey had done a guard's dirty work.

TU on Alcatraz was not much different from the Segregation Hole at McNeil Island, same type of cold damp cells, and nothing to keep warm with except the nightly blanket.

It was a little over two years since Whitey was last in Segregation, but nothing had changed. Here he was again in the hole trying to keep warm by doing pushups. Then he began jumping up and down until he tired and started pacing the floor, as he did so, his thoughts were on Soda, and again (as with LeRoy Jackson) he was planning ways of doing him in.

On the fourth evening in the darkness of his cell he was lying on the floor panting rapidly after vigorous exercise. He had started off with pushups, and had continued doing them until he could no longer push his body off the floor. Then immediately pulled himself to his feet, and began to jog on the spot, lifting his knees as high as he could. Perspiration flowed freely, but he kept up the pace until he felt exhausted. Then he began doing more pushups until his arms no longer supported his weight. In total exhaustion he collapsed to the floor gasping for breath. As Whitey lay there he enjoyed the warmth he had generated. Perspiration was trickling down the sides of his cheeks, he became drowsy and his eyelids slowly closed, and as he lay there his thoughts were on Soda.

Suddenly a soft breeze drifted across the floor. Whitey began to stir as the soft breeze developed into a gentle wind. Where was it coming from? His cell was completely sealed off. He felt the impact of the wind as it became stronger. His body became numb, and except for his eyes he could not move. The wind was building into a whirling cyclone, and in it's raging fury it felt as though his body was being tossed about. The sound of the wind was so devastating he felt his eardrums would burst.

As abruptly as it started it ceased—it became incredibly quiet and his cell began to illuminate, getting brighter and brighter to the brilliance of a morning sunrise. He attempted to sit up, but his body would not respond; a shocking fear electrified his mind. What was happening to him? He couldn't move, he couldn't talk, he couldn't even shout or scream. His eyes rolled from side to side. Whitey had known physical fear, but now he was experiencing a petrifying fear of the unknown. His vision focused from one wall to the other; he could feel cold beads of perspiration running over his skin. Is this the way it feels when you die?

Like the wind that came from nowhere, a whispering could be heard, "Whitey, Whitey you are living—Whitey you are living," the voice got louder and louder penetrating his mind. "Whitey, Whitey you are living—you are living."

He moved his eyes in the direction of the sound, his vision was blurred, but slowly cleared, and an apparition appeared. He was totally astonished, for he saw a young woman standing there. It was Rose, he recognized her voice. He could see her plainly as she stood by his side, he tried to speak to her, but was unable to open his mouth. Silently he watched her, and in a moment she commenced to

219

fade until she and the brilliant light had disappeared altogether.

In total darkness, Whitey lay there trying to understand what he had just seen. It was Rose, that much he was sure of, but what was she trying to tell him? Was she telling him not to kill Soda? That he still had a chance to make a life for himself? Rose's love was stronger than he realized, for he was sure her spirit had come to guide him to a better life.

Again Whitey thought about Soda, and came to the conclusion that he wasn't important anymore, his fate would have to be in someone else's hands—not his.

CHAPTER 35.

After serving his tenth day Whitey was released from TU, and it was quite a relief to get back into the daily routine after the close confines of the hole. His friends greeted him back into the population, and Chili pumped his hand on his return to the Glove Shop.

"Glad you back," Chili said, "Tank you, you beat So-So for me."

"Wait a minute Chili, I didn't do it for you or anyone else, you get that straight now,"

"All same, you beat bul-ly good. Ever-thing I do for you, you let Chili know."

"No no, Chili, you don't have to do anything for me, you understand?"

"Make no mind for me. You beat up Mex-can, all same I fix So-So one day, he get you TU, you friend, I fix So-So good, you see."

"Forget Soda, Chili" Whitey told him. "By the way where is he now?"

"He was in the hospital for over a week, matter of fact he just got out day before yesterday. You sure fucked his face up." Russell told him. "Look there he is now with the Brush crew."

Whitey looked, and sure enough there was Soda with a patch over his nose. Soda turned in time to catch Whitey looking at him, he quickly looked the other way.

At noon when Whitey returned from work, it was like old home week when he walked into the Dining Room for lunch. From all directions of the Hall someone called to him.

Johnny House was on the steam line, and when he saw Whitey he called out, "Hey slugger! How you doing pal? I'll see you in the yard Saturday, right?"

"You got it House, I'll be there."

The next day at lunch, Whitey was standing at the rear of the line waiting his turn to be served. He sensed something was about to happen, what it was he had no idea, but he felt uneasy. He was the last man in line with no one behind him, but yet he kept looking back to make sure no unseen person was slipping up on him. He turned his head forward in the direction of the steam table when it happened—pop-slap; that same familiar sound followed by a sharp grunt, and a sickening thud as someone fell to the floor, striking their head on the concrete.

Chili had been near the head of the line and had no trouble slipping up behind Soda, and without any indication, he ran a ten-inch shaft (similar to an ice pick), right through his lower back. The shock of the impact was so great, Soda lost control of his bowels.

The Lieutenant was behind the steam table when the incident occurred. Chili, still holding the weapon in his hand stood over his victim and did not see the Lieutenant coming. Without a struggle the Lieutenant retrieved the weapon from Chili's hand. Then a guard escorted him out of the Dining Room straight to TU, and as they passed Whitey their eyes met. Chili, with a faint smile on his face nodded his head, "You see White-tee I tell you I fix So-So."

Shortly after Chili was escorted out of the Dining Room, Soda was placed on a stretcher, and under the supervision of the M.T.A. he was rushed to the hospital. The hospital was located directly over the Dining Hall.

Nonchalantly the food handlers continued filling trays for the parade of prisoners who filed by. Each one sat at their respective table eating their food as though nothing had happened.

The next morning at work, Russell told Whitey he had some news about Soda.

"Whitey you're going to enjoy this, Soda is on the critical list, he is not expected to make it, and you know what? I heard this morning they brought a chaplain over from the City last night to give him his Last Rites. You know when they took him to the hospital," Russell continued, "all they did for him was put a Band-Aid over the puncture, they put one on both sides. You know the shaft went right through him! After the M.T.A. put the Band-Aids on him he was taken straight to TU, and early this morning when the guard opened his cell door, he found Soda in shock. They rushed him back to the hospital, and that's when the chaplain or priest, or what the hell ever you call them, gave him his Last Rites."

222

"Well I sure hope the son of a bitch don't croak for Chili's sake."

After an extensive operation, Soda hung on, and slowly he began a long but steady recovery. The surgery was successful, and his miraculous recovery continued. When he was released from the hospital, he was a changed man—almost a shy man, for he seldom spoke to anyone, and kept to himself. His close brush with death made him see life in a new perspective.

As for Chili, he was not charged with the assault, therefore never went on trial, but Whitey never saw the little guy again. It was years later he learned that Chili finished his prison term in TU, and when his sentence was completed, he was deported to his native country, Chile.

Soda was also deported to Mexico on completion of his term.

In most assault cases on Alcatraz, rather than have a costly trial, the officials meted out their own punishment and seldom were charges ever filed.

The next few months passed slowly and uneventfully for Whitey. He spent endless evenings chatting with his neighbors, and occasionally he would just sit quietly on his bunk staring at the bars on a window across from his cell.

The view from this window was breathtaking, especially after nightfall. Across the Bay in all her splendor, lay the Berkeley coast line with a multitude of lights, each single one reflecting it's own glow in the water, giving an illusion—instead of thousands of lights—millions of them. The first time Whitey looked through the window and saw this sight, he became momentarily spellbound, it was an extraordinarily beautiful picture. For one brief moment Whitey was a part of this picture with the night wind tearing at his face. He was on a motorcycle speeding along the Freeway toward the Oakland Bay Bridge. The lights from his cycle were reflecting into the water, blending in with millions of other ones. For a second or two he felt he was part of the free world. Then a sudden sadness shadowed over his thoughts, for he realized he was in a prison cell, and he was not part of the coast line, nor was he on a motorcycle. He sensed a feeling of utter loneliness, and quickly focused his eyes back within the walls of prison so that he would no longer see the lights of Berkeley.

Inside these prison walls was reality, his cell, the steel bars, the concrete, his fellow convicts and the guards, this was his life, this was reality, and nothing existed beyond that window. It was all a dream out there, and the only thing that existed for him was the prison in which he lived.

Many months would go by, but Whitey never glanced beyond the window again.

The monotony of time was a killer, and simple things would amuse a prisoner. When he was not chatting between cells or reading a book, he would pace back and forth in his cell.

Whitey, as of yet, never went to see any of the bimonthly showing of movies. One Sunday just to break the monotony he decided to go. The title of the movie was, "The Magnificent Seven." One of the stars was Charles Bronson, and as he sat there watching the movie, it wasn't Charles Bronson, but instead it was Whitey Thompson himself riding a horse across the silver screen. For almost two hours his imagination took him out of prison, Whitey was one of the Magnificent Seven galloping across the Badlands of Mexico. When the movie came to a conclusion and the lights came on, the reality of where he was, and being in prison left him in a depressed frame of mind. From that day forward he never went to another movie.

On Alcatraz Island, commonly known as the Rock by the inmates, there were no educational classes, or any type of rehabilitation program. Other than his regular job, To Whitey, life seemed to become more meaningless than ever, and at times he felt he was indeed a part of the living dead.

One Saturday morning in the autumn of 1960 Whitey was sitting in his usual spot at the top of the bleachers. He did not notice Johnny walking up until he spoke.

"Hi Whitey, what's wrong? You look like you lost your best friend."

"Hi Johnny. No, I didn't lose a friend, I'm just fed up. I hate coming to the yard, and I hate staying in my cell—there's no in between."

Johnny realized the meaning of what Whitey said. In reality he was giving up, and in a matter of time he would go for it, and let the guards shoot him off the wall.

"You should get into a hobby Whitey to occupy your mind, you know, like oil painting."

"Shit I can't paint House, I don't have the talent."

"You don't need talent Whitey, don't make no difference whether you can paint or not. The idea is to do something to occupy your time. Little kids in kindergarten don't know how to paint but they have fun smearing it all over the place. Why don't you give it a try?"

224

"House you flipped a screw, does this place look like kindergarten? This is the Rock man, Alcatraz."

"You missed the point Whitey, I know this isn't kindergarten, all I'm trying to say is, you might enjoy fooling around with oil paints. Look I'll tell you what, I've got some bottles of paint left over from a paint by numbers kit. Also I have a few brushes and a canvas board, would you like to try your hand at it? What do you say?"

"I'm not really interested House, but what the hell I'll give it a try. If it don't work out you can be sure the bottles of paint will end up flying off the tier."

Johnny laughed at the remark. "Listen, I have to return to the kitchen at 2:30 this afternoon. On my way back to work I'll ask the Cell House Officer if I can run the paints up to your cell. Okay?"

That afternoon Whitey was on his bunk snoozing, and had forgotten all about Johnny's offer until he called his name.

Johnny stood just outside Whitey's cell with a canvas board and paper bag, which he handed through the bars to him.

"The guard is waiting for me," Johnny said, "I have to run, see you later."

"Hey thanks House," Whitey called after him.

The bag contained fifteen small bottles of various colored paints, and two brushes. He placed them on the wall table along with the canvas board, and lay back down on his bunk.

Whitey had accepted the art supplies from Johnny because he did not want to hurt his feelings by refusing. He knew he was trying to be a friend, and the least he could do was to accept the gift.

That evening Whitey sat on his bunk staring at the little bottles of paint. What the heck, he thought, I'll give it a try, no one can see the mess I'll make. He propped the canvas board up against the table with the base of the board resting on his knees. He unscrewed the bottle caps, picked up a brush and began to paint. He was at a disadvantage having only two brushes to work with; he had to frequently clean them to apply various colors. He did not have the slightest idea what his subject would be, but the moment he applied paint to the brush, his hand went straight to work as if it had an independent brain of it's own. Back and forth the brush went, from the paint bottles to the canvas, and like magic an elephant began to take shape, even to the jungle foliage.

Whitey was not pleased with his workmanship, but he continued on regardless. He was so engrossed in what he was doing that he lost track of time, suddenly his cell lights went out.

"You son of a bitch! What happened to the lights? Turn on the lights," he yelled.

"Hey Whitey," Blake, his next door neighbor called, "it's nine-thirty man, lights out."

He sat motionless on his bunk, he was afraid of getting paint all over himself, and he had to wait until his eyes adjusted to the semi-darkness. In a moment he was able to see. After he put the paints and brushes away he laid the canvas board flat on the floor under his bunk where no one could see it. It was an enjoyable evening for him, time had slipped by before he knew it. He was anxious for the next morning to arrive so he could resume painting.

The next morning, Sunday, yard call sounded. Whitey remained in his cell, and when no more movement could be heard on the tier, he quickly got things set up and began to paint.

Again he lost track of time. He was so absorbed in his work that he didn't hear approaching footsteps until a voice said, "Hey Whitey, I didn't know you could paint."

Whitey was like a little boy who had been caught with his hand in the cookie jar, the voice startled him! He turned his head and was surprised to see Blake standing outside his cell. Whitey was first startled, followed by embarrassment that quickly turned to anger.

"What the hell you sneaking up on me for Blake?"

"I didn't sneak up on you. What're you painting?"

Whitey's anger subsided as he replied, "I can't paint, I'm just screwing around."

"Let me see it anyway," Blake insisted.

"Okay you bastard, but if you laugh I'll put your lights out."

Whitey turned the canvas board around so that Blake could view it.

He showed pleasant surprise and said, "Hey Whitey, not bad at all, I really mean it."

"Come on Blake, who the hell do you think you're kidding?"

"I'm not kidding, I think it's good. What're you going to do with it when it's finished?"

"I don't know—throw it off the tier I guess."

"Hell no man, don't do that, give it to me."

The fact that Blake liked and wanted the painting was all the inspiration that Whitey needed. When it was completed, he gave it to Blake who hung it on the wall in his cell. Whitey was so inspired by his acceptance of the painting he could hardly wait to get started on another one. He borrowed a canvas board from a friend, and this

226

time he began to paint a snow scene. It turned out much better than his first attempt, and he sold it for three packs of Wings cigarettes to James, a convict who celed on the Flats. Whitey was so thrilled with the expectation of his paintings that he placed an order for art supplies that included canvas, brushes, linseed oil, turpentine, clear varnish, Winsor Newton oil paints, and many more necessities. It would take the order approximately a month before he would receive it. First it would have to be approved by the Counselor, but only if he had adequate funds on the books to pay for it. Whitey had more than enough money from prison industry earnings.

Two days after placing his order, he received a notice that it had been approved. All he had to do now was wait for it to come in, but a month was an eternity for him to wait. He was anxious for the supplies as this was the first time in years he actually had something to look forward to.

Johnny was happy when he heard that Whitey had put in an order, and offered to loan him enough supplies so he could continue painting until his order came in, and paint he did! Every evening found him hard at work.

Everyone who saw his finished paintings thought he was doing well, but even with their praise Whitey still didn't think he could paint. The truth was, he could actually paint, and he was exceptionally good at it.

It did not matter to Whitey if he could paint or not, he was having fun. His mind was at work, time was moving quickly, and that was all that mattered. The irony of it was he had a natural talent, and never knew it until he came to Alcatraz. For Whitey, oil painting was just what the doctor ordered. He needed something to occupy his mind, and oil painting seemed to be the answer. It was a new experience for him and it gave him something to look forward to. All thoughts were pushed from his mind except for the current painting that was appearing before him on canvas. He felt as though he was handed a new lease on life—something to hang onto, and above all it was an escape from reality. He was indebted to Johnny House.

On their way to or from work, or other activities, prisoners would stop at Whitey's cell to admire his paintings. It gave him a great deal of encouragement and drive to keep on improving. The daily routine of prison life no longer bothered him. He was feeling good about himself, and when the wake up horn sounded on each new day, he would bounce out of his bunk, quickly wash up, and get his cell in order before the count buzzer went off. He was no longer depressed about working in the Glove Shop. The money he earned would keep him in art supplies, and each morning he was happy to go to his job, for he knew when the day's work was over, he had three and a half hours to paint in his cell.

Whitey lost track of how many times he was caught at 9:30—lights out, with his pallet board full of paint, dirty brushes, and tubes of paint all over his bed. In the darkness of his cell he would strain his eyes cleaning his brushes and tidying up.

Whitey purchased a wooden board twenty by thirty by one inch thick. He would sit on his bunk with the board resting on his knees, and the top end propped against the table. The canvas was thumb-tacked onto the face of the board, and with his pallet lying to his right side on the bunk, he would paint. He worked in that position hours at a time, and there were a number of occasions—by accident, he would sit down on his pallet board full of paint! Each time it happened, did he ever sound off! He could be heard yelling clean over in C Block!

His friends would laugh and shout, "Whitey did it again! He sat on his pallet board! He's the only man I know of who paints with his ass!"

"Fuck you guys," he would yell at them.

Another voice, "Hey Whitey what happened man?"

"You'll find out in the morning when they unlock these doors, wise guy."

Whitey whole attitude was changing, he was more outgoing and cheerful, and the day his art supplies arrived he was beaming with delight. Immediately he put in another order, a larger one to eliminate the fear of running out of supplies. Painting was becoming an obsession with him. Things were going well, and for the first time since his incarceration he felt he might have a future, and why not? Why not start right here in this cell on Alcatraz? It was better to plan now than not to plan at all.

He started to laugh when he thought about his future as an artist. He visualized people asking him where he started to paint, and he would say, "On Alcatraz man, in a cell on Alcatraz."

The daily routine was bearable now that he found an escape in his art work. One evening while painting a Swiss Alps scene, he began to visualize himself up in the very mountains he was painting. With a little imagination, he could feel the wind tearing at his face as he skied down the slopes. What a discovery! He realized he could escape to any place in the world, and he could even escape out of this world

228

if he so chose.

Once he did a painting of a ship on the high seas. While his brush moved gracefully over the canvas, he felt he was standing at the helm of the ship while the ocean spray engulfed him. It was wonderful, all he had to do was start a painting, and his mind was transported there. Many times while finishing a canvas, he would be planning on his next oil painting. Time went by so fast he hated to be interrupted by the daily routine. On Saturdays and Sundays he began skipping lunch, so he could continue painting. He became so obsessed he even resented shower and clothing exchange; however, these things had to be done.

As the months passed by, and the novelty wore off, he was able to adjust to the regular daily activities in conjunction with his painting. It was all a challenge for him, and he enjoyed each day, but there were occasions when he had setbacks, and he would experience some bitter feelings.

CHAPTER 36.

One afternoon while at work in the Glove Shop, the Industry Officer approached Whitey's machine.

"Thompson there's a Custody Officer here for you. He has orders to escort you to Control."

Whitey was surprised, "A guard for me? For what, what've I done?"

"I'm sure I don't know Thompson, but you have to go with him."

"Yeah okay, okay, but I know it's a bum-beef."

Anger showed on Whitey's face. The old defensive feeling began to churn, and his thoughts flashed back to another day on McNeil Island. He was thinking of the time when the two members of the Goon Squad had come into the Shoe Shop and dragged him out. Of the beating that followed, and the endless days of isolation.

"Come on Thompson, I haven't got all day," the Custody guard called.

Stalling for time to get his thoughts together, Whitey slowly rose from his seat. For a fleeting moment he was confused. Should he go with this officer peacefully, or put up a fight? What have I done wrong? He could not figure it out.

"Come on Whitey," the Industry Officer said, "you've done nothing wrong, so why worry? Go with the guard and find out what they want."

Whitey walked to the shop entrance where the Custody guard was waiting for him.

"What does Control want me for?"

"You have two visitors," the guard replied, "so let's go Thompson we're losing time."

"Visitors!" Whitey was totally surprised. "Hey you're bullshitting, I don't have no one to come visit me."

"Look Thompson, all I know is I have orders to pick you up and escort you to the Visiting Room."

"Something is wrong here, I don't have anyone to visit me."

"I can't help it Thompson. You got a couple visits now, so let's go."

There was a time when Whitey would have told the guard to get lost. They would have had to drag him bodily to Control. But his attitude had changed, and he realized the Custody Officer was merely carrying out his orders.

Whitey walked through the doorway with the guard accompanying him. Together they walked along the roadway, up the cliff side steps with Whitey going through the metal detector. They continued their journey on up through the Sally Port, and as they started across the yard Whitey said to the guard, "Are you sure it's a visit, not a beef?"

"Look Thompson, all I know is that two people are here to see you, who they are, or what they want, I have no idea."

Whitey and the officer proceeded up the stairs into the Cell House and down Broadway. Facing Broadway was the solid steel door, standing next to it waiting for them, was the Cell House Officer. He opened the heavy door and re-locked it after they passed through. They approached the barred gate with the metal shield cover over the lock; the Cell House Officer gave a nod to the Armorer inside Controls. The Armorer glanced into the mirror and saw all was clear. Then he pressed a button that released the shield allowing the Cell House Officer to insert the key and unlock it. After passing through he relocked it, and the metal shield slid back in place.

Whitey and the guard entered the Visiting Room, and found two middle-aged men dressed in dark gray business suits waiting for them. At a glance Whitey knew they were FBI agents, and it proved to be true when they showed their credentials.

One agent was rather tall and slim with a receding hairline, and reddish complexion. The other agent was the same height, dark completion, brown hair, heavy set with piercing brown eyes.

"My name is Martino, he said, "and this gentleman is my partner, Agent Meyers."

Whitey said nothing as he stood there staring.

"Sit down right there," Martino ordered pointing to a chair.

"I'm okay, I'd just as soon stand."

"I said sit down," the agent shouted.

In the same tone as the agent, Whitey barked, "Fuck you, I'll stand if I please."

Again Martino ordered him to sit, but got no response, and looked to the guard for help.

The guard looked from the agent to Whitey, and said in a cold

231

voice, "He don't have to sit down if he don't want to."

One thing about the guards of Alcatraz—they did not care if you were an FBI agent, or whatever title of authority you may carry, you did not come into their prison and give orders to anyone—not even convicts.

"All right Thompson," Martino said, "if you wish to stand, then stand."

"What the hell do you want anyways?" Whitey asked.

Agent Meyers spoke for the first time, "Thompson would you state your full name."

"Sure why not, Leon Warren Thompson."

"I just wanted to be sure you're the man we're looking for," Meyers stated. "Now then, when you were arrested, there was some luggage picked up that belonged to you. We've held it in storage all these years, it's too expensive to just throw. . . ."

"What the hell you talking about?" Whitey cut in. "I never had any luggage."

"Like I was saying Thompson," Meyers continued, "we've held your luggage a long time, and we just came by to see what you want done with it."

"Lookit, I never owned any fucking luggage," Whitey retorted sharply.

"Damn it Thompson all we're trying to do is return what's yours. Just cooperate and tell us what to do with it."

"You know what you can do with it! You can shove it up your ass! I don't own and I never did own any luggage."

"Thompson let's quit this horsing around, we know that luggage belongs to you; when you were arrested your luggage was picked up also, and now we just want to return it."

"Do you take me for a fool? First off, you and your pal here are not the ones who arrested me, second, I don't own any fucking luggage, nor did I ever own any. The only thing I had when I was busted was a double barrel sawed-off shotgun, the Feds got that. So don't give me any crap about luggage."

"Damn it Thompson, can't you get it through your head we mean you no harm? Just tell us it is your luggage, and how you want to dispose of it. Maybe you have a friend or someone who can claim it for you until you get out."

Whitey was losing his composure and yelled at the agents, "Goddamn you people, how many fucking times do I have to tell you that luggage don't belong to me." Turning to the guard Whitey asked,

"How about taking me out of here? I've nothing more to say to these people."

"Sorry Thompson," the guard replied, "you have to stay until they're done talking to you."

Whitey's hatred returned in full force as he faced the agents, "Look, let's cut the goddamn bullshit, I'm no juvenile, so let's get to the fucking point, why the hell are you trying to connect me with that luggage?"

"Okay," Meyers said, "we'll cut the corners and get right to the point. We have reason to believe that you killed and robbed a motel owner, and also. . . ."

"Hey hold it right there man," Whitey interrupted, "you got the wrong pigeon here, I didn't kill no son of a bitch."

The accusation did not surprise Whitey, nor did it catch him off guard for he had anticipated something like this. He knew the FBI would not go through the expense of making a social call on Alcatraz, just to return something out of the goodness of their heart.

"We believe you did Thompson. You held up a motel right here in San Francisco. You killed and robbed the owner of ten thousand in cash. You placed the money in a suitcase, and then shipped it to San Diego by way of Greyhound bus. Once you felt the luggage was safely on it's way, you yourself started for San Diego by other means of transportation to pick up the money, but you never made it, because on your way down there you robbed a bank. You were arrested, convicted of bank robbery, and sent to prison, and here we are. Now just try to deny it Thompson."

For the first time Whitey sat down, and he seemed to be relieved as a knowing look appeared on his face. He looked from one agent to the other, and there was no attempt to conceal his hatred.

"What's wrong Thompson?" Martino asked, "cat's got your tongue? You can't talk? Well you'll get your chance to talk in a court room right after we book you for murder. We'll be back in a day or so with the indictment papers."

Turning to the guard the agent said, "Okay officer, we're done for now."

Whitey jumped up out of the chair and bellowed at the agents, "Hey wait just a fucking minute! You bastards come in here like gang-busters, and say you're going to slap a murder charge on me. I never killed no one and you can't prove I did."

"Oh we'll prove it Thompson," Martino sneered, "you can count on that!"

Whitey began snickering, "Okay fools, arrest me, take me to court and you'll prove what fools you really are."

Meyers said to the guard, "I guess that wraps it up for now. We'll be back in a few days with the papers."

"Save yourself a trip copper, you ain't taking me no place unless it's a frame-up."

Ignoring Whitey's remark, the agents started for the door.

"If you bastards are charging me with murder," Whitey shouted after them, "I got a right to know when it was supposed to of happened—when did this robbery take place?"

Both agents paused and whispered to each other, then turning around they walked back to Whitey.

"This crime took place in June of 1958," Martino stated.

"June 1958!" there was sarcasm in Whitey's voice, "June 1958?"

"That's the date Thompson, I'm sure you know it well," Meyers said.

Whitey stood there quietly, and as he did so a smile was appearing on his face that turned into a broad grin. He was on the verge of laughing, but he kept his composure and held it back. The agents were surprised at his actions, and looked from one to the other, then to the guard, and back to Thompson.

Finally Whitey spoke in a cocky voice, "You know-it-alls, you're so smart you think you know everything. Well know-it-alls, June 1958 I was pulling time, I been in prison for the past eleven and a half years. So go ahead—charge me with murder! You'll have a better chance of convicting your own mothers than you'll have of convicting me. So shoot your best stick!"

The agents were taken aback by this change of events. Still, they were skeptical, and turned to the guard.

"Is this true?" Meyers asked.

"Thompson has been with us for a while now, but we can check his prison records," the guard replied. The guard walked to the Visiting Room entrance, and spoke to another officer who was standing just outside.

"Would you call the Classification Councilor and ask him if he could possibly come to the Visiting Room, and to bring the records of Leon W. Thompson AZ 1465."

Whitey was desperately trying to keep his equanimity. He sat down again and began to roll a cigarette. A few minutes elapsed before the Councilor appeared in the doorway.

"Yes?" he asked the agent, "What is it you would like to know?"

234

"I would like to know," Martino said pointing to Whitey, "was this man in custody during June of 1958?"

The Counselor opened up his folder and as he leafed through the pages he mumbled to himself, "Let's see, Thompson 1465. Ah yes here we are." The Councilor addressed Martino, "Yes Thompson was incarcerated during June of 1958, he was serving time at the Federal Penitentiary, McNeil Island, Washington, in fact he has been in custody for the past eleven and a half years."

Martino could not believe what he had just heard. "May we see for ourselves?" he asked.

Both agents examined the documents, and the records confirmed what the Classification Officer had just told them; they were satisfied.

The Cell House Officer with a grim expression on his face appeared in the doorway.

"It seems like you agents got your wires crossed. We sent a teletype to the Bureau of Prisons, their reply was, the Leon Thompson you are seeking is incarcerated in Leavenworth, Kansas. He is at this very moment serving fifteen years for bank robbery."

Meyers immediately turned to Whitey, "Thompson we owe you an apology."

Whitey could no longer hold his animosity as he shouted at the agent, "Apology! Apology hell! You can stick your apology up your ass! If I didn't have a perfect alibi, you would of hung a murder rap on me and sent me to the chair."

"It was a mistake Thompson, and honest mistake. His name was the same as yours, and whether you accept it or not we truly are sorry, we do apologize."

"No doubt about it, you're sorry all right! You can't even find a man who's locked up in prison."

"Okay Thompson," the guard intervened, "let's go, I don't think you are needed here anymore."

Whitey was escorted out of the Visiting Room, and as they walked by the Armorer Whitey said to the guard, "Hey—ah, thanks for not making me sit down."

"That's okay Thompson," the officer said, he paused, then spoke again, "This may come as a shock to you, but I'm glad you had a perfect alibi."

Whitey glanced at the guard, then turned his head forward and continued walking.

They returned to the Cell House desk, seated behind it was the Lieutenant busily leafing through his reports; he looked up as they approached.

"It's too late to report back to work Thompson," the Lieutenant stated. "You are accounted for, so just returned to your cell."

"Okay Lieutenant." Whitey turned and walked toward B Block, and as he started up the stairs it was the guard's turn to be shocked when Whitey called back to him, "Hey officer, thanks, thanks a lot." Without waiting for a reply he continued on up the stairs, and disappeared around the corner of the Cell Block.

Whitey returned to his cell with bitter feelings. He felt he had been violated by the harassment of the agents. But once his cell door closed behind him the incident was forgotten, for he immediately lost himself in work on one of his paintings.

His popularity as an artist was beginning to grow, and on numerous occasions he would sell paintings to other prisoners for art supplies, and Wings cigarettes. The inmates were not allowed to give or sell paintings to one and other, but there were ways of getting around this rule. All a prisoner had to do was to put in a request to order art supplies. Once it was approved he could order any time he wanted, and was permitted to have paintings in his cell, or send them home. Most of these men did not know how to paint, so Whitey would do the painting, and they would pay him for his services with art supplies.

At one time the convicts were allowed to send their paintings to San Francisco where they were put on display and sold. The money would be put in a trust fund for the inmate. In 1960 Warden Madigan put a stop to this practice, consequently, not being able to send their paintings to San Francisco, they no longer had an outlet for their finished work.

Whitey painted mostly for pleasure, but soon he had no more room in his cell for the finished art. For an outlet for his paintings he began to write to his older sister Marge in Connecticut. He sent her many paintings as a gift, more or less in payment to her in return for holding well over a hundred paintings for him.

After she received all these paintings, she stopped writing. He lost contact with her, never hearing from her again. This was hard for Whitey to accept because when he was a small boy she was the only one in the family that ever showed him any kindness. As for the paintings, he would never know what happened to them.

It came as a surprise but one morning the cell next to Whitey was empty, Blake had been transferred to the Federal Penitentiary at

Atlanta, Georgia. At the time of his transfer, there was a prison breakout from the North Carolina penitentiary. Five men had made a daring escape, but were recaptured within ten days. One of the escapees was Whitey's old friend from the chain gang days, Yank Stewart. After Stewart's capture he was turned over to the Federal Bureau of Prisons, and sent to Alcatraz.

One afternoon shortly after Blake's transfer, Whitey had just returned to his cell and was surprised that someone was already occupying Blake's cell.

"Hey old-timer, where did you drive up from?"

"I come in on a chain from Atlanta. Yank Stewart is the name, what's your handle?"

"Whitey, Whitey Thompson. "

"Whitey! I knew a Whitey a long time ago on the chain gang in Durham, North Carolina. He was a blond-headed kid we called Cotton. I remember him climbing up a flag pole. "

For a moment there was silence. Then there was a sudden eruption of sheer excitement, "That kid was me! They used to call me Cotton. That's me Yank! How the hell are ya?"

A muttering reply of joy came from Yank's cell, "I'll be damned, I can't believe it! Cotton!" Then Yank raised his voice, "Cotton, is that really you Cotton?"

"Yeah it's really me Yank, nobody else. How ya doing old buddy?"

"Just great Cotton. Damn it's a hundred years since Durham! Hell you was nothing more than a skinny little kid, I can't believe it's you Cotton."

"It's me all right, but they don't call me Cotton anymore, just call me Whitey okay?"

The two men were happy that fate had brought them together again, and to be able to bring their long forgotten memories into their present life.

One evening Big Longo yelled up to Whitey from the second tier, "You know this cell next to me? The one right under you? It's going to be empty soon."

"Hey Longo, you told me that two fucking years ago and it still ain't empty."

"I know, but Bob just told me he's going to McNeil. You should put in for his cell now."

Whitey thought it would be a great improvement to cell down by Longo and Warren, for both of them were accomplished artists who specialized in portraits. Whitey was more versatile, he painted everything from portraits to land and seascapes. All three of these men admired each others work, especially Warren, for during Whitey's first few months as an artist, Warren paid him a very high compliment.

"Goddamn Whitey," he said one day, "you learned more about oil painting in six months than I learned in ten years. You do beautiful work."

Below Warren on the first tier, there celled a prisoner called Tennessee. Tennessee was a happy-go-lucky man. He had a terrific sense of humor, and was always ready for a joke. With his attitude, he gave the impression he was serving a short term, but this was not the case, for he was doing twenty years for the Federal Government, and when that time was terminated, he had ninety-nine more years to serve in Tennessee. He was a very gifted guitar player, and on any given night you could hear sounds of beautiful music drifting from his cell.

Two days after Whitey moved to cell B-204, he put in for a job exchange from the Glove Shop and went to work in the Clothing Factory. Big Longo and Warren also worked in the Clothing Factory.

One evening Longo and Tennessee were calling bets back and forth on a basketball game which could be listened to on the headsets.

"Hey Tennessee, I'll give you four points and the Dons," Longo called to him.

"Hell, no way man, you give me six points and the Dons, and ya got a bet."

"You crazy? You take me for a sucker? I'll give you four points and that's it, besides you still owe me a pack."

"You creepy Texan, I don't owe you nothing."

"What? What did you call me?" Longo roared.

"I called you a creepy Texan, now you're a creepy fucking, take-it-up-the-ass Texan, and I still owe you nothing."

"Damn you Tennessee, if you don't pay up, I'll have to rub you out. I'm gonna rub you out anyway for what you just called me."

"Hey Longo, hey Big Longo," Whitey interrupted.

"What do you want Whitey? What're you sticking your nose in for?"

"You want Tennessee knocked? I'll do it for a small fee, two sacks of Stud tobacco!"

"You got a deal Whitey! Hey Tennessee, I got a man up here who says he'll rub you out for two sacks of stud."

"Yeah, who the hell is it?"

"Whitey, Whitey Thompson."

"Hey Whitey," Tennessee yelled loudly, "what's the deal? Longo tells me you're going to snuff me out for two sacks of Stud."

"He told you right Tennessee, you're days are numbered!"

"Goddamn Whitey, you're a regular killer!"

Laughter sounded from the tiers.

"Okay Killer, you got a deal," Longo called to Whitey.

"Did you hear that Tennessee?" Whitey shouted.

"Yeah I heard," Tennessee replied, "I don't want to mess with no killer. Hey Longo, you got the bet, and I'll pay the pack, okay?"

"Okay," Longo answered, "but what kind of Texan am I?"

"Hey you're the best Longo," Tennessee laughed.

Ever since that day Big Longo stuck Whitey with the nickname—Killer!

CHAPTER 37.

One Saturday afternoon, half the population was attending the movie, while the other half was out for recreational period.

Whitey was busy in his cell putting the finishing touches on a painting. He spent practically all of his spare time at his art work. He loved this pastime, and discovered that if he let more than two or three days elapse between painting, he suffered a mood change; an angry tension would start to build. Now that he was aware of this mood, and when it would start to occur, he would immediately begin another painting.

On this particular day he was very busy when someone stopped in front of his cell, he looked toward the bars and saw Archie standing there.

"Hey Arch how ya doing old man?" Whitey said cheerfully.

"Okay Whitey, what're you painting?"

Whitey turned the canvas so that Archie could get a better view of it.

"It's Jacqueline Kennedy when she was a little girl, I'm just finishing it."

"I sure do love your work Whitey. Hey I gotta go here's the bull to lock me up."

At that moment Officer Collins walked up. He stood beside Archie, and looked through the bars at the painting Whitey was holding.

"Is that Jacqueline Kennedy as a child?" Collins asked.

Whitey was beaming with delight at the officer's recognition of the painting.

"Yes sir, it sure is her."

"It's beautiful, really beautiful work." Then turning to Archie he said, "Come on Archie, I'll lock you up."

Officer Collins went to the control box at the end of the tier, and pulled the bar for Archie's cell door.

Collins was known to the inmates as "Punchy." He had been a hero of World War II, and had received the Congressional Medal of Honor. For his act of heroism, President Truman had given him a lifetime job with the Federal Bureau of Prisons. He had previously

240

done a great deal of boxing while in the service, and that was how he got the nickname "Punchy" from the convicts. He was well liked by most prisoners, and it was told that he had never written a disciplinary report on any man.

Archie lived three cells down. After Collins locked him up, he returned to Whitey's cell.

"That sure is a beautiful painting," he said again. "It's so realistic with her holding that a kitten. I'd sure love to own a painting like that."

Before Whitey realized what he was saying, he said, "When it's finished it's yours."

Collins looked surprised and said, "Thanks for the offer, but you know I can't accept anything from an inmate."

"Ah bullshit! Who the hell's going to know I gave it to you? And you know for sure I won't tell anyone I gave something to a screw, except a hard time!"

Collins chuckled at what he said, "It sounds tempting, but still I better not accept it."

"Ah shit, it's just between you and me. When the painting is ready, I'll roll it up, and all you have to do is slip it inside your coat. No one will know it's there and that's all there is to it."

"I appreciate that Thompson, I sure do. Okay let me know when it's ready."

Collins nodded his head at Whitey and departed. After he had gone Whitey thought over what he had just said to him. He couldn't believe it! Has something come over me? I must be getting weak! To hell with it! If I want to give that bull a painting, it's my business, I'll give him a painting.

The painting was twelve by twenty inches, and when it was ready he gave it to Officer Collins, who picked it up just as he was going off duty. Whitey never expected anything in return for the gift.

CHAPTER 38.

It was Wednesday morning, and while at work Whitey began to feel a pain in his right side. It started off as a dull ache, but became quite severe; he decided that right after lunch he had better report to sick call. He had seldom been sick in his entire life, and the pain in his side had him worried.

After lunch he told the M.T.A. of his problem. This was Whitey's first time in the sick line since his arrival over two years ago.

"How long have you had this pain?" the M.T.A. asked.

"It started this morning," Whitey replied. "At first it was just a dull ache, hardly noticeable, then it began getting stronger."

"How about right now, can you feel it?"

"Just slightly, it's not too bad now."

The M.T.A. decided to admit Whitey to the hospital, but first he must return to his cell for the 1:00 P.M. count. When it cleared the M.T.A. told him to return to the Lieutenant's desk.

Count cleared, and he returned to the desk as instructed. There was a guard waiting for him.

"Thompson 1465."

"Yeah that's me," Whitey replied.

"Good, I've been waiting for you, I'm going to send you right up to the hospital."

The guard opened the big barred gate to the Dining Room, after they passed through the doorway he re-locked it. To their left was another barred gate covered with heavy wired mesh. To the right of the gate was a push button that the guard pressed, and when he did, a bell upstairs in the hospital sounded. This was a signal to the hospital guard alerting him that a convict was on his way up. The hospital guard in turn pressed another button that caused a red light to flash at the gate below. It was a signal to open the gate and send the prisoner up. The guard unlocked the gate, and as soon as Whitey passed through he re-locked it, and returned to his post at the desk.

Whitey walked up a flight of concrete stairs, and on the second floor he was confronted by a heavy steel barred gate. A guard was waiting for him there, and once he passed through the heavy gate was re-locked behind him. The officer escorted Whitey down the corridor. The operating room and the M.T.A.'s station were on their right, and on the left side were a number of rooms behind solid wooden doors.

Further along to the left, was Robert Stroud's cell, "The Birdman of Alcatraz." He should have been call, "The Birdman of Leavenworth," for it was at Leavenworth where he started studying birds and became an authority on bird diseases. During his seventeen years on Alcatraz, he wrote, but did no bird research. His hospital cell was three times bigger than a regular cell, and in comparison to the other prisoners, he lived rather comfortably with all his books and information. Stroud was psychotic and not popular with all Alcatraz convicts. His health was failing, and he spent the last few years on Alcatraz in the hospital. He was later transferred to the Federal Medical Prison in Springfield, Missouri where he died on November 23, 1963.

Halfway down the corridor in front of Stroud's cell, was the Security Guard's desk. Whitey was ordered to stand there and wait.

Whitey took his place beside the desk while the guard opened the door and disappeared into a room. As he stood there he noticed a pack of Camel cigarettes lying on the desk top. He had not seen a Camel since his train ride to Alcatraz. He furtively looked up and down the corridor to make sure no guard was about. Seeing no one, he took two cigarettes out of the package, placed them in his shirt pocket, and resumed his position by the desk.

"Hey fellow, what's your name?"

The voice startled Whitey for there was no one in sight. Then he noticed Robert Stroud peeking through the tray slot in his door, at that moment the guard reappeared with the M.T.A.

"Just follow us Thompson," the officer said.

The guard and the M.T.A. accompanied Whitey to the far end of the corridor to another steel barred gate. The officer unlocked it, admitting them into the ward. There were six huge cells, three on either side, and Whitey was placed in the middle one on the left. After locking him up the guard departed leaving the M.T.A. just outside.

"Pick any one of those beds," he said, "and take it easy until the doctor sees you. He'll be here at approximately ten o'clock tomorrow morning."

"Tomorrow morning!" Whitey shouted, "Hell I could be dead by then!"

The large cell contained six unoccupied hospital beds. Apart from Robert Stroud who was in the hospital for protection, Whitey was the only patient. There was a thick impenetrable cell window that was located on the west side of the hospital. If one could see through it, he would have a bird's eye view of the yard, and beyond it, the magnificent sight of the Golden Gate Bridge.

243

At the base of the window stood a white table with a single drawer. Cautiously Whitey opened the drawer and found it contained a number of hardback books. One title caught Whitey's eye, *"Battle Cry."* He selected the bed nearest the bars, and lay down to read.

He found the bed quite comfortable with a thick mattress, clean sheets, pillow, and a blanket. It was a complete contrast to the hard solid steel slab he had become accustomed to. The last time he had lain on a similar bed was in the hospital at McNeil Island.

With a good book in hand he let out a sigh of contentment at the thought of the Camel cigarette he was about to light up. Just then he heard the outer gate open; he hurriedly returned the cigarette to his pocket. A moment later the guard appeared in front of his cell. He opened the door and ordered Whitey to get up off the bed.

"What the hell for?" he asked.

"Just get up, that's all."

Whitey slung his feet over the side, and sat on the edge of the bed. The guard went directly to him, reached in his pocket and removed the two cigarettes.

"Where did you get these from?" he asked.

Whitey sat there a moment and then answered, "From your desk, where else?"

The guard was taken aback by his honesty, and asked, "What gave you the right to take them?"

"The same right that son of a bitch had to snitch me off."

"Why do you say that?"

"Look, you didn't know you were missing any smokes, someone had to tell you, the only one who could of seen me was that fucking `Mockingbird.' "

There was a frown on the guard's face, he was undecided as to what to do or say or do next. His features seemed to relax somewhat and he smiled.

"All right Thompson," he said at last, "you were honest, you told me where you got the smokes, we will say no more about this." He tossed the two cigarettes on the bed and started to walk away.

"Hey wait a minute, you're not doing me no favor."

The guard turned to face Whitey and said, "Would you think it was a favor if I took those two cigarettes back, and wrote a report on you?"

"Hey if you got the guts go ahead and write a report, and tomorrow you'll be pounding the bricks looking for a job."

"Just what the hell are you talking about Thompson?" the guard was showing signs of anger.

"Just this, when you were in training to be a guard, one of the first things they tell you is to never leave anything laying around within reach of a convict, and that goes for keys, money, cigarettes, or

244

anything a prisoner can use."

Whitey picked up one of the cigarettes lying on the bed, and nonchalantly placed it between his lips lighting it up, and in a very causal voice he said, "Pretty good cigarette."

Without a word the guard turned and stormed out of the ward, slamming and locking the heavy barred door behind him.

Chuckling to himself, Whitey lay back on the bed to enjoy his cigarette and book.

He dozed off, and was awakened suddenly by the sound of keys. It was the guard unlocking the ward door. Along with the officer a convict entered pushing a food cart, and behind him followed the M.T.A. The inmate immediately filled a tray and slid it through the slot in the door, followed by a cup of coffee.

"How you feeling Thompson?" the M.T.A. asked.

"I still feel the pain. It seems to be hurting a little more than it had been, but it's bearable."

"If it gets worse let me know."

Twenty minutes later the guard returned with the inmate to pick up the empty food tray, cup and silverware. After they departed, the corridor and hospital ward became very quiet, almost an eerie quiet. For the remainder of the evening no one appeared except for the guard making his regular rounds.

At 8:00 or so, the pain in Whitey's side began to increase to a point so severe he could no longer keep his mind on the book.

"Hey M.T.A." he shouted.

He listened for sounds of activity, hearing none he called out again, "Hey M.T.A." again there was no response. Whitey was getting angry now, "Hey you fucking quack, you jive-ass pill-pusher get your ass in here, I need help. Heeeeeeeeey out there!"

He listened again for sounds, at last he heard it—keys.

He began to mumble under his breath, "A guy could croak in here."

A guard appeared at the inner door, "What's all the yelling about Thompson, what's wrong?"

"What's wrong? My side is killing me, I need something for it."

"Okay I'll tell the M.T.A.," the guard said as he relocked the ward door and left. He returned shortly with the M.T.A.

"What is it Thompson? The pain acting up?" he asked.

"Yeah it hurts like hell. I've been yelling for over an hour! I need something for it."

"Sorry Thompson I can't give you anything until the doctor sees you. You'll just have to tough it out until morning."

"I could be dead by then! Come on, give me something to ease the pain."

"I'm not allowed to prescribe anything. You'll have to wait damn it." The M.T.A. was losing his patience.

"If you can't do nothing, what the hell good are ya? A boy scout could do your fucking job, and do it better."

The M.T.A. did not deign to reply, he turned and stormed out.

At 9:30 the lights went out, simultaneously the dim overhead light came on, casting a ghostly twilight on the ward. The night's silence was disturbed by an uproar that came rocketing into the hospital. It was the hoarse bellowing of foghorns, one after the other from either end of the Island. A dense fog had drifted in again on the night wind from the Golden Gate.

Whitey was awakened the next morning by the sound of keys as the guard entered the ward with the food runner.

He was just finishing his breakfast when the M.T.A. came in.

"How's the pain this morning Thompson?"

Ignoring the question Whitey asked, "When's that doctor gonna show up?"

"He should be here soon. Now tell me, is the pain any worse?"

"It's about the same, if I don't move around it doesn't hurt too bad. I get sharp pains when I climb in and out of bed."

"Well the doctor will find out what's causing it. Then we can treat you. In the meantime just lay still until he gets here."

"Just lay still! Shit, a man could die before that fucker shows up."

"Just be patient Thompson, relax and you'll feel better."

"Yeah that's easy for you to say," Whitey retorted as the M.T.A. departed.

He attempted to read, but could not concentrate on the book because of the nagging pain.

After two hours of waiting his patience ran out, and he hurled the book at the opposite wall.

"Where is that fucking quack? Goddamn where is he?" he yelled.

He was still yelling when the outer door opened admitting the guard, followed by the doctor and the M.T.A.

"Jesus Christ, it's about time you got here! What did you do, stop for a drink?"

The doctor ignored Whitey's remarks while he waited for the guard to unlock the door.

Standing at his bedside the doctor said in a sarcastic voice, "Never mind the greetings, Thompson. I'm told you're suffering from a severe pain. Would you show me just where it is."

Placing his hand to his right side Whitey said, "Right here is where it hurts."

The doctor ordered the M.T.A. to take his temperature, as he was doing this the physician pulled down the bed covers, and probed around asking where it hurt the most. He then removed the

246

thermometer—the temperature was normal. Next he took his pulse and listened to his heart. When the examination was completed, the doctor informed the M.T.A. that all Whitey had was a slight internal infection, nothing at all to worry about. He prescribed penicillin, one shot a day for the following three days, and that should clear it up. The doctor immediately turned to leave.

"Hey," Whitey called after him, "what if it don't clear up?"

The doctor chose to ignored the question and left the ward.

"Hey you fucking quack, what if it don't clear up?" Whitey shouted again.

The M.T.A. followed the doctor out.

A few minutes later he returned to administer the first injection, and as he did so he said to Whitey, "You know Thompson, if you'd be a little more quiet you would get more attention!"

"If I didn't yell, I'd get no attention at all! Just give me the shot boy scout, not a lecture."

After the M.T.A. had left, Whitey lay quietly in the bed, and soon after the pain began to subside. The relief was well received, he dozed off until lunch time; then again until dinner.

That evening he asked the M.T.A. about a shower, and he was told he would have to wait until he was discharged from the hospital, unless he could talk the guard into letting him use the hospital bathtub.

That evening he asked the guard if he could take a bath in the tub that was located at the end of the ward. At first the guard flatly refused him, but Whitey was persistent in his winning ways. The guard finally approved.

"I'll be damned!" Whitey exclaimed as he proceeded to take his bath. "I haven't seen a tub in over twelve years! Wow weeeeeeeeee!"

The guard stood there a moment, and smiled at Whitey's pleasure as he turned the water valves on full force, filling the tub to capacity.

Whitey removed his robe, and climbed into the tub. Holding his breath he slowly submerged until he was completely under water. He stayed that way for a few moments, then his head popped above the surface.

"Damn this is luxury—real luxury!"

The antibiotics administered to Whitey cleared up the infection, and he was released from the hospital.

CHAPTER 39

It was a chilly foggy midsummer morning of 1961, and according to the weather it was hard to believe it was the middle of July.

It was unseasonably cold for that time of the year. From the Golden Gate a frigid blanket of fog had drifted in on the early morning wind. There would be no work today.

The weather played a big role for the prisoners; no matter what time of the year it seemed unbearable. The winters were no exception, if anything it was even more miserable, for they had the rain to contend with as well as the cold.

On this particular morning Whitey was lying on his bunk enjoying a cigarette when he heard unfamiliar voices. A few days earlier there was a strong rumor that a transfer was coming in from Leavenworth Federal Penitentiary. As he lay there the voices got louder and seemed to be coming from the Flats below. Whitey was curious as to who it was. He got out of his bunk and stepped to the front of his cell, and looked through the bars to investigate.

Down on the Flats standing next to the wall was a guard, and five convicts dressed in white coveralls. Whitey had an excellent view, and he carefully scrutinized the prisoners to see if he might recognized any of them. There was one tall man in particular with a shaved head who caught his attention. Whitey's pulse picked up speed, and he could not believe his eyes.

"Lou, is that you Lou?" he shouted.

The tall convict glanced around the Flats trying to distinguish where the voice came from.

The moment the big man turned, Whitey knew for certain it was his buddy, Lou Peters.

"Up here you dumb fucker! Up here on the second tier." Whitey had both arms thrust through the bars frantically waving them. Lou looked up, and the movement of Whitey's arms immediately caught his attention, his face lit up.

"Whitey—Whitey you little termite! I'm happy to see you man, how's it going?"

"Everything's fine Lou "

From the end of the tier Warren called to Lou, "Hey Lou, my name is Warren. You didn't know it but the Killer has been riding the broom on you ever since he's been here."

"Yeah I know he has, I could feel a magnetic pull!"

"All rights, you transfer, let's move out," the guard ordered. "Head straight for that door." The officer pointed toward the door leading to the clothing exchange and shower room.

"I'll catch ya in the yard this Saturday Lou," Whitey called after him.

"Hey Killer," Longo called, "That the guy you were telling me about?"

"Yeah Longo that's him, that's Lou."

"Hey Killer?" Warren shouted. "Next time I see your buddy Lou, I'm going to tell him how you ran him down, and called him a big fucking sissy!"

"I'm gonna sissy you Warren when these doors open up.!"

"Oh-oh," someone hummed.

Another voice called out, "Hey Killer."

"What the fuck do you want Mondoza? You gotta stick your two cents in now huh?"

Mondoza lived four cells to the right of Whitey on the same tier.

"When I see your buddy," Mondoza shouted, "I'm going to tell him you blame him for being shipped to the Rock."

Whitey didn't reply, instead he called out to Warren, "Warren, you fuck-head. I'm gonna waste you. Then I'm gonna kill me a fucking Mexican! Do you hear me Mondoza? You fucked up Wet-Back."

From the cell next to Mondoza another voice shouted, "Hey Killer."

"Yeah Archie you old fart! I knew you had to get in on this, now what do you want?"

"Nothing much Whitey, I'm gonna tell Lou I was talking to Yank Stewart out in the yard, and Yank told me that when you and he were on the chain gang, you was his cotton-head boy!"

"Woo-wooo-woooooo!" someone hummed.

"That's a goddamn lie," Yank's voice bellowed out from above, "don't you believe a word he says Whitey, he's full of shit, I never said anything about you."

Ignoring what was said, Whitey called out to Warren, "Hey Warren, I want you to add Archie and Yank to the hit list, I'm sending them down the drain too!"

"Oh-oh," the voice hummed.

This kidding in the Cell Block and was called "Playing the Dozens." They would laugh and kid back and forth with each other; this time Whitey was the scapegoat. They would not let up on him for days to come—or until they found a simple reason to get onto someone else.

Whenever a transfer came to Alcatraz, it was the talk of the Cell

House, and the highlight of the year. In a years time maybe five or six prisoners might transfer to the Rock, and perhaps five or six transferred to another prison. There was very little turnover on Alcatraz.

During dinner on the day of Lou's arrival, he and Whitey were seated at opposite tables, but managed to talk to one another.

"When you coming off Broadway Lou?" Whitey asked.

"This Saturday. I sure hope there's an empty cell near you Whitey. Anyway I'll see you in the yard Saturday."

That evening back in the cells Longo was talking to Whitey, "Yeah I think he could get into the Clothing Factory, I'll speak to Mr. Lang tomorrow."

"Okay Longo. Now all we need in an empty cell at this end of the tier."

"You'll have one tomorrow," a voice called from the next cell over. "I'm leaving in the morning, I'm on a chain for Leavenworth."

"That's great Kayo you lucky fucker!"

Whitey did not get a chance to talk to Lou until Saturday morning when they met in the yard. It was just like old times for the two friends as they shook hands.

"Damn Lou, I didn't expect to see you again. How come they sent you to the Rock?"

"About four months after I was sent to Leavenworth, a chain came in from McNeil and Blackie and Shorty were on it. You see, Blackie and Shorty screwed up again and were shot to Leavenworth .When I saw them I was disappointed not to see you with them, but they told me how you were shipped to the Rock the day after I left. When I heard about it I started to screw up hoping to get here myself. For the past three years I went to the hole at least a dozen times, but the bastards never transferred me until I punched out a bull. Next thing I knew I was on my way to Alcatraz, and here I am."

"Three years, can you believe it Lou? It's been three years since we left McNeil. Oh by the way, did you move yet?"

"Not yet the Lieutenant told me they'll call me off the yard when it's time to move."

"Hey that's good, listen, the cell next to me is empty, it's B-206, remember that. Tell the Lieutenant you want to go into B-206, okay?"

While they were talking, Longo, Warren, Mondoza, Archie, and Yank Stewart approached, and Whitey formally introduced them to Lou.

"We heard a lot about you from the Killer. He said you're good people," Longo told Lou.

Smiling, Lou thanked Longo for his compliment, and then he turned to Whitey and asked, "What the hell is this Killer business?

How come they call you Killer?"

"Ask Longo here, he can tell you how I got tagged with the name."
Longo barely finished explaining about the nickname when an announcement sounded over the PA system.

"Lou Peters, report to the Lieutenant for cell move, on the double, NOW!"

"Don't forget, cell B-206," Whitey shouted, "Also this afternoon the Classification Officer is going to see you. Tell him you want to work in the Clothing Factory, that's where we work, the fix is in, okay?"

The yard recall sounded, Whitey returned to B Block and found Lou had already moved into his new cell B-206.

A guard pulled the bar, and Whitey went into his cubicle, and the door closed behind him.

"Hey Lou," Whitey called. "You're some kind of a nut to get yourself sent to Alcatraz."

"Yeah I'm a nut and so are you Whitey. You haven't changed a bit have you?"

"Yeah I'm still the same, but I didn't deliberately get my ass shipped to the Rock."

"Fuck you Whitey, but to change the subject, I peeked in your cell, those are some really nice paintings you have in there. I didn't know you could paint."

"Neither did I until a couple of years ago, that's when I got started."

"There're good, real good—some of the best work I've seen. You've got a real gift there."

"Coming from you Lou I know that's a compliment. Thanks."

"By the way Whitey what is the hole like here?"

"You won't believe me, I was in there once, and that was over two years ago."

"You're right Whitey I don't believe you, I think you're lying."

"Hey man, if I'm lying I'm dying! I haven't had a shot on me in over two years."

"Hey Whitey this is Lou, I know you bro, you can't stay out of trouble a week."

"Hey Longo," Whitey called. "Will you tell this fuck-head buddy of mine the last time I was in the hole."

"Sure I'll tell him. Hey Lou he just got out last week!"

"You're full of shit," Whitey shouted. "You're lying like hell Longo, I'll see you when the doors open."

Laughter could be heard issuing from Longo's cell.

"Hey Warren old buddy," Whitey called. "You and I are tight, right pal? Will you tell this fool how long it's been since I been in the hole."

"It's been just about four days," Warren called to Lou.

"Hey you bastard, Warren, I'm gonna cut your tongue right out of your fucking head!"

Above the sound of laughter, Warren again called out to Lou, "Hey Lou, I was just kidding you. It's been over two years since the Killer has been in TU."

"That's right," Longo cut in, "he's a regular Sunday-go-to-meeting boy!"

By now everyone was joining in the playful harassment.

"Hey Lou," Archie called, "the Killer is a little Lord Fauntleroy!"

"All right Archie, I'm putting a contract on you and all you other bastards! And that goes for you too you fucking Wet-Back!"

"What!" Mondoza exclaimed. "Hey Whitey man I haven't said a word, I been just sitting here listening. I thought you and I were tight."

"We're tight, only if you keep a clamp on your big lip!"

Later on in the afternoon the Classification Officer came by, and approved of Lou's assignment to the Clothing Factory.

The following Monday morning Lou was put to work at the string table—it was an easy job pulling loose thread off the finished garments.

The two longtime friends, Whitey and Lou, soon took up where they had left off at McNeil Island—watching each other's back.

CHAPTER 40.

Two weeks before Lou's arrival, Warden Madigan took over as head man at McNeil Island. He was replaced by Associate Warden Blackwell, who took over the top position as Warden of Alcatraz. On November 26, 1961, he was officially named Keeper of the Rock. Arthur N. Dollison, Superintendent of the Shop Industries, became the Associate Warden.

One Saturday afternoon Whitey was working on a painting, and did not notice a pack of Pall Mall cigarettes and an orange lying on his bed until he reached for a tube of paint.

Whitey quickly peeled the orange and flushed the evidence down the toilet; then he split the orange in half. In a quiet voice he told Lou to stick his hand out between the bars. Lou complied, and Whitey placed half a section of the orange in his hand.

"Wow, I'll be damned! Where did you get this from?"

"Just dummy up and eat it!"

Allowing Lou time to eat the morsel, Whitey again told him to hold out his hand. This time he laid ten Pall Mall cigarettes in his palm.

"Wow! You hit the jackpot! Where's this shit coming from?"

"Never mind, just enjoy it and dummy up, I been receiving this stuff for sometime now."

"What's your connection Whitey? It must be a bull, right?"

"What the fuck's wrong with you Lou? You know better than to ask questions. Never look a gift horse in the mouth."

Lou was curious, he was curious about the Pall Mall cigarettes, for the only place they could come from was the outside world. The only one with access to the outside were the employees of Alcatraz. Lou knew a guard had to be giving him the cigarettes, why, he did not know, unless Whitey had something on the officer. As for the orange, there was nothing unusual, for there were ways of getting it from the Mess Hall.

Whitey had friends who worked in the kitchen. One of them was Johnny who on occasions would manage to get fresh coffee grounds to give to him. Whitey would put some into a clean Stud tobacco sack and like a tea-bag, put it into a hot cup of water. It didn't make the best coffee, but when one is in prison, anything is better than nothing.

Three days later Whitey shared an apple with Lou, and ten more cigarettes. Lou was baffled, he couldn't understand it; he was with Whitey every minute of the day while they were out of their cells. He decided to keep an eye on all activity on the runway. He didn't really care where the gifts came from, but his curiosity was getting the best of him.

Three days later Whitey again gave Lou half an orange and ten cigarettes. Putting two and two together Lou realized it was every third day he would receive these gifts from Whitey.

Three more days went by, Lou was watching the runway, and was prepared when Officer Collins came walking down the tier. Lou was standing at the front of his cell holding a mirror behind him while waiting for the guard to pass, and the moment he did so, he quickly put his mirror out between the bars at an angle just in the nick of time to see Officer Collins flip the gifts into Whitey's cell. The guard's action was so precise he did not miss a step as he hurried past. A few minutes after Collins went by Lou received half an apple and ten cigarettes. Lou thanked Whitey for the gifts, and knowingly he smiled to himself.

One Saturday afternoon Officer Collins while making his rounds confiscated a grapefruit from a prisoner on the west side of B Block.

"Are you going to write a shot on me Mr. Collins?"

"No, I'll give you a pass this time, next time I'll write you up."

Collins continued making his rounds, and as he passed Whitey's cell he tossed in the grapefruit, and walked away.

Whitey was grateful for the gift, and immediately began to peel it, and flushed part of the skin down the toilet. He was so engrossed in what he was doing he did not see another guard approach his cell. Whitey had his back to him as he dropped the remainder of the skin into the toilet.

"What did you flush? What have you got there Thompson?" Officer Murdock asked.

Without turning around he quickly dropped the biggest part of the grapefruit into the toilet bowl, and pressed the flush-button. He hastily stuffed the remainder into his mouth.

"What did you flush? What are you hiding?" Murdock demanded.

With his back still turned toward the officer Whitey chewed on the piece of fruit, and then hurriedly swallowed it. Halfway down his throat it got stuck and he began to choke.

"Turn around," Murdock ordered. "Turn around damn it, what have you got there?"

Lou, who had been asleep, woke up when he heard the guard

254

yelling.

"What the hell are you yelling at? " He shouted, "get the hell outa here with that noise."

Murdock paid no attention to Lou, "Turn around Thompson, show me what you're hiding."

Whitey was choking violently, and was at the stage of panic as he fought for air. He ran his index finger into his mouth in an endeavor to dislodge the piece of fruit. He was desperate, and fighting for his life. Repeatedly he tried to cough it up.

Lou recognized the choking sound, and knew Whitey desperately needed help.

He shouted at the guard, "Open his door you dumb bastard, can't you see he's choking."

Officer Murdock shouted, "Collins, open B-two-oh-four."

Whitey could feel his strength draining, His legs trembled, and he was ready to fall.

Officer Murdock yelled. "Come on Collins damn it, open B-204 damn it."

Whitey's body was shaking violently, and he dropped to his knees. Again he thrust his finger into his mouth; as he did so Murdock began shouting again.

"Don't you dare swallow it Thompson, I want it for evidence. Collins open this door!"

Subsequently there was a terrific roaring explosion as a ten-inch salt water main burst in the tunnel behind Whitey's cell. Thousands and thousands of gallons of salt water came gushing through the Cell Block.

At the precise second the water main let go, Whitey made a final effort to dislodge the piece of grapefruit from his throat. Starting from the pit of his stomach with subhuman dying strength, he came up with a tremendous cough. The piece of fruit flew out of his mouth landing on the floor. His strength gone, and gasping for air, he fell over backwards onto his bunk.

The Cell House was in a state of confusion. The sound of gushing water was deafening to the ears as it roared out of the tunnel through the vents into the cells. Guards appeared from all directions shouting orders, but no one could hear them above the roaring water.

Whitey lay on his bunk panting and gasping for air; his right arm hung over the side with his hand in the flowing water. After a few minutes the roar of water began to subside somewhat, and the guards' commands could be faintly heard.

One guard in particular was shouting, "Get the plumber, call the plumbing crew."

In the distance a prisoner was shouting above the noise, "Turn off the water you fucking hacks, I'm gonna drown in here!"

"Swim you dumb bastard," someone else yelled.

Lou held his mirror at an angle, and saw Whitey's lying on his bunk.

Whitey was breathing much easier now, and as he lay there he felt something bump against his hand. Straining to move his head he looked over the side of his bed just in time to see a piece of grapefruit as it floated under the bars of his cell onto the tier!

Officer Murdock was still in front of Whitey's cell, and happened to glance down and see a wedge of grapefruit brush against the side of his shoe. Floating on the water he saw his evidence go over the edge of the tier and disappeared down a drain.

CHAPTER 41.

It was nearing the end of the year and the Christmas holiday was just a week away. The inmates were informed they could put in a request for a two-pound box of See's Candy. Of course this only applied to inmates who had money in their prison funds. On Alcatraz the spirit of Christmas was absent. Except for a lone Christmas tree mounted in the Dining Room, there was no evidence to indicate that the holiday was imminent. There was no enthusiasm for the Holy Day, and the inmates ignored the decorated tree.

On Christmas Eve the convicts came out of the Dining Room on the return trip to their cells. The Captain and Mr. Dollison were waiting to check their name and number off a list, and hand them their box of See's Candy as they passed by. As they did so they wished each convict a Merry Christmas.

A Merry Christmas on Alcatraz, what a joke, Whitey thought as he returned to his cell. Immediately after his cell door slammed shut, he opened his box of candy. He could not believe what his eyes were feasting on—such a wonderful sight! He had to tease himself before he popped a chocolate into his mouth. He didn't chew or suck on it—he just let it lie there and melt on his tongue. For a number of years he had been starving for sweets, and it was hard to believe that a single moment could be so blissful as it was when he put the first piece of chocolate into his mouth! To Whitey it was better than having sex for the first time, and he began popping them into his mouth one after another. He was shocked when he realized in such a short time he was working on the second layer of candy. I want to save some for tomorrow he thought, and it took all his willpower to place the box of candy on the top shelf out of reach from his bunk.

There were a few prisoners who had an extra sweet tooth, and paid as high as $80. worth of art supplies to other inmates for a box of candy. Although Whitey had numerous offers he would not sell his candy no matter what price was offered.

For Whitey, New Years Eve was a little more exciting than the previous ones. At 9:30 P.M. the lights went out, and again a ghostly twilight settled throughout the Cell House. In the semi-darkness

257

Whitey and Lou had a quiet conversation. With the cell wall between them they could not see each other, but they could easily talk.

"Be quiet a minute Lou, I swear I just heard a chick's voice."

"You're dingy Whitey, you're hearing things."

"So I'm hearing things—hey Longo," Whitey called. "Did you hear a woman's voice?"

At that precise moment there was the distinct sound of a woman's voice.

"Yeah, I can hear it Whitey, I can hear it now," Lou said.

Wasting no time Whitey jumped up onto the cell bars. A second or two later inmates on the east side of the Block were climbing up on their bars trying to get a better view of the Bay where the sound of voices was coming from. Like monkeys, the convicts were hanging onto the bars all excited over the sound of a woman's voice.

"Hey, shut up, you guys," Whitey yelled, "shut up and listen."

He turned his attention to the windows. He could see rays of light casting shadows across the water, and riding on the gentle swells was a wealthy looking yacht.

"There it is, look toward the buoy, see it?" Whitey cried excitedly.

Everyone focused their eyes toward the buoy. A number of silhouettes could be seen moving about on the yacht, and by the sound of their voices, they must have been intoxicated. They were no doubt celebrating the oncoming New Year. There was laughter and merriment aboard, and from across the water a woman's voice called out.

"Hey you jailbirds—hey you jailbirds!" the voice carried on the night breeze through the open windows of the Cell House, giving it a musical tone as it drifted throughout the Blocks.

The yacht was riding dangerously close to the buoy, and each ground swell was bringing it nearer and nearer, but miraculously with only the luck of a drunk, the boat missed the buoy. It was now inside the two-hundred-feet limit, a no-man's-land for the unauthorized.

Suddenly from the gun tower a guard threw a switch, and a gigantic searchlight came on illuminating the area. The darkness no longer concealed the boat or the people aboard; they were at the mercy of the guard in the tower.

"This is a Federal Prison, you're in restricted waters," came loud voice from a bullhorn.

"This is a free country," the intoxicated woman shouted. "We can go where we please."

The bullhorn blasted again, "This is a warning. Get that boat out of here."

"To hell with you, this is our country, you can't make us go," was the reply.

The silence of night was broken by the unmistakable sound of a machine gun. A burst of fire came dangerously close to the boat. Like some giant monster letting go with a raucous roar from the deep depths of its throat, the bullhorn sounded, "You had your last warning!"

There was an echoing sound of an ignition, the deep bellow from the exhaust pipes as the powerful engines took hold, followed by a mighty roar as the throttle was pushed forward. The yacht picked up speed and disappeared into the darkness. After the yacht disappeared you could hear her wake splashing loudly against the cliffside, and off in the distance there was the distinct sound of her engine fading into the night, and so did the year of 1961.

CHAPTER 42.

Unlike the previous New Year, 1962 was a good beginning for Whitey. True he was still in a cell, but he had escaped the prison of his own making, he had torn down the shell that had engulfed him for so many years. He was becoming more of an extrovert and was developing new feelings for himself as well as for other people.

Many times he would think about animals, especially the ones in the zoos, and he wished that he had the power to set them free. He thought it was extremely cruel to put a wild animal in a cage for the sole purpose of human pleasure. Man could be locked up for a violation of law, and know why he was incarcerated, but one of God's creatures could spend its natural life pacing back and forth in a cage, and never understand why it was there. He often visualized how he himself would feel to go to bed at night without locked doors or steel bars around him.

Whitey's birthday, January 23, rolled around, but like all his previous ones, it was merely another day for he had completely forgotten his thirty-eighth birthday.

As usual when the work day was over he returned to his cell, and like hundreds of times before, he checked it out for any planted contraband. Finding nothing, he turned his attention to his bunk, and ran his hand over the covers. Suddenly his hand, as if it had a mind of its own recoiled from the blanket. It had made contact with a hidden object. Being extremely careful, he slowly pulled back the covers. To his surprise, lying there under the sheet was approximately thirty dollars worth of art supplies along with a note which read,

> "Whitey, no excuse, now do me a
> painting. Happy Birthday.
> Johnny."

The unexpected gift was very touching to Whitey. In return he not only did one painting, he did a total of six. This pleased Johnny immensely, and shortly after they were finished he sent them to a friend in Anchorage, Alaska.

A few weeks later on February 11, 1962, Sunday morning started off like any other Sunday. The inmates had just returned to their cells from breakfast, and were impatiently waiting for church and yard cal—especially yard call!

The baked chicken on Alcatraz was excellent—one of the prisoners favorite meals.

"Hey Killer," Longo called, "We're having baked chicken for dinner. I'm taking yours."

"You taking it before or after the fight?" Whitey asked.

"I guess it'll have to be after the fight," Longo laughed, then he called out to Archie, "I'm taking your chicken today."

"Ah goddamn Longo, not again," Archie sighed.

Laughter sounded, followed by other prisoners yelling playfully to each other.

"Hey Cowboy," someone yelled. "I'll trade you my next two sausage dinners for today's chicken dinner, okay?"

"Are you nuts?" Cowboy returned, "shove that Polish sausage up your ass."

"Oh-oh," someone hummed.

The good-natured banter continued until it was interrupted by church and yard call.

Whitey remained in his cell to paint. He barely got started when Chino dropped by. He was very interested in art work, and on weekends he visited Whitey on a regular basis.

"Hey Whitey how's it going? Say that's a nice painting your working on."

"Thanks Chino, how are things going with you and Johnny House?"

"Hey everything's cool man—say I gotta split, I'll catch you later." Chino took off at a run down the tier, and Whitey resumed painting.

Shortly after 10:00 A.M. Whitey heard footsteps and looked toward the front of his cell just in time to catch a glimpse of Archie walking by. This was unusual, for Archie always stopped for a chat on his return to his cell. Whitey was concerned and felt something was wrong. "Hey Archie," he called after him, "what's up?"

There was no reply, so Whitey held out his mirror, and three cells down he viewed Archie leaning over the runway rail.

Still holding him in view he called louder, "Hey Archie are you okay?"

Raising his head slightly from the rail, and in a faint voice Archie replied, "I don't feel well Killer, I—I just don't feel well. I felt bad out in the yard, that's why I came in early. I just want to get in my cell and lay down."

At that moment a guard pulled the bar admitting Archie to his cell. Whitey returned to his painting.

Whitey became deeply engrossed in his art work, and did not realize how fast the time had gone by until he heard the heavy trooping tread of the inmates returning to their cells.

Whitey called to Mondoza as he passed by, "Hey Mondoza, come here a minute."

"What is it Killer, what'd you want?" he asked.

"Look, Archie came in early, he's not feeling well. Look in on him as you pass his cell." "Yeah, I'll check on him right now," Mondoza replied, and started back down the tier stopping at Archie's cell. He found him lying on his bunk.

At that moment the guard pulled the bar, and Mondoza, along with the others prisoners on the runway retreated into their cells.

"Hey Killer what's wrong with Archie?" Longo called over to Whitey.

"I don't know what's wrong Longo, he just isn't feeling good—hey Mondoza! Put your mirror on the old man will ya, make sure he's okay."

Mondoza held his mirror outside his cell bars, then he maneuvered it at an angle to view the interior of Archie's cell. He was surprised to see an empty bunk, Archie could not be seen.

"Hey I can't see him," Mondoza yelled. "He must be on the—wait a minute, I see him now, he fell out of his bunk, he's on the floor."

Sounds of a gagging cough began issuing from Archie's cell.

"He's having a fit," Mondoza shouted again. "It might be a heart attack, he needs help."

Quickly Whitey jumped to the rear of his cell, grabbed his tin cup off the shelf, and in one bound he was back at the front of the cubicle. In a sweeping motion like one paints a wall, he ran the cup back and forth across the steel bars. Other prisoners followed suit.

"There's a man down—a man down! Get some help up here quick! There's a man down!"

Above the noise of clattering cups and shouting, a guard's voice could be heard, "What cell is he in? What's the number?"

"Two-one-oh!" came the reply. "Get some help up here quick, Archie's having a heart attack!"

The moment the inmates realized help was on its way an eerie quietness settled over the Cell Block. Except for the kicking and gagging sounds issuing from the old man's cell, you could hear a pin drop.

The sound of running feet could be heard as a guard charged down the runway past Whitey's cell. One glance at Archie told him the situation and he shouted an order for the Lieutenant to call the hospital for the M.T.A.

A few anxious minutes elapsed while Whitey and other convicts stood at the bars of their cells waiting for help to arrive. Finally the M.T.A. accompanied by the Lieutenant and two guards, came dashing down the tier to Archie's cell. More crucial moments passed as Whitey stood with a trained ear listening to the voices.

"Lift his head up. Hold him here, watch out now, watch it, okay, pick him up, pick him up. Easy now—easy."

All along the tier there were a dozen or more mirrors being held out of various cells, as the convicts watched the activity on the runway. Except for the Lieutenant and a guard leaning against the rail, no one else could be seen on the tier.

Suddenly from Archie's cell two guards appeared carrying him on a stretcher. As the small procession quietly made its way along the runway, a sadness settled over the Cell Block.

Long after the stretcher-bearers had passed, Whitey stood to the front of his cell with his forehead resting against the bars.

"Hey Whitey," Lou called. " Do you think Archie will be okay?"

"He would be if there was a doctor on duty. It'll take a couple of hours to bring one over from the mainland. Hell Archie could be dead by then."

"You really like old Archie don't you Whitey? I remember a time when you hated everyone, yourself included."

"Ah shut up Lou, just shut the fuck up."

After lunch was served yard call sounded, but Whitey remained in his cell. The afternoon seemed interminable, and to take his mind off Archie; he began to oil paint.

Along about 3:15 P.M. he was still busy painting when he heard someone calling up to Longo from the Flats.

Whitey set his painting aside, moved to the front of his cell and looked out over the tier at the caller. Standing below was a convict hospital worker called Phil.

"Longo's out in the yard, what'd you want him for?" Whitey called down to him.

"I just wanted to tell him about Archie. Archie died at ten minutes past two." Without waiting for a reply, the hospital worker walked away.

Whitey stood there staring down at the vacated spot where Phil had stood. He could hear his words lingering in his mind, "Archie died at ten minutes past two." The words were echoing in his ears. Damn it all, why did he have to die on Alcatraz? He deserved better than that.

Whitey took the old man's death very hard, and at dinner that evening he seemed to be in a trance—in fact all the occupants at the table were stunned. This was the first time in years old Archie was not sitting with them. The irony of it all was that at this particular

263

meal they were having baked chicken—Archie's favorite.

For this group of men at mealtime, especially dinner, was a fun-loving time. They would kid, joke, laugh, and harass each other in playful fun. Longo, Warren, Mondoza, Lou, Whitey, and of course Archie, who was a part of this select group, but now, except in spirit, he was not with them anymore, he was sorely missed.

At the dinner table Longo was sitting opposite Whitey who was seated with his back to the Dining Room gate.

"Look Killer—look!" Longo exclaimed. "Look the other side of the grilled gate."

Whitey spun his head around, and just beyond the gate were two guards carrying Archie out on a stretcher. He was wearing handcuffs with his arms folded across his chest, and his legs were bound in irons. Archie's body had to be taken to the morgue. All traffic to and from the hospital had to travel through the Dining Hall. But to move him at dinner time was uncalled for, especially for his friends, who watched the guards carry their dead comrade out in irons.

Prison regulations stated that no prisoner, dead or alive, could be transferred to or from Alcatraz, without wearing handcuffs or shackles.

"The filthy bastards," Whitey was angry, "Look at the dirty scum. They had to pick chow time to move him so we could see his dead body in irons, and they say *we're* not human."

Lou tried to calm Whitey down by placing his arm over his shoulder.

"Cool it Whitey," Lou told him. "It won't do Archie any good to get yourself fucked up."

"Yeah I guess you're right, but the sons of bitches piss me off, the dirty bastards, they had to wait until mealtime to put on that display. Shows how sick they are."

That night after 9:30 lights out, the Cell House remained silent. On this evening before going to sleep, the usual chatter, catcalling and laughter was missing. In its place there was absolute silence, for everyone knew Archie was gone.

Whitey lay there hardly daring to breathe for he could sense Archie's presence still within the Cell House. He felt his spirit would always be there, for even in death, there was no escape from the Rock.

His thoughts were broken when Longo softly called, "Gus, hey Gus."

Gus lived on the third tier directly over Whitey, and in a muted voice he replied, "Yeah Longo what do you want?"

"Gus do you know how to play Taps? If you do how about playing them for the old man, I'm sure Archie would like it."

Gus gave an affirmative reply. Then from his harmonica came the sweet and mournful sound of Taps. No bugle or trumpet could have sounded better as the soft notes flowed gently throughout the Cell Block. Every corner, every crack, every bit of space within the walls of this ancient prison felt the soft vibrations from this mournful tune. While Gus was playing Taps, Whitey lay on his bunk listening. When the tribute was finished, he could hear the echo of the notes fading quietly throughout the Cell House. He was thankful for the darkness and the confines of his cell; no one could see the tears. There were many more silent tears shed that night.

During his life Whitey had witnessed any number of deaths, and was not affected by any of them. Archie was special.

Archie's remains were to be shipped back east to his sister for burial. The inmates of Alcatraz put in a request for permission to take up a collection for flowers, and a little extra money to send to Archie's sister. The request was denied.

Two weeks after Archie's death, a number of convicts in TU set their blankets on fire. It was 12:30 A.M. and it was quiet in the cells, for the prisoners had settled down for the night. Officer Jamestone had just finished his rounds, and was seated comfortably in a chair reading a magazine. This particular guard was thoroughly disliked by the general population. Whenever he was on duty, the inmates would go out of their way to try to make his shift as miserable as possible, including the flooding of their cells, and regularly cussing him out. This time they succeeded.

As Jamestone leafed through his magazine, he felt relaxed thinking he had TU secured and well in hand. Suddenly the quiet evening erupted when a prisoner shouted, "Fire! Fire!"

Jamestone jumped out of his chair and ran for the wall extinguisher, then he charged to the cell that contained the fire. Just as he arrived to extinguish the flaming blanket, another prisoner called out, "Fire, fire, my cell's on fire!"

All hell broke loose with a chorus of voices, "Fire! Fire! Help my cell's on fire!"

In the excitement the guard ran from cell to cell shouting orders. It was becoming too much for him, and he quickly pressed the emergency button to summons help; then again he turned his attention to the business at hand. He was furious as he screamed at the prisoners to put out the fires. Jamestone was at the verge of panic. TU was beginning to fill with smoke making it difficult to breathe.

Again he began to scream, "Put out them fires you fools, put 'em out!" He was desperate now, very desperate, and he quickly pressed the emergency button again.

"Where the hell are they? I need help in here."

He ran down the Flats desperately trying to combat the flames, but it was all in vain. The howling convicts, the fires, the smoke, trying to breathe, the excitement of it all was too much for Officer Jamestone. The extinguisher slipped from his hands and fell to the floor, and with a cry of pain he grasped his head. To the enjoyment of the cheering convicts, his body twisted like a corkscrew before falling to the floor with a sickening thud.

Officer Jamestone had suffered a stroke leaving his left side partially paralyzed. After his recovery he was no longer able to work in the Cell Blocks, but he was still capable of shooting a rifle, and was assigned to a gun tower.

Shortly after the fire incident a notice was posted asking all inmates to donate to a fund for Officer Jamestone and his family. The prisoners of Alcatraz had nothing against the officer's wife and family, but their dislike for this particular guard was so strong that none of them would donate so much as a dime.

The Warden would not let the prisoners take up a collection for Archie who was one of their own, but had the audacity to expect a group of felons to donate a sum of money to a guard who was cruel and inhumane to every convict he encountered. When the inmates received the notice asking for donations, some laughed, some cussed him out, while others shouted, "Take up a collection for that prick? That no-good son of a bitch! He's nothing but a pussy, a no-good clapped-up pussy! I hope the bastard has another stroke and lands in hell! If he does, Archie's got seniority down there, he'll be there waiting for him to punch his lights out!"

CHAPTER 43.

The normal daily routine was soon resumed, and Whitey returned to his favorite pastime—oil painting. He had become accustomed to working in the cold dampness of his cell. Over the years many windows had been knocked out and never replaced. Whitey would hang a blanket over the lower section of his cell bars in an endeavor to keep out some of the cold drafts. Of course each time a standing count was to be made, he would have to remove the blanket, and after count cleared he would rehang it. No matter how cold it became it did not deter him from painting. Often he could be found in his cell wearing a pea coat under his bath robe with a blanket draped over his shoulders.

Toward the end of March, Whitey had a number of new admirers who would stop at his cell to view his paintings. The most recent admirer was Mickey Cohen, the alleged gambling czar and syndicate front man. Whitey had never known Mickey on the outside, but naturally everyone knew of his reputation. His reputation meant absolutely nothing to Whitey, he couldn't care less, but both men loved art work, and when time permitted, they would talk for hours on end.

Mickey Cohen, who had a penchant for ice-cream, was the owner of a number of ice-cream parlors in the Los Angeles area. On Alcatraz for desert, ice-cream was served once a week, and he had a tremendous craving for it. Whitey had never known another human who loved it the way Mickey did, so whenever it appeared on the menu he would give his portion to him.

"I sure appreciate this," Mickey would say, "and if I can ever do you a favor Whitey just let me know."

Cohen worked in the clothing department down in the shower room, and one Saturday morning Whitey asked him for a favor.

"My pants are getting kind of threadbare, I wonder if you could slip a new pair into my clothing bin."

On Tuesday the following shower day when Whitey turned in his dirty clothes, Mickey handed him a new pair of trousers.

If Mickey had been caught giving Whitey the new trousers without authorization he would have been sent to TU.

Whitey was not the easiest man to make friends with, but he liked Mickey the first time they met. On occasion the two of them, sometimes with Lou, could be seen in the yard sitting on the top bleacher step talking.

Cohen was a big-time syndicate man from the Los Angeles district, and the authorities tried to keep an eye on his activities.

"That's right," Mickey told Whitey and Lou one day, "they sent me here on a bum-beef. The law couldn't nail me for any illegal activities, so they hit me on a phony income tax charge, and here I am with fifteen years."

A short time after Mickey came to Alcatraz, Frank Carbo was sentenced to twenty-five years. He was also known as a notorious syndicate gambler. The sentence he received was for putting the fix in on topnotch boxers.

As Mickey and Carbo were both syndicate men, one would assume they had a lot in common. Instead there was friction between the two mobsters, and they never had anything to do with each other—not so much as a hello. Whitey never asked Mickey about it, he felt it was none of his business, and sometimes the less you knew about something like this, the better off you were.

Whitey knew Carbo by sight, but never exchanged words with him; when he was standing close by, Whitey did not like the vibes he received, so consequently he never liked the man.

It was Wednesday evening and the inmates were waiting to be released for dinner.

"Damn it's Wednesday, that means Polish sausage. I'm fed up with it. How about you Killer, are you tired of it?" Longo asked.

"No, I like Polish sausage, and I never get tired of it."

At that moment the Cell House Officer called out, "Chow down. Let go outside B-1!"

After the trek to the Dining Room, Whitey took his seat at the usual table with Longo, Warren, Lou, and the others. He noticed that no one was eating their sausage. It had been on the weekly menu for years, and most of the inmates were tired of it.

"Fuck you guys, I'm gonna eat!" Whitey picked up his fork and started to eat.

"Fuck this shit!" said Longo, and he threw his sausage across the Dining Room striking an inmate on the back of the head. Longo's victim spun around glaring from one man to the other, hoping to find the perpetrator. Not knowing who threw it, he in turn picked up his sausage and flung it with force. It bounced off the head of a man sitting two tables down from him! The second victim made a grab for his head, and looked around for the sausage thrower. Unable to identify him, he became furious, and hurled his sausage at another unsuspecting person!

In seconds Polish sausage came hurling from all directions. The meticulous complexion of the Dining area rapidly took on the aspect of a battlefield, it was truly a "Mess" Hall now! The only possible thing for the guards to do was to stand by and watch as the missiles flew. They were reluctant to push the button to release the tear gas, for that would surely set off a riot, and someone, including the guards, might get killed. However the officers knew the sausage throwing would only last a few minutes, and then come to a stop. They knew no real harm would be done, because this was the convicts way of letting the Food Manager know they didn't want any more Polish sausage on the menu.

Whitey sat there ducking and dodging the missiles as he tried to eat. He was really enjoying the sausages until one struck him on the back of the head. With a growl he reluctantly started hurling sausages with the rest of them.

It was like an orderly play period, for the inmates remained in their seats throwing and ducking Polish sausages. Now and then a prisoner would catch a flying missile, but most of them were picked up off the floor, and would be sent hurling through the air again.

Needless to say that was the last time Polish sausage was on the menu! Alcatraz food was well prepared, but now and then a menu change was needed.

CHAPTER 44.

It was the second Saturday in May; a beautiful spring day, and Whitey decided to go to the yard for the recreation period.

You could walk out to the yard any time of the year, and be greeted by the same scene, inmates jogging around the borders of the yard like boxers in training. A softball game would be in play with the usual big league intensity; while along the foot of the concrete bleachers four inmates would be playing shuffleboard on a long cement slab. Over to one side of the yard a few bridge experts, and dominoes' players sitting at their game, while other groups of men just stood about chatting.

As Whitey walked down the steps, he cast his eyes about taking in the yard scene, there was a game of handball in progress up against the west wall, and the two participants leaping about were Longo and Warren.

Whitey descended the stairs and made the trek toward them.

"Hey guys who's winning?" he greeted them.

"Who do you think?" Longo said with a smile. "You want to take on the winner?"

"No, I don't think so," Whitey replied, "I'll catch you later."

Whitey eased over to the dominoes' players, and was watching a game when Johnny approached him. He called Whitey over to one side, and said, "I'm having trouble with that fucking loud-mouth Chino again. You remember quite sometime ago I told you how he tries to bully us around in the tray room, and if he kept it up he's going to get hurt?"

"Yeah I remember Johnny. I had a talk with him a long time ago. I told him he'd better back off. What's happening now?"

"The son of a bitch is trying to push his weight around again, you know, loud-talking about things he don't know nothing about, sticking his face in where it don't belong, things like that. You know what I mean?"

"Yeah I guess so, but I don't know what to tell you Johnny."

"It's not me that has to be told, it's Chino," Johnny's voice carried a tone of anger.

"I understand Johnny, but I'm not his wet nurse."

"I know you're not Whitey," Johnny's voice softened, "I just thought you could talk to him, being as you know him so well."

"Okay House, I'll do it for you, but I can't guarantee nothing. Do you know where he is now, is he in the yard?"

"No, I think he stayed in. He's in the Cell Block."

Whitey didn't see Chino until the following morning when he yelled from the Flats.

"Hey Whitey, come to the front of your cell, it's me Chino."

Whitey complied and looked down to the Flats. Chino was in clear view leaning against the radiator next to the wall.

"Chino, you're just the guy I want to see, come up here a minute will ya."

"I can't slip up there this time Whitey, the bull's right there at his desk."

"Ah you fucking sissy! You can get by him, come on up here."

When the guard wasn't looking, Chino slipped up to the second tier to Whitey's cell.

"What'd you want man?" Chino asked. "Hurry up before the bull catches me."

"I got the word you're doing some loud-talking in the tray room."

"So what's it to you?"

Whitey's face turned red with anger, "It's nothing to me, absolutely nothing. Just get lost, get the fuck outa here!"

"Hey wait a minute Whitey, don't get mad at me, just what the hell are you getting at?"

"I have a good buddy who works in the tray room, he don't like your bullying shit. If you don't get your act together you're a dead man."

"Hey man, no one is going to fuck up Chino! I can take care of myself."

Whitey grabbed hold of the bars, and gripped them so tight his hands turned white, he was furious with the Mexican's stupidity.

"I ain't got no more to say to you Chino, just split, get the hell outa here."

Chino hurried away. Whitey stood at the bars shaking his head in disgust.

The tray room was located just off the main kitchen, the only access to it was through a single door from the interior of the kitchen. There were no windows except for the west wall that had a section removed to serve as a counter for dispensing trays to the Dining Room. Against the east wall were two huge stainless steel sinks used for washing and rinsing the large cooking pots. To the right of the sinks bolted to the wall were a number of racks for storing pots and pans. On the south side of the room, sitting there like a steam-puffing mechanical monster, was the sterilizing machine for all utensils and flatware. The crew consisted of five inmates, and between the operation of the machine and the men working, the noise was deafening.

The atmosphere in the tray room reminded one of a boiler room gang, for each inmate was stripped to the waist, perspiring freely in the one hundred-and-ten-degree heat.

Lunch had just finished; the trays were coming in fast and furious. The prisoners labored at their tasks, trying to keep up with the flow. Under these conditions' tempers were always short, and it was dangerous for anyone to say a wrong word.

In both pot washing sinks there were removable brass overflow water pipes. The pipes were eighteen inches in length, and weighed approximately a pound and a half each.

Johnny House was up to his elbows in pots and pans, and was scrubbing feverishly at the grime and grease. This was the peak of the work period; the pots and pans were piling up, while from the Dining Room the flatware was pouring in.

"Come on you bastards get a move on," Chino yelled above the noise, "come on let's go you fuckers!"

"We'll get done quicker if you shut your mouth and get the fuck to work," Bart, one of the crew workers yelled at Chino.

"Fuck you Gringo! I'll break your neck, just get the fuck to work! That goes for the rest of you punks too, you hear me?"

It was not long before the pots, flatware, and all the utensils were washed and stored away ready for the next meal. All that remained now was the cleaning up of the tray room, mopping the floor, wiping off the counter, and sterilizing machine.

"Come on Johnny, grab a fucking mop, let's go!" Chino ordered.

"Hey drop dead Chino you mother-fucker! You're no boss in here," Bart shouted.

"I told you I'd break your fucking neck," Chino made a grab for Bart, and as he did, Johnny struck him across the head with one of the overflow pipes. It was a sickening blow. Chino fell to the wet floor; blood was gushing from the back of his head. As he lay there Johnny swung the pipe again, catching his victim across the forehead. There were no outcries from the fallen man; he was knocked unconscious the moment he received the first blow. Again Johnny swung the pipe, hitting him on the bridge of the nose. It was a crushing blow that tore the left eyeball clean out of its socket.

"Hit him again! Kill the bastard!" Bart shouted as he kicked Chino in the ribs.

"Shut up Bart, shut up, and help me," Johnny ordered.

Both men grabbed hold of the victim and pushed him bodily under the sink. When this was accomplished, Johnny washed the blood off the pipe and replaced it in the sink. Bart turned on the water hose and began hosing down the floor, washing the blood down the drain. Johnny grabbed the big rubber squeegee, and pushed the loose water toward the drain. Then the crew together pitched in with mops. Once the job was finished and the tray room secured, the inmates wiped the perspiration from their faces, put on their shirts, and straightened themselves up. Then nonchalantly they walked out into the kitchen, and calmly waited for the guard to inspect their job area.

The officer went into the tray room, and immediately came charging out, dashed to the kitchen phone and rang Control.

After the noon meal Whitey returned to his cell, and when yard call sounded he remained in to paint.

Shortly after 2:00 P.M. Lou returned from the yard, and while waiting for the guard to open his cell, he spoke to Whitey. "I heard someone got piped in the tray room."

Whitey's countenance turned white as he spun his head from his painting to look at Lou.

"Who was it?"

"I don't know Whitey, all I know is someone got it. They tell me Custody questioned the tray room gang, but no one knew anything, no one would cop out."

"How about Johnny House?" Whitey asked anxiously, "did you see him in the yard?"

"No. When I came in Johnny and the rest of the kitchen crew were just coming out of the Dining Room. I don't think they busted anyone, hell they can't bust the whole kitchen crew."

The news had taken Whitey aback, he was almost positive it was Chino who had gotten piped, he hadn't expected anything to happen so quickly. But if it was Chino, then Whitey was sure that Johnny was the assailant. He had to find out.

"Look," he said to Lou, "quick before the screw pulls the bar, run down the tier and see if you can find out who it was that got it."

Lou walked off, and in a few minutes he returned.

"Nothing Whitey. I got to go and lock up now, Collins is on his way to pull the bar."

After Lou was secured in his cell, Officer Collins stopped to chat with Whitey.

"Hello Thompson," he said, "what are we painting now?"

Whitey turned to face the officer, "Hi there Collins, bust any heads lately?"

The guard chuckled, reaching in his pocket for cigarettes, he offered one to Whitey.

"I hear someone got it in the Culinary this noon, anyone I know?" Whitey asked.

"Yes it was Chino. They found him under the sink in a pool of blood. The Lieutenant immediately inspected the rest of the crew for signs of blood, but everyone was clean. Chino's in critical condition, he'll be lucky if he makes it."

The conversation was interrupted with yard recall, and Officer Collins beat a hasty retreat down the runway.

Whitey stood at the bars trying to grasp everything that had occurred. He was thankful Johnny was not busted, but similarly, he had feelings for Chino and wished the incident had not happened. But it did happen and there was nothing that could be done about it. Chino was not a bad sort, he just didn't know how to keep his mouth shut.

That evening at dinner time, Whitey was standing in line waiting to be served. He saw Johnny just behind the grilled gate to the kitchen. The distance was too great for them to talk without shouting. Johnny nodded his head in acknowledgment, and Whitey reciprocated as he walked to the front of the steam table to receive his ration.

The dinner was well prepared, but it was tasteless to Whitey, and as he sat there eating, his thoughts were not of food. He wished he were far away from the rat race of prison. He visualized himself living up in the mountains; doing woodwork, oil painting, and not having to worry about anything or anyone; with the nearest neighbor living miles away.

He finished his meal, and as he was walking out of the Dining Room he saw the M.T.A. coming through the screen door from the hospital. The M.T.A. walked out of the Dining Room and stopped at the Lieutenant's desk. Whitey followed him.

"How's Chino?" he asked.

The M.T.A. turned around and looked at Whitey for a moment. At first it seemed he wasn't going to answer. Then suddenly his expression turned into a concerned look.

"He's alive," he said, "that's about all. If it wasn't for his excellent physical condition, he would be dead right now, but how much longer he can last I have no idea. The scalp and bone structure was shattered badly from the blows, and his left eye was torn out of his head. Except for the movement of his right eye, his body is completely paralyzed. He can't talk or utter a sound. There is not much we can do for him here, and if he is still alive tomorrow morning he will be flown to Springfield Missouri Medical Center. Outside of that Thompson, there is not much more I can tell you."

Early the next morning Chino was transferred to the Springfield Medical Center, and rumor had it he passed away shortly after his arrival.

CHAPTER 45.

It was shortly after 4:00 P.M. on the last Monday in May, when the quietness was broken by the heavy trooping of convict workers returning from the Industry Mills. After traveling through the electronic detector, the single line of men split up forming the usual two lines. One moving toward C Block and the other to B. Whitey climbed the stairs of B Block followed by Longo, Lou, and Warren.

As they approached their cells Whitey commented, "Hey look, there's dust all over the place! What gives?"

"I know what it's from," Warren stated. "It's from A Block, a couple of maintenance bulls are knocking a cell wall out with a jackhammer. They're going to widen the cell. They want to make it big enough for the Classification Officer, they're going to move his office in there."

That evening shortly after the 9:30 lights out, Whitey had just crawled into his bunk when Lou called to him in a hushed whisper.

Whitey scooted himself up so his head was touching the bars, and in a quiet voice he said, "Go ahead bro, what's on your mind?"

"There's going to be a breakout, did you know that?"

"Yeah I know about it, I've known it for weeks."

For the next two weeks the maintenance officers worked the jackhammers in the empty A Block section. What Warren had said was true, for they were taking out the dividing wall between two cells to make a small office for the Classification Office.

The Cell House guards were unaware of what was occurring at the precise time the maintenance officers were running the jackhammers. Four convicts who lived on the Flats of Michigan Avenue directly across from A Block, were working at the vents at the rear of their cell undercover of the noise of the jackhammers. They too had a hammer, but it was a small homemade electric chipping hammer. For days on end you could hear the sound of the huge jackhammer, and if one had a talented ear, he could distinguish the sound of the smaller hammer blending in with the noise of the jackhammers. No one was the wiser as to what was going on, except for a number of trustworthy convicts.

On the night of June 10, 1962, there was the usual amount of noise in the Cell House, but anyone with a sharp ear would have realized the tone was a trifle louder. The guitar players were strumming away, while the chess players were calling out their moves, "King knight to black bishop three." A grumpy response, "Queen pawn captures."

In adjoining cells on the third tier an argument was developing, the pitch was rising. The confusion continued after 9:30 P.M. lights out, and under the commotion Whitey and Lou lay on their bunks whispering to each other. At the same time in the pale light they could see a guard in the south east end of the gun gallery reading a magazine. To the Gun-Rail Officer the confusion in the Cell House was the usual nightly noise, and he paid no attention to it.

"They're out Whitey," Lou whispered, "I can hear them going up through the tunnel."

At that moment a clanging sound echoed throughout the Block. Both men quickly looked toward the gun gallery guard, but he seemed to take no notice of the clanging noise.

One of the escapees had let a pipe or pinch-bar slip out of his hand, and the object had fallen the distance of a three-story building, striking the plumbing pipes in between cells on its way down. Clang—bang—bang, it hit the bottom at last.

Whitey's eyes were riveted on the guard during the fall of the object. He was relieved to see that the officer paid no heed to the sound, and continued to read his magazine.

Approximately 10 or 15 minutes later you could hear the sound of footsteps going across the roof of the Cell House, and the customary sea gulls that roosted on the roof had been disturbed. They could be heard squawking and screeching in protest.

Whitey thought it strange on the part of the tower guards; they were well trained in their profession, and had been employed on Alcatraz for quite some time. On this particular night they either were asleep, or felt the disturbed sea gulls did not warrant an investigation.

Some of the prisoners who were still up shucked off their clothes to settle down for the night. Their movements filled the Cell House with a sound like rustling leaves on a gentle wind.

In the quietness of his cell Whitey lay there straining his ears for any telltale sounds. He heard none; all was quiet, and he hoped they made it.

The following morning—June 11th, 1962—the Cell House was shaken alive by the usual raucous blast of the rise and shine horn that jarred the men awake. Twenty minutes later a guard shouted, "Count time, standing count."

276

Simultaneously the guards, one on each level, started their trek around the tiers making their count.

Whitey heard the distant voice of a guard over in C Block getting on to a prisoner who was not standing up to the bars, "Stand up for count, what the hell's wrong with you?"

Down on the Flats another guard with the nickname of Tiny (the name given to him by the inmates because of his huge size), was approaching the corner of B Block making his count.

Officer Collins was working the second tier, and hurried by making his count run. After he passed by Whitey remained at the bars listening to the forward movement of the guard below.

On the Flats Tiny was hustling along making his count when suddenly he broke stride, and skidded to a halt. There were three cells in a row with lights out, and the occupants appeared to be sleeping.

"Get out of those bunks," the officer ordered. "Count time, come on move it."

The prisoners did not stir. Tiny moved up to the bars, reached in to shake the inmate's shoulder, and as he did so, the head rolled over the edge of the bed onto the floor. The guard emitted a frightened scream; at the same time he jumped away from the bars with the intensity of a man who had been stung by a bee!

"It's a dummy! It's a dummy!" the guard shouted. "Lieutenant," he called out as he ran down Michigan toward Times Square.

The Lieutenant heard the commotion, and came rushing around the south east corner of B Block barely avoiding a collision with the terrified guard.

Gasping for air, the overweight officer stood in panic trying to collect his wits about him. The Lieutenant grabbed him by the shoulders and shook him violently.

"What the hell is the matter? Speak up," he ordered.

"There's been a breakout Lieutenant, a breakout'"

The Lieutenant and the officer rushed back to the cell. Morris was gone, and in his place was a dummy. In the next cell they discovered another dummy left by John Anglin, and next to him was his brother's cell, Clarence Anglin, he too, was also gone, leaving behind a dummy. In the cell next to Clarence was Alan West.

Along with the other three prisoners Alan had attempted to escape. But at the moment of departure he was unable to make it through the aperture in the rear of his cell. He was terrified; a few days previously he had put temporary mortar in the hole to pass the inspection of regular cell shakedowns. Alan did not know when he was closing the hole with temporary mortar, he was sealing himself in more effectively than the original concrete.

On the previous night Alan chipped madly in a last desperate attempt for freedom, but to no avail. Frank Morris and the Anglin brothers were long gone through a vent in the Cell House roof. Alan West was horrified, he knew he could not make it for time had run out. Exhausted, he fell back on his bunk to await morning and the inevitable.

The Lieutenant charged back to the Cell House desk, Control was immediately notified, and all hell broke loose. Horns sounded as the Lieutenant returned to the cells of the escapees. Guards appeared from all directions, storming the Cell Blocks.

The Lieutenant ordered a guard to open Alan West's door so that he could be taken to TU. Later the rumor was out that the guards (though this was never proven) beat him mercilessly, endeavoring to find out the escape plans and destination of Frank Morris and the Anglin brothers. As far as the convicts knew, Alan West never talked.

The next two days Alcatraz was locked down. Whenever there was an escape, or an escape attempt, the Rock generally was locked down for at least a week, but in this incident it was only for two days. The reason for such a short lock down was that Custody wanted the inmates out of the Cell House so they could go through each cell with a fine tooth comb.

On the first day of work after the escape, Whitey returned to his cell and found it in total disarray. Custody had gone through his personal belongings discarding them onto the floor; these items were followed by his blankets, sheets, pillow and pillow case. His oil paintings, paints, brushes, and the rest of his art supplies were also strewn all over the floor. The rear wall of the cell had the paint chipped and scraped off, and ground into his bed clothes and art supplies. The tubes of paint had been stepped on squirting the contents all over the floor.

Whitey was furious as was every other prisoner on Alcatraz He was at the exploding point, and felt like attacking the first guard that came near him. But he did not let this happen, Whitey knew he must keep himself under control at all cost. It was touch and go, and he had to keep a grip on himself until this all blew over. He knew that Custody had been humiliated through the escape, and to retaliate they had to strike out at someone. So they destroyed his personal property, but Whitey was not the only scapegoat, for the guards tore up many of the other cells. Custody was so furious, if you looked the wrong way at a guard you would end up in TU! Whitey attempted to get his cell back in order; it wasn't easy.

For the ensuing weeks there were continuous shakedowns, and the break up of the cells. All a prisoner could do was grit his teeth and bear it, for Custody was looking for the slightest excuse to rough a convict up and put him in TU.

A young inmate called Dugie, had an extra pair of socks in his cell, and an officer who shook his cubicle down, found them. The guard confronted him with the extra socks. All Dugie had to say was, "Gee I'm sorry about that, I didn't realize I had an extra pair." The guard no doubt would have just confiscated the socks and that would have been the end of it.

But no, Dugie was mad, and had to open his mouth, "You dumb sons-of-bitches," he ranted, "you can find an extra pair of socks in a cell, but you couldn't see a man-size hole knocked out of a cell wall!"

For this remark he spent the next two weeks in the Special Treatment Unit.

Immediately after the breakout the FBI was called in. A dozen or more inmates were questioned each day, but no one talked. Whitey knew it would be a matter of time before they called him in for questioning. He had become quite popular amongst the inmates with his art. , and it was a known fact someone supplied the materials, and painted the faces on the dummies.

One week after the escape the prisoners were waiting for work call. Officer Collins stopped at Whitey's cell, and told him, "Don't come out when work call sounds. It's the FBI Whitey, they want to have a word with you. I'm not supposed to tell you this, but they're going to question you about art supplies."

"Art supplies? You mean what I've got *left* of them."

"Look Thompson, just between you and me, I don't give a shit who painted the dummies, or anything about it. But when you go in there for questioning don't get mad and flare up. Just answer their questions in a normal tone. Don't give them an excuse to screw over you."

"I'm pissed off about my supplies. I don't give a fuck if they knock my head in, they won't be getting a cherry."

"That's not it Thompson, you've been clean for quite some time now, keep it that way."

"Okay Collins, thanks for the advise. For a screw you're all right," Whitey smiled.

After Collins left, Lou called out to Whitey, "Hey Killer what the hell did that bull want?"

"Nothing much," Whitey replied, "he told me not to come out for work call."

"Why? Did he say why?"

"No, he didn't Lou, he didn't tell me why."

Shortly after work call, Officer Collins called out to Whitey as he pulled the bar opening his cell, "Okay Thompson, let's go."

Whitey stepped out onto the runway, and with Officer Collins acting as escort, he was taken to the Visiting Room.

279

Seated at the far end of the room behind a table, were the Associate Warden, Captain, Counselor, and an FBI agent. Whitey took his place in front of the table with a guard standing to one side of him.

"Well Thompson," the Counselor said, "it's been a few years since you had a disciplinary report, and I've received a number of outstanding progress reports on you. I'm pleased in your change of attitude. Now to the business at hand. This gentleman is with the FBI and would like to ask you a few questions."

Whitey shifted his eyes toward the agent.

The agent said, "I'll get right to the point. I understand you are quite an artist. We know it took someone, an artist perhaps, who had the knowledge of how to mix the color of flesh tone for the dummy heads. I understand neither Morris nor the Anglin brothers had that knowledge, so that means someone with that knowledge helped them, and it could have been you."

"It could of been but it wasn't," Whitey snapped back.

"Okay Thompson, if you're holding back information, we'll certainly find out about it."

Whitey gave a short derisive laugh and said, "I don't know nothing."

"Okay Thompson, that will be all." Turning to the guard the Counselor said, "Return him to his cell and bring in the next man."

Returning from work, Lou and Longo stopped in front of Whitey's cell.

"Hey Whitey what happened?" Lou asked.

"They took me to the Visiting Room for questioning, they're trying to find out who supplied the paint for the dummy heads. I told them nothing."

"Do you think they'll be questioning me?" Longo asked.

"Shit I don't know Longo, they said they were gonna question all the artists in the joint."

That evening returning from the Mill Whitey found his cell in a turmoil. All his possessions along with his art supplies were strewn all over the floor. He went into a rage, and grabbing the bars he kicked and yelled.

"You dirty bitches, you low-livered bastards! Look at that cell, they tore it up again."

"I know you're mad Whitey, but cool it. Hell, look at my cell, it's all fucked up too."

Whitey looked into Lou's cell; sure enough, his things were scattered all over the floor.

Whitey was mad, and turning to Lou he said, "You know why they tore up our cells? It's because of the escape, that's why. Fucking

280

bulls are taking it out on us, the mother-fuckers."

"Easy Thompson, just take it easy now."

Neither man had seen Officer Collins walk up behind them. Whitey spun around to confront the speaker and recognized the guard.

"Look at my cell Collins, look at it. Were you in on this?"

"No, I wasn't in on it. I can't say that I blame you for being mad, that's why I took the time to come by. I don't want you to screw yourself up."

"Mad! You're goddamn right I'm mad! They destroyed my art work, and all my supplies, am I supposed to be happy?"

"I know Thompson, I know how you feel, but you been here long enough to know this will all blow over in a few weeks. So just hold yourself together, take it easy and don't foul up."

"He's right Whitey," Lou said. "Hell I'll buy you some art supplies and help you replace what you lost, okay?"

"No Lou, but thanks anyway." Whitey's temper subsided somewhat as he turned to Collins, "I guess you're right, I'll cool it, but they're still a bunch of sorry pricks."

Collins turned to leave, and Lou called after him, "Hey Collins I heard a rumor that they going to shut the joint down, is that right?"

The guard continued down the runway, and as he walked away he called back, "I don't know, it's just a rumor—could be though."

Shortly after Collins left, Longo, Warren, Mondoza and a few more inmates came walking down the runway.

"Goddamn they did it again!" Longo shouted.

"They hit everyone's cell," Lou told him, "They got mine and Whitey's too."

"I guess after yesterday they're pissed off," Warren volunteered. "J.V. Bennett, you know the Director, he flew in yesterday from D.C. He was steaming mad about the breakout. After he got here, he called a staff meeting. From what I heard, he chewed some ass out. He sure got on the bulls, he told them, 'Just because you officers have an inmate locked up, you think you can start daydreaming and forget all about him. Well you're wrong, you can lock up an inmate, but you can't lock up his mind. While you smart officers goof off, the inmate is using his brains, and that is something you officers don't have! I hate to say this, but I have to admire Frank Morris and the Anglin brothers for their daring escape, but if you officers had kept on your toes instead of getting lax and lazy, I would be admiring you instead of them.'"

"Get into your holes," a guard shouted, then he pulled the bar sliding all doors open. Whitey, Lou, Longo, and the rest of the inmates retreated into their cells. The doors slid shut behind them with the customary clang-bang.

281

As for Frank Morris and the Anglin brothers, no substantial proof was ever found that they drown. It would seem that if they had, at least one out of the three bodies would have turned up. They made their bid for freedom, and quite a number of Alcatraz inmates felt that they had made it, but the majority felt they hadn't.

One thing was certain; whether they made it or not, they would never be completely free of Alcatraz. Dead or alive, no matter how a prisoner may leave the Rock, a part of him will always be there, and remain there forever.

At the time of the Morris/Anglin brothers escape, Alcatraz had been condemned for over ten years, but the June 10 break out was the final cinch to shut her down. The rumor was strong throughout the prison that the Rock was finished, but if you asked a guard if Alcatraz was being closed down, he would say, "Hell no, they will never close the Rock?"

The truth of the matter, the staff members, and guards did not want Alcatraz closed down because it was good duty for them.

Alcatraz was dying, it was past its time, there was no longer a need for a Devil's Island in the United States. However the officials cried, "We need the Rock," and they went as far as to try to get the inmates to riot so they could say to the public, "You see, we need Alcatraz, we need it for these mad-dog killers! We can't close the Rock!"

The prisoners of Alcatraz no longer received the good meals they were accustomed to. The quality of food had fallen off, but the convicts were wise to the ways of the officials; a riot would benefit them, not the cons. Consequently word was passed around from prisoner to prisoner, "Whatever the guards do, don't lose your cool, just be calm and hang tough. It's the only way we can beat them. They will have to close the Rock."

When they closed Alcatraz there would be no winners or losers—for they all paid a price, and if there is a winner, it would be the sea gulls.

For the inmates the next few weeks were agonizing ones. Whitey lost track of how many times he returned from work to find his cell in total disarray. Each time he did, he would keep his cool and calmly straighten it again.

In a five day period, it seemed as though he had his clothes off more often than he had them on! Every guard he chanced to meet would make him strip on the spot. One afternoon when he came up for lunch, he had to undress six times on shakedowns he received between the Industry Mills and B Block. He was almost insane with rage and at the boiling point, but to all outward appearances' one

282

would never know it, for he kept his expression calm and collected.

It was like a game of chess, you make your move, then I will make mine, only in this game, Custody was making all the moves while the prisoners stood pat. Custody tried to convince the inmates into thinking Alcatraz would remain open. To prove their point, they tore down the old fences, and then erected new twelve foot chain link double fences that ran along the west side of the Island. Why would they put up new chain link fencing that ran into thousands of dollars if they were going to close down Alcatraz?

Then they tried to prove their point further by installing thousands of dollars worth of sound devices throughout the Cell House. The officials went through a large expense account trying to convince the inmates that Alcatraz was not closing. But it was all in vain, the prisoners of Alcatraz would not riot. The chess game was over, the convicts had won.

CHAPTER 46.

August came and went, and by late September all was quite on Alcatraz, the guards were back to normal again, and the quality of food picked up. Whitey no longer feared his art work would be destroyed, and was able to resume his painting.

Again the daily routine was in play; time moved slowly, and on the morning of October 20 the rise and shine horn sounded just like any other morning. After count cleared the inmates made their morning trek to the dining room. When breakfast was over, they returned to their cells to wait for work call to sound. It would be late today for on the early morning breeze a fog bank had swirled in from the Golden Gate.

A calmness settled over the Cell House, this was not unusual for the inmates were disappointed, disappointed because of the fog that had rolled in at this late hour. They had anticipated freedom from their cells, but as long as the fog held, there would no work today.

Whitey was lying on his bunk with his head rested against the bars talking to Lou.

"What do you mean something is going to happen? You mean a riot or something like that?" Lou was asking.

"No man not a riot, nothing stupid like that. I wish I could explain it but I can't. I just have a feeling—you know what I mean, like something good is gonna happen."

"Like someone is going to give you a blow job?"

"Oh-oh," someone hummed.

"Nothing like that you dirty fucker! Get out of the gutter Lou."

"Hey Killer who's giving the blow job?" Longo called.

"You are you punk."

"Oh-oh," someone hummed again.

"Hey Killer, all kidding aside," Longo continued, "you say something good is going to happen, like what?"

"Hell I don't know," Whitey replied. "I was just telling Lou I felt like. . . ."

Whitey did not finish the sentence for his cell door began to slowly open, he quickly jumped off his bunk, and stuck his head out the doorway.

The guard who had just pulled the bar called down the runway, "Thompson, report to the Classification Office, the Counselor wants to see you."

Whitey stepped out on the tier, and peeked into Lou's cell.

"You see fucker, I told you something was gonna happen. No doubt they're going to apologize and turn me loose!"

"Turn you loose! Ha-ha-ha, all that Counselor wants is to let you know a hold has come in on you."

Whitey turned down the runway, and as he walked by Longo's cell, Longo called after him, "Hey Killer, so it's the Counselor who's giving the blow jobs!"

"Woo-woo-woooooo!" the hummer sounded.

As Whitey walked down Michigan Avenue work call sounded, the fog line was lifted. All cell doors along the Flats slid open. Simultaneously the inmates stepped out of their cells, and just as quickly the doors closed behind them.

The long line of convicts tramped toward the north end of B Block, while Whitey continued south on Michigan Avenue to the end of A Block. In their respective turns other cell doors throughout the prison clattered open. Immediately followed by many stomping heels as the human chain of men descended the steel stairways, and tromped across the concrete floor.

At the south end of A Block, Whitey turned left at the corner, while up in the gun gallery a guard observed his every move.

After all these years, Whitey still resented being stared at by a guard. He stopped in his tracks and glared up at the gun gallery guard. At first he was going give him the finger, but changed his mind and continued to the Classification Office.

The Counselor heard Whitey approach the doorway and looked up from his desk.

"Ah Thompson I've been expecting you. I want you to state your full name and number."

"You know my name and number, you know every man on this Rock."

"I know Thompson, for the record I have to ask you your name and number."

"Okay, Leon W. Thompson AZ 1465."

"Very good Thompson, now I have some good news for you."

"Last time I heard that, they tried to hang a murder rap on me."

"Nothing like that Thompson," the officer assured him. "I received a letter from the court clerk to have you ready for release."

"Are you fucking with me?" he took a threatening step forward, "Counselor or no Counselor, I don't go for your fucking jokes."

"Easy Thompson, easy," the Counselor reminded him. "It's true,

I have my orders to release you just as soon as the papers come in from the court. This letter was in advance to notify us to have you ready. You're as good as a free man, you'll leave in a few days."

It took a few moments for Whitey to grasp the meaning of what was said. Suddenly he executed a deep knee bend, and then with all his strength he sprang straight up in the air, legs wide apart and with arms waving he shouted, "*Heeeeyheeeeey, whoooooo-eeeeeee!* I don't believe it!"

The Counselor let him have his moment, and then he tried to calm him down.

Whitey's face was animated with excitement; his heart was pounding with joy. The feeling was contagious to the Counselor; for he too felt a sense of joy at seeing this man overwhelmed with happiness.

"I don't know just how soon your release papers will be in Thompson, but we have to be prepared, and get you ready."

"Get me ready! Man I've been ready for years! Just open the gates and turn me loose!"

"Well it's not quite that easy. Now just let me tell you why you're being released early."

"I don't give a damn," Whitey cut in, "as long as I go free. After fourteen and a half years, no doubt the judge realized he got the wrong man!"

"No, no," the Counselor laughed, "I'm afraid you were the right man Thompson. Anyway the reason for the release is that the sentence you received was illegal. Now the robbery charges were within the law, but the shotgun charge was wrong. You see the District Attorney had charged you with failing to register a sawed-off shotgun. Well under the Fifth Amendment it states that a man doesn't have to say or do anything to incriminate himself, and if you had tried to register the weapon, you would have incriminated yourself. It would have been admitting that you had an illegal shotgun. The D.A. should have charged you with possession of a sawed-off shotgun instead of failing to register a sawed-off shotgun. Do you understand? But anyway the sentence was illegal, and the judge had no alternative but to terminate your sentence, and order your release. You see Thompson, another prisoner was charged with failing to register a saw-off shotgun, and he filed a writ in Federal Court stating the Fifth Amendment. No person has to say or do anything to incriminate himself. The writ was upheld, and the laws were changed, and the court was forced to free all Federal Prisoners on this charge, and you happened to be one of them."

The Counselor offered his hand to Whitey, "Congratulations. I guess that's about it Thompson. After you return to your cell and officer will come and escort you to dress out."

Whitey thanked the Counselor and departed. As he made his way back to B Block, he had a new skip to his walk.

It was a wonder the south gun gallery guard didn't think something was wrong with Whitey the way he skipped by. He was going faster and faster then started to run. Suddenly he came to a skidding halt looking up toward Lou's cell. Then he remembered the fog line had been lifted, and Lou must be at work.

"Hey Lou are you up there?" he called anyway.

"Yeah I'm up here, where the hell did you think I'd be?"

"They're cutting me loose Lou, I'm getting out," Whitey yelled excitedly.

"No kidding, is that right Whitey?" Lou was excited. He thrust both arms through the bars and waved frantically. "Hey that's great Whitey, it's fantastic, I can't believe it."

"Well you better believe it Lou, it's true. Look I'm going to slip over to see if House is in his cage, I'll be right back."

Whitey hurried around the north end of B Block, and as he rushed passed the Lieutenant's desk, the Cell House Officer called after him, "Hold it right there Thompson, where do you think you're going?"

Whitey paid no attention and continued down Broadway. The officer took after him in hot pursuit.

Whitey came to a skidding halt in front of Johnny's cell and shouted, "Hey Johnny"

Johnny had been sleeping, and as he dropped his feet to the floor he recognized Whitey.

"What's all the excitement about?" He asked.

"I'm leaving Johnny, I'm getting out."

"You're getting out? You mean you're going free?"

"Yeah that's right, I'm. . . ."

Whitey was interrupted by the guard's harsh voice, "Just what do you think you're doing Thompson, you don't belong in this area."

"I know it. I just wanted to tell my friend I'm leaving, I'm getting out."

"So that's why the Counselor sent for you. Well, congratulations Thompson. But I got to return you to your cell now."

"Hey man, that's sure great news Whitey, when will you be leaving?" Johnny asked.

"I'm not sure, in a few days I guess when the papers come in. Look I gotta go Johnny, I'll catch you later."

Whitey returned to his cell and the guard locked him up.

At that moment the yard door opened. The Industrial Mill workers were returning for lunch.

Twice a day the inmates make their trip to the Industrial Shops, and from the moment they leave the Cell House building they are quiet and orderly until the return trip from work. The moment they

287

step through the threshold into the Cell House building, the loud shouting and noise begins. The sound magnifies three to four times its intensity.

Whitey heard Longo calling before he came into view, "Hey Killer I hear you're leaving. I just seen Johnny going into the Chow Hall, he told me you're getting out. That's great news man." Then at the top of his lungs he shouted, "Hey Tennessee, Yank Stewart, everybody, the Killer's leaving us, he's getting out."

The entire east side of B Block went into a roar of congratulations.

"Whitey, good luck pal," someone yelled out.

"Hey Killer you lucky bastard, take the first drink for me!"

On and on they yelled, one after another wishing him good luck. The congratulations were genuine, for the men of Alcatraz were always happy to see a fellow inmate go free.

Since Alcatraz opened in 1934 as a Federal Prison, and until the day of its closure in 1963, only six prisoners were ever freed directly from Alcatraz. On October 25, 1962, Leon W. Thompson was added to this rare list of names. In most cases an inmate was transferred back to McNeil Island, Leavenworth, or Atlanta Federal Penitentiaries. Where after a short period of time, if a man was scheduled, he was released.

After lunch was finished, and count cleared, Whitey was escorted to dress out. At the dress out he settled for a brown pair of dress pants, white shirt, yellow tie, brown jacket (Eisenhower style), with brown socks and shoes.

The remainder of the day passed by uneventfully, and the evening was spent chatting back and forth with Lou.

"What are your plans Whitey? What are you going to do when you get out?"

"I don't know Lou. I guess I'll go back to Sacramento. But right now I'm gonna try to go to sleep. I feel tired pal, I'll see you in the morning."

"Yeah sure, okay I'll see ya."

Whitey lay there with his eyes wide open; sleep evaded him for he had too much on his mind. At 1:00 A.M. when the guard made his count, he was still awake. He was thinking about his discharge papers, and was hoping there was no mistake, but maybe there was. His thoughts were running at random, and maybe the court had him mixed up with another Leon Whitey Thompson! Ah this is crazy thinking, of course he was going free, didn't they take him to dress out? And when you dress out it means you're getting out. Then a new thought struck him. He was worried the release papers might have gotten lost in the mail, or maybe the judge forgot to have his clerk send them out. At this very moment the papers might be sitting on the clerks' desk! The dumb bitch, Whitey thought, she forgot to mail them! Ah relax, he told himself, the papers will be here in a day or so.

At last he felt drowsy, and moments before he fell asleep, his thoughts were of Rose.

The following morning shortly after work call sounded Whitey's cell door opened. This is it he thought! With excitement flowing through his veins, he jumped off his bunk and stuck his head through the open doorway.

"Is this it?" he shouted to the guard.

"No I'm sorry Thompson, you're wanted in the hospital."

"Shit!"

Whitey reported to the Cell House desk where the Lieutenant was waiting for him.

"Good morning Thompson."

"Good morning Lieutenant Ordway."

In disbelief he raised his eyebrows, "I can't believe you said good morning, Thompson."

Whitey stared at the Lieutenant, and wondered what the big deal was.

"For the past four years every time I said good morning to you Thompson, you never answered," Lieutenant Ordway told him, "but today you said good morning, what's the difference between this morning and all the other mornings?"

"There was nothing good about all them other mornings Lieutenant. Now that I'm going free, it is a good morning from here on out!"

Smiling the Lieutenant said, "Yes I know you're leaving us Thompson, and I think congratulations are in order. How are you feeling physically?"

"I guess I'm a little on edge," Whitey replied. "These past few days were a little rough waiting for my papers to come in."

"I know how you feel Thompson. I'll have the M.T.A. give you something to calm you down a bit. You're going to be with us until Monday or Tuesday. I'm sorry to say we received word that your release papers were sent to McNeil Island by mistake, otherwise you'd be leaving this morning."

"What a fucking bummer—that's just great! I figured something like this would happen. That stupid court clerk sending my papers to the wrong prison. I have to spend three more days in prison because of her stupid error."

"I'm sorry Thompson. Come on let's go up to the hospital."

The Lieutenant unlocked the gate to the Dining Room, and after relocking it they made the trek up to the hospital, where they were admitted by the M.T.A. who was waiting for them.

"Who've we got here Lieutenant? Is this Thompson?"

"Yes, and look, he's a little on edge, so I want you to give him something to calm him down."

"Okay Lieutenant, will do." The M.T.A. turned to Whitey, "So you're leaving us Thompson, well before you go we have to give you a physical."

"What for? You think I'm contagious with something? You think I might contaminate the free world?"

"You never know Thompson, better safe than sorry!" The M.T.A. laughed, then ordered Whitey to remove his shirt, and proceeded with the physical examination. When it was completed, he administered medication to settle Whitey's nerves before he was returned to his cell.

At 11:45 A.M. the inmates returned from the Industry Shops.

Lou stopped in front of Whitey's cell, "Shit you're still here, I thought maybe you'd be gone."

Longo, Warren, and a few other inmates also stopped in front of Whitey's cell. They were disappointed to see he was still there.

"What happened Killer, no news yet?"

"The Lieutenant told me my release papers were sent to McNeil," Whitey replied. "I won't be getting out until Monday or Tuesday."

"Hey Whitey are you still here?" a voice called from the Flats. Then another voice called out. Soon everyone was yelling to find out if he had gone.

Whitey raised his voice to the top of his lungs and yelled, "I'm still here goddamn it!"

For the remainder of the day time passed by slowly for Whitey, and the sleepless night was even longer.

Sunday morning finally rolled around, and after breakfast count had cleared, Whitey decided to go to the yard. It would give him a good chance to say farewell to his buddies.

It seemed like everyone was out there except for Lou who remained in his cell. Whitey spent the next half hour talking to different inmates, and then he and Johnny sat on the lower bleacher chatting with each other. They were interrupted by Mickey Cohen.

"Whitey," Mickey called, "can I see you a moment."

"Sure Mick, I'll be right with you." Whitey turned to Johnny, "I'll catch ya after a while House, okay?"

Whitey caught up to Mickey who was waiting for him at the north end of the bleachers.

"I hear you're getting out in a few days," Mickey stated. "What are your plans? I may just have a deal for you."

"What kind of a deal we talking about?" Whitey asked cautiously.

Mickey looked sharply around the yard before answering, seeing no one standing nearby, he replied, "How would you like to pick up ten grand?"

Absorbing what Mickey had said, Whitey stood there a moment, then he replied, "Yeah sure, who wouldn't like to pick up some extra bread? But what has to be done for it?"

"Nothing much, just a quick job Whitey, but you'd have to go to L.A. You won't be there long, just long enough to make contact with one of my people."

"I don't know if I like what you're getting at Mick. I don't think it's my type of work."

"Don't give me that shit Whitey, I know a little bit about you. When you were at McNeil Island, you were a Collector, you used to cave in heads just for cigarettes. Well I'm offering a little more than cigarettes. You been down fifteen years, and it's going to be tough on you out there. All you have to do is go to L.A., stay there two, possibly three days at the most, and come away with ten Gs. That's not bad money for just a few days."

"Look Mick, I got a good idea what the job is, but why don't you cut the crap, come right out and tell me what I have to do."

Once more Mickey looked around, and in a very hushed whisper he said, "It's a hit job. Five grand in advance, and five when it's over."

"I kind of figured that's what it was, but I think I'll pass on it."

"Don't be a fool Whitey, it's a good chance for you."

"I don't know Mick. By the way, how come you're asking me to pull this job?"

"Because nobody knows you Whitey, none of my people know who you are, and above all, my enemies don't know you at all. You're perfect for the job. Besides how much going home money will you have?"

"I'll have over eighteen hundred."

Mickey laughed, "Hell that's no money! What are you going to do when it's gone?"

"I won't wait until my money is gone. I'll look for work as soon as I get out."

"Whitey, be realistic, who's going to hire an ex-con from Alcatraz?"

"I'll worry about that when the time comes."

"You don't have to worry at all Whitey, just tell me it's a go and I'll set it up. You'll receive five of the ten grand just as soon as you hit L.A., what do you say, is it a go?"

"Tell me more about it."

"All right, here's how it is, the day you get out call CH2-4037. Can you remember that?"

"Yeah I'll remember."

"You call that number," Mickey continued, "and ask for Ben. When he asks who you are, you reply by saying 'All's well in October.' That's all you have to say. He'll know I sent you and give you further instructions. You got that?"

"Yeah, yeah I got it, but suppose I change my mind?"

"If you do, you better change it before you make that phone call."

"Okay Mick, I guess this conversation is over."

"It's not only over," Mickey stated, "it never took place, right?"

After lunch Whitey remained in his cell, he had a great deal of meditating to do. He wasn't quite sure about the Cohen deal. He thought about his release papers, and hoped they would arrive tomorrow.

Monday was uneventful. On Tuesday morning the rise and shine horn jarred him upright, and he was about to hop out of bed when Lou called, "Whitey, today's the day."

"Yeah Lou," Whitey replied, "I hope you're right."

After breakfast, work call sounded. As the inmates on the second tier passed Whitey's cell, they bid their last farewells.

When the Cell House guard was not looking, Yank Stewart and Shorty McCoy, sneaked up to Whitey's cell to wish him well.

"I hope it's not another twenty years before I see you again Whitey, but no matter, it's been a pleasure to know you pal."

"Same here Yank, if we ever meet again, I hope it's on the outside, that goes for you too Shorty. I hope you both get out soon."

After shaking hands, Yank and Shorty fell in line with the parade of inmates walking by.

Prisoners on the first and third tiers who were on their way to work, were not in Whitey's vision, but he could hear them as they passed by above and below. They too called out good wishes and good luck. Longo, Warren, and Mondoza stopped long enough for a few words.

"So long Killer, good luck," Longo said.

"Yeah that goes for us too," Warren and Mondoza added.

"So long you guys," Whitey called after them. The three men fell in line with the workers, and disappeared around the corner of the Cell Block.

Lou had waited until everyone else had passed by and was gone.

"Well old buddy this is it," he said.

"Yeah Lou, hopefully when you return from work I won't be here."

"You'll be gone Whitey, I'm sure of it. This is your day," Lou said as he reached into Whitey's cell to shake hands, and as they did, their eyes met and locked.

"There isn't much to say Lou that we haven't already said, so I guess it's goodbye for now."

"So long Whitey, good luck to you pal, and take care."

292

The moment Lou disappeared from in front of his cell, Whitey began to pace back and forth. He attempted to light a cigarette, but had trouble holding the match; after two tries he finally got it lighted. He was feeling nervous and was trying to control himself.

With the inmates at work the Cell House had a deserted feeling about it. It was quiet—a ghostly quiet, and Whitey felt a loneliness engulfing him, but the feeling immediately vanished when a guard walked up to his cell door.

"Are you ready to go Thompson?"

Whitey spun around on his heels to face the speaker, Officer Collins was standing there.

"Does a bear shit in the woods? You know I'm ready to go."

"Okay Thompson, then this is it. Grab your box while I open your door."

Whitey had his personal belongings packed in a cardboard box; he held it under his arm waiting for Collins to pull the bar for the door's final opening, which it did with its usual loud bang.

Whitey stepped through onto the runway; he waited a moment to watch the heavy barred door close for the last time. How nice, he thought, never to hear it slam shut again.

Collins was waiting for him at the end of the tier. As they started down the stairs Whitey asked him if he could walk over to Broadway to say goodbye to a friend. Collins approved.

When Whitey and the officer walked up to his cell Johnny was lying on his bunk. At the sight of Whitey he jumped up, reached through the bars and grabbed hold of his outstretched hand. For a brief moment they stood there speechless.

Whitey broke the silence, "Well this is it old buddy, I'm on my way."

"You sure are Whitey, and I want to wish you all the luck in the world."

"You're going to have to cut it short Thompson," Collins reminded, "we're running a little behind time."

Still holding Johnny's hand, Whitey choked up a bit as he said, "It kind—it's kind of hard to say so long, you've been a real pal Johnny, and I know we'll never see each other again."

"Yeah that's the way it goes. So long Whitey, it's been my pleasure."

Whitey released his hand, and with the guard at his side they started to walk away.

"Hey Whitey," Johnny called.

Without breaking his stride, Whitey looked over his shoulder toward Johnny's cell, "Yeah Johnny?"

"So long pal, good luck."

At the end of Broadway, Collins unlocked the barred door, "This is as far as I go Thompson, I want to wish you luck also."

"Thanks Mr. Collins, you know coming from you that means a lot to me. Like I told you once before, you're okay even if you are a screw!"

Officer Collins smiled, and after shaking hands Whitey continued on through the barrier of steel doors. As he reached the last door a guard was waiting for him, and led him into the Visiting Room area.

The guard pointed to the set of civilians' clothes draped over the back of a chair and said, "There you are Thompson, you can get dressed."

This was the first time in almost fifteen years that he was putting on something other than prison clothes. He was happy everything fitted perfectly, even the shoes, but he was having difficulty tying his tie.

"What's wrong Thompson?" the guard asked. "You forgot how to tie a tie?"

"Looks that way don't it?"

"Here let me do it for you," the officer volunteered.

This took Whitey by surprise; he couldn't believe this guard was actually tying his tie. At that moment the Classification Officer came in with his release papers. After Whitey signed them, he received his Industry work check for eighteen hundred dollars, along with sixty dollars in cash.

The Classification Officer extended his hand to Whitey, "I want to congratulate you Thompson, on your release."

"Yeah thanks a lot, say how about Warden Blackwell, isn't he going to shake my hand and wish me luck?"

The Classification Officer merely smiled as he shook his head.

"How disappointing," Whitey gave a mock sigh, "I've been in a number of joints, and I've done a lot of time, but know what, I've never had a warden shake my hand yet—coming or going! I've seen a lot of Hollywood movies where the warden always shook the convict's hand just before he went free, but I'm a son of a bitch if a warden ever shook my hand!"

The Lieutenant had entered the room and smiled at Whitey's remark. "Are you all set Thompson? Are you ready to go?"

"He's all yours Lieutenant," the Classification Officer told him.

Carrying his cardboard box on his shoulder, Whitey left the Visiting Room with the Lieutenant. Together they walked out of the building, down the short flight steps to a waiting bus.

As Whitey boarded the bus, his mind flashed back to the day of his arrival wearing shackles and irons. But today the picture was in reverse, for he was without restraint, and there were no armed guards to watch his every move—it was a pleasant feeling.

After he was safely seated in the bus, the driver closed the door;

started the engine, and with the sound of gears grinding, he jammed the stick into first.

The bus creaked and rattled its way down the twisting route, nothing like the day of arrival when it had labored up this narrow and tortuous road.

A few minutes later, Mondoza, who was working the docks, watched Whitey as he stepped off the Carryall bus.

"Good luck Whitey," he called out.

"So long Mondoza, take care man, play it cool."

"What else I can do pal?"

The Warden Johnston had just pulled into the slip and grated against the landing as the passengers disembarked, four guards and two civilians.

"Okay Thompson," the Lieutenant said, "you can go aboard now."

With the Lieutenant directly behind him, Whitey stepped aboard, and selected a seat in the passenger cabin.

Mondoza was still watching from the dock as the lines of THE WARDEN JOHNSTON were cast off. With a thunderous roar the engines came alive. As the boat backed out of the slip the skipper pulled the cord, and the shrilling sound of the horn echoed across the Bay.

Once clear of the slip, THE WARDEN JOHNSTON began to move in a forward motion toward San Francisco. As the huge craft pulled away, Mondoza started to wave. Whitey walked out onto the weather deck, and waved back to him. Both men continued to wave until they were out of sight.

Whitey lowered his hand, and then focused his attention on San Francisco. *The Warden Johnston* was on a direct course now as she plowed across the Bay. Seemingly, down by the bow, she plunged through the waves rather than over them keeping the deck and pilot windows awash. Soon the outline of the Fort Mason dock loomed up ahead. The skipper cut back on the throttle, and the vibrating boat went silent as she glided in toward the dock. Quickly she came alive again with a mighty roar of the engine as the skipper gave her full throttle astern, and then, All Stop.

Whitey picked up his box and made for the gangway.

"Well this is where I leave you Thompson," the Lieutenant said. "I hope you won't be back!" He held out his hand, and Whitey accepted it.

"This is it Lieutenant, I won't be back."

"I hope not, you go with Officer Turner, he'll drive you to the Bus Depot. Good luck to you."

Turner accompanied Whitey to a government car, and after placing his box on the rear seat, they were on their way. It seemed rather strange for him to be sitting in the front seat beside a guard.

traffic, giving Whitey an opportunity to take in the sights. At a crosswalk waiting for a red light to change, two young girls passed in front of the car; the one nearest to Whitey looked through the windshield at him. For a moment their eyes met and held. Whitey's heart picked up a few extra beats. A female, he thought, a real live female! And a very pretty one at that! Quickly he lit up a cigarette, and while doing so an unusual feeling came over him, he was sure he knew how an alien from another planet would feel.

"Well here we are," Officer Turner announced. "The Greyhound Depot, we have about a twenty minute wait."

Whitey stepped out of the car, and opened the rear door to retrieve his box. Officer Turner also got out, and came around the side of the car just as Whitey was closing the door.

"I'll go to the depot with you Thompson," the guard said.

"No need for that," Whitey said sharply. "Just give me my ticket and I'll be on my way."

"Sorry, I have my orders. I have to stay with you. I'll give you your ticket just before you board the bus."

Whitey was getting a trifle mad, "Hey what the hell is this shit, I'm a free man now."

"Not yet Thompson, not for twenty-four hours," Turner said with a smirk.

"Hey, I don't need no babysitter to wait for a bus, don't you understand, I'm a free man now."

"Not quite Thompson, for the next twenty-four hours you will still be under the jurisdiction of Alcatraz, then you are a free man."

"I don't give a shit what you say, I don't want people seeing me standing here next to a bull. Just give me my ticket and go."

"I told you I can't do that, you'll just have to wait until you board the bus," Turner said with authority.

"Fuck your ticket! I'm not on parole, I'm discharged." Whitey's anger was at a danger point. "I'll buy my own goddamn ticket." With that he started to walk into the depot.

"Wait a minute," the guard ordered, "just wait one minute. What did you just say?"

Whitey turned around to face the guard, and in a sarcastic voice he said, "I'm not on parole, I'm discharged, so shove your ticket!"

"Can I see your papers?"

"Hell yes you can see them," Whitey reached to the inside of his jacket, extracted the document, and handed it to Turner.

The officer read the paper, and as he did so, his face began to redden.

"I'm—I'm sorry Thompson, I was under the impression you were going out on C.R, (conditional release) I didn't know you were discharged."

"Well you know now. You have no jurisdiction over me."

Turner handed Whitey his papers along with the bus ticket to Sacramento.

"Okay Thompson," he said as he held out his hand, "I guess you're on your own."

Whitey ignored the guard's hand, and turned to walk away.

Officer Turner shrugged his shoulders, "Well good luck anyway Thompson." He turned to the car, and just as he reached for the door handle, he heard Whitey call his name.

"Hey, hey Officer Turner."

"Yes Thompson."

"Thanks, thanks a lot."

Officer Turner smiled and waved as he entered the car and drove away. With him went Whitey's last tie to Alcatraz—or was it?

With his box under his arm, Whitey went inside the depot and entered the cafeteria. He walked over to a vacant table where he left the box. Then went up to the counter to place his order.

Seated to his left were two bus drivers having coffee, and to his right, a woman and three men were eating their meal. The cafeteria was humming with activity, from the behind the counter came the sound of clicking dishes, along with small talk from the waitresses.

A nervous feeling came over Whitey when he saw a pretty waitress coming his way. He made out he did not see her approaching, and pretended to be studying a large menu mounted on the wall behind the counter.

"Good morning sir, can I help you?" the young waitress asked Whitey as she set a glass of water in front of him.

Whitey was afraid to speak; his mouth was dry and felt like it was full of cotton. He was worried if he tried to talk no sound would emerge.

God, he thought, how do you talk to a girl?

The smiling waitress spoke again, "Can I help you sir?"

With a slight tremor Whitey replied, "I'll—I'll have a cup of coffee.'

Still smiling, the waitress turned to the coffee maker. Whitey watched her movement as she filled the cup. She set it in front of him and pushed the sugar bowl within his reach.

"Would you like some cream?" she asked.

"No, no thank you."

"Is there something else you would like?"

Is there something else I'd like? He thought, *ooooooo-weeeeeee* is there! But I sure as hell can't ask her for that!

"No thank you, the coffee is fine—oh wait a minute, do you have any cigarettes?"

Pointing beyond the cash register, she answered, "Yes sir right there in the machine."

"I'll need change." Whitey produced his wallet and handed her a ten-dollar bill. "Take out for the coffee also," he added.

The waitress took the ten and made change.

"Here you are sir," she said as she counted it out to him, "five, six, seven, eight, nine dollars and twenty-five, fifty, seventy-five, eighty, and one dime makes ninety—nine dollars and ninety cents, thank you sir."

Whitey felt embarrassed when he handed her a ten-dollar bill to pay for a ten-cent cup of coffee, he wished he had ordered something to go with it. Self-consciously he picked up his change from the counter and returned it to his pocket. He picked up his cup of coffee, and started across the dining section to his table. As he walked across the room his hand was trembling, causing the cup to rattle in the saucer, spilling a small portion of the liquid on the floor.

At last he made it to his table and quickly set the cup down. He sat a moment trying to get his nerves under control; then reached for his coffee. Again his hand shook, but he managed to take a sip before setting the cup down. He was getting mad at himself for acting so nervously.

Come on, he thought, get a hold of yourself, what's wrong with you? Relax, try it again, drink some more coffee, you'll be all right.

He made another attempt at the cup—this time he was successful and found the coffee delicious, it certainly beat the coffee on Alcatraz.

With his nerves seemingly under control, he rose from the table and walked over to the cigarette machine. There was a sign posted on the glass front that read,

CIGARETTES 30 CENTS
DEPOSIT CORRECT CHANGE
NICKELS AND QUARTERS ONLY

Selecting the right change, Whitey dropped the coins into the cigarette machine, and pressed the button for a pack of Camels. He returned to his table and sat down to enjoy a cigarette with his coffee. As he did so he watched the movement of the people around him.

After finishing his coffee he lit another cigarette, picked up his box, and walked out of the cafeteria into the waiting room. Off to one side he noticed a row of telephone booths. He entered one of the empty booths, lifted the receiver off the hook, deposited a dime and dialed the operator.

"What city?" the operator asked.

"I want to place a call to Los Angeles," Whitey replied.

"What number please?"

"Ah let's see—CH2-4037."

"Thank you sir, one moment please."

After a short pause he heard the voice say, "Please deposit fifty-five cents for the first three minutes."

"Operator, I only have two quarters and a dime in change."

"That's quite all right sir, if your call is within three minutes, just give me your mailing address and the nickel will be refunded to you."

"Ah forget it operator." Whitey dropped the two quarters and dime into the slot.

"Here is your party, go ahead sir."

"Thank you. Hello—hello."

From the other end of the line he heard a soft female voice reply, "Yes, who is this calling?"

"I want to speak to Ben, tell him it's a friend."

"I'm sorry mister," the soft voice said, "he won't take the call unless you tell him just who you are."

"I can't tell him who I am because he don't know me, he won't recognize my name."

"Well if he don't know you," the voice persisted, "and if you don't know him, then why are you calling?"

"You dumb bitch, get him to the phone."

"He won't answer the phone unless I give him a name or something."

"All right, all right, just tell him, 'All's well in October.'"

Whitey could hear a mumble of voices at the other end of the line, but he could not make out what was being said.

A few tense moments passed, then a gruff voice sounded, "Ben speaking, who am I talking to?"

"Just a friend."

"Okay friend how soon can I expect you?"

Thinking, Whitey stood there holding the receiver to his ear.

"Well friend, answer me, how soon can I expect you?" the gruff voice of Ben was becoming angry. "I asked you how soon can I exp—never mind that, just who the hell are you?"

Whitey stood there a moment longer with the receiver to his ear, then suddenly he hung up the phone, and stepped out of the booth into the waiting room. It was none too soon, for his bus to Sacramento was now loading.

Quite a number of passengers boarded the bus. Whitey was lucky to find a vacant seat halfway down on the right-hand side. He quickly placed his cardboard box on the aisle seat to discourage anyone from sitting next him. Seated opposite him was an elderly rich-looking couple.

Most of the passengers had a cheerful look about them, and at a quick glance Whitey could tell the majority of them were tourists.

At last the operator boarded the bus. He took his seat behind the steering wheel, and turning the key he pressed the ignition button, igniting the explosive mixture in the cylinders of the big diesel engine, the Greyhound bus came alive. Slowly it pulled out of the depot, and made its way through the heavy traffic of San Francisco en route to the Oakland Bay Bridge. Once on the bridge the bus gathered speed.

Seated in front of Whitey was a teenage girl listening to a transistor radio, Tony Bennett was singing, "I Left My Heart In San Francisco." This was the first time Whitey had heard this song, and he had never heard of Tony Bennett. For Whitey the timing of the song was wrong, and he immediately disliked the singer as well as the song.

The rich old couple seated across from him caught his attention when he heard the lady say to her husband, "Oh look George, isn't that Alcatraz?"

Whitey turned his head and looked beyond the couple. Sure enough, out there in the Bay was the grim outline of Alcatraz, it's massive bulk remarkably like an obsolete battleship riding at anchor.

"Yes that's Alcatraz," her husband replied.

"Oh George, just seeing it gives me the shivers."

"It should, every man on that Island is there for life."

"Really George? All of them?"

"Yes sweetheart, all of them are notorious killers, and they deserve to be there."

"It gives me the shivers George, I don't know what I would do if I ever met one face to face. I'm sure I would die of fright!" She turned her head away from the Island, and looked at Whitey, and smiled at him.

There was no return smile, he stared coldly at her and thought to himself, I wonder how the old gal would feel if she knew that the man she just smiled at was one of the so-called notorious killers of Alcatraz! Should I tell her I just left the Rock an hour or so ago? And that I am no killer? Ah to hell with her!

He turned his attention to the window and looked out across the Bay toward Alcatraz, it was a clear beautiful day—a day to be free!

PART 4.

FREEDOM

CHAPTER 47.

It was two and a half hours since Whitey's release. To him it seemed like a miracle to be sitting on a bus instead of in a cell on Alcatraz. Except for the seat next to him, the bus was loaded to capacity, and he was sure all eyes were focused on a neon sign strapped over his head. From this neon sign brilliant lights were flashing words, "Ex-con, Ex-Alcatraz Convict!" Unconsciously his right hand shot to the top of his head, feeling no neon sign there he quickly glanced across the aisle at the elderly couple, but they were taking no notice of him for they were viewing picture postcards. Hastily he scanned the interior of the bus, taking in each passenger as he examined them closely, and found no offensive eyes staring at him. He heaved a sigh of relief for he realized he had let his imagination run rampant, but he now had it under control, and he knew he must keep it that way.

"Vallejo—Vallejo," the bus driver called to the passengers.

The Greyhound rolled into the depot parking area, and came to a grinding halt.

"Ten minutes, there will be a ten minute stopover," the driver announced.

Whitey remained in his seat and watched the people as they scurried past him, and when the last passenger had departed, he lit up a cigarette. He had felt somewhat nervous moving about with strangers, so he decided to stay on the bus. The quiet moment alone with his cigarette was relaxing to him.

Again the passengers were seated as the big Greyhound bus edged its way through town toward the freeway on ramp.

It won't be long now, he thought, next stop Sacramento; as he drew nearer to his destination, a feeling of apprehension came over him. He was uneasy and fearful about the future, the unknown future, for he had no idea what to expect. He had been out of circulation nearly fifteen years, and while he was incarcerated, progress on the outside continued, but for Whitey, time had stood still. Today everything was changed, nothing was the same anymore, even to the people he once knew—they were gone now, and he had no one to turn to.

Having no pre-release program on Alcatraz had its affect on Whitey. One day he was a prisoner serving time, and then suddenly without warning; he was set free to face the world he left fifteen years ago.

Everything was in reverse for him. While incarcerated he had become accustomed to the ways of prison life. So much so that he actually felt he was free while in prison, but now—today as he rode on the bus, he had no comprehension of freedom. He didn't feel safe, he felt he didn't belong, and he was afraid.

Upon release the first few hours are critical, and right now it was a critical time for him. He needed someone he could trust, someone to talk to and help channel his thoughts to the right side of life.

He knew in order to give himself a chance he had to give society a chance. He had to face things as they occurred, and he must make the right decisions, that's all one could do.

Whitey was not sure when he dozed off, but he woke with a start when the driver called out, "Sacramento—Sacramento. We have a twenty minute stopover here."

It was 1:00 P.M. when the Greyhound bus arrived at the Sacramento Depot. Whitey waited until everyone disembarked then he stood up, and picked up his box. He then made his way down the aisle to the front of the bus. The driver was standing just outside the doorway, and as Whitey stepped down their eyes met. The driver smiled at him, then he glanced at the box under Whitey's arm, almost as if he knew he had just been released from prison he said, "I hope you had a nice trip, good luck to you mister."

Whitey's only response was a nod of the head as he stepped off the bus and walked toward the depot entrance. Just short of the doorway he stopped to light a cigarette. He stood there a moment or two watching people move about. They all seemed to know where they were going. He took a deep drag on the cigarette and mumbled to himself, "Look at all those people damn it, they all have some place to go, and they all know how to get there!"

Whitey didn't know where he was going, or what direction to take. He took a final drag on the cigarette and flipped it to the pavement; he turned on his heel and entered the depot. Once inside he went to the cafeteria for a cup of coffee. This time he did not feel quite so nervous when the waitress asked him what he would like.

"Just a cup of coffee," he told her.

He finished the first cup and one refill, and after paying the cashier he tucked the box under his arm and walked out to the street. He stood at the curb to light another cigarette, then he casually leaned against a telephone pole to watch the people walk by. He was hoping by chance that he might see a familiar face, but he knew it was hopeless—hopelessly impossible. He realized he could stand there for days on end and never see a familiar face. At this moment he realized more than ever, that he was alone—absolutely alone with no one to turn to. The feeling was frightening, and for a brief moment he wished he was back on Alcatraz in his cell where he would be safe.

Damn it all, he thought, what the hell is wrong with you? Get that kind of thinking out of your head stupid, or you'll never make it. Come on, come on get yourself together.

He took another drag on the cigarette; he began to feel a little more confident in himself, and his nerves were calming down.

With his box under his arm, he flipped the cigarette into the gutter and started down the street. He had no idea where he was going and after three blocks he pulled up short. He was getting nowhere, he had to know what he was going to do and where he was going. He was feeling tired, and felt like lying down, but he knew he could not lie down in the street! The best thing to do, he thought, was to find a cheap hotel and start from there.

He had been walking down G Street, and a short distance up the road he saw a sign, "ROOM AND BOARD." He approached the boarding house and rang the bell, and almost immediately the door opened revealing a pleasant middle-aged woman.

She greeted him with a pleasant smile and said, "Yes sir?"

"Hello, I seen your sign 'Room and Board,' do you have a vacancy?"

Glancing at the cardboard box she replied, "Yes I have one room vacant, would you like to see it?"

"No, I'm sure it's all right. How much is it a week?"

"It's fifteen dollars in advance."

"Okay I'll take it."

The landlady stepped aside and beckoned Whitey to come in. He stepped through the doorway into a very clean and orderly living room.

"Follow me," the woman said as she led him through another door into a large but airy dining room. He noticed how spotlessly clean the area was, and in the center of the room was a dining table that would accommodate ten people.

"Won't you sit down?" she said politely as she walked over to her desk, and after retrieving a receipt book and a key from a drawer, she returned to the table. Whitey took three tens out of his pocket and handed them to her.

"You need only pay fifteen in advance," she reminded him.

"Thank you, but I'd just as soon pay for two weeks."

"That's fine with me," she said as she tucked the money into her dress pocket, and reached for the receipt book.

"What is your name?"

"Thompson, Leon Whitey Thompson."

She wrote out a receipt, and as she handed it to Whitey she said, "My name is May Hanny, you may call me May."

"Thank you, and you can call me Whitey instead of sir."

"All right, Whitey it is, now I'll show you to your room."

As he followed her down the hallway she talked over her shoulder, "We serve breakfast every morning from five to seven. Lunch is from eleven forty-five to one P.M., and dinner is from six to seven. On Sundays, there is no lunch, and dinner is always served between three-thirty and four P.M."

At the far end of the hallway, May unlocked a door to his room and handed Whitey the key.

"Here you are Whitey. I'm sure you'll find the room comfortable, and if you need anything, don't hesitate to call me."

"Thank you May, thank you very much."

May returned to the front of the house, and Whitey entered the room closing the door behind him. He found the room rather small, but very large in comparison to his cell on Alcatraz. It was a tidy room with a single bed equipped with box springs and mattress, and to one side stood a lovely antique dresser with five drawers. On the other side was the door to the bathroom.

Whitey inspected the facilities, and was pleased to find it contained a full-sized bathtub and shower. No more standing in long line waiting his turn to shower, for he now had his own private bathroom.

A contented smile lit up his face; for he was happy with his new quarters. He charged out of the bathroom making a beeline for the bed; he leaped high in the air, landing square in the middle of the mattress!

"*Oooooooo-weeeee* this bed feels good! I wonder what them poor fools on the Rock are doing now."

He had no sooner uttered the words when a sad expression appeared on his face. He knew very well what his friends were doing. The enjoyment of his new-found luxury was marred by the thought of his buddies still in prison. He realized his old friends on Alcatraz would never see or know the enjoyment of this room.

He decided to wash up, and after doing so he smoked a cigarette, then he extinguished it; pulled off his shoes, and sprawled across the bed. The hour was early, but he was exhausted, and promptly fell asleep, so ending his first day of freedom.

CHAPTER 48.

The following morning shortly after 6:00 A.M. Whitey was sure he heard the count buzzer go off. Startled, he bolted upright in bed.

"Damn it all, I didn't hear the rise and shine horn!" His eyes were full of sleep as he reached over the side of the bed for his pants. Not finding them, his hand was like a blind person, and seemed to panic as it frantically groped around the floor.

"Where are my pants, goddamn it, where the fuck are they?"

The upper half of his body was stooped over the edge of the bed, when suddenly he realized where he was. The mad expression on his face turned into a smile as his eyes took in the sights of the cozy little room.

"This is no cell, this is a mansion!" He jumped out of bed, quickly removed his clothes, and dashed into the bathroom to fill the tub.

After his bath he hurriedly dressed and left the room. He had no idea what time it was until he saw the clock on the wall, 6:45 AM. He was extremely hungry for he had nothing to eat since his release the morning before. He walked through the living room into the dining room and was greeted by the appetizing fragrance of home cooking.

At the dining table two elderly men sat eating their breakfast. They both smiled at Whitey when he entered the room, and then quickly turned back to their meal.

The table had been pre-set with plates, cups, silverware, and napkins.

"Does it matter where one sits?" Whitey asked the nearest man.

"You sit wherever you please, but before you do, it is customary to go up to the kitchen counter and let May know you are here, then she will wait on you."

Whitey smiled and thanked the man. Then he walked over to the counter at the end of the room. There was an opening above the counter, and looking through it he saw May cooking over a stove. He watched her for a moment before he called her name. Being a middle-aged woman did not take anything away from her attractiveness. She was full breasted, and as she bent over the stove he could see the fine outline of her body. She was very attractive, but for Whitey, just being released from prison, any woman would seem attractive, after all it had been almost fifteen years since he had so much as touched one!

"Good morning Whitey, can I help you? Good morning Whitey—Whitey!"

At the sound of her voice he jerked his head up, and his face turned red when he realized she had caught him staring.

"Good morning Whitey," May said again in a cheerful voice. "Did you sleep well?"

"Yes I did, I had a very good night's sleep, thank you."

"I'm glad you slept well. Now for breakfast you have a choice, you can have sausage and eggs with hash-browns, or bacon and eggs and hash-browns, which would you prefer? And how do you like your eggs?"

"I'll have the bacon, and over easy with the eggs."

"Over easy it will be. Just help yourself to the coffee, it's out there on the stand."

"Thank you." Whitey turned to the coffee maker and poured himself a cup. Then he selected a seat at the table near the counter. It wasn't long before May came through the swinging doors from the kitchen, and placed his breakfast in front of him.

"Here you are Whitey, I hope you enjoy the meal. If there is anything else you need, please just call out."

"Thank you, thank you very much."

May turned to leave, and as she did so she gently brushed her hip against Whitey as she walked away. He was not quite sure if it was intentional or not, but the incident was forgotten as he dove into his bacon and eggs.

He had just finished his meal and was about to wipe his hands on a napkin, when he noticed that May was standing on the far side of the counter staring at him.

She called across the room, "How's the meal Whitey? Did you get enough to eat?"

"It was perfect, and yes I had plenty. Oh by the way is it all right to smoke in here?"

"Yes sure. As a matter of fact I was just about to have one myself, I'll join you."

As Whitey lit up a cigarette, he wondered why she was being so nice to him, or does she treat all her tenants this way?

The kitchen door swung open, and May walked through going directly to the coffee stand, poured herself a cup, and after lighting a cigarette she sat down next to Whitey.

"A cigarette tastes twice as good with a cup of coffee, don't you think so Whitey?"

Whitey smiled at May and nodded his head yes.

She smiled back and continued talking, "I always enjoy my first cup of the day with a smoke. I just can't get started without my coffee and cigarette." She nudged Whitey with her elbow. "How about you?"

"I can take it or leave it, it don't make no difference."

"Oh you're kidding," she exclaimed with a laugh as she nudged him again.

"No, I'm not kidding. In the morning when I wake up, I'm used to smoking a cigarette without coffee."

"Oh how can anyone enjoy it without coffee, how can you?"

"Hey I like coffee and I like cigarettes, I like them alone or with each other, it don't matter."

"Oh I have to have them together, that's the only way I enjoy them. By the way would like another cup of coffee?"

"Yeah please, I would like another cup."

May walked over to the coffee stand; returned to the table, and set the two filled cups down. She pushed her chair closer to Whitey; so close her thigh was pressing against his, causing an exciting hot surge to run through his veins.

Whitey picked up his cup of coffee and discovered his hand had a slight tremble to it. To stabilize the shaking cup he gripped it with both hands, and as he drank he thought, what is this old gal trying to do, don't she realize her leg is touching mine? I bet she know's it, and if I don't get out of this chair soon I maybe in trouble!

Whitey tried to shift his leg somewhat to relieve the pressure between their thighs. Slowly he moved his leg away from her's; she immediately used this opportunity to remove her hand from the table and place it on her knee. Then ever so carefully she began to stroke her leg, and in doing so she let the back of her hand rub up and down against his thigh.

It was no longer just a surge running through his veins, it was a tidal wave! He had to get away from her. This was too much. Just as he started to gulp down his coffee one of the tenants walked into the dining room.

"Morning May, I'm running late. I'll have my usual order and be on my way."

Whitey was not sure, but he thought he heard May say, "Damn!" under her breath.

"Good morning Joe," she said with a half smile, "I'll have your breakfast ready in a jiffy."

As she pulled her hand out from under the table she gave Whitey's thigh a knowing squeeze, "Sorry but I have to get back to work, I'll see you later Whitey."

"Yeah I gotta get out of here myself, so long, see you later May."

Whitey got up from the table, and after placing his dirty dishes in a pan provided for such, he returned to his room.

He lit a cigarette and lay down on his bed, and as he lay there enjoying the smoke, he tried to get his thoughts together. He had to decide on a plan of action for job hunting that day. He wondered where he should start to look for employment. At a trucking company, where else? You're a truck driver—a rusty one, but you are a driver. That's it, he thought, I'll go to every trucking company in town, I'll get me a job, I'll find employment someplace.

He had a great deal of confidence as he walked out the front door of the boarding house. As he started down G Street he mumbled to himself, "Damn that fucking May, hell I have enough problems ahead of me without her making me start my day off with a hard on!"

Whitey's first stop was Valley Motor Lines. As he approached the personnel office he hesitated a moment, his self-confidence had deserted him, and he stood staring at the door.

Posted on the door was a sign, "APPLICATIONS ARE BEING ACCEPTED." Whitey read the sign but was hesitant to enter the office. He was feeling self-conscious and was ready to walk away.

What the hell is wrong with you? He thought, you always had self-assurance, and you never felt self-conscious when it came to holding up a bank!

"Shit!" Whitey said aloud, and boldly opened the door and walked in. He was greeted by a young woman who came out from behind her desk, she stepped up to the counter, and with a welcoming smile she asked, "Can I help you sir?"

"Yeah, I'd like to fill out an application if you got one."

She replied, "Yes sir we have plenty of them. What position are you applying for?"

"Truck driver."

She reached under the counter for an application and handed it to Whitey. "Here you are sir, you may fill it out right here if you like."

He began to study the application while the young woman returned to her desk.

He commenced to fill out the form starting with his name, age, and Social Security number, but halfway down the sheet he was stumped by a question he was not sure how to answer. The question read: "Have you ever been convicted of a felony?" Whitey was bewildered trying to decide what to write for an answer. The young woman looked up and noticed Whitey was having a problem.

"If there are any questions you don't understand, leave them blank and go on to the next question. I will help you with the unanswered ones when you have finished."

Whitey froze as he stared at the question, and as he stood there leaning against the counter, his eyes slowly moved, and when he had the young woman in view, he spoke in a very cold and sarcastic voice, "Hey I know how to read, I don't need help with these stupid questions. I have the answers, I just don't know if I want to put them down or not, okay?"

The young woman felt embarrassed, and quickly turned her attention to her work, while Whitey continued on to the next question—'List all employment for the previous ten years.' Again he froze and his eyes burned at the question.

"Shit to hell with it!" he said out loud, and slammed the pen down with such force it bounced off the counter, skidded across the floor striking the receptionist's desk. She looked up aghast as Whitey tore up the application, threw it to the floor, and stormed out of the building.

It turned out to be a very long and tiring morning for Whitey as he walked from trucking company to trucking company.

At each company the job applications were similar—'Have you ever been convicted of a felony—have you ever been convicted of a felony—list of employment for the previous ten years—list of employment for the previous ten years—have you ever been convicted. . . .'

Each company he went to he was handed an application, after a quick glance at it, he would hand it back, and without saying a word he would walk out. By noon he was tired, but after having coffee and donuts he felt much better.

With renewed energy he was again on the streets walking. His route took him to numerous trucking companies, but he had not filled out one application. He could feel himself slowly being pressed against the wall, and he was nonplussed as to what he should do. He finally decided there was only one thing he could do, just write the truth on the application and see what happened.

He found himself in the personnel office of the Sacramento Freight Lines, and asked the receptionist if they were accepting applications.

"For what position sir?" she asked.

"Truck driver," Whitey returned, "what else?"

Smiling she handed him a form, and without any hesitation whatsoever he filled it out and returned it to her.

"Thank you sir, we will notify you by mail if you are accepted."

"Why not save the postage and let me know now."

"All right sir, I'll see if Mr. Sherman is in his office." She disappeared through a doorway leading to an inner office, and a few minutes later she reappeared accompanied by a tall slim-looking middle-aged man. He wore a well-tailored gray business suit, and he had a wealthy air about him as he walked across the floor. He had a pencil striped mustache that was almost invisible on his protruding upper lip. Most of his gray hair was gone, but his balding head seemed to give him a mark of distinction.

"Ah Mr. Thompson," he said in a guarded voice, "we are in need of

311

a driver, but I don't think you fit the bill."

"Why not? I can drive as good as any man you got here."

"Maybe so Mr. Thompson, but to be frank with you, it is not our policy to hire ex-felons, I'm sorry."

"Hey I paid my debt to society, I'm a damn good driver."

"I'm sure you are Mr. Thompson, but it's not our policy to hire people we cannot trust, and you should know that."

"Hey if I wasn't honest I would have lied on that application. I need a job," Whitey began to raise his voice.

"May I ask you where you were incarcerated, and how long, and what for?" he asked.

By the application, Mr. Sherman knew Whitey had just been released from prison, but he was not prepared for the answer he received.

"I just finished doing fifteen years for bank robbery," Whitey replied, "I was released from Alcatraz yesterday morning."

Both Sherman and the receptionist were taken aback, and before the color had a chance to return to his face, Sherman said in a stern voice, "I'm sorry we don't hire your kind."

His words felt like a slap across the face to Whitey, and he fought to keep his temper under control. For a tense moment it looked as though he was going to attack the man. He was so furious, and it took all his willpower to control himself from a violent reaction. Whitey immediately realized that if he did any harm to this man he would definitely be in the wrong. So the best thing to do, was to leave at once.

"Okay Mr. Big-Shot, you're right, I'm not your kind." Just before Whitey reached the door he finished with, "And I hope I never am!"

It was quite depressing for him. At each company he went to he told the truth, and each one of them promptly informed him that they did not hire his kind.

The hour was getting late, and he was very disillusioned about his first day of job hunting. Damn it, he thought, I should have taken that hit job, it's still not too late, and I could use that ten grand. Maybe that's what I should do, maybe I should pick up a gun and take the job.

Don't be a fool you idiot, get that kind of thinking out of your mind. What the hell, you've only been out one day. Give yourself a chance!

"Yes that's right," Whitey said aloud, "I've only been out a day for Christ's sakes. Fuck it, I'm gonna get drunk!"

He made for the nearest barroom and got good and drunk!

It was shortly after eleven when he returned to the boarding house. Only the night lights were on in the living room and hallway, and there was no one about as he made his way to his room. He was trying to be careful not to make any noise as he did not want to disturb the tenants. But he had difficulty trying to unlock the door to his room. The night light was dim, and he fumbled with the key endeavoring to get it in the keyhole.

"Son of a bitch," he mumbled, "where's the fucking hole?"

The hallway was silent, so silent the sound of his mumbling seemed extra loud, and the noise of the key was thunderous as it scraped over the door panel in its search for the keyhole.

The door to May's room was directly across the hall, and he did not see her peeking out to investigate the sound. She was surprised to see Whitey in his drunken condition fumbling with the door lock.

"Are you having trouble with the key?" she asked him quietly.

"Who said that?"

"It's me Whitey, I'm right behind you."

He turned around, and in the semi-darkness he saw May standing in her doorway clad in a revealing nightgown.

"Oh hi May, sorry I disturbed you."

"You didn't disturb me I was already awake. What's wrong with your key?"

"Nothing's wrong with the key, I just can't find the hole."

May laughed and said, "Here give it to me I'll open it for you."

Whitey handed her the key; she opened the door and turned on the light for him. Then reaching back she took a firm hold of his hand, and guided him across the floor toward his bed.

"Looks like you had a few too many, come on I'll help you." She immediately began to unbuckle his belt. What the hell, he thought, if she wants to undress me, let her undress me I don't care. Once she had the belt undone, she gave him a gentle push onto the bed, and after removing his shoes and socks, she fumbled with his fly, and as she did so she pressed her hand against the bulge that was protruding under his trousers.

"My my, what have we got here?" she said in a soft cooing voice.

Whitey was quietly lying there in anticipation of her next move. He didn't have long to wait; she began to pull on his trouser legs, slipping his pants off him. All that remained were his under shorts and shirt which she promptly removed.

The excitement was building up, and he was sure she would remove her nightgown and lay down beside him, then he would carefully ease himself up on top of her.

What occurred next was altogether different from what he had anticipated. The only noise in the room was a rustling sound, and Whitey opened his eyes a fraction. Through squinting eyelids he saw May slipping out of her nightgown, and at the sight of her nude body he felt he was ready to erupt. The next sound he heard was the light switch, and he opened his eyes to total darkness.

313

What is taking her so long to reach me? Damn it's only a few steps from the light switch to the bed. His mind was running wild anticipating her next move. He felt the bed sag, and as she lay down beside him her fingers began to explore. As they moved over his body, the sensation was more than he could bear. He silently screamed, quit screwing around damn it! Whitey began to squirm from side to side, and in the same motion he raised his midsection up and down, up and down, building up speed.

"Oh you poor boy," May cooed, "you must be in a hurry and can't wait. Well we'll take care of that!" She suddenly took hold of him, causing his scalding blood to shoot through his speeding heart on a rapid course to the brain. She tightened her grip on him, and his whole body quivered with delight. They were both in motion and the speed was building up. He placed both hands behind her head. The sensation was too much for him, and with an upward drive, his gushing hot blood reached his brain and the sky was full of exploding rainbows.

The following morning when Whitey woke up he was so groggy it took a few minutes before he could remember the night before. He pulled himself out of bed and made his way to the bathroom. After a hot bath he was again himself, and he was in good spirits when he entered the dining room.

May was busy cooking when he called in his order, "Hi May, I'll have the bacon and eggs, okay?"

May looked toward the caller, and when she saw it was Whitey her face lit up with a smile, "Coming right up," she replied cheerfully. "Have a seat I'll be right with you."

There were four elderly men already seated having their breakfast.

Whitey poured himself a cup of coffee, took a seat, lit a cigarette and relaxed while waiting for May. The wait was short, barely enough time to finish his cigarette before she brought out his plate of bacon and eggs. While he was eating, two more tenants entered the dining room; May returned to the kitchen to wait on them.

After she had finished she hurriedly returned to the table, and quickly sat down next to Whitey who was wiping up the remains of his eggs with a slice of bread. After sitting down she nonchalantly slipped her hand under the table, and placed it on Whitey's lap. Her fingers immediately went to work on his fly.

"Don't May, don't do that," he whispered.

"Why Whitey, don't you like it?"

"Not now," he replied, "damn it all, yesterday I went looking for work with a hard on because of you, and now you're trying to send me off with another one!"

"Have no fear," she whispered, "I'll be finished in the kitchen shortly, so if you want to wait around I'll take care of it for you."

Whitey turned his head to look at May, and in a serious voice he asked her, "What is it with you May, how come you want it from me?"

"Take a look around, what do you see?" she asked in a somber voice.

"All I see is a few old men eating, what else is there to see?"

"That's what I'm getting at, that's all there is around here, old men. I have nine tenants not counting you, and the youngest one is seventy-one years old."

"Why don't you get younger tenants in. . . ."

"Wait a minute," she interrupted, "my husband died eight years ago, and eight years ago we had ten tenants in here, well they're all still living here except one, he died last week."

"I'm sorry."

"Don't be sorry, he was eighty-two, he had a full life, so you see it was his. . . ."

"Wait a minute, just what the hell are you trying to tell me?" Whitey interrupted.

"I'm trying to tell you this, in plain English I have not had any sex since my husband died eight years ago. Not that I didn't want it, because I did, but I'm not the type to go bar hopping looking for it. My tenants are old men, so what was I to do? I couldn't kick any of them out, that wouldn't be right."

"I see what you mean, and when one finally died, you rented his room to me, right?"

"That's right," she returned.

"Why did you rent to me? Why didn't you rent to someone else?"

"I'll tell you why and the truth, I rented to you because you are at least ten or twelve years younger than me, and I know you just got out of prison."

Her words took Whitey by surprise, he was taken aback.

"What? How the hell did you know I just got out of the joint?"

"Oh, just the way you acted, and when I saw that cardboard box; most men who get out of prison don't have much more than the clothes on their back, and a cardboard box. Where did you come from? San Quentin or Folsom?"

"The Rock! I come from the Rock."

It was her turn to be surprised by Whitey's words.

"You mean—you mean Alcatraz?"

"Look May I don't want to talk anymore about it. Does it make any difference where I come from? If it does I'll leave."

"No Whitey, no it don't make any difference. You're welcome here as long as you want to stay."

"Thank you May. Look I have to get going, I've got to land a job, and I won't find one sitting here."

"Okay. Say would you like me to make you a lunch to take along, I would gladly do it."

"No that's okay, I'll just stop for coffee someplace. I'll see you later."

"All right Whitey, I hope you land a job."

But he didn't, he found no job that day. The next four mornings he got up bright and early to look for work, but with no success. It had been a long time since he had done so much walking, and at the end of each day he was more discouraged than the previous one.

"I don't know why it is," he was telling May one night, "but the moment I mention Alcatraz they show me door."

"Don't tell them you were on Alcatraz, don't tell them nothing. You're a good man Whitey, you just need a chance."

"Yeah, but how do I get that chance?"

CHAPTER 49.

It was the morning of the eighth day, and Whitey was again looking for work as he walked over the M Street bridge to West Sacramento. He traveled the length of West Capital Avenue out to the Motor Speedway, and it was the same old story at each place he inquired about work. Sorry we're not hiring today. Sorry we don't hire ex-felons. No one would offer him a job, and he was about to give up hope.

Across from the Speedway he noticed a tavern called "The Roadhouse." He decided to walk over to have a beer, but changed his mind when he noticed a number of used trucks for sale parked in a lot. Just off to right of the vehicles was a huge repair garage. The location of the business office was at the entrance to the lot, and mounted over the establishment was a large red, yellow, and black sign that read:

> **STRANGE TRUCKS**
> **NEW AND USED TRUCKS FOR**
> **SALE.**

Curious, Whitey decided to get a better look at the used equipment. One rig in particular caught his eye. It was a two-axle 1948 red Peterbilt, powered by a 220-Cummins diesel. The truck had a new paint job, and the 11 by 22 tires were in excellent condition. After lifting the hood to check the motor oil and radiator, he knelt down to take a look under the truck at the drive shaft and running gear. He found no trace of oil lying on the ground to indicate any seal leaks. With total disregard for his clothes, he lay flat on the ground and rolled under the frame of the truck for a closer inspection. The springs, overload springs, and tie rod seemed to be in good shape. With both hands he took hold of the drive shaft and turned it enough to take up the slack, then turned it back. He did this a number of times to try to determine how badly the universal joints were worn. They seemed to be in order.

He crawled out from under the truck, and after brushing himself

317

off he walk toward the sales office. The approach to the building had a short walkway to a flight of steps leading to the entrance. He took the stairs three at a time, opened the door and walked in.

The interior was furnished in expensive taste with wall to wall wine colored shag carpet. There were two huge windows that overlooked the truck yard with red drapes of a fine texture. In front of the draped windows polished with a mirror-like gloss, set an antique reddish brown mahogany desk, and just behind it sitting in a matching chair was a middle-aged man. He was heavy set with graying hair, and a reddish alcoholic complexion, and as Whitey entered the room he stood up. The first thing noticeable about the clean shaven man was his warm smile, and the glitter of a large diamond ring he wore on his hand as he held it out to Whitey.

"Come in, come in," he greeted in a cheerful voice. He held Whitey's hand in a firm grip and introduced himself, "The name is Cliff Strange, and you, who may you be?"

With a slight trace of a smile Whitey replied, "They call me Whitey Thompson."

"Glad to make your acquaintance."

"The same here sir."

"We don't sir around here, just call me Cliff. Now how can I be of service to you?"

"I'd like some information on one of your trucks out there, the red '48 Peterbilt."

"Oh yes, she's a good truck, her price is $3,800.00. let's go out there and start her up."

Leaving the office both men walked outside, and as they approached the truck Cliff handed Whitey the key.

After unlocking the door Whitey climbed into the cab. He sat there a moment to get the feel, for it had been many years since he had been behind the wheel of a diesel rig. After turning the ignition switch to the on position he pulled the compression release, and simultaneously pressed the starter button and held it there with his finger. The engine began to turn over, faster and faster, until she was whirling. Whitey released the compression release, and the diesel engine immediately ignited with a deep hollow roar. Her sound was good and healthy; he let her run while he checked out the gages on the dash panel. The AMP indicator showed the generator was working. The oil pressure was good, and the engine was idling at 500 RPMs. Satisfied, he turned the switch off shutting her down, and stepped out of the truck.

"Well what do you think of her?" Cliff asked.

"Not bad. She sounds real good, but there's more to a rig than just the engine."

Cliff replied, "Yes, but there's no need to worry, all of my trucks have been gone over right here in my garage, they're in good shape or they wouldn't be up for sale."

"What's the minimum you'll take down on her?" Whitey inquired.

"Well let's see, the full load, not counting the registration will run somewhere in the neighborhood of twelve fifty to thirteen hundred dollars."

"Shit," Whitey said in disgust, "I guess there's no deal then."

"Hold on a minute, let's go into my office, I'm sure we can come up with something."

After returning to the office Cliff asked, "Well if you want the truck, tell me how much money you have to put down, then we can go from there."

"Hell I don't know—I don't know if I really want to buy it or not. If I did, I would have to find work for it right away so I can pay it off. Hell I don't even have a Class One license."

"You don't have a Class One?" Cliff exclaimed with surprise.

Whitey thought, ah to hell with it, tell him the truth and see what happens. Looking straight into the big man's eyes he said, "Look I just got out of the joint eight days ago. For the past seven days I've been pounding the beat looking for work. I've gone to every trucking company in town, nobody will hire me." On that note Whitey turned and started for the door.

"Hold it a minute," Cliff ordered. "Where did you serve time, and what for?"

Whitey turned his attention back to Cliff, "I was on the Rock, I went to prison behind some bank jobs, okay?" He reached for the door handle. . . .

"Hey hold it wait a minute."

Still holding the door knob he again turned to face Cliff.

"I like your honesty, maybe we can work something out."

With renewed hope Whitey returned to the desk.

"All right now," Cliff said, "let's get down to business. First off I don't give a damn if you are an ex-con, but being that you are, no one has to know anything about it, okay?"

"Now, how much money do you have to put down?"

"When I was discharged I received a check for eighteen hundred dollars and that's it. The best I can put down is a grand, I have to have money to live on."

"That's good enough, I'll accept the thousand down. There's no problem there, but you'll have to have work for the truck."

"That's right, if I can't work it, I'll just be throwing a grand away for nothing."

"I understand that, and I'll tell you what I'm going to do. I'm going to call a friend of mine who is the owner of Senator Trucking Service. He has a lot of lease drivers working for him, I'll see if he can use

319

you. If he can, then I'll sell you the tractor. How does that sound?"

"Yeah sure, that sounds okay," Whitey said excitedly.

Cliff made the call to S.T.S. and was told they were in need of another lease truck and driver.

"Well Whitey it looks like we got a deal," Cliff said as he held out his hand. "I'll accept a grand for the down payment, and you don't have to worry about financing the balance. I carry my own paper. Now do you have the check with you? If so I'll draw up the papers, okay?"

"Yeah go ahead, I've got the check here."

After the papers had been drawn up Whitey signed them. Cliff cashed the check for eighteen hundred dollars, and gave Whitey eight hundred in return, and a temporary registration to the truck.

"Well that's settled, now we have to see about getting you a Class One driver's license."

Cliff made a telephone call to his garage, and told the foreman to send Ed in. A few minutes later a tall thin man in his middle forties entered the office. He was wearing a pair of dirty blue coveralls, and was in dire need of a shave. Regardless of his appearance he was an A-1 mechanic.

Cliff introduced Ed to Whitey. Then he explained to his mechanic how Whitey had just purchased the Peterbilt, and he wanted him to hook it up to a set of double trailers. After hooking up the rig he was to take Whitey to the Motor Vehicle Department.

Whitey waited in the office talking to Cliff, while Ed hooked the truck up to the trailers.

When they were ready to leave, Whitey took the wheel and did the driving. Once a truck driver, always a truck driver, he had no trouble whatever handling the big rig.

At the Motor Vehicle Department he passed the written exam and driver's test with ease, and received his temporary license.

After they returned, Whitey walked next door to Senator Trucking Service, and a lease was made out.

Early the following morning he hitched his truck to a set of Senator trailers, thus starting his first day of work. The hours were long, but the pay was good. The cargo he hauled was material for construction sites.

His average monthly income was right at $2,000, and after making his truck payment; plus fuel bill, and other truck related expenses, he would clear approximately $1,500. He was doing exceptionally well; technically he was his own boss and he loved the feeling of independence.

May Hanny was happy for him, but now that he was earning a sizable amount of money, she was afraid he might decide to move to a more appropriate location. But he assured her he would be there for some time to come.

He was progressing right along, it was an uphill climb, but one that he enjoyed. Two months from the day he acquired the truck; he purchased a 1950 Chevrolet. The upward swing for Whitey was great, for he not only had a truck, he had a car and money in his pocket.

The routine of his daily life was beginning to get him down. He loved hard work, and it did not matter to him if he was on the road day and night. Everything was fine while he was working, it was the off duty hours that were hard on him.

When he came off the road from a trip he would park his rig at the S.T.S. yard. Then he would drive home to the boarding house, and stay there until his next trip. He would go to work, then come home, then go to work and. . . .

Whitey had great difficulty in relating to people and making friends. Other than May, he had no one to talk to. He was lonely—a very lonely man, and it was inevitable that he began to bring home alcoholic beverages as a crutch to help him during the difficult off duty hours.

CHAPTER 50.

May knew Whitey was doing a great deal of excessive drinking, and each time she cleaned his room she was disturbed by the increase of empty beer cans and whiskey bottles. She became even more disturbed on weekends; without fail, each Friday night Whitey would return from work, and disappear into his room with a fresh supply of alcoholic beverages.

On one particular weekend she was more than concerned. She was worried for it was Sunday evening, and she had not seen or heard from Whitey since his arrival the previous Friday night. She was hoping he would appear in time for dinner. When he did not, May became alarmed. She went to his room, and knocked lightly on the door.

"Yeah who is it?" Whitey called.

"It's me Whitey, May, can I talk to you?"

"The door's unlocked, shoot your best stick!"

May opened the door, walked in, and was greeted with an overwhelming smell of cigarette smoke, stale beer, and whiskey.

Whitey, clad only in a pair of undershorts, was sitting in the recliner smoking a cigarette and sipping on a can of beer. May was distressed at the sight of the mess, for there were bottles and cans strewed about the room. She immediately proceeded to gather them up, and carried them out to the trash container. Quickly she returned to the room and began tidying up while Whitey sat there in silence. He watched her in amazement for she had the touch of a magician. Within a few moments she had the room looking fairly respectable.

She started to empty his ashtray, and as she did so she said, "I didn't come in here to clean, I came in to see if you were all right and to talk."

"Well talk then, who's stopping you?" Whitey retorted in a sarcastic voice.

"Whitey why are you doing this to yourself?"

"Doing what to myself—what the hell are you talking about?"

322

"All you do is come home from work and stay in your room and drink. It's no good cooping yourself up every weekend. You don't even come out to eat."

"What the hell's it to you? I pay my board on time, so why should you care what I do?"

"I just don't like to see you so all alone. I don't mind you drinking, but at least go somewhere, meet people and enjoy yourself. Don't stuff yourself up in this room, it's no good."

"What the hell is it to you May? Why do you care what I do, why?"

"Because I care that's why, I care what happens to you. Go out, enjoy yourself, meet some girl, you've been locked up long enough. Don't waste what life you have left in this room."

Whitey stood up and put his arms around May, "You're okay May, I didn't know you were that concerned about me. I'm gonna take your advice."

"I'm glad Whitey. Now wash up and get dressed, when you're ready, come to the dining room and I'll fix you something to eat."

May walked out of the room and closed the door behind her. As she started down the hallway toward the dining room, she began to smile. From Whitey's bathroom came the sound of off-key singing.

The following Friday evening Whitey returned from work, and after a bath and a change of clothes, he went to the dining room for dinner. Stepping up to the counter he called out to May, "What have we got for dinner May?"

"Hi Whitey," she called back, "we're having fillet of sole, can't you smell it?"

"Hell yes I can smell it. It smells good, bring me the works when you get a chance."

There were three tenants seated at the table eating, and when Whitey sat down with his cup of coffee they nodded to him.

Shortly after May brought him his dinner.

"Well look at you!" she exclaimed. "All dressed up, you must be going out on the town."

"That's right, I said I was going to take your advise. Well there's a place called 'The Raven' out on J Street, I thought I'd go out and have a few, and maybe pick up a chick."

May turned from the table and started toward the kitchen, "I've got to get to work," she said. "Have a good time, tell me about it tomorrow."

"Wait a minute, come back here."

May returned to the table, "Don't hold me up too long Whitey, I've got to get back to the kitchen."

Whitey reached out and pulled her nearer to him, and whispered in her ear, "If I don't score tonight, when I come home I'm going to

323

crawl in with you."

May pulled away from him, as she returned to the kitchen, she said, "Like hell you are!"

After Whitey finished his meal he walked over to the door, and as he opened it May called out to him, "When you come home tonight, if you still want to, it's okay with me."

"I might just do that May," Whitey called back to her as he closed the door behind him.

The Raven Club was a singles bar catering mostly to neighborhood trade. Whitey had driven by there a number of times on his way to the liquor store.

The only occupants in the club were two middle-aged men seated at the bar talking to the bartender. When Whitey made his entrance, the bartender and his two patrons gave him a stern look as though he had just invaded their privacy. He walked past the proprietor who was in the act of pouring drinks for the two men, and selected a stool at the far end of the bar. .

When the bartender was free he called out to Whitey, "What will it be sir?"

"I'll have a Bud," Whitey replied.

The bartender set his order in front of him, "That will be forty-five cents sir."

Whitey pulled out a dollar bill, and handed it to the bartender.

Turning on his stool, he glanced at a row of booths in a dark section at the rear of the room. Except for one booth the rest were empty. It took a moment for Whitey's eyes to adjust to the darkened area, and when they did, he noticed the occupant was a young woman sitting alone. She was no more than twenty-eight years old, with brown eyes, long brown hair, slim well-proportioned body, a very attractive girl to say the least.

He finished his beer and called out, "Hey barkeep how about another Bud?"

The bartender set another bottle of beer in front of him, and as Whitey paid for it he said, "Say barkeep who's the girl back there?"

Looking toward the booths the bartender answered, "That's Brenda Cox. She comes in once in a while. She used to come in with her old man, but he took off about four months ago, left her with a couple of kids. They were just shacking up, you know, but they were his kids."

"How do you know so much about her, did she tell you all this?"

"Yeah she came in right after he left her. She got drunk and told me the whole story. From what I've heard she's not a bad sort. Whenever she comes in here she's always alone."

"Whatever she's drinking, give her a drink on me will ya?"

324

Whitey watched the bartender as he set a beer in front of her. The girl looked in his direction, and with a slight nod she picked up the beer. Whitey did the same.

To the left of the booths was the men's restroom; Whitey used it as an excuse to walk in front of the girl.

As he passed by her he smiled and said, "Hi there, you look lonely."

With a trace of a smile she replied, "Looks are deceiving, I'm not lonely."

As Whitey opened the restroom door he said to her, "Deceiving or whatever, I still think you're lonely."

She was unable to reply for Whitey disappeared into the restroom. He felt he must remain there at least a few minutes to give the impression he needed to use the facility. He lit a cigarette, and as he did so he watched his reflection in the mirror. He liked what he saw, and flashing his strong white teeth he began to smile at his image. Then he dropped his cigarette to the floor, and after grinding it with the heel of his boot, he removed his comb from his pocket. He ran it through his hair a number of times; then he paused to inspect his handiwork. He was not satisfied and continued combing until he was absolutely sure every hair was in its proper place. Returning the comb to his rear pocket, he viewed himself again, and after looking at it from every angle, he decided it was too prim and proper. He quickly ran his fingers through the soft blond hair, then shook his head to let the strands fall naturally. Satisfied with the rough look, he walked out of the restroom.

This time when he passed, the girl spoke first, "Thank you for the beer."

"You're welcome," Whitey returned, "are you sure you're not lonely?"

"I told you looks were deceiving, I'm really not lonely."

He had just about passed her when he suddenly stopped to face her, "Well maybe you're not lonely, but I am, can I sit down?"

Momentarily indecisive she hesitated before answering, "Well as long as you remember who the lonely one is, you may sit down."

"Thank you, let me get my beer off the bar, I'll be right back."

He returned with his drink and sat down opposite her offering a cigarette. As he did so he said, "My name is Whitey, Leon Whitey Thompson. The bartender tells me your name is Brenda, Brenda Cox, is that right?"

"As if you didn't know! What else did the bartender tell you?"

"Only that your old man ran off and left you with a couple of kids, that's all."

Brenda's cheerful expression changed, "That's all?" she snapped, "Hell he told you everything!"

"No, he didn't tell me everything," Whitey was trying to make light of it. "He didn't tell me where you lived."

"The son of a bitch didn't know, that's why he didn't tell you—the bastard!"

"Ah come off it, don't be so hard on him, he felt sorry for you, he thinks it was a dirty deal your old man running off like he did."

"How about you?" she asked, "What do you think?"

"To be truthful, I don't know what to think."

"And just what the hell do you mean by that?"

"Just what I said, I don't know what to think—maybe your old man did you a favor when he ran off. Have you ever thought about that?"

"Done me a favor? Are you crazy? He left me with two kids," Brenda was angry now.

"Hey don't get pissed at me girl, all I meant was maybe he wasn't good enough for you, and when he split, maybe he did you a favor only you didn't know it—that's all I meant."

She began to smile, "I'm sorry Whitey, I misunderstood you."

"Forget it. How old are the children?"

"Mary just turned eight, and Jackie is five."

"Hey that's nice," Whitey returned. "A little girl of eight, and a boy of five, you're lucky."

"Yes I guess I am lucky, only I have two girls, you see Jackie is a girl too. But forget about us, how about you? Are you married? Do you have any children? Tell me about yourself."

"No, I'm not married, as for children, there may be some around that I don't know about! There's not much to tell about myself."

"Sure there is—you have a New York accent, you don't come from California, and you haven't told me what you do for a living."

"You were pretty close when you said New York, but I come from New Haven, Connecticut. Where do you originally come from?"

"Tulsa, Oklahoma. I left home when I was seventeen, and I came to Sacramento and I've been here ever since. Tell me Whitey what do you do for a living?"

"I'm a truck driver, just a plain old truck driver. I have my own rig, I'm leased to Senator Truck Service over in West Sacramento."

Brenda's face lit up at the mention of him owning his own rig.

They had several more beers; finally Whitey suggested they go out for a bite to eat.

"I'd like to go, but I better go on home, you see my children are home alone. I can't afford a babysitter. I never leave them for more than an hour or so. Anyway I'd love to get something to eat with you, but I really must get home."

"Say I got an idea Brenda, if it's okay with you. How would you like to go to a take-out restaurant? I'll get some burgers and fries to go.

I'll get some for the kids too, what do you say?"

Brenda hesitated, and then said, "Why not? If you want to treat us to burgers and fries, it's just fine with me."

They got up to leave, and as they passed the bar, the bartender spoke to them, "You people come in again, hurry back now."

"Sure okay, goodnight."

Whitey turned the car around, and drove toward the main section of town.

It was a short trip to Kelly's Drive-In on West Capitol Avenue where he bought the hamburgers and fries. Subsequently at the nearest liquor store he bought a six pack of beer, and Colas for the children. It was a short drive to her home.

Brenda's home was a small wooden frame dwelling built during the late 1920s. The house consisted of two small bedrooms, one bathroom, living room, and kitchen. For its age, the old building was in good condition, but in dire need of a paint job, and other minor repairs.

Brenda informed Whitey that when it came to the rent, the landlord always collected on time, but when it came to repairing the house, he was always too busy.

There was a glow of light shining through the windows. They entered the dwelling into a brightly lit kitchen.

"Damn kids," Brenda grumbled, "I've told them to turn off all lights when they go to bed."

"Ah they're just kids," Whitey told her, "probably afraid of the dark."

Brenda started to say something, but was interrupted when two sleepy-eyed children came into the kitchen. At first they didn't notice Whitey standing there, and when they did, Jackie threw her arms around her mother's legs and began to cry. Brenda reached down scooping the child up in her arms, and assured her that the visitor was not going to hurt her.

"This is Whitey, Jackie, he's a nice man. He bought all of us some burgers."

Reaching for the bag Mary cried, "Oh boy, hamburgers! I want a hamburger."

Taking control of the paper bag, Brenda ordered the children to sit at the table.

Whitey was amazed at how quickly the children devoured the hamburgers They're starving he thought, and he wondered when they had last eaten.

Brenda excused herself and left the room. The moment she disappeared into the bedroom, Whitey divided his own hamburger and fries between the children.

When Brenda returned to the kitchen she was wearing a house

327

coat and slippers. The children had finished eating their burgers and fries, and sat there hungrily watching their mother eat hers.

"How about a beer, aren't we going to have one?" she asked Whitey.

"Yeah sure, I'll have one, do you have a church key?" (beer can opener.)

Brenda went to the silverware drawer, retrieved an opener and handed it to Whitey, who opened the beers and two Colas for the children.

When the children finished their refreshment, Brenda ordered them off to bed.

While Brenda was putting the children to bed, he decided to put the remaining cans of beer in the refrigerator. He was shocked when he opened the door, except for a half empty container of mustard and an empty bottle of ketchup, the refrigerator was bare. After storing the beer, he quickly looked into the cupboards, and they too were empty. There was absolutely no food in the house, and he realized now why the children were starving.

When Brenda returned to the kitchen he was seated back at the table.

"Come on," she said, "let's sit in the front room."

As was the rest of the house, the living room was poorly furnished with an old studio couch, two apple boxes for end tables, a coffee table, two straight-back chairs, and a TV set.

Sitting next to Brenda, Whitey took out his cigarettes and offered one to her. After lighting up he said, "Those girls of yours are sweethearts. Who watches them when you work?"

Brenda smiled and replied, "Your kinda nosey isn't you? But if you must know, I'm on Welfare."

"How about the kids' father, don't he send money for them?"

"That son of a bitch! I don't even know where he's at."

He put his arm around her shoulders, and in a sympathetic voice he said, "Sorry Brenda, I'm not trying to be nosey, I'm just concerned."

She turned her head slightly to look at him, and as she did so he took her in his arms and gently kissed her.

"Would you like to stay the night?" she whispered.

"I'd be lying if I said no."

Brenda was sleeping soundly, and did not hear the voices that had awakened Whitey. The children were up bright and early, and were watching the Saturday morning cartoons on TV.

Trying not to disturb Brenda, Whitey reached for his cigarettes on the night stand. After lighting up, he relaxed as he thought of the events that occurred the night before. Brenda had responded to his

328

desires far beyond his imagination, an evening of fulfillment, and one to remember.

He lay there looking at Brenda while basking in his thoughts. Then he suddenly hopped out of bed and got dressed. Before leaving the room, he took a long look at the sleeping girl. She looked so young and innocent with her long brown hair streaming across the pillow. It was all he could do to resist removing his clothes, and crawl back into bed to make love again. Instead he made his way to the bathroom and washed up.

The children were so engrossed in watching the cartoons that they didn't see or hear Whitey go into the kitchen. He wanted to inspect the refrigerator and cupboards to reassure himself that they contained no food. After his inspection, he peeked in on the children, and then quietly left the house.

Startled, Brenda sat upright in bed. She was not sure if she had been dreaming or not, for she thought she had heard an automobile start up, and the sound of it speeding away. Whitey, missing from the bed confirmed her thoughts.

"Damn!" she groaned. "Damn—damn—damnit." She quickly jumped out of bed, and without taking time to cover her nude body she dashed to the bedroom window. Seeing Whitey's car gone, she ran to the living room.

"Turn off that damn TV—turn it off," she shouted.

The children were startled and somewhat frightened by their mother's voice. They were lying on the floor rug, and before Mary could respond to the command, Brenda had already turned off the TV.

Jackie immediately began to cry, "I wanna watch cartoons—I wanna watch cartoons."

"Never mind the damn TV. Did he say where he was going? Is he coming back?"

The children had no idea what she was talking about.

"Who Momma? Who is coming back who?" Mary was on the verge of tears when her mother began to shake her.

"Whitey, I'm talking about Whitey, stupid. Did he say if he was coming back?"

"I don't know Momma, we didn't see him. Honest we didn't."

It was then Brenda realized that the children didn't know he had stayed overnight.

"I'm sorry Mary, Momma's sorry, just forget what I said. Go ahead, both of you, watch TV if you want to."

She was furious at Whitey. The dirty bastard, she thought, he's just like the rest of them. All he wanted was sex, and once he got it he split. The son of a bitch! I sure wished I had gotten his address, I'd give him a piece of my mind! Ooooh that bastard! I could scream.

Damn it all, I wish I had a good old man to take care of us. Damn that Whitey Thompson.

Brenda went into the bathroom, and after a hot shower she felt somewhat better.

The children were still in the living room when Brenda appeared in the doorway, "Mary," she called, "I'm going out for a while, I'm going to try and get some money for. . . ." She didn't finish, she heard a car pulling into the driveway, and a few seconds later there was a knock on the door.

"Mary, go answer the door, if it's the landlord, tell him I'm sick in bed. Tell him I can't pay the rent until next week sometime. Hurry now, go answer it."

Brenda ran into the bedroom closing the door behind her. She quickly began to wipe off her lipstick, and just as she started to ruffle her hair, Mary called from the kitchen.

"It's Whitey, Momma—it's Whitey."

Brenda hurried to the kitchen in time to see Whitey going out the back door; setting on the table was a large bag of groceries. A smile replaced her grim expression as she hurried out the door after him.

"Where you going Whitey? Wait a minute," she called out. She ran around to the side of the house, and immediately she felt embarrassed when she saw Whitey standing behind his car with the trunk open.

"Come on," he told her, "give me a hand with this stuff."

Inside the trunk were four more large bags of groceries, and a ten-pound sack of potatoes.

Brenda was excited, and threw her arms around Whitey and cried, "Why didn't you wake me? I would of went along to help you."

"You were sleeping, I thought I'd be back before you woke up. I bet you thought I'd left for good."

"No Whitey, whatever makes you think that? I knew you were coming back, honest."

"I want you to know I'm no hit and run guy! I just wanted to get some groceries for you."

The children were excited, they had never seen so much food at one time in their home. The kitchen table was literally covered with all sorts of eatables and household items.

Brenda, with the help of Mary went about putting the groceries away. When the chore was finished she asked Whitey if he would join them for breakfast.

"No, no thanks Brenda, you and the children go ahead, thank you."

"Come on Whitey, sit down, I'll make you some nice bacon and eggs. What's the rush anyway? By the way, you never did tell me where you lived."

330

"I live over on G Street in a boarding house."

The bacon and eggs were good, but the enjoyment of watching the small children dig into their food was a delight to Whitey's eyes.

Brenda noticed Whitey watching the youngsters, and said, "You like kids don't you?"

"Yeah I guess you can say I do. Kids are a treat."

"They need someone like you Whitey, would you like to stay with us?"

Whitey was taken aback; he wasn't prepared for a proposition such as that. Before he could answer her, the children started cheering.

With the anticipation of having a father, the girls were all excited, and began to jump up and down with joy.

"Hold it down girls," Whitey ordered. "I didn't say yes. Before I say anything, there's something I must talk over with your mother first, okay?"

Brenda agreed, and when the meal was over she told the girls to play in their room while she had a chat with Whitey.

"Look Brenda, I appreciate you wanting me to move in, but I think you should know a few things about me first. You know, like who I am, what I am, and where I come from."

"You told me all that when we first met, what more is there to know?"

"Not much more, only that I'm an ex-con."

Brenda had been smiling, but the smile faded, "You mean you were in prison?"

"Yeah that's right, close to fifteen years for armed robberies. I was on Alcatraz"

"You're kidding me. You was never in prison, especially Alcatraz."

Whitey took hold of her arms, and shook her firmly but gently. "Brenda I'm not kidding, don't you understand, I don't kid about things like that." He released his grip and continued, "Look maybe I just better split."

"No, no Whitey, I believe you. It don't make any difference to me. Honest."

"I've only been out a few months, you better think about it first."

"It don't matter to me. I like you Whitey, and the children adore you. We want you to move in."

At the boarding house May was sorry to see Whitey leave, but she told him that any time he wanted to come back, she would make room for him, no matter what. She also said that if he ever needed help, remember, she was his friend.

Whitey moved in with Brenda that day, and the couple seemed

compatible, making the first year a joyful one.

He had taken over the full responsibility of the household, including paying the rent, utilities, and all other bills. He readily accepted the responsibilities of a family man. He loved Brenda, and he adored the children. To Whitey, it was a ready-made family, and he was the happiest man in the world.

His first week in the house he furnished the kitchen with all necessities, including installing a freezer in the garage. At every opportunity he would add a new item to the home.

Being a truck driver, his nightly hours of driving over the road were tedious, but he was devoted to his job and family. He was a happy man. The first year was a prosperous one; for he paid off his truck. Then he traded it off on a new Kenworth diesel, and shortly after he was able to purchase a new Chevy Super Sports Coup Impala.

One night while getting ready for work, he suddenly realized he was on his second year of freedom. He could hardly believe how the time had flown, and everything was going extremely well. He no longer had feelings of rejection. Being a family man suited him, and he was truly enjoying the fruit of life.

Looking at his watch he realized he had better hurry. He was running a little late; the time was 9:45 P.M. He had to drive his car to King's Truck Stop to pick up his rig, and be on the road by 10:00 P.M.

Whitey never left the house without looking in on the children, as usual, they were sound asleep. Just before leaving he gave Brenda a warm hug and kiss.

He walked directly to his car, opened the door, and paused for a moment before getting in. He was in deep thought; the warmth of Brenda's embrace was still with him, and the two sleeping children were pictured in his mind. He felt elated as he looked toward the brisk evening sky. He held his hands up reaching to the heavens, and quietly whispered, "Thank you Lord—thank you."